INTERNATIONAL
NON-GOVERNMENTAL
ORGANIZATIONS

INTERNATIONAL NON-GOVERNMENTAL ORGANIZATIONS

THEIR PURPOSES, METHODS, AND ACCOMPLISHMENTS

BY

LYMAN CROMWELL WHITE

[*The author is a member of the Secretariat of the United Nations; the views expressed, however, are personal and not necessarily those of the United Nations.*]

ASSISTED BY

MARIE RAGONETTI ZOCCA

RUTGERS UNIVERSITY PRESS   NEW BRUNSWICK

1951

Copyright, 1951, by the Trustees of Rutgers College in New Jersey

Designed by Edward L. Mills

Manufactured in the United States of America

TO THOSE WHO SERVE IN
                INTERNATIONAL SECRETARIATS

PREFACE

PERHAPS NO aspect of international relations has received less attention, even from students of international organization itself, than the part which international non-governmental organizations have played in world affairs. This is indeed surprising when we consider the facts presented in this book. There are now in existence more than a thousand such organizations, not counting the numerous international business and commercial enterprises. Their activities cover practically every phase of man's interests, from theology to the Olympic Games, from child welfare to astronomy, from cancer to the problems of labor, from aviation to human rights. These international non-governmental organizations, referred to herein as *INGO's,* have made, we shall show, a significant impact on international life, an impact which promises to be still greater in the future. Yet they remain the great unexplored continent in the world of international affairs; no survey of their activities and accomplishments has been made up to the present time; the study of their functions has been almost completely ignored in textbooks, in university courses, and in the training of those who represent governments in international negotiations.

For the first time their importance was officially recognized on an extensive scale when the Charter of the United Nations was framed at San Francisco. Article 71 of the Charter specifically provides that the Economic and Social Council may make arrangements for consultation with non-governmental organizations, and as this volume is being prepared for publication, eighty-seven of these have "consultative status." Each organization had to pass a severe test, for the principles which govern these consultative arrangements with the United Nations clearly specify that such arrangements "are to be made on the one hand, for the purpose of enabling the Council or one of its bodies to secure expert information or advice from organizations having special competence . . . and, on the other hand, to enable organizations which represent important elements of public opinion to express their views."

Today it is granted by almost all serious observers that if there is to be peace, the world must develop an international mind, a mind which fully appreciates the interdependence of our world; and that if the United Nations is to succeed, it needs behind it the wholehearted support of the peoples of the world, for cooperation on the official level alone is not enough to guarantee a dynamic peace. An enlightened world public opinion is an essential factor in the successful functioning of the UN. A large measure of that basic understanding and necessary support is to be found in the efforts of the *INGO's* which, crossing national frontiers, are the channels through which private citizens in different countries unite to promote their common interests. We find these *INGO's* acting as agents of international understanding, as molders of public opinion, and as pressure groups both on the national and the international level. Often they are organized to meet specific needs which official bodies either cannot meet or, equally important, are not willing to meet.

Therefore, we should not think of international relations and international organizations in terms of official action alone. We must take cognizance of the important role of the *INGO's*. Just as the study of political science expanded to include, in addition to the structure, powers, and functions of government, the role of political parties and pressure groups in national life, so the study of international relations today must be expanded to include the activities of the non-governmental organizations.

Several handbooks have been published, listing many of these groups and giving a general description of their membership, interests and activities, but so far no publication has been devoted to a study of their functions, accomplishments and influence. This volume tries to fill that gap. This is not a definitive study; instead, this is a survey intended to help officials and students of international affairs, as well as members of the general public who are interested in the organization of peace, to gain insight into the activities of the major private organizations and to understand better the part which they have played in world affairs. This survey covers the period from the middle of the nineteenth century, when international organizations began to gather impetus, to the beginning of World War II. It does not deal with the activities of these *INGO's* during the recent war or during the present reconstruction period; the assembling and evaluation of this material must be the subject of a later volume. It is, as a matter of fact, too early to consider the period since 1939. During the war the *INGO's* were generally inactive. The time from V-E day, May 8, 1945, through the summer of 1947, or even later, was a period of reorganization. Thus the *INGO's* have since 1939 been active for the most part only from two to three years. Furthermore, these last few years have been a time of rapid change. Many new organizations have been founded. Some are being torn apart by the East-West conflict. The Americans, the Dutch, the British and others, for example, have left the World Federation of Trade Unions, and a rival organization, the International Confederation of Free Trade Unions, has been set up. It would be premature under these conditions to attempt to tell the story of the *INGO's* since 1939. It is clear, however, that the influence of the *INGO's* has already surpassed that of the pre-war days and that in a few more years there will be an even greater story to tell than the one we now submit.

The writer first became interested in the activities of the non-governmental organizations when, as a student at the Graduate Institute of International Studies at Geneva, Switzerland, in 1929–30, he had an opportunity to visit the headquarters of many of these groups in Paris, Brussels, London, Geneva and other cities and to observe their work at first hand. From this experience grew the first book which treats of the subject, *The Structure of Private International Organizations*, published in 1933. In 1936 he saw something of the work of these organizations in Hawaii, Japan, and China. Again in 1937–38, eight more months were devoted to personal visits to the European headquarters of these groups. In 1945 he visited numerous ones having their headquarters in London and in 1948 he called upon some fifty organizations in Geneva, Fribourg, Lucerne, Rome, Paris, Brussels and London. In all, the writer has visited the headquarters of about two hundred and fifty international organizations and has gathered material by correspondence with many others.

"International non-governmental organization" is an all inclusive term, defined by the Economic and Social Council of the United Nations to mean any international organization which is not established by an agreement among governments. Within this category fall organizations which, although not intergovernmental, have a distinct official character. This study is, however, primarily devoted to international organizations composed of private citizens or private bodies, with less attention to those organizations which upon examination the writer felt were largely official in character.

The author imposed a further limitation upon himself by restricting his study to nonprofit organizations, thus excluding the numerous international business enterprises, such as the International Telephone and Telegraph Company, the great oil corporations and automobile companies. In addition, this study does not include those national organizations which are engaged in activities outside the boundaries of their own countries. However, this area of activity should not be minimized, since it encompasses such widespread operations as the programs of national philanthropic foundations in foreign countries, the missionary work of national churches, and such activities of the profit-making institutions as loans from a private bank to private companies within other nations.

Part I of this volume is devoted to the role of non-governmental organizations in world affairs.

Part II is an analysis of specific organizations classified, under twelve main headings, according to their major field of interest. Of course, in many instances, their work overlaps into more than one field of activity, and here, wherever it seemed necessary, there is a footnote reference. For the reader who wishes to note the impact of *INGO's* on a particular subject, the index will supply the necessary references.

The author would have preferred to submit what he has written in this part to each *INGO* concerned, as he did with his previous book, but this procedure has not been feasible with the present volume. He trusts, however, that he has been accurate in the use of the information supplied to him by the officials of these groups, and for any errors or misinterpretations he assumes full responsibility.

Part III deals with a study of the relations of these private organizations with intergovernmental organizations, ending with a discussion of their probable future. The author is confident that these organizations will be more and more effective in their contribution to the building of the peace.

An appendix listing the *INGO's* which have been granted consultative or similar status by the Economic and Social Council and by the specialized agencies has been included.

The author wishes to extend his most sincere appreciation to the officials of the numerous non-governmental organizations, who, though often overworked, found time to grant him interviews, supply him with documentation and assist him in gathering the necessary material for this volume. He also wishes to express his great debt to Marie Ragonetti Zocca, without whose editorial assistance the publication of this volume would have had to be postponed. To his step-father Mr. Joseph Lush he owes a very special debt of gratitude for the financial help which has enabled him to press forward toward the conclusion of this book. And, as always, the author owes much to his wife who has been a constant help in every way.

He wishes to dedicate this volume to those men and women who serve in secretariats of *INGO's* and hopes that they, through seeing their own individual organization in the light of the over-all picture presented here, will intensify their faith in the importance of what they are doing as a part of a great fundamental movement which is uniting mankind. May this volume also prove useful in bringing a larger measure of moral and financial support to their organizations both from their own constituents and from the general public.

LYMAN CROMWELL WHITE

CONTENTS

PREFACE vii

PART I THE ROLE OF INTERNATIONAL NON-GOVERNMENTAL ORGANIZATIONS (*INGO'S*) 3

PART II THE CONTRIBUTION OF *INGO'S* IN SPECIFIC FIELDS

    1 BUSINESS AND FINANCE 19
    2 COMMUNICATIONS, TRANSPORT, AND TRAVEL 54
    3 LABOR 75
    4 AGRICULTURE 89
    5 ARTS AND SCIENCES 94
    6 PRESS 121
    7 EDUCATION 124
    8 RELIGION 133
    9 SOCIAL WELFARE 166
    10 SPORTS 198
    11 INTERNATIONAL LAW AND THE LEGAL SETTLEMENT OF DISPUTES 201
    12 PURSUIT OF PEACE 213

PART III RELATIONSHIP OF *INGO'S* WITH INTERGOVERNMENTAL ORGANIZATIONS 243

CONCLUSIONS PARTNERS FOR PEACE 273

NOTES AND REFERENCES 279

APPENDIX *INGO'S* OFFICIALLY RECOGNIZED BY THE UNITED NATIONS AND THE SPECIALIZED AGENCIES 305

BIBLIOGRAPHY 312

INDEX 315

PART I

THE ROLE OF INTERNATIONAL NON-GOVERNMENTAL ORGANIZATIONS (*INGO'S*) IN WORLD AFFAIRS

I THE ROLE OF INTERNATIONAL NON-GOVERNMENTAL ORGANIZATIONS (*INGO'S*) IN WORLD AFFAIRS

THE STUDY of world affairs has, from the beginning, been largely confined to the relationships between states. It has been concerned primarily with struggles for power, wars, the resulting problems and the efforts of states to obtain cooperation for peaceful and constructive ends. That study is still, therefore, in a stage of development similar to the study of political science in the United States some decades ago when students gave attention only to the formally constituted branches of the government, not recognizing as they do now the important role of political parties and "pressure groups," e.g., trade unions, chambers of commerce, churches.

The time has come to realize that the unofficial side of world affairs has developed to the point where it should be given consideration as an important aspect of international life. In particular, the students of international organization should recognize the immense contribution of those organizations composed of unofficial groups in different countries which have come together to promote common interests through international action. These were known as "private international organizations" before the war but, following the terminology of Article 71[1] in the Charter of the United Nations, "international non-governmental organizations" has become the commonly accepted term. This term has since been defined by the Economic and Social Council to mean "any international organization which is not established by intergovernmental agreement."[2]

Our study of these "international non-governmental organizations," which we will refer to as *INGO's,* will be concentrated on the international aspect of their activities. It is recognized that the importance of an *INGO* is to be measured not so much by the importance which its national member organizations may have in their own countries as by the importance of the work which they do together on the international level. This point is kept in mind throughout this book, which is a study of *international NGO's* as such and not a study of *national NGO's* (*NNGO's*). The statements which follow, therefore, refer to the *international* aspect of these organizations unless otherwise stated.

The *INGO's* greatly outnumber the organizations composed of governments, which are known as "intergovernmental organizations" (*IGO's*), and have a far wider range of activities. *INGO's* are to be found in the economic and social fields, in agriculture, science, education, religion, the arts, law, communications, sports—in fact, in every known field of man's interests. From 1850 to 1939 they held approximately six thousand conferences. More individuals are directly engaged and, up to 1939, probably more money was spent in carrying on their programs.[3] They have played an important part in the establishment of many of the intergovernmental bodies themselves and have significantly influenced the work of *IGO's*.

HISTORICAL DEVELOPMENT

Although some form of international organization has existed since early times, notably the Roman Catholic Church and the religious orders (i.e.: the Franciscans, the Jesuits, the Dominicans, etc.), it was not until the second half of the nineteenth century that, impelled by the forces released by the industrial revolution, the modern movement toward international organization began to gather impetus. As the world grew more and more interdependent and smaller and smaller in terms of travel and communication, international organizations grew faster both in number and importance. In every known field of human endeavor man set up international organizations, for both selfish and idealistic reasons.

Contrary to what might be expected, the first *INGO's* to be organized were not primarily concerned with the betterment of international relations, for it was not until 1892 that the International Peace Bureau was created, although its founding had been preceded some twenty years by two international law societies, and four years by the Inter-Parliamentary Union. The earliest *INGO's* are to be found mainly in the humanitarian and religious fields. Because they answered an easily recognized need and were generally not of a controversial nature, these *INGO's* increased more rapidly than any other type of organization, and today are still more numerous. Particularly noteworthy is the World Alliance of YMCA's, which from the date of its foundation in 1855 was truly international with member associations from Belgium, England, France, Germany, Holland, Scotland, Switzerland, and the United States. It was probably the first true international non-governmental organization to be established in the modern movement.[4]

It is interesting to note that this early religious and humanitarian *INGO* (the *YMCA*), with the exception of the Central Commission on the Navigation of the Rhine (founded 1815), was established before any of the official bureaus. Those relating to telegraphy, the postal service, weights and measures, industrial property, artistic and literary property, the Pan-American Union, slavery, customs tariffs, sugar, agriculture, public health, were all founded in the forty years from 1865 to 1906.

A study made by the author of 546 organizations in 1938[5] showed that only two health organizations were founded before 1900, whereas from 1900 to 1914, thirty-eight more were established, a greater proportional increase than in any other area of work. The reason for this probably was that before 1900 both medical science and popular interest in health had not been highly developed. Of the eighteen agricultural *INGO's* studied, only one had been founded before 1900. The same held true in education. The business world did not set up its international network until later, although before 1906 there were *INGO's* concerned with questions of railroad transportation and with navigation and maritime matters. Labor had begun to establish its international organization in the 1890's; its driving force lay in the desire to improve social conditions.

Before World War I, international non-governmental organization was still in its infancy. Compared with the work of the postwar period, it was visionary rather than practical; it existed more for the sake of being international than for the sake of getting something accomplished; debate rather than action was the rule, and consequently in the pre-1914 period the organizations on the whole exerted less influence than they did after 1919. Likewise, the structure of these groups was not as highly developed as that of their postwar counterparts. They were willing to get along with little in the way of permanent headquarters and few of them saw the need of setting up permanent committees for continuous study. Their members met in international conferences, many of which were held at irregular intervals.

During World War I, nearly all *INGO's* ceased their activities for, with the exception of bodies like the Red Cross, there was little they could do but wait until the war was over. It was almost impossible to hold international congresses. Revenues declined, and supporters were busy fighting. However, recognizing the catastrophe of war on a global scale, a few *INGO's* were created to prevent its recurrence. Among these was the Women's International League for Peace and Freedom, founded under the leadership of Jane Addams in 1915. But it was not until a year or two after the Armistice that conditions became settled enough to enable international organizations to function normally. Some *INGO's* welcomed the Germans without hesitation; others excluded them until hatreds died down and the need for ex-enemy cooperation was revealed.

The war taught the people of the world that international organization was inevitable. The peace settlement brought into existence such great intergovernmental bodies as the League of Nations, the International

Labour Organization, the World Court, and the Bank for International Settlements. In the private field this great stride was paralleled by such associations as the International Chamber of Commerce, representing over three million firms, the International Cooperative Alliance, with seventy-one million members, and the International Federation of Trade Unions, with twenty million members. Their budgets matched the phenomenal rise in membership: Rotary International had an income of a million dollars a year and the Jewish Agency for Palestine had over four million a year. Hundreds of new organizations were created, and those which had survived the war expanded their membership and activities far beyond their previous status. International organization marched on; the future seemed assured.

Then came the depression, followed closely by the Japanese seizure of Manchuria in 1931, the failure of the disarmament conference, the rise of Hitler to power in 1933, the conquest of Ethiopia in 1935, the war in Spain, a new conflict in the Far East in 1937, and the seizure of Austria in 1938. Nationalism gained over internationalism. Trade barriers were raised to new heights. Millions who had put their faith in the League of Nations were disillusioned. The verdict that international organization had failed was almost universally accepted.

However, during these troubled years a vast majority of the private organizations kept up their activities. In spite of depression, fascism, and war, some of them grew in importance and even new *INGO's* were established. On the whole, beginning with 1932, the great decline in income slowed down the extension of activities for several years. In some cases the regular international conferences had to be postponed, but not a single organization which had attained any importance before the depression failed to survive. It should be noted, however, that many entered the depression in good financial condition, with sizable surpluses.[6]

The rise of fascism had both negative and positive effects on the life of the *INGO's*. Its rise in Germany led to the withdrawal of important national groups from certain organizations, especially those dealing with international relations, labor, reform, and religious matters. This action weakened some *INGO's*. For example, the International Federation of Trade Unions lost several million members when the German trade unions were forced to withdraw in 1933. In August 1937 the Rotary Clubs were banned in Germany, and Nazi party members, Reich officials and military men were ordered to withdraw from the organization.[7] German groups, however, continued to participate in cartels and in organizations concerned with economic, scientific and health questions, sports, and general technical or administrative matters. In fact, the participation of Germans in international organizations was far more extensive than might have been expected; in many cases this participation can be credited either to their desire to make use of these *INGO's* for propaganda or in order to receive information. The suppression of the free trade union movement in Italy was keenly felt, while Japan, which controlled its national organizations, did not abolish them or compel them to withdraw from *INGO* participation, at least until after the beginning of the war in 1937.

On the other hand, the growth of fascism stimulated many groups to redouble their efforts. This was especially true of those concerned with peace, religion and labor. The experience of the International Federation of Trade Unions typifies the reaction. The membership of its national units became greater in number and more determined in action as the threat of fascism spread, and this, together with the addition of new members, including the American Federation of Labor, more than made up for the loss of the German trade unions within the *IFTU*. Speaking for his own organization, the World's Student Christian Federation, but expressing what had occurred in others, W. A. Visser't Hooft stated, "these last years have been years in which the process of interchange and of deepening our consciousness of belonging together has intensified."[8]

In the late thirties, the year just before the outbreak of World War II, there were over a thousand nonprofit *INGO's* in existence, enveloping the world in a net of influence. Later we will describe in some detail what this influence has been, but first let us look at the over-all picture.

MEMBERSHIP OF *INGO'S*

The composition of the *INGO's* is varied. In a few instances, the members are individuals from various countries who have joined the international organization directly, but generally the members are national organizations from two or more countries. A small number are composed of international associations. Most have permanent central offices with a secretariat; a few have merely a permanent committee. Nearly all are governed by a constitution, by-laws, etc. In all instances, the structure and control are on the international level.

While in most *INGO's* this control is exercised by the members through their voting rights on policies and actions of the organizations, there are cases where the control is vested in a single authority, which we can consider as having an "international personality." Such international authorities are to be found in the Roman Catholic Church and other religious bodies, or in organizations like the Salvation Army where the highest official exercises autocratic control over the personnel, finances and actions of the organization.

The majority of *INGO's* are composed of national groups whose members are private citizens. However, we find that the term "non-governmental organization" applies also to some groups which have a distinct official character, even though their existence does not depend upon some form of intergovernmental agreement. There are, indeed, varied gradations between the private and the intergovernmental organization which need examination, particularly since we are interested here in evaluating the achievements of private citizens who are trying to solve international problems through their joint efforts.

In this examination the first step must necessarily be to ascertain to what degree the membership or control of an *INGO* is official or private.

Some *INGO's*, like the International Criminal Police Commission, are composed of representatives appointed and instructed by, and consequently responsible to their governments even though these governments have not entered into any intergovernmental agreement. Side by side with these groups are those *INGO's* whose members are officials acting in their official capacity, or whose members are government agencies, such as state educational bureaus, agricultural experiment stations, forest research institutions, etc. These agencies, composed, of course, of state employees, are in reality arms of the state. As a result, it is difficult to conceive of these agencies ever acting in international organizations, such as the International Union of Forest Research Organizations or the International Union of Local Authorities, in any private capacity.

On the other hand, there are *INGO's* composed of officials who are free to make decisions on their own authority or in accordance with the opinions of a private association with which they are connected. Typical of this category is the Inter-Parliamentary Union, whose members, despite their official status as members of parliaments, act within the organization as private individuals. The Union is composed of members and former members of national parliaments; in some cases even the parliament as a whole has joined, and it has become a frequent practice for national legislatures to authorize appropriations for its support. Since the purpose of the Union is to study all questions of an international character suitable for settlement by parliamentary action, with the ultimate aim that a World Parliament or a World House of Commons will be established, it is evident that the decisions of the Union are independent of the function of these officials in their respective legislatures. The *INGO's* of this type are in reality private, regardless of the official character of their members, for in the ultimate analysis the decisions of the organization are made without government control, each member acting as a private and independent individual.

Some organizations are made up of both official and private members and may be classified as either "privately controlled mixed organizations" or as "officially controlled mixed organizations." The determination of the exact status of these *INGO's* is often difficult, since it may require a study of each of their member organizations. For example, the International Broadcasting Union was composed primarily of the national broadcasting systems in Europe, with associate membership open to all non-European systems. Of the thirty systems functioning in Europe in 1938, only three were privately owned and operated. Of the remainder, thirteen were government owned and operated; nine were government monopolies operated by autonomous public bodies or partly government-controlled corporations; four were physically operated by the government but privately serviced for programs. In two countries, France and Jugoslavia, government and privately run organizations existed side by side.[9] In 1938 all but one of these thirty broadcasting systems, the Russian, were members of the International Broadcasting Union.

Another difficulty may be illustrated by the International Federation for Housing and Town Planning, which is governed by a Council which at times has a majority of representatives from official agencies, and at other times a majority of representatives from private bodies, depending upon the chance variation in the number of delegates attending. However, it appears from a study of these mixed groups that their decisions are mostly of private character.

Sometimes there are cases where the membership is private, but the control is definitely official. One of the most interesting examples illustrating this aspect of the problem is the recently dissolved Permanent International Commission of Agricultural Associations. This Commission was created by an intergovernmental body, the International Institute of Agriculture. It was composed of representatives of agricultural associations, which are distinct private entities. However, the membership of these associations in the Commission was determined jointly by the International Institute of Agriculture and the respective governments. The Institute called the meetings of the Commission and specified the agenda. The Commission was obliged to give the Institute its opinions on all questions submitted. The powers of both the agricultural associations within the Commission and of the Commission itself were strictly limited. True, the associations could select their representatives on the Commission, and, in turn, this commission elected its own officers. However, the Commission was in no way controlled by its members, but by the official Institute which had created it.[10]

Many national organizations have come under the control of their governments. Naturally, when this occurs, even though the organization proclaims its private status, it no longer can be classified as private. Germany under Hitler, for example, completely controlled many nominally independent German organizations which belonged to *INGO's*. If an

INGO ever had a majority of such state-controlled units it could no longer be classified as private.

In discussing control, the question of finance also arises. In many instances *INGO's* have received financial aid from an intergovernmental organization or from a government directly. Again, as in the question of membership, when the members of the association are free to make their own decisions, the financial aid does not alter the private character of the *INGO*. In cases where states are promoting private activity, we find *INGO's* composed of state-subsidized groups—churches, airlines, shipping companies, etc. These *INGO's* also must be considered private in character, for their control is not official.

In addition, we have to consider the extent of the official character of an organization, if it is called upon to serve as a secretariat or perform other services for an intergovernmental agency. For example, the International Committee of the Red Cross was given authority through an international convention to act as the secretariat for the intergovernmental International Relief Union;[11] the International Broadcasting Union was officially recognized as the technical expert of governments in international broadcasting matters.[12] In practically all cases studied, although the *INGO* was performing official acts under the authority of an intergovernmental decision, it was doing so as an exception to its regular private activities; it accepted the official duties voluntarily, and on its own authority could vote to discontinue the action. An organization remaining under private control can be classified as private in character despite official services it may be performing.

FUNCTIONS OF *INGO'S*

Some *INGO's* are organized to promote the interests of a particular group, industry or profession—steel, cocoa, cooperatives, nursing, chemistry. Some are created to advance a movement—arbitration, standardization, world federation, calendar reform; some to perform a particular task—facilitate the exchange of students and teachers, administer relief, prevent blindness, promote religion. Others engage in scientific research and the exchange of information.

The *INGO's* usually function as agents of international understanding, as molders of public opinion, and as pressure groups, both on the national and international level. Frequently, they are pioneers—the first to recognize a need, the first to do something about it, either in study and research or in a program of action.

It is only natural that the businessman, the labor leader, and the social welfare worker should be the first to feel the need for intergovernmental action in his field. It is also an obvious fact that government is slow in extending its public services and often lags behind public opinion in assuming new tasks. Consequently, it is not surprising to discover that it is the *INGO's* which often point the way for intergovernmental action.

At times we will find these private groups pioneering far ahead of public opinion, working to meet a need that only relatively few persons recognize, and which cannot be met by official action because of the lack of support from public opinion itself or because of public opposition. Consequently, the *INGO's* represent in international affairs not only the interests of majority groups but also the aims of minorities—aims which often become commonly accepted within a few decades.

As Agents of International Understanding. As existing *INGO's* grow and as new ones are created, bonds of friendship are strengthened and better international understanding results. These organizations make it possible, through their national members, for the countless number of people participating in local groups in all countries to become part of an international community. Their horizons are raised; their allegiance is extended beyond national frontiers. And the *INGO's* are steadily embracing more and more people within their activities, as they organize new member associations and assist their national units to widen their own membership, reaching out to the grass roots of their countries. Many individuals from different countries, often influential in their communities, come to know each other personally through the international conferences and congresses which are held by the *INGO's*. The number involved is astonishingly large: twenty thousand Catholics attend an Eucharistic Congress; fifty thousand Boy Scouts from forty-two countries meet in a World Jamboree; twelve thousand dentists hold a congress of the International Dental Federation; four thousand engineers and technical experts take part in a World Power Conference.

The leaders of *INGO's* act as ambassadors of good will; their ever-increasing corps of specialists are true members of an unofficial international civil service. Within the *INGO's,* men exchange experiences and discard their differences in behalf of the common cause. At times these organizations bring together in friendly discussion persons from unfriendly nations, in some cases helping to improve relations between countries themselves. In this respect, President Eduard Beneš considered the peace work of the Inter-Allied Federation of Ex-Service Men "incomparably more effective than that of the diplomats"; King Alexander of Yugoslavia gave credit to the World Alliance for International Friendship Through the Churches for the cessation of bad feeling between Bulgaria and Yugoslavia and the resulting pact of friendship between the two nations.

Perhaps no greater contribution is now being made to world understanding than that of the private organizations through their programs of study and research. Here is carried on that exchange of information and personnel which is so necessary today in our world of specialization. And, as a result, a more realistic approach is made to international problems, an approach based on facts and figures instead of sentiment and guesswork. No longer need the isolated worker guess at what is being done elsewhere; no longer need the expert in a remote part of the world remain unknown. For the *INGO's* reach the former and discover the latter.

We find these organizations stimulating the investigation of common problems and research into the ever-widening circle of man's knowledge. In this sphere of activity we should note that the private *INGO's* often have the advantage over official agencies in being able to release and publish findings without being hampered by political considerations.

Since they are able to gather facts from all parts of the world and from actual experience, they are in a position to estimate trends. Often their reports are the first comprehensive study made of a particular problem; frequently they become the basis of official discussion. In Part II of this book we shall come across many specific illustrations of this kind of work.

Needless to say, it is the very nature of these *INGO's* which makes them so important a factor in spreading international understanding. But perhaps it is worthwhile to point out that these *INGO's* are equally a powerful instrument in working toward the goal of *one world*. They are building the organization of interests on a world basis, thereby exerting a profound influence toward world unity, each *INGO* contributing a segment of world unity for the particular interests with which it deals.

As Molders of Public Opinion. Reasonably enough the *INGO's* are concerned with building up support for their specific interests or aims. Their members naturally express a unified opinion in support of certain objectives, but the *INGO* is equally anxious to reach the individual who is not directly connected with its activities. The *INGO* is seeking general public approval, within countries and among other international agencies. To this end, extensive public relations programs are undertaken and widespread distribution of publications, which may be regular periodicals or special reports, ranging from one-page propaganda fliers to studies of many volumes, is sought. As a result, although the *INGO's* in one particular field may be functioning to advance their own self-interest, often through increased public understanding of the issues involved, their specific goals come to be accepted as goals of general concern, and become identified with the objectives of many different associations. Their congresses play an important part; the conclusions reached at these meetings are translated into programs of study and action sponsored not only by their own member units but by other national associations as well. Thus we find policies which originally were of basic interest only to a particular group of *INGO's* coming to be backed by a vigorous public opinion.

Constantly, the *INGO's* utilize this world opinion to bring about official action.

As Pressure Groups. We find that as pressure groups the *INGO's* are often directly responsible for intergovernmental action; they exert pressure simultaneously on national governments and on international agencies. We see them participating directly in the committees and commissions of intergovernmental bodies. We find them demanding new services, and often it is only long after the private groups have pressed for specific action that it comes within the province of intergovernmental activities.

We find them criticizing intergovernmental organizations, or governments, and demanding changes in policy. The moral weight alone which they exert has at times changed the policy of a government in regard to a minority group under its jurisdiction, particularly in the field of religion.

Their work has proved to be the basis of much of the international legislation in existence today. At times it has been at their insistence that an official conference has been held. At other times it has been their spade work which made the conference successful. We will encounter ample evidence of such achievements. For example, it is an acknowledged fact that the calling of the Hague Peace Conferences of 1899 and 1907, which constitute the first important action of governments in the modern peace movement, was greatly influenced by the work of the Inter-Parliamentary Union, but, as Elihu Root stated before the American Society of International Law, ". . . it is not generally understood that the first conference at the Hague would have been a complete failure if it had not been for the accomplished work of the *Institut de Droit International.*" The eleven conventions, codifying various aspects of international law adopted by the 1928 and 1933 Pan-American Conferences, were based on projects of the American Institute of International Law, which is composed of eminent lawyers of North and South America.

In evaluating the *INGO's* as pressure groups, we need to be reminded that intergovernmental agencies formulate international legislation in the form of conventions but do not have the power to enact it into law. This must be done through ratification of these conventions by states. In this connection the *INGO's* operating through their national units perform an important task as pressure groups which persuade governments to ratify. On the national level also we see their members urging legislation to affect international policy, as was done by many American national groups in 1934 in pressing for revision of the neutrality laws so that U.S. policy could parallel action of the League of Nations.

One achievement, which is not generally recognized, is that the *INGO's* are frequently responsible for establishing international standards which have as much authority as if they came into being through governmental action. These standards are brought about when the *INGO's* adopt agreements which either regulate the relations among their national member groups or which substitute one single international regulation for the many national practices. For example, no athletic association would care to violate the rules governing international competition which have been laid down by some thirty international sporting federations; business firms frequently accept the provisions for arbitration set up by the trade associations in standard commercial contracts. One startling example is to be found in the field of air transport, where the air transport companies as members of the International Air Traffic Association unanimously decided to apply the provisions of an official convention, dealing with the carrying of passengers and goods, in countries which had not yet ratified the convention!

Also, we will come across ample evidence of the fact that the *INGO's* have influenced the actual establishment, as well as the policies, of official administrative agencies. At times, an *INGO* has evolved into an intergovernmental organ, as was the case with the International Bureau of Education, and the Tin Producers Association, which is now the International Tin Committee.

As pressure groups we find that the *INGO's* have even helped to create nations, the most recent example of which we have witnessed in our own day—the birth of Israel. *INGO's* played a role in the historical development of both Germany and Italy. Simeon E. Baldwin, an early president of the American Political Science Association, wrote, "The empire of Germany is more the fruit of the Zollverein of 1833 than of any of the political confederations by which it was preceded; and the Zollverein itself might never have spread so far, had it not been for the sentiment of nationalism so passionately voiced by the gathering of the Burschenschaft at Eisenach, only ten years after the Congress of Vienna." The Burschenschaft was a gathering of German university men from various separate German states who pledged themselves to work for unification.[13] Mazzini's organization, "Young Italy," was a major factor in the unification of the Italian states and in the creation of modern Italy.

INGO's RELATIONS WITH EACH OTHER

In recent years there has been a noteworthy advance in regard to cooperation among the *INGO's* working in related fields. Sometimes two or more organizations will maintain one office and secretariat or divide a field of work in order to avoid overlapping and conflict. There is also a growing tendency to set up special liaison committees or other bodies, thus creating what might be called "super-*inter*-national" organizations, that is, those composed of international organizations each of which is in turn composed of national associations. This developed to a great extent in the field of labor, with the creation of the prewar International Federation of Trade Unions and its affiliated Trade Secretariats—the International Transport Workers Federation, the International Federation of Textile Workers Associations, etc.; it has also occurred among the women's international organizations and those *INGO's* concerned with peace, religion, sports, science, and education.

It is, moreover, a common practice for one *INGO* to invite other *INGO's* to participate in its international conferences, and sometimes special congresses are held which bring together the representatives of a large number of international organizations. For example, in 1928 the International Federation of League of Nations Societies held at Prague a conference on economic problems in which thirty-three *INGO's* participated; in 1927 a World Congress of Documentation was held in Paris at which forty international organizations were represented, twenty-nine of which were nonofficial.

It is surprising how much cooperation has resulted from the efforts of individual leaders of *INGO's* who, taking an active part in the work of two or more associations, act as a connecting link and are able to perform many useful services of a coordinating and informational character. This at times has resulted in formal collaboration between groups. Names such as Dr. René Sand, for many years Technical Counsellor of the League of Red Cross Societies and associated with many organizations working in the field of health, and John R. Mott, Chairman of the World's Alliance of Y.M.C.A.'s and active in many international religious organizations, stand out prominently in this connection.

There are many other ways in which the *INGO's* cooperate. For example, the employment of a joint secretary-general; cooperation in research; exchange of publications; arrangement of conference schedules so that delegates traveling long distances can attend several meetings in one trip; joint appeals to official agencies and to governments; joint campaigns to arouse public opinion on specific questions. Also, one organization sometimes assists another by providing secretariat services, giving financial assistance, or making local arrangements for the latter's international conferences.

However, the *INGO's* working in completely unrelated fields feel little or no community of interests. In addition, all is not harmony in the relations between certain *INGO's*. There have been quarrels over the division of activities and over "credit" for what has been accomplished. Also, there are, of course, cases where *INGO's* by their very nature are in direct conflict, as the World's Woman's Christian Temperance Union with the Permanent International Committee on Wine Growing, and the International Federation of Trade Unions with the International Organization of Industrial Employers.

* * *

To anyone who has read this far it is obvious that the accomplishments of *INGO's* have been greater than is usually realized. To neglect the nongovernmental aspect of international organization is to neglect the very foundation of international life as well as the most encouraging and constructive aspect of international affairs.

PART II

THE CONTRIBUTION OF *INGO'S*
IN SPECIFIC FIELDS

I BUSINESS AND FINANCE

WITHIN THE field of business and finance some of the most powerful international non-governmental organizations (*INGO's*) control and regulate vital segments of world economy. During the prewar years, these *INGO's* also directly affected international trade and had a considerable influence on the economic standards and practices which were adopted on a world basis, coming into existence at times through the voluntary self-regulation assumed by these organizations, at other times through their influence on official international action. Also, the credit for the progress achieved in the peaceful settlement of business disputes is almost wholly theirs.

We shall begin our examination with the *INGO's* concerned with economic affairs as a whole and then consider those with specialized interests.

INGO'S CONCERNED WITH ECONOMIC AFFAIRS AS A WHOLE

International Chamber of Commerce

Beginning in 1869 a series of periodic conferences of commercial and industrial organizations was held, the last of which met in Paris in June, 1914.[1] But it was not until after the war, in 1920, that a permanent association for the business interests of the world was established. Today, the International Chamber of Commerce has become the most important *INGO* working for the improvement of international economic relations, providing the means for constant contact and for cooperative effort between the businessmen of many countries.

The reasons for creating a permanent body were explained at the time by John R. Fahey, Chairman of the Organization Committee:

> The world's business is handicapped at present, not only by a lack of dependable information to guide it, but also by hundreds of needless obstacles and inconsistencies in the laws affecting the business in all the countries. Scores of these laws have not been changed in a hundred years or more.... Today these regulations and statutes mean delay, confusion and waste, representing unnecessary cost in the distribution of the world's merchandise amounting to an almost unbelievable sum. A systematic survey of these laws and constructive suggestions from the business men, presented through their organizations, should prove helpful in eliminating these difficulties

and making the commercial laws of all the countries consistent, where there is no sound reason for difference.[2]

The chief functions of *ICC*, then as today, are: to consider laws affecting commerce and to suggest changes and the enactment of new measures which will improve conditions; to bring about through the initiative of the members themselves reforms in business customs and practices; to gather and distribute information essential to the better conduct of commerce; and to suggest to governments improvements of the machinery for commercial relations.

Since the membership embraces practically every important business association in the world—chambers of commerce, industrial, banking, shipping and other economic organizations as well as individual firms and corporations—it is no empty boast when the *ICC* claims that "its recommendations represent the concensus of world business opinion, arrived at after expert investigation and after full consultation of all its national groups."[3]

Its prewar activities were being carried out by a staff of over forty employees, from its headquarters at Paris, with the assistance of forty-seven working committees concerned with practically every phase of commercial and financial life—advertising, international fairs and exhibitions, trade expansion, monetary policy, highway, rail, sea, and air transport, commercial arbitration, and customs procedure. To sum up its achievements from 1920 until the outbreak of the last war is not an easy task, for the *ICC* has exerted its influence on many economic fronts.

To begin with, the *ICC* has been responsible for a constant flow of informational and technical reports on all types of international economic problems.[4] One of the important publications in this field is its periodical, *World Trade*, to which many of the world's most prominent businessmen and economists have contributed. In addition, it has maintained a World Business Information Centre for the use of its members as well as trade associations and economists. This Centre replies to inquiries on many matters ranging from financial and commercial policy to details on customs tariffs and trade statistics; it analyzes economic information received from the leading countries, and conducts studies on vital problems. Its job is to coordinate "the information available which will provide business leaders and executives with significant analyses of practical value in planning production or organizing their markets."[5]

ICC's international congresses are considered a world parliament of business. Not only have they brought together delegates from all quarters of the globe for a discussion of important economic problems, but they have also framed, through the resolutions adopted, a platform of world action in the economic field. They have been widely attended by other international organizations, and have received wide press coverage.[6] At the 1931 Washington Congress, twenty-five international organizations, some official, were represented; a hundred special correspondents were in daily attendance, and U.S. papers alone devoted a total of 25,419 inches of editorial comment to the proceedings.

A major part of the work of the *ICC* has been devoted to the expansion of international trade, particularly to "oiling the wheels of trade." It has carried on a constant campaign for the lowering of trade barriers, attacking the obstacles to multilateral trade—import quotas, barter, and foreign exchange restrictions.[7] Although it must be admitted that the *ICC* achieved a limited success in securing governmental action along these lines before World War II (no other *INGO* or official agency had enjoyed more), its constant campaign of education among businessmen and the general public has been an important contribution.

It played a leading part in the International Economic Conference of 1927, one of the most important official conferences held up to that time on world trade problems. It collaborated in gathering the documentation for the Conference and participated in the work of the Preparatory Committee. The Report of its Trade Barriers Committee was presented to the Preparatory Committee in 1926, which accepted it as a basis for discussion in preference to the documentation of the Secretariat of the League of Nations.[8] The Final Report of this *ICC* Committee was considered one of the most important reports submitted to the Conference.[9] At the Conference, the *ICC* was represented by five delegates and six experts; indirectly, however, its influence was very much stronger, for among the members of the national delegations, appointed by governments, sixty-four were members either of the *ICC* Council, Working Committees, or of its National Committees.[10] Its contributions were considered invaluable, and many of its recommendations were incorporated in the final report of the Conference. The President of the Conference in his closing speech stated:

> The Conference has met after a long and elaborate preparation extending over a year. It has had at its disposal a documentation which derives its value from the collaboration of distinguished experts and of both official and private organizations throughout the world, and is remarkable alike for its range, its fullness and its authority. I would mention for example the International Chamber of Commerce, whose written and personal contributions—based on previous consultations of national committees in many countries—have throughout been of the greatest assistance.

The President of the Conference then referred to intergovernmental organizations saying that, "We have also been fortunate in obtaining the help, in every stage of our work, of the International Labour Office, the International Institute of Agriculture and other bodies."[11] The *ICC* participation in this Conference might be called the high water mark of private collaboration in intergovernmental conferences during the period preceding World War II.

The *ICC* was directly represented also at the 1928 Conference of the League of Nations which dealt with the problem of export and import restrictions, and it is significant to note that its delegation head signed the final act of this Conference.

Again, its proposals for trade expansion were incorporated in the famous van Zeeland Report of 1938 on *International Economic Reconstruction* which the former Prime Minister of Belgium prepared for the French and British Governments. This report was composed in part from the findings of the *ICC* and of various committees of the League of Nations.[12] Mr. van Zeeland pointed out in his report that on most of the proposals he put forward, detailed studies were already in existence, having been made by the *ICC* and the economic committees of the League of Nations, and therefore plans to put the recommendations into effect "could be quickly drawn up with the assistance of specialized organs such as the Economic and Financial Committees of the League of Nations, the Bank for International Settlements, the International Chamber of Commerce [which is the only *NGO* mentioned in the Report], the International Institute of Agriculture, et cetera."[13]

Further, in the field of trade, the *ICC* has fought against the "invisible" barriers to trade, working for the simplification of customs procedure and for uniform interpretations of trade terms. At the invitation of the Council of the League of Nations it participated in the International Conference on Customs Formalities of 1923, being represented by eight delegates and nine experts. Here again we see the head of an *ICC* delegation signing the final act of an official conference which accepted practically all this *INGO's* recommendations.[14]

Its attack on the problem of conflicting interpretations of trade terms —such as F.O.B.—was inevitable, for the confusion and loss of time and money was anything but efficient. For example:

> A seller may enter into a contract with a foreign buyer for the sale of goods on, say F.O.B. terms, under the impression that it is clearly understood that he is undertaking simply to put the goods on ship at his own expense . . . and may then find out, when it is too late to avoid unpleasantness, that the buyer expects him to insure the goods as well.[15]

To avoid such misunderstanding and wrangling on the part of businessmen in their foreign transactions, the *ICC's* Committee on Trade Terms produced a *Digest of Trade Terms* giving the exact and full interpretation placed in thirty-five countries on six commonly employed terms,[16] and a publication, *Incoterms,* giving a standard international interpretation for each of eleven important terms. By placing a reference to *Incoterms* in contracts, the meaning of the term becomes definite.

Just before World War II, a similar activity in relation to international rail transport was under way in an attempt to define both goods and tariff terms, which likewise differ in meaning in various countries. In this task the *ICC* was collaborating with the International Union of Railways and anticipated, with reason, that their efforts to establish a goods nomenclature would "facilitate the designation of goods in consignment notes and, where necessary, their translation"; and that their efforts to establish an international definition for the most common tariff terms would "enable shippers to avoid risks of confusion when drafting sales contracts for abroad," and would also "facilitate the establishment of international tariffs by the railway administrations."[17]

This effort to remove specific barriers to trade was initiated also in the field of shipping. Here, the *ICC* was instrumental in establishing two important international standards, rules for uniform bills of lading and the almost universal acceptance of the principle of reciprocal tax exemption for ocean carriers.

The lack of any uniform law in the shipment of goods had been a real obstacle to international trade, sufficiently serious for the newly organized *ICC* to tackle at its first Congress in 1921. It secured the cooperation of the International Law Association[18] and the International Maritime Committee (both *INGO's*),[19] with the result that the former called a private conference which drew up the Hague Rules for uniform bills of lading, and the rules were supported by the expert authority of the International Maritime Committee. Diplomatic conferences in 1922 and 1923 put these Rules into a Convention which, through ratification by governments and the action of the Japanese shipowners in adopting the Rules voluntarily, covered more than 75 per cent of the world's tonnage.[20]

The significance of this achievement is clearly brought out in the following statement by Charles S. Haight:

> The importance of the reform cannot be missed by any one who stops to consider the facts. Every export shipment *must* have five parties connected with it—shipper, carrier, discounting banker, cargo underwriter and consigner. In most cases three or four of those parties are of different nationalities and not infrequently five countries are represented. Under such circumstances, it was absurd to handle our international trade under the handicap which was inevitable when the law of every country differed from that of every other country on important questions affecting the rights

of cargo owners and the obligations of the carrier. The only possible result was friction and litigation constituting a serious trade barrier which was of benefit to no one and prejudicial to all.[21]

It is commonly accepted that without the support of the *ICC* the Hague Rules would not have been accepted officially.

The following instance, in the field of shipping, is a typical example of how the *ICC* through the cooperation of its individual members is able to bring about international action essential to the welfare of business. Here, the *ICC* brought about general adoption of the principle of tax exemption, on a reciprocal basis, of income derived from traffic originating in one country but terminating in another. The problem was created by the U.S. Revenue Acts of 1916, 1917 and 1918 which made taxable all freight and passage money collected by foreign steamship companies on outward-bound traffic originating in the United States. Because of wartime conditions this tax in some cases amounted to approximately 65 per cent of the total net earnings of a company. Since the foreign companies had been permitted to delay the filing of their tax returns, it was not until about 1920 that they realized what the American tax meant. There was tremendous resentment and retaliation seemed inevitable. The *ICC* through Charles S. Haight, Chairman of its Bills of Lading Committee, persuaded the foreign owners not to demand from their governments retaliatory taxation against the United States. During the year and a half that elapsed while the problem was being worked out in the United States not a single retaliatory move was made. Mr. Haight was instrumental in drawing up a bill which was incorporated in the Revenue Act of 1921 upon the advice of Professor Thomas S. Adams, who at that time was expert adviser of the House of Representatives on tax matters and also a member of the *ICC* International Committee on Double Taxation. This bill abolished retroactively the tax on condition that similar exemption would be granted to American steamship owners. By 1925 the principle of reciprocal exemption was in operation in fifteen countries.[22] By 1938, this principle was accepted almost universally, with the conclusion of a chain of agreements in the negotiation of which Mr. Haight took an active part.

The *ICC* has been influential also on other fronts in the field of transport. In air transport, it urged official ratification of the 1919 Convention regulating aerial navigation, its resolutions along these lines both at the 1925 and 1927 Congresses having had, according to Pierre Etienne Flandin (in 1925 serving as Chairman of the *ICC* Committee on Air Transport and later Premier of France), "practical results in bringing new members" into the official International Commission for Air Navigation.[23]

It also helped to bring about in 1935 revision of this Convention so that the requirements of air traffic companies could be met.[24]

The *ICC* pioneered to bring about insurance for international air transport personnel long before the International Labour Organization or the League of Nations took cognizance of the problem. According to Laurence C. Tombs in his study on *International Organization in European Air Transport*, as early as 1926 the *ICC* had submitted to the *ILO* a draft convention on the subject; on the other hand, the Air Transport Cooperation Committee of the League of Nations was not established until 1930, and only then, at its first meeting, was it decided to examine the question, inviting the *ILO* to participate in the study. The *ILO* secured the technical assistance of the official organizations, the International Commission for Air Navigation and the International Technical Committee of Legal Experts on Air Matters as well as the International Air Traffic Association,[25] to undertake this study.[26]

Perhaps one of the *ICC's* greatest achievements in the field of transport has been the extension of international air mail. When, by 1926, the official International Commission for Air Navigation had not taken steps to organize international air mail, the *ICC* submitted to the governments its proposal transmitted officially by the postal administration of the U.S.S.R., that a special conference be held for the purpose of arriving at an international agreement. As a result the first official conference to deal with the organization of air mail convened at The Hague in 1927. At this conference, in addition to the thirty-eight postal administrations, including several non-European, which were represented, fourteen European air transport companies participated as did the International Air Traffic Association, which submitted suggestions that were placed before the conference.[27] The *ICC* played a major role and saw many of its recommendations adopted.[28] The scope of this conference was naturally limited, for it dealt with the initial problems of organization. Ever since the conference, the *ICC* has pressed for the adoption of the principle, "all the first-class mail by the quickest available route," and has seen the extended use of the airplane as the normal means of carrying mail, with the abolition of the surcharge adopted on more and more international routes. At the Postal Conference at Cairo in 1934 it was decided that the "Administrations have the option of charging no special fee for the transmission by air, provided that information is given to the country of destination and previous agreement is reached with the transit countries."[29] At a restricted meeting of Postal Administrations in 1937 it was concluded that the airplane must be considered as a normal means of transport for letters and postal cards, and used by the postal administrations as other means of transport are utilized, without surcharge.³⁰ In 1938 this principle was finally adopted for Europe by the Air Mail Conference at Brussels.

Still in the field of transport, we find the *ICC* making other valuable contributions. For example, it has tackled many phases of highway transport, particularly those concerned with the problem of highway finance, to which it has given special attention, convinced that an expanding program of road construction was necessary to meet not only the needs of increased automobile traffic but also the problem of world-wide prewar unemployment. Its publications, "Road and Rail in Forty Countries," and "Highway Finance and Administration in Fifteen Countries" provided information on a comparative basis which received universal attention. Moreover, it followed closely questions of railway transport, promoting the interests of the users, and was instrumental in bringing about effective changes along these lines in the new international convention for the carriage of goods and rail which came into effect in 1938. In the new convention of 1933 (which came into force in 1938) the *ICC* worked to extend the obligations of the railways in regard to the users. For example, the *ICC* fought to reduce from three months to six weeks the period reserved by the railways for payment on C.O.D. shipments. Also, the *ICC* secured increased liability of the railways in cases of abnormal damage or the loss of whole packages.³¹

In the field of communications, the proposals the *ICC* put forward in 1935 "for more efficient international telephone service, speedier connections, increased facilities for users, were adopted in large part by the International Consultative Telephone Committee of the official International Union of Telecommunications and put into effect in 1937."³² The *ICC* has also benefited cable users "by obtaining rate concessions and watching their interests whenever code regulations and cable rates are modified."³³

In 1936, faced by the possibility of an increase in telegraph rates at the Cairo Conference scheduled for 1938, the *ICC* reacted strongly. It immediately launched an inquiry, which lasted for two years, among more than two thousand firms in thirty-three countries, and these findings together with its recommendations were submitted to the Conference. In its report, entitled "International Telegraph Regulations and Rates," which was distributed to the governments and telegraph administrations of the world, the *ICC* warned that any increase in rates for any category of telegram and especially for extra-European code messages would force business to reduce the number and length of their messages and to make increased use of other means of communication. Needless to say, the Cairo Conference of telegraph administrations, probably recognizing that business was "their best and principal client," eventually met the demands of the *ICC*.[34]

We have seen how effective the *ICC's* activities have been in the fields of trade, transportation, and communication. Now we turn to the field of finance, and here, too, the role of the *ICC* has been impressive.

One of the principal problems tackled by the *ICC* at the time of its establishment was double taxation. It was the first international organization to deal with this question after the war, not only for income tax purposes but also because double taxation had the disastrous effect of encouraging the export of factories rather than the export of goods. The *ICC* cooperated with and stimulated various activities of the League of Nations concerning this question, and was the only *INGO* represented at the 1928 conference of fiscal experts called by the League to consider the problem. This conference drew up model bilateral treaties, which have served as a basis for the 145 treaties on double taxation concluded by 1938, and led to the establishment of the Fiscal Committee of the League of Nations on which the *ICC* was regularly represented in a consultative capacity. The *ICC* also assisted Mitchell B. Carroll in securing information for his report to the Fiscal Committee of the League of Nations on *Taxation of Foreign and National Enterprises*, which was utilized in preparing the Draft Convention for the Allocation of Business Income Between States for the Purpose of Taxation.[35]

The part the *ICC* played in bringing about the Dawes Plan has been widely lauded, for the idea of a committee of experts to deal with the problem of reparations was put forward by the *ICC* at its Rome Congress in 1923. Francis Delaisi in his *The Contradictions of the Modern World* points out that this proposal was strongly urged upon the U.S. Government by the *ICC* American National Committee, and that leading members of the Chamber were appointed to serve on the Dawes and McKenna Committees—Mr. Owen D. Young, Mr. Henry G. Robinson, Mr. Alberto Pirelli and Mr. Mario Alberti. He states:

> The Dawes Plan was really the work of the International Chamber of Commerce. Without official standing, without any means of coercion, by the sole force of its competency and the weight of the interests it represents, the International Chamber of Commerce was able to play a decisive part in the settlement of a great international question. . . . In brief, what thirty-two diplomatic conferences with the help of countless meetings of ambassadors and interviews between heads of governments were unable to achieve, has been done by a private business organization.[36]

M. Albert Janssen, then Belgian Minister of Finance, also gave credit to the *ICC* for this achievement.[37]

The *ICC* was also instrumental in effecting the Hoover moratorium of June 20, 1931 on the payment of war debts, its efforts culminating at its 1931 Washington Congress where a revision of payment of war debts was strenuously pressed. The *ICC* considers this Congress an important illustration of how an aroused public opinion can alter governmental policy within a relatively short span of time. The *ICC* points out that on May 3, the opening date of the conference, the American Government's attitude was that "it could not contemplate any change in the intergovernmental debt arrangements," and this was the opinion also of both the European and American press. The widespread and extensive newspaper publicity given to the statements made by world leaders of business aroused "public interest in a most dramatic fashion. Almost overnight the whole world was talking international debts and their relation to trade depression." On May 11, President Hoover had already decided on a change in policy. The *ICC* states:

> A government is free to act only within the bounds imposed by the limited understanding that exists in its country of other people's problems and of the extent to which every nation is affected by conditions outside its own national borders. The key to the situation is the change which took place in public opinion, and the impetus to the movement which brought about this change came from the Washington Congress of the International Chamber.[38]

The *ICC* work on stabilization of currencies started with its action in regard to German reparations, and it long fought for the economic stability and development for which the International Bank for Reconstruction and Development and the International Monetary Fund of the United Nations were established. As early as 1933, in its Report to the Monetary and Economic Conference, it advocated the creation of a currency stabilization fund, urging "immediate de facto stabilization and a return at the earliest possible moment to a regime of stable foreign exchange notes." This Report was concerned also with the control of prices, the need for debt readjustments to promote the resumption of the movements of capital and the sanctity of contracts related to foreign investments. In 1935, at its Paris Conference, the *ICC* agreed to undertake a joint study with the Carnegie Endowment for International Peace of the problems of economic reconstruction; a major part of this study was devoted to the question of monetary stabilization, calling for economic reforms which were echoed later in the van Zeeland Report of 1938.

There have been other important achievements of the *ICC* in the field of finance. Costly confusion has been eliminated by the *ICC's* "Uniform Rules and Practices Concerning Commercial Documentary Credits," now used throughout the world by the leading banks in international trans-

BUSINESS AND FINANCE

actions. Its banking committee, before the outbreak of the last war, was working on uniform rules for determining the responsibility of banks which honor invalid or forged checks in good faith, a study which will undoubtedly prove equally useful. It was also at work on a comparative study of measures in operation in various countries for the control of banking activities and the protection of savings.

The *ICC* pioneered for unification of laws on bills of exchange, promissory notes, and checks, and influenced the four official conventions in this field which by 1938 had been ratified by twenty-eight countries.[39] Arthur K. Kuhn, in his article in the *American Journal of International Law* on the international conferences held to bring about unification in this field, gives full credit to the *ICC* for the new impetus given to the movement for unification after World War I, and states that upon the insistence of the *ICC* the League of Nations assumed responsibility for the continuance of the work with the cooperation of the Dutch Government. The final outcome was the three conventions relating to bills of exchange and promissory notes signed at Geneva on June 7, 1930.[40] The convention on checks was signed in 1931.

Also, the *ICC* established a Stock Exchange Bureau which has promoted coordination and cooperation between the twenty-two stock exchanges which are members, and has studied remedies for difficulties arising from arbitrage in securities and other problems arising from the purchase and selling of stocks internationally.

There can be no question that the *ICC* has greatly advanced peaceful business relations on the international level. To this end, perhaps, no greater contribution has been made by the *ICC* than through its Court of Arbitration which since its establishment in 1923 has dealt with over a thousand commercial cases. The creation of such a Court, which only a powerful *INGO* such as the *ICC* could possibly organize, filled a need which no official agency could meet. This need was explained by its president, Nicholas Politis, in the following terms:

> We know the difficulties encountered in settling foreign commercial disputes by means of a recourse to law: which to choose of the national or of the foreign court? If the national court is applied to, its judgment will have to be enforced abroad and this is, in general, a matter of considerable difficulty. If a foreign court is resorted to, the issue is submitted to judges whose language and legal spirit are often unfamiliar to the plaintiff, who only too often may feel—rightly or wrongly—that this foreign court is inclined to be somewhat biased in favour of its compatriot. In either alternative, the plaintiff lays himself open to often enormous costs, interminable delays, a series of instances, and also to a final breaking off with his former client or seller who will not care to resume business relations with a firm which has brought a lawsuit against him.

It was, therefore, natural that an effort should have been made with a view to substituting private arbitral jurisdiction for State courts. This . . . has been successfully achieved in a series of organised trades and in the stock-exchanges of great commercial centres.[41] But besides these categories for which powerful professional associations have framed precise rules and model contracts whether applying to corn or cotton, to timber or oils, there is an unlimited field of unorganised trade which calls for the creation of an arbitral organisation open to all industries and trades: it was this gap that the International Chamber of Commerce has sought to fill.[42]

This Court provides the means for settling disputes arising out of transactions between businessmen of different countries, many of whom in their contracts include the arbitral clause drawn up by the *ICC* Court: "All disputes arising in connection with the present contract shall be finally settled under the Rules of Conciliation and Arbitration of the International Chamber of Commerce by one or more arbitrators appointed in accordance with the Rules."[43] In each case, instead of having the parties appoint the arbitrator themselves, as is the usual practice in arbitration, the Court appoints the arbitrator, whose nationality is not that of either of the two parties.[44] This procedure is possible, Mr. Politis maintains, since the Court is able to find especially qualified men to serve as arbitrators "only because of the unique organization of the *ICC*." The arbitrator gives his award in a form which will meet the legal requirements of the country in which the award may have to be enforced by its Courts; however, in 87 per cent of the cases the award of the *ICC* arbitrator has been accepted and executed without resort to any national court. Mr. Politis explains that the Court of Arbitration "reappears at the closing stage to control the form of the award and make sure that the latter is in harmony with the legal requirements of the country where the award may have to be enforced."[45] In the other instances, the Courts have with one exception enforced the arbitrator's decision.[46] This decision of the arbitrator is final and without appeal.

It should be noted that before proceeding to arbitration, an attempt at conciliation is usually made; in recent years before the war 81 per cent of the cases were settled in this manner.[47]

The cases have dealt with many different types of disputes, for example, "the execution of contracts drawn up in currencies subsequently devaluated, the quality of various products (raw materials, foodstuffs, machinery, textiles, etc.), the payment of royalties on licenses and commissions, the validity of banking documents, the winding-up of companies, the appointment of markets between members of a cartel, etc."[48] The average cost of arbitration has been 1.2 per cent of the amounts involved in the disputes, with the largest amount known to have been involved about ten million French francs. There have never been any complaints as to either the expense or the impartiality and competence of the arbitrators.[49]

The work of the *ICC* in this field has influenced national legislation and the efforts of other international organizations, both private and official. Manley O. Hudson in discussing the resolution of the League of Nations on January 28, 1932, which adopted rules of procedure for the optional friendly settlement of economic disputes between states, said, "These rules suggest a borrowing of ideas from the Permanent Court of Arbitration as well as from the Permanent Court of International Justice. They are also to be compared with the rules of conciliation and arbitration of the International Chamber of Commerce. . . ."[50]

As already indicated in this chapter, the relations of the *ICC* with official international activity have been both widespread and decidedly important. The Chamber was represented at twenty-nine official conferences from 1927 to October, 1932, at times with full voting rights, at other times in a consultative capacity.[51] In addition to the instances already discussed, the following should also be mentioned.

The *ICC* was directly represented on the Economic Consultative Committee of the League of Nations which was set up after the 1927 Economic Conference. Although the *ICC* had the right to appoint three members to the Committee, often its indirect representation was in reality even greater. For example, in 1929 in addition to its three appointed representatives, the President of the Economic Consultative Committee itself, M. George Theunis, was at the time president of the *ICC;* two members of the Committee, Sir Arthur Balfour and M. F. von Mendelssohn, were vice-presidents of the Chamber; and three members of the Committee, Robert Olds, M. de Peyerimhoff De Fontenelle and Dr. F. Hodac, were members of the *ICC* Council. The direct representation of the *ICC* on the Committee was irritating to the president of the International Institute of Agriculture,[52] and also brought objection from the International Co-operative Alliance, which stated: "Our attention has been drawn to the extraordinary claims which have been publicly made that the organized private traders of the world had not only succeeded in entrenching themselves at Geneva in the authorities of the League on a basis of equality of voice and voting with the National Governments, but wielded such influence on behalf of their clients—the capitalist private traders—that they practically dominated the situation and were even able to repudiate their own National Governments. . . ."[53]

The *ICC* took a very prominent part in the Diplomatic Conference on International Exhibitions of 1928. Before the Conference the Chamber had, on the request of the French Government, undertaken the study of the international regulation of fairs and expositions, setting up a special committee which met both in Paris and Cologne. The principles established by this committee were embodied in the draft convention submitted to the Conference by the French Government, and many of its recommendations are to be found in the final convention.[54]

At the invitation of the French Government, the *ICC* was represented at the Conference by a delegation acting in an advisory capacity. However, the *ICC* had made a special appeal to its national committees to propose members of the Chamber's Committee on Fairs and Exhibitions as representatives on the national delegations. As a result, fourteen members of this *ICC* Committee were official representatives at the conference. Needless to say, the views of the *ICC* had a ready backing on the part of the governments.[55]

The Conference set up the International Exhibition Bureau in which the *ICC* has since taken part regularly, in a consultative capacity, in the Administrative Council and the Classification Commission. At the Conference real doubt was raised concerning the advisability of inviting the *ICC* to participate in the Bureau's Council, fearing that a precedent might be established in admitting an *INGO* to a governmental organ concerned with administrative matters. However, the Conference (since it was strongly argued that the *ICC* members were most directly concerned in exhibitions; that its opinions had always proved valuable; and that since the *ICC* would be admitted only in a consultative capacity such action could not create a "troublesome precedent") finally provided in Article eleven of the Convention that the Administrative Council be authorized to invite in a consultative capacity two or three persons designated by the *ICC*.[56]

Also, the *ICC* participated actively in the International Conference on Economic Statistics of 1928, being directly represented and signing the final act of the Conference. President of the Conference William E. Rappard, in acknowledging the assistance of the *ICC*, stated that the importance of its proposed resolutions could not be overestimated, and the Conference in its final recommendations expressed its gratitude and recognized the lesson which it had learned concerning the role which *INGO's* could perform: "Because of the great appreciation that it desires to express for the preparatory work for this conference done by the International Institute of Statistics and the International Chamber of Commerce, consideration should in the future always be given to the scientific work and the technical advice of the competent international organs."[57]

International Co-operative Alliance

Functioning in a capitalistic world and representing institutions of relatively little wealth, the International Co-operative Alliance naturally was not able during the 1920's and 1930's to secure as much public attention, exert as much influence, nor carry on as extensive activities as the International Chamber of Commerce. However, there has been a continuous advance in the growth of co-operative societies both in membership and in the amount of their business since the early days of the establishment of the *ICA* in 1895, an advance which was particularly marked during the years of depression and political upheaval, until the Alliance now represents several hundred million consumers throughout the world.

In 1913 the membership of the Alliance consisted of fifty-five national co-operative organizations in twenty-three countries; this comprised 3,871 societies and two million members. In 1920 its membership had jumped to forty-four national organizations in twenty-four countries, comprising sixty thousand societies and thirty-one million members. Sixteen years later Germany and Italy alone of the great powers were unrepresented; and the Alliance included 141 national organizations in thirty-eight countries; this membership then comprised 123,000 societies and seventy-one million members. If one estimates that each member represents an average family of four, the *ICA* therefore embraced 284 million consumers throughout the world.

The Alliance, naturally, is concerned with promoting and protecting the interests of the co-operative movement in all countries; it aims also to promote trade and other economic relationships between the nations, to develop a "solidarity" that will "maintain peace by means of a true league of peoples." It seeks to change the present economic order from a competitive system to one of co-operation, and tries to see that it does not lose ground to capitalist enterprise. The Alliance considers that one of its major functions and responsibilities is to be watchful that no new law places an "embargo" on the co-operative method or gives an advantage to the capitalist system that is not "equally shared" by organized consumers.[58]

An important part of *ICA* activities is devoted to gathering and disseminating information which will help its societies to advance. From its headquarters at London, the *ICA* publishes the *Review of International Co-operation* monthly; likewise it releases a monthly summary of the co-operative press. Bi-weekly it distributes general co-operative and economic information; and annually it publishes statistics on its member national associations. The proceedings of its triennial congresses are also released. The *ICA,* in addition, undertakes widespread research, and its special reports deal with detailed problems of production and marketing as well as general questions of concern to the co-operative movement. These reports are on such subjects as: Planned Economy and Its Effects Upon the Co-operative System; Costs of Retail Distribution; Private

Monopolies in the Production of Essential Commodities; and Collective Marketing of Agricultural Commodities and Raw Materials.

The Alliance has organized several significant auxiliary organs: an Insurance Committee which acts as a research and documentation centre for co-operative insurance and workers' societies; the International Co-operative Banking Committee which is concerned with a study of the activities of co-operative banks in relation to those of private institutions and with the problem of financial aid to national co-operatives; the International Co-operative Women's Guild, composed of national organizations in twelve countries, which promotes the interests of the co-operative movement among women and is equally concerned with the investigation of social and welfare problems; and the International Co-operative Wholesale Society which the *ICA* considers the chief achievement in the international co-operative movement.

This Society, a nontrading institution, was established in 1924 with the primary purpose of promoting trade among the co-operative societies of the world. This trade amounted to $245,000,000 in 1938.[59] Since it does not release reports for general publication, but only yearly confidential reports to its members, it is impossible to summarize or evaluate its activities. However, in a letter received from its secretariat, we learn:

> Since its inception, the Society has carried out the investigation of many problems which have been brought before it by various members, and it may be said that its chief function is that of an advisory or consultative body. Many of the problems which have engaged its attention have been uniquely co-operative and of a confidential nature, but to quote one example I may mention that the possibility of joint purchase of commodities in general use has received careful consideration, and a scheme has been evolved which has achieved a considerable measure of success.
>
> One outstanding result of the Society's work has been the formation of an International Co-operative [Trading] Agency, which was established in London in October last [1937] for the purpose of purchasing goods on behalf of Society members and for the sale of their products abroad.[60]

According to its president, the Society's "chief merit has been the development of international relations and a better understanding of the general or peculiar economic conditions of each country."[61]

Despite the international outlook of co-operatives, none has been organized on an international basis with the exception of this Agency and the Scandinavian Co-operative Wholesale Society (Nordisk Andelskorfund) which was established in 1918.[62]

Another example of the type of work the *ICWS* has undertaken is to be found in its agreement with the International Commission of Agriculture (see p. 90), under which the latter supplied information regarding the butter which its members had available for export and the *ICWS* in turn passed on this information to its own members. On the other hand, the *ICWS* informed the Commission of the goods of interest to rural householders which the wholesale co-operatives had available for export.[63]

In addition to its auxiliary organs, the International Co-operative Alliance maintains an International Co-operative School which each year holds a two-week session for approximately a hundred students from nearly twenty countries.[64]

In 1927 at its Stockholm Congress, the *ICA* took steps to bring about closer relations between the societies of consumers' co-operatives and those of agricultural producers', where no formal liaison was then in existence. As a result, the International Committee of Inter-Co-operative Relations was organized in 1931, with Albert Thomas, Director of the International Labour Organization, who had been instrumental in bringing this Committee into existence, as President. Its task was to promote national committees for inter-co-operative action, and to collect information on both the marketing requirements of agricultural co-operative societies and, on the other hand, the supply requirements of distributive co-operative societies. Its purpose also was to undertake other special studies which would help to bring about closer cooperation between the two types of co-operatives. The secretarial work of this Committee, which had the support of the League of Nations, was done by the co-operative section of the International Labour Organization.[65]

In the political field, the *ICA* strongly opposed fascism; here the policy of the co-operatives was closely associated with that of the trade unions. In Italy and Germany the co-operatives were forced to withdraw from participation in any international agency. In Spain, the Alliance sent goods and supplies to aid the Spanish co-operatives and had raised by 1937 over fourteen thousand pounds for their relief in the firm conviction that the Spanish members were fighting not only for their own liberties but also for the principles of freedom and democracy "which form the precious heritage of co-operators in nearly every land, and which lie at the root of our co-operative system."[66]

International Organization of Industrial Employers*

Composed, before the war, of the national confederations of industrial employers in twenty-seven countries (the United States was not represented until after World War II), the International Organization of Industrial Employers is concerned with all social questions affecting industry and labor, and specifically those questions which are being dealt with, or

* Its name was recently changed, omitting the word "Industrial" from the title.

which are likely to be dealt with, by the International Labour Organization.

Its publications are not available to the public, but the author was permitted the use of a comprehensive report by H. C. Oersted, Chairman of its Executive Committee, and the following information on the work of the *IOIE* is based on that publication.

This report clearly points out that the employers were forced to organize internationally to cope with the organized efforts of labor which had long had experience in international activity, while the businessmen in 1919, when the first *ILO* Conference was held, "were absolutely disunited." When they met in Washington for the Conference, Mr. Oersted stated, "they did not know each other; neither had they exchanged any views as regards the serious problems with which production was directly concerned, namely as regards the questions of the forty-eight-hour week or eight-hour day. They knew nothing about their respective positions, had no mutual connection nor knowledge of what they would and could accept." As a result, the *IOIE* was founded the following year, with headquarters at Brussels, to defend within the *ILO* "the interest under the Employers' management and responsibility with regard to all social claims."

The constitution of the *ILO* provides that its Governing Body shall consist of thirty-two persons, eight of whom are to represent employers; eight, the workers; and sixteen, its government members. This tripartite representation is carried out also in the annual Conference of the *ILO,* where each national delegation consists of four representatives: two representing the government, one the employers, and one the workers. At the Conferences, the delegates in each category elect their own representatives to the Governing Body. Even with this direct representation, it is obvious that only a few employers come into direct contact with the *ILO.* Yet, as we know, for the successful functioning of the *ILO* it is essential that employers know the specific goals of the *ILO* and equally essential that the *ILO* know the opinions and reactions of employers regarding the various questions under consideration. Consequently, one of the major contributions which this employers' *INGO* is making is in its efforts to keep employers informed, and help them to arrive at an employers' policy, on questions before the *ILO.*

How thoroughly the *IOIE* examines these questions is explained by Mr. Oersted, and it is understandable why the *ILO* Director, Albert Thomas, in 1925 said: "It is perfectly clear that the Employers' group is provided with information for the debates of the Governing Body and the Conference by a well-developed research organization. The publications of the Office and documents circulated at meetings are consequently criticized carefully and in detail. Although the criticisms are occasionally somewhat severe, they are of the greatest value in promoting the scientific authority of the Office." We will describe this activity in Mr. Oersted's own words:

> Before a question is placed on the agenda of the Conference, it comes under discussion two or even three times in the Governing Body. This gives our Secretariat the opportunity of considering the proposals, of consulting our Members as to their preferences. . . . The Secretariat thus knows, from the very beginning, the Employers' opinions. It keeps the Executive Committee informed and the latter, after having discussed the matter, decides on the policy to be adopted in the Governing Body of the I. L. Office [International Labour Organization]. Once the question had [sic] been placed on the agenda of the Conference, the Office prepares a grey report. The latter is circulated to the various Confederations which are Members of the *IOIE* and which are requested to give their advice and to submit their objections, if any. A preparatory report on the matter is drawn up by our Secretariat previous to the Conference.
>
> At the opening of the Conference, Employers are summoned to a group meeting by the Secretariat of the *IOIE;* the work has been prepared and no time is lost when the attitude to be adopted is considered. In the course of the Conference's work further exchange of views takes place between Employers; the Secretariat draws up the notes or statements which are considered necessary and arranges the whole work.
>
> When a blue report, that is to say a proposed draft convention, is concerned, such report is analysed with all due care before the Conference. The objections of the various Confederations are gathered, as well as their attitude as regards the question under consideration. If the matter is worthwhile or if it is a special one, our Secretariat convenes a Committee composed of experts sent by the various affiliated Confederations. We have analysed and prepared in this way the work of the Employers' Group at the Conference when conditions of labour in coal mines, in glassworks, in iron and steel works, etc. came under consideration. . . .
>
> Immediately after the Conference, the Secretariat of the *IOIE* sets up a general report on the Conference's work. . . .
>
> As regards the work of the *Governing Body* of the International Labour Office, our Secretariat proceeds in the same way. . . .

The *IOIE* controls the election of the employers' representatives to the Governing Body. Before the war, it included in its slate an employers' representative from the United States, in spite of the fact that the American employers' organization was not then a member.[67]

> Apart from Conferences and meetings of the Governing Body, many *Committees'* meetings take place, which I referred to previously. The work of such Committees when it is a matter of general interest is also summed up for the Members of the *IOIE*. Our Secretary attends the meetings of most Committees.

Mr. Oersted acknowledges that of necessity the employers have defended their interest in the ILO but feels that their cooperation has been "fair and frank":

> They harshly struggled against inadmissible draft conventions or pretences aiming at the suppression of an industry which it was sufficient to regulate (white lead), or at a useless suspension of production, contrary to all scientific progress, under the pretext of giving a collective rest to workers who could as well rest otherwise (suspension for twenty-four hours in the glassworks). They even claimed from The Hague Court an advisory opinion as regards the Employers' own work which, in their opinion, had been restricted without right in the convention on night work in bakeries.
>
> But, when the question was of acknowledging the workers' right of association, of securing protection to women and children, equality of treatment to foreign and national workers, victims of accidents, compensations for such accidents, social insurances, etc., did the Employers not vote in favor of such matters without any restriction?

The report includes a detailed chart of the employers' votes on particular labor conventions in support of this statement. At this point Mr. Oersted emphasizes the attitude which has governed the employers in regard to proposed *ILO* conventions, and warns that a convention, "if it is wished to be a useful one and to be ratified—should not contain exaggerated provisions. It should not be the 'Optimum,' but should simply codify the average suitable to most countries. It, thus, represents a slow but steady progress in international legislation."

International Industrial Relations Institute

Organized in 1925, with headquarters at The Hague, the International Industrial Relations Institute has been concerned with the "study of working conditions in all Industry." In a report dealing with a decade of work, the Institute described its function as follows:

> The phrase "industrial relations" refers to the associating of groups and individuals whose working together constitutes economic life. These relations may be regarded as satisfactory when they permit all groups concerned to function effectively toward a socially desirable end.
>
> A meeting ground is thus offered within Industry itself for the fulfillment of these aims by study and discussion among individuals whose functions in relation to industry lie within the fields of the technical and managerial professions, labor, and the social sciences.
>
> There exist few platforms which offer an opportunity for the dispassionate study and consideration of the basic problems of Industry from the points of view of these related groups. To provide such an inclusive platform is precisely the aim of the Institute, open as it is to all alike in the industrial community. It draws together individuals from different nations

in order that they may become aware of their common problems in modern industry. This international character also makes possible comparative studies in different economic systems.[68]

In 1938, its individual members represented twenty-seven countries. They have met in annual Assembly. To promote the exchange of ideas and experiences, the Institute has held international conferences, summer schools and discussions, has arranged intercountry visits for its members, and has appointed a number of special study committees. The Institute has emphasized the need for world social planning, and before the war published a number of books including the well known *On Economic Planning* (1935).[69] It has substantially assisted the International Foundation for the Promotion of Visual Education which has done much to create interest in the "Neurath" or "Isotype" method of presenting economic and other facts (i.e., by symbols each representing a certain quantity), now quite commonly used.[70]

INGO'S CONCERNED WITH STANDARDIZATION*

International Federation of National Standardizing Associations[71]

The chief purpose of standardization is to reduce, as far as possible, the number of different models or sizes of manufactured articles in order to lower the cost of production. Experience has shown that considerable savings can be thus achieved. Standardization also makes possible a greater exchange of goods on the international level and helps to reduce materially the size of inventories. It has also helped to increase safety, as, for example, in the standardization of aircraft and airfield lighting, and in the standardization of the height of automobile bumpers above the ground. It makes possible the interchangeability of parts, and is of advantage to manufacturers, sellers and the general public. Today, standardization has become most important in the field of logistics, with standardization of gun parts, gauge of a railroad, etc., important elements in joint military action.

In every important industrial country there are a number of standardization associations operating in various branches of industry. In more than twenty countries these are organized in National Standardization Associations, many of which have been established as governmental agencies, with the purpose of developing uniform standards in each country.[72]

Standardization on a national level is directly connected with international trade. Maurice Berger, President of the International Bureau of

* See also World Power Conference, p. 96; International Commission for Testing Materials, p. 100.

Automobile Standardization, presents the practical attitude of France: "From the international point of view, we . . . see even better the importance that we should attach to standardization in our country and the interest that we have in collaborating closely in international agreements in order that our standards be proposed and adopted internationally as far as possible. Otherwise we would take the risk of waking up some day to find ourselves completely isolated in world production."

The International Federation of National Standardizing Associations (*ISA*) was organized in 1928, with headquarters at Basel, Switzerland, in order to assure closer cooperation between these national units in the attempt to unify standards as far as possible on the international level. Through the international meetings of its committees, which brought together "the most highly qualified experts of the various industries of different countries," the *ISA* achieved practical results in the field of international standardization.

The *ISA* established forty international committees, each dealing with a particular branch of industry, which normally convened once a year. When they reached agreement on a new proposed standard, it was presented to the member countries for acceptance. If accepted by all the members, the agreement was published as an international standard by the Federation in its *Bulletin*. About fifteen Bulletins were issued, each dealing with the standardization of more than one item.[73]

Maurice Berger points out in a lecture on standardization that the work of the *ISA* has contributed to undermining the objections of Great Britain and the United States to the adoption of the metric system: first, by establishing a greater number of international standards in metric terms; and, secondly, by helping to unify the standards of the metric countries. This greater unification, he pointed out, would force both Britain and the United States to produce metric models for export purposes, a step which would assure "a much better chance of universal adoption of the metric system."

International Electro-Technical Commission*

To promote the unification of standards in the electrical field, the impetus for which originated in official action, the International Electro-Technical Commission (*IEC*) was formed in 1906 as the result of a resolution passed by the Chamber of Government delegates at the St. Louis Congress in 1904.[74] Located in London, it was composed of twenty-eight national committees, almost all of which received government financial aid; some were, in fact, governmental agencies. The *IEC* received additional sup-

*In 1947, the International Electro-Technical Commission became the Electrical Division of the International Organization for Standardization.

port from various electrical institutions as well as the backing of associations of manufacturers of electrical equipment. Embracing practically every branch of the electrical industry, the *IEC* was "universally recognized as the official organization for the promulgation of recommendations in regard to international standardization in the electro-technical field."[75] Most of its work consisted

> in the preparation of internationally agreed rules and standards intended to facilitate international trade in electrical machinery and apparatus. These internationally agreed recommendations give the purchasers an equitable basis for the comparison of tenders from whatever country they may emanate, safeguard the manufacturers from unfair competition and so promote fair dealings all round. The Commission also dealt with the question of the naming of electrical units, the standardisation of Letter and Graphical Symbols used in Electrotechnical Vocabulary and other electrical questions of unification which are of interest to the people of all countries.[76]

To carry out this work it had established twenty-eight international advisory committees, such as Rating of Electrical Machinery, Insulating Oils, Rules and Regulations for Overhead Transmission Lines, and Electrical Installations on Ships. The Commission cooperated with many international organizations concerned with the problem of standardization. Beginning in 1921 a series of international conferences dealing with questions of electric power were held under its auspices.[77]

Naturally, the national rules for standardization in this field have been greatly influenced by the work of the *IEC,* with many of them based on *IEC* recommendations. In the field of radio it set up the International Special Commission on Radio Interference (*CISPR*) which, composed of the representatives of six international organizations, deals with the means of suppressing the interference caused by electrical machinery and equipment.[78] Also, as a result of *IEC* activities, the use of metric units in the field of electricity has been officially accepted by Great Britain and the United States.[79]

INGO'S CONCERNED WITH PARTICULAR INDUSTRIES

Cartels

Within the category of nonprofit *INGO's* in the field of business and finance fall the twelve hundred or more international cartels[80] whose influence, whether good or bad, undeniably has been extensive. It has, in fact, been estimated that 42 per cent of world trade between 1929 and 1937 was cartelized or influenced by loosely knit associations or conferences.[81] Their action has often been more important than the decisions of many of the smaller nations of the world. It is not within the purview of this volume to judge whether or not these *INGO's* are economically necessary or desirable. This question must be left to the competent economists familiar with the field; certainly, sufficient material has already been produced, both pro and con.[82] Here, instead, we are considering their organization, activities, and influence in international relations. Of course, it is impossible to state categorically what their effect on world economy has been, or whether they have or have not been a force working for peace, for, indeed, there exists too great a difference of opinion on these questions. The truth undoubtedly lies a little on both sides, since at times the cartels have made a positive contribution to international life while on other occasions, having been administered as world monopolies interested only in higher profits, they were definitely detrimental to world stability.

By grouping the national producers of a particular industry within an international organization, the cartels, often aided by national governments, have controlled the production, export and price of many of the most important commodities in world trade. In *Cartel Problems,* Karl Pribram points out, in a statement that also gives some indication of the extent of international cartelization, that: "Of the industries which have been made the object of international cartelization, only a few in number have been covered by world-wide agreements: potash, aluminum, copper, probably also rails and steel tubes and incandescent lamps. With other industries, producers of a limited number of countries arrived at international understandings. Such is the case in the mining industries with lead, zinc, magnesium, bismuth, antimony, nickel, quicksilver, ferromanganese; in the iron and steel industry with pig iron and various kinds of steel and steel products; in the metallurgical industry with sheets and wires; in the chemical industry, in the dyestuffs, nitrogen, superphosphate, etc.; in the textile industries with velvet, silk, sewing thread, and silk furnishing; and in other industries with cement, glass, linoleum, paper, ceramic products, and the like."[83]

For example, the membership of the international aluminum cartel consisted of the producers of all countries which were exporting aluminum, since the Alliance Aluminum Cie. was comprised, in 1937, of the aluminum industry in Germany, France, Switzerland, Great Britain, Canada, and part of the Norwegian industry. The production in Austria, Spain, Norway and Sweden was also controlled by the Cartel, for some of its members or the Alliance itself controlled plants in these countries.[84] On the other hand, the Steel Cartel was a regional grouping, the steel producers of Belgium, Germany, France, Luxembourg, the Saar, Austria, Czechoslovakia, Hungary and Poland adhering to the International Steel Agreement [Entente Internationale de l'Acier] concluded in 1926 to regulate the steel output in Europe. However, special agreements were made with the Swiss, Norwegian, Finnish and Dutch steel plants, and with the British Iron and Steel Federation, organized in 1935.[85] Also, as regards the North American plants, early in 1938 it was reported that the Cartel and the Steel Export Association of America had entered into an export agreement.[86]

Usually, as pointed out by the Report of the World Economic Conference of 1927, cartels are found in those industries which are already highly centralized, and come into being when world economic conditions are greatly disturbed. The *ICC* report on cartels substantiates this view.[87] In fact, there was a rapid development of cartels during the industrial depression of the thirties; Ballande points out that of eighty-one cartels existing in 1937, six were founded from 1879 to 1914; twenty-seven during the six years preceding the debacle of 1929; and forty-eight during the period of 1930–1936.[88]

By treating each industry as a world problem, these combines have controlled the production and sales of essential raw materials and products, and their economic agreements often have significant political implications in international relations. As typical of their activities, we will examine the work of three cartels, in the fields of aluminum, steel and tubes; the information for this summary is based on material in Clemens Lammers' Report for the International Chamber of Commerce.

In the aluminum cartel (The Alliance Aluminum Cie.) questions of policy were determined by a General Assembly, Board, Control Committee and the Management whose decisions the members were bound to accept. Production quotas were established by periods of three months, and the members could not go beyond their quotas except on payment of a tax, which was graduated according to the amount by which the quota had been exceeded. In addition, the Alliance regulated the stocks of aluminum held by its members, bought up excess stocks and sold these to members in need of additional supplies. Fines were imposed on members whose stocks surpassed the normal amount. Mr. Lammers reported:

> The fixed costs of the members were reduced after the constitution of the Alliance. In view of the reserves held by the Alliance for purposes of adjustment, it was possible for the members to hold smaller stocks and the fact that it was possible to reckon with the buying up of unsold quantities by the Alliance enabled member plants to organize their production on more regular lines and better to exploit their capacity.

This, according to Lammers, proved a contributing factor in reducing the price of aluminum, which, contrary to what had happened in other nonferrous metals, *"constantly* sank during the past ten years."[89]

The Steel Cartel, on the other hand, controlled not only the output of crude steel but also the production and export of many steel products. Lammers reported that this cartel went through five different periods of development between the time of its inception and the outbreak of war, involving during the different stages: first, the control of the amount of crude steel produced with fixed production quotas for the different countries; then, the control of steel exports; and finally, from 1933 on, fixed quotas for the export of crude steel and the control of steel products.[90] At this time, to control the sale of steel products a series of "comptoirs," or international sales organizations, were established.

Clemens Lammers classified the comptoirs in three categories, according to their relation with the Cartel:

(1) Those which were directly subordinated to the Cartel, such as the International Comptoir for Semi-Finished Products (established in 1933); and the International Thick Plates Comptoir (1933).
(2) Those which are more or less affiliated with the Cartel, such as the International Wire Rods Comptoir (which also fixes quotas for the domestic markets) (1928), and the Tin Sheet Comptoir (1936).
(3) Those which appear to be independent of the Cartel: The International Rail-Makers' Association (already established in 1926) and the Sheet Piling Association (1936).[91]

From 1933, the Management Committee, in an attempt "to adjust offer on the export markets to the actual demand," decided the total amount of crude steel which could be exported. This amount was then divided on a quota basis among the different countries. Groups which exported more than their quota were fined proportionately according to the excess of the exports; the money served to reimburse those groups which exported less than their quota.

The sales "comptoirs," numbering fourteen, were concerned in regulating the exports of special products such as thick plates, wire rods and sheet piling. These comptoirs, international organizations in themselves, controlled all the steel exported by the member countries; their membership embraced not only the steel producers within the Cartel but the producers of other countries, including Great Britain, the United States and Italy. These sales organizations determined the export quota of each country for the products under their jurisdiction, and fines were used to enforce the decisions. These comptoirs were concerned also with the "fixing of the export prices and of the sales conditions, the classification of the products according to grade and the elaboration of provisions concerning the activity of agents and traders." These questions were determined by a Management Committee, which decided all questions affecting the comptoirs, and its decisions were absolutely binding.

Relating to sales, an agreement had been made with the shipping companies "concerning the East Asiatic market, the excellency of whose functioning is very much appreciated in the cartel circles"; and, in addition, special market organizations were founded in eight countries through which agreements with local consumers to buy exclusively from these organizations in return for "tonnage rebates and bonification" had been made.[92]

To ensure the execution of the Cartel decisions, the Steel Agreement called for "the deposit of guarantees on the part of members for the observance of the undertakings, the checking of all figures by a Trust Company and, finally, the arbitral settlement of any eventual disputes."[93]

The third cartel we will examine is the Continental Tube Cartel,[94] for under the administration of a central office, whose functions and powers were most extensive, it regulated the domestic as well as the foreign sales of its members, including, too, their percentage of profit. As described by Lammers:

> The neutral central office of the Cartel was the Abise . . . an organization newly constituted for the purpose. The management was vested in a Committee of three members, elected by the Group Conference for a period of two years. The Abise was entrusted with the task of supervising the regular distribution of orders. It distributed among its members all larger orders, from 500 tons upwards, according to their rights and obligations, and with due reference to the business relations of the Groups, the requirements of the consumers and the geographical position of the various plants. It had to see that each Group received as far as possible its normal share of orders for the different categories of tubes. In the event of differences of opinion among the Groups concerning the questions dealt with in the Agreement, the Abise was empowered, if requested to do so, to take a binding and immediately enforceable decision. It issued fortnightly tables based on communications from the Cartel Groups, showing the extent to which the quotas had been utilized. The Abise was further called upon to supervise foreign sales in order to prevent the undercutting of the fixed export prices. For this purpose, the Groups had to send in regular duplicates of shipping documents and invoices.

During the ten years of its existence, the Cartel was successful in maintaining fixed prices.

> At the end of June and December of each year, the Groups proceeded to a distribution of export profits among themselves. In view of these settlements, the Abise calculated, according to a detailed scheme, the average profit per ton made on export products covered by the Agreement. On this basis, it then determined the sums which Groups with higher profits per ton had to remit to the others.

Lammers also points out that the Abise, on authority of the Group Conference, could "take appropriate steps to cope with disturbances of Cartel policy in the form of lock-outs or strikes."

Fines were imposed for any breach of the Agreement, and any dispute in relation to the Agreement had to be settled by arbitration if the attempt at conciliation failed.[95]

Most cartels utilize a system of sanctions to enforce their decisions. On this point Alex Skelton in the *International Control of Non-Ferrous Metals* comments, "The battles may be terrific during the negotiations for agreement and for renewal, and the differences may there prove irreconcilable, but if the agreement is signed it is usually observed. Accusations of bad faith are not, of course, rare, and if a cartel is approaching dissolution evasion may become general, but considering the inadequacy of enforcement facilities the record is remarkably good."[96] In this connection, it is interesting to note the experience of the private tin cartel, the Tin Producers' Association, established in 1929, which failed partly because the producers were not centralized, and partly because it was a loose organization whose agreements or sanctions could be enforced only by governments. The regulation of the tin industry became possible only by the establishment of the official International Tin Committee in 1931.[97]

That cartels were able to control so major a sector of world economy is a fact which cannot be ignored in the field of international organization. Whether their role helped to cushion the economic disorders before World War II is a moot question. Advocates of the cartel system argue that cartels contributed to world stability. These combines, they contend, reduced the economic evils of overproduction, thereby helping both manufacturers and labor alike. At the same time, they point out, the cartels through their quota system kept in operation plants which otherwise would have had to close. For example, during the thirties the consumption of non-ferrous metals was greatly reduced; without the protection of the cartels a large percentage of the world's metal industry would have gone into bankruptcy, plants which later would have had to be rebuilt.[98] Furthermore, they argue, cartels have curtailed widespread price fluctuations (and, therefore, speculation), and by removing the fear of a sudden rise in prices, enabled manufacturers to engage in long range planning. Further, they remind us that cartels have opened new fields of production through their research and promotional activities, as for example, the achievements of the International Office for the Application of Aluminum, which, established by the Aluminum Cartel, led "to increased possibilities for the household use of aluminum articles," and a more expanded use for alloys.[99]

The political contributions of these economic combines are, indeed, difficult to judge. However, certain facts can be stated. Cartels did achieve a measure of success in curbing unbridled competition and hostility in the world of business; their agreements often came into effect because of the pressure of governments. Widely recognized, also, is the fact that cartels have affected the commercial policies of governments, witness the power of the steel cartel. For example, beginning in 1925 the commercial negotiations between the French and German Governments were at a standstill. The steel cartel, in bringing about the industrial agreement between the producers of these countries (the agreement of November 4, 1926, known as the Lorraine-Luxembourg Quota Agreement which regulated the exports of Lorraine and Luxembourg steel entering Germany), laid the basis for the commercial treaty which soon followed. Further, the cartel agreement with the producers of South Africa resulted in the repeal of the antidumping duty which had been imposed on European imports, and through the agreements with the producers of Switzerland, Finland, Norway and the Netherlands "it was possible to avoid an increase of duties and other measures of trade protection."[100] Still to be ascertained is whether cartels through their international set-up contributed to the lessening of nationalism. W. Y. Elliott in the *Introduction* to the cartel study in the field of non-ferrous metals raises a real doubt, maintaining that these organizations took on "national color": "Although [cartels] have risen out of the dislocation produced by nationalism, they are attempting in some way to remedy it. Yet they can only act through national governments to achieve some of their ends, and they are not able to alter many of the fundamental attitudes of nationalism. They must convince every government that agrees to enforce limitation of production that its own producers will be benefited by the common 'benefit' of 'stabilized' (higher) prices. For this reason, organization of national producers into international cartels offers a useful special example of the difficulties of a piecemeal internationalism."[101] On the other hand, Sir Arthur Salter takes an affirmative position, maintaining:

> International cartels, when national associations already exist, have a . . . significance and value of great interest. They cut across national frontiers and help to eliminate them as factors in the world's economic life and competitive struggle. They thus create interests and forces which will tend to counteract the competitive nationalism which is the world's chief danger. Every grouping of the world's activities and interests along lines different from those of the national frontiers is a help in this direction. Whenever the citizens of different countries meet on a basis of common interest that transcends and cuts across frontiers . . .; whenever organisations develop on lines determined by their special purpose . . . and draw their members indifferently from every country, the foundations of international relations are broadened, and international unity no longer rests precariously on purely political foundations.[102]

International Association of Department Stores

A unique experiment in international organization is the International Association of Department Stores which, composed of seven major department stores of seven European countries, attempts to improve the management of each on the basis of data supplied by the affiliated firms. This *INGO* was organized in 1928 with headquarters at Paris. Its meetings are devoted to a discussion of common problems and a critical examination of the organization and operation of the member establishments. For these meetings, the department store to be studied submits detailed information in advance, and international subcommittees are set up to consider particular problems. Undoubtedly this survey of their work by a group of international experts has been of great value to the member stores. Also, at these meetings the action and plans of the department stores in dealing with economic changes are discussed, giving each member the benefit of the opinion of all. This type of direct contact between the members has become more and more frequent as they learned to know each other better.

The Association has organized a thorough information service for its members, collecting and distributing detailed statistics on sales, overhead expenses and other questions affecting management. The Association is also concerned with setting up standard procedures for the operation of department stores, as for example its manual of budget control which serves as a guide to the members.

What its influence has been is indicated in the following statement by Werner Kaufmann:

> Certain of our stores have made savings directly attributable to the influence of the Association amounting to millions of francs. It is impossible for me to calculate or even estimate the total amount of savings and still less the increased profits or the amount of losses prevented. . . . Under the impulse of the Association some of . . . [our members] have transformed their traditional attitude of empirical management into that of scientific management, and throughout, their attitude toward their business problems has become more objective and professional.[103]

International Credit Insurance Association

To serve as a clearing center for credit insurance companies, the International Credit Insurance Association, with headquarters in London, was founded in 1928. It was composed of thirteen leading firms from eleven countries, mostly European but including also La Buenos Aires Insurance Company and the National Surety Corporation of the United States. Its most useful executive activity has been in connection with its Evidence Bureau, established in Amsterdam. This Bureau enables the members who are interested in insuring the same risks, or who are approached from different quarters to insure the same risks, to compare notes and information. This consultation makes it more difficult for any buyer to obtain excessive insurance against credits by approaching several different companies.

Almost 10 per cent of the risks handled by the members has been registered with the Bureau; for example, up to February 14, 1933, 8,288 risks were insured involving an amount of £6,855,781. Of these, 688, or approximately 8 per cent, were registered with the Evidence Bureau. Yet the cost for this clearing service during the same period amounted to only about £156.[104]

International Federation of the Building Trades

The International Federation of the Building Trades was founded in 1905 at Paris, with a two-fold purpose: to promote the formation of employers' groups and their association in national federations; and, to initiate, coordinate and supply information on all questions relating to the general international activity in the building trades. In 1938, its membership included federations in twenty-two countries.

It has held international conferences dealing with the problems affecting the building trades; has published a monthly *Bulletin,* supplying information to its members; and has been concerned with government regulations in the field. For example, it secured in the *ILO* convention on the eight hour day the adoption "of the principle of the French law which permits the number of hours of work per year to be 2,400, with a possible increase to 2,500, and permits the making up during the good weather season of time lost during the season of bad weather."[105]

International Federation of Master Cotton Spinners and Manufacturers' Associations

Located at Manchester, England, the International Federation of Master Cotton Spinners and Manufacturers' Associations, more tersely known as the International Cotton Federation, was established in 1904. In 1938 its membership reached twenty-three countries. It has maintained statistical and research activities which are held in high esteem in business circles. Since 1906 it has issued half-yearly statistics on cotton mill consumption and stocks, "which are recognized throughout the world as the most reliable figures published." It has "studied and acted upon" such questions as "cotton mill fire insurance, revision of contracts, cotton baling, cotton standards, damp in cotton," and various other technical subjects. Since 1922, it has surveyed and reported directly to its members the state of the U. S. cotton crop (the United States before the war was the only important cotton country not represented in the Federation).

It has set up panels of arbitrators "to deal with disputes arising out of yarn or cloth transactions in various countries." It has held international congresses, the proceedings of which have been published in several languages. It has published also the *International Cotton Bulletin* which "contains original articles on cotton as well as reproductions of important subjects and articles on cotton matters which have appeared in any part of the world." It has maintained close contact with governments concerned with cotton; for example, its Joint Committee composed of cotton spinners, Egyptian Government officials and cotton exporters was able to bring about "important reforms" in Egyptian cotton.[106]

International Hotel Alliance
and
International Hotelmen's Association

In 1938 the Hotelmen's Association had been in existence for sixty-nine years, and its membership included hotel proprietors from thirty-five countries, covering a goodly portion of the favorite tourists' areas. From its headquarters at Cologne, Germany, it published several important periodicals of basic value to the hotel industry. Its weekly publication, *Hotel*, appeared in several languages and dealt with "all the acute problems of international hotel and tourist traffic trades of the various countries"; its *Technical Supplement to the Hotel* also appeared in several languages and was concerned "with the latest questions of hotel technics and hygiene." Its *International Hotel Guide* supplied information on the hotels represented in its membership, and contained the *International Hotel Telegraph-Code* for ordering rooms, which had been in existence for some time and was revised by the *IHA* to meet present-day conditions. It also issued a mimeographed bibliography, "Professional Literature on the Hotel Industry."

It maintained an Employment Bureau for both trained and untrained employees which, together with the employment advertisement section of its weekly publication *Hotel*, was able to satisfy quickly the demands of the hotel trade and the wants of men and women from all countries who were seeking hotel employment.

The Association had a widespread information service, giving legal and advertising advice, releasing lists of unreliable advertising firms, of travel agencies worthy of recommendation, etc. Part of its public relations activities were devoted to keeping the press informed on the hotelmen's point of view.[107]

The International Hotel Alliance is a more recent *INGO*, set up in 1921 with headquarters at London. Its membership comprises national hotel associations in twenty-seven countries. To avoid duplication of activities and other possible conflicts, an agreement has been worked out with the Hotelmen's Association.

The activities of the Alliance were manifold. For example, agreements were effected with the International Federation of Travel Agencies covering such questions as payments to hotels by travel agencies, and one of a similar nature was concluded with l'Association entre les Grandes Organisations Nationales de Voyages et Tourisme (*AGOT*—mainly official).[108] It carried out various investigations of interest to its members, as, for instance, an international comparison of hotel prices, cost of gas, water, and electricity, and government aid to the hotel industry. It drew up an international set of model rules for hotels, *Règlement International des Hôtels,* setting forth such principles as the rights and duties of a guest (i.e. payment for damages caused by the guest). It published a trade *Bulletin.* It was concerned with achieving international uniformity in hotel legislation and lessening the official barriers to touring. In cooperation with the International Union of Official Organisations for the Promotion of Tourist Traffic, the Central Council of International Touring, the International Touring Association and the other organizations mentioned above, it drew up a memorandum on the *Necessity of Liberating International Travel from its Present Fetters* (March, 1937) which was presented to governments, and pressed for the principle that taxation should be based on net income rather than on the value of property.[109]

International Office for Cocoa and Chocolate

The International Office for Cocoa and Chocolate, composed of chocolate and cocoa manufacturers from twenty-six countries, was established in Brussels in 1930. Its objects, as defined by the League of Nations *Handbook of International Organizations*, are:

> To study all questions relating to the cultivation of cocoa and to the chocolate and cocoa industry; to promote the solution of problems of mutual interest; to bring these solutions to the notice of national associations; to collect and circulate all material of interest to manufacturers of chocolate and/or cocoa and the associations to which they belong. It is the duty of the Office to do everything possible to carry out all decisions taken by its constituent organs—its Governing Body and Congress.[110]

The office has adopted definitions for chocolates and cocoa; its definition of a "healthy cocoa bean," for example, has been approved by many governmental authorities. It has been concerned with the question of international standardization of the weights and forms of chocolate for sale, and has collected scientific studies on the fat content of chocolate and cocoa. It framed standard contracts, as the "Draft Standard Contract for Cocoa, sold Cost, Freight and Insurance." It issued a study for cocoa planters giving the exact requirements of the manufacturers, which proved to be of great economic benefit to the cocoa bean producing territories in assuring bigger sales and less waste. The government administrations of these territories welcomed the study and "assured the Office of their entire collaboration" in meeting the requirements, and commended and thanked the Office for preparing and distributing "this important work."[111]

In 1932, on the request of the Office, the Belgian Government convoked an official conference of nineteen cocoa bean producing States, in which the representatives of the Office took a prominent part. This conference approved a project for the organization of an international campaign in favor of cocoa products which was proposed by the Office to increase cocoa consumption. The funds for this campaign were to have been raised by a small tax on all cocoa beans exported and to have been administered by the Office.[112] However, no action was taken before the war, although information had been collected on national campaigns.

International Wool Textile Organization

Founded in 1928, at Bradford, England, the International Wool Textile Organization, representing the wool textile industry of Europe, has accomplished much in promoting its interests. It has drawn up model terms of sale for various commodities such as Raw Wool, Semi-Manufactured Wool and Wool Yarn, which are incorporated in the contracts of firms who wish to buy and sell on these terms. Most important, it has established by international agreement the amount of moisture which various wool textile commodities should contain. This, as explained by the Organization, was essential for the protection of buyers. Most products of wool, with the exception of cloth, are sold by weight, and part of this weight is the natural moisture contained in the textile. For instance, it is usual for Wool Yarn to contain what is called a re-gain of 18¼ per cent of moisture. With no regulation, unscrupulous sellers could add more moisture, which is cheaper to provide than the actual yarn, thereby defrauding buyers.

The Organization has established a Technical Committee for research purposes. Members are connected with the research organizations in various European countries, such as the Wool Industries Research Association, Torridon, Leeds; the scientists who have been "thus enabled to come together have benefited materially from the interchange of views and thoughts." The *IWTO* has also endeavored to effect a world-wide reduction in the duties levied on wool textile products. The only achievement along this line was an agreement between Belgium and France in 1934, which also benefited the countries which had "Most Favored Nation" treaties with the two countries.[113]

The *IWTO* has at various times intervened with national wool producers successfully; for example, defective packing of wool from the Union of South Africa caused many complaints, and this was corrected when the matter was brought to the attention of a government official.[114]

A requirement of membership is adherence to the *International Wool*

Textile Arbitration Agreement (which has been called the "foundation stone" of the International Wool Textile Organization), by which the member associations "agree strongly to recommend to their respective members to submit all disputes to arbitration. . . ." No international court has been set up, but disputes are submitted to national Chambers of Commerce.[115] Buyers who, after accepting the arbitration clause in contracts, refuse arbitration or mediation are put on an international "black list."[116]

Permanent International Bureau of Motor Manufacturers

Representing the automobile manufacturers of twenty-four European countries, the Permanent International Bureau of Motor Manufacturers, founded at Paris in 1929, controls automobile exhibitions and races and contests, which in Europe are a leading sport, and are organized also to advertise the different makes of cars. Its members have agreed not to participate in any such event which has not received the authorization of the Permanent Bureau or, in countries represented in the Bureau, the endorsement of the member national Group. It has laid down various regulations concerning these events, which if violated can call forth sanctions. If a national Group pronounces sanctions on a manufacturer (as, for example, exclusion from its exhibitions for a period of two years) and wishes to have these sanctions applied against the manufacturer in other countries, it takes the matter to the Permanent Bureau which decides on the issue. In cooperation with the International Association of Recognized Automobile Clubs (see p. 100), such international sanctions have been applied once or twice.

The Bureau endeavors to secure the international unification of automobile terms (not standardization, which is done by the International Bureau of Automobile Standardization, but the definition of terms) such as, "useful load of Vehicle."

It produces a number of statistical and informational publications among which are its monthly statistics on the sales of new cars by makes for about thirty-five countries; statistics on exports and imports; its annual *Review of the European Motor Market;* the periodical *Administrative and fiscal regulations concerning the motor industry in the various countries;* and its *Information Bulletin.*[117]

Widely recognized is the fact that the research undertaken by these Groups for racing has contributed in producing better and safer automobiles, with the "racing car of yesterday becoming the touring car of today."

2 COMMUNICATIONS, TRANSPORT AND TRAVEL

SINCE THE means of communication and transport have been government-operated in most countries, in this field, unlike the area of business and finance, the intergovernmental organizations have always been very influential. Foremost among these are the intergovernmental International Union of Telecommunications (formerly the Telegraphic Union) concerned with international communications by telegraph, telephone and radio, and the Universal Postal Union which is the international agent for postal affairs. There has never been an intergovernmental organ for railway transport; however, since most railways, particularly in Europe, have been government-owned and -operated, almost all the international non-governmental organizations concerned with international railroad transport, like the International Union of Railways and the International Railway Congress Association, have been truly official in character. Consequently, in this field of communications and transport the prewar role of the private organizations was an indirect one, to make known the wishes of their members and to endeavor to influence official action accordingly. Nevertheless, in radio broadcasting, shipping, air, and automobile transportation, the private *INGO's* played an important part directly as well as indirectly through their influence on official action.

We have already seen the significant contributions of the International Chamber of Commerce in this general field. Later on we shall see the extensive contribution of the international law societies. Here we are interested in the work of those *INGO's* which have been directly concerned with communications and transport as well as those devoted to the promotion of international travel. The *INGO's* concerned with railroad transport, however, have been dealt with very briefly because of the official character of their membership.

INGO's CONCERNED WITH COMMUNICATIONS

International Broadcasting Union[1]

Within a few years after the first World War, the rapid increase in the number of radio broadcasting stations, from two in 1920 to 1,105 in 1925,[2] soon threatened chaos, for governments were almost totally unprepared for their new task—the governing of the air. Frequently, in assigning wave lengths to new stations they failed to assign one which would be free from interference by a station already functioning. Sometimes, one government would find upon investigation that for a certain wave length no interference would be likely from any existing station and would assign this wave length to a new broadcasting unit. In the meantime, for exactly the same reasons, another government would have assigned the same wave length, or one very close to it, to a new station within its boundaries. As more and more stations, and more and more powerful ones, started to broadcast, the interference became increasingly serious. The listener often found himself tuning in on two musical programs jumbled together with the added attraction of loud and rasping buzzes emitted by one or more spark stations using the Morse dot and dash code. The very nature of wireless telegraphy and of radio broadcasting (the sending out of electrical waves in every direction which cannot be kept within the bounds of the sending country nor excluded by any country which would prefer not to be invaded by foreign electrical waves) is such that it can be regulated only by international action.

In 1925, at Geneva, the International Broadcasting Union was organized to take the necessary international action in the European zone to put an end to the disorder that was so serious an obstacle to the successful advancement of broadcasting. Starting with only a few members, the *IBU* soon included as full members all units in the European zone which broadcast on a national scale. Some of these systems, as explained earlier, were wholly or partially controlled by governments and some were privately owned (see p. 9). Associate membership was open to non-European broadcasting organizations, and in the United States, for example, such units as the Columbia Broadcasting System, the National Broadcasting Company, and the National Association of Broadcasters were associate members. Every continent was represented in its membership before the war, and it was estimated that the programs of the members were available to fifty-eight million homes or two hundred and thirty million people.[3]

To cope with the problem of interference, beginning in 1926 the *IBU* divided the wave lengths among the European stations under the "Plan of Geneva" accepted by its members. From time to time changes were made in these designated wave lengths. At Prague in 1929 and at Lucerne in 1933 intergovernmental agreements, known as the European Radio Conventions, were concluded between twenty-seven countries of Europe and the Mediterranean region; these established the partition of wave lengths in operation before the war. The 1933 Convention was based on a plan prepared by the *IBU* at the request of the official International Conference of Telecommunications held at Madrid in 1932.[4]

To assist radio stations to check the accuracy with which they maintained the wave length assigned to them, the *IBU,* through its Technical Commission, developed a very accurate wavemeter of which more than 250 were in use in 1935. From the beginning, the *IBU* itself kept a very close watch. In 1927 it established at Brussels a sort of "air police." After that time the wave lengths of all European stations were checked and registered every day, many of them several times a day. By 1935 some eight hundred thousand such recordings had been made, and about ten thousand telegraph or telephone messages had been sent to radio stations informing them of failure to keep to the assigned wave length. Consequently, at many times the duration of serious trouble, affecting perhaps millions of listeners, was greatly shortened. The radio broadcasting organizations have always received the messages from the control center favorably and without protest. The publication of the measurements of each station created a healthy international rivalry tending toward perfection which, in the absence of sanctions or punishments for failure to maintain the allotted wave length, proved both useful and effective.[5]

The writer was privileged to visit the new building of the *IBU's* Technical Observation Post at Brussels, the center of the activities of the *IBU*, where these technical measurements are still being made with the finest instruments of an almost unbelievable accuracy. The explanation of the technical difficulties involved and the means used to overcome them were completely engrossing, even for a layman, and indicated the tremendous service which the *IBU* was rendering to international broadcasting.

The Union has concerned itself not only with the distribution of wave lengths but with all matters of interest to broadcasters from an international point of view, and prior to the war some twenty-eight employees located in Geneva and Brussels were devoting their time to its activities.

The Union has collected a vast amount of information on broadcasting for the use of its members, and its research work is especially noteworthy. In the European Radio Convention of 1933 it was officially recognized as the technical expert of governments in radio broadcasting matters.[6]

The League of Nations invited the Union to be represented at various meetings concerned with radio broadcasting. Many international organizations have utilized its cooperation in their technical research, including the official Comité Consultatif International Télégraphique (CCIT), International Advisory Committee on Wireless Communications (CCIR) and the International Electrotechnical Commission, already discussed.

In 1925, the *IBU* requested the then official International Consultative Committee on Long-Distance Telephonic Communications (now the CCIT) to give serious consideration "to the creation of an international network of telephonic circuits suitable for the long-distance relaying of not only high-quality speech but the best musical performances. This request was favorably received, a study was made—and still continues—and today most of the countries of Europe are linked together by such telephonic circuits."[7]

The *IBU* assisted the League of Nation's International Institute of Intellectual Co-operation in collecting "voluminous documentary material on the experiments in school broadcasting" which were being carried out "in most countries of the world."[8]

In its prewar work the *IBU* did much to create better understanding between peoples through the use of radio, since it not only worked to secure the necessary technical conditions which would permit the international exchange of programs, but also promoted several series of special programs devoted to that end. Among these were the "National Concerts" for which the broadcasting unit of each European country represented in the Union devoted one program a month, on the same day, at the same hour, to the music and literature of a particular nation. Preparation for each broadcast was begun four months in advance and carefully followed through by the Geneva office.

When, on its initiative, technical improvements made possible the international exchange of musical programs by long-distance telephone, the *IBU* replaced the National Concerts with "European Concerts." As described by the *IBU*:

> The "European Concert" is a monthly manifestation organized in honour of a country in the European zone, on a system of rotation and for a date fixed several weeks in advance. . . . The programmes and essential publicity material are distributed by the Geneva office of the International Broadcasting Union about three months in advance of the concert, and every month, immediately after the concert, each participant in a "European Concert" forwards to Geneva its observations concerning the technical quality of the relay, any difficulties encountered telephonically, the acoustic quality of the performance, its impressions as to the composition and execution of the concert, the announcements, and the general presentation of the programme. The opinions of the Press and of the listeners are also given. These criticisms are circulated, subject to the approval of the organiser of the relay, amongst all Members of the Union. By this procedure all are able to profit by the experience gained.

In 1936, a series of "World Concerts" was initiated based on the experience gained from the European Concerts, and here too the *IBU* collected criticisms from all the participants, which were circulated in order to improve the quality of broadcasts.

There were also "International Concerts" at which each member of the Union contributed the "cream of its musical programme." As a result of this pooling, these concerts included "performances from the Bayreuth,

Glyndebourne and Salzberg festivals, and selections from the great opera seasons of Berlin, Brussels, Budapest, Florence, London, Milan, Paris, Rome, Vienna, and Warsaw, symphony concerts of the highest order, and first class performances of lighter music from the European spas and watering places." The number of such offers made through the Geneva office increased steadily from 123 in 1932 to 881 in 1936 (exclusive of Olympic Games broadcasts).

Special programs were organized for children. In 1935, for example, the *IBU* sponsored a program entitled "Youth Sings over the Frontiers," which the Union considered "the most elaborate and impressive collective manifestation" it had organized up to that time, in which "choirs of children and young people in thirty-one countries situated in five continents sang to each other, and to the world at large, the songs they love."[9]

The work of the *IBU* has been highly valued both in private and official circles, not only for its technical contributions but also for its efforts to promote international good will, coupled with its policy of discouraging the use of any material likely to cause ill-feeling. For example, the 1937 Report of the International Committee on Intellectual Co-operation of the League of Nations states, "There has always been complete agreement that, on the international plane, technical problems relating to broadcasting can be dealt with only by the Union and by the organs it has created for the purpose; the [Technical] Commission and the Supervising Centre at Brussels."[10] The appendix of this Report includes a special summary by Professor Gilbert Murray on the "Use of Modern Means of Spreading Information in the Cause of Peace" in which he stated that the *IBU* had done "a great deal to bring about the broadcasting of matter calculated to further the objects set out in the [League of Nations] Assembly's resolution"—the furtherance of international goodwill. He reported that it was the opinion of the Advisory Committee on the Teaching of the Principles and Facts of International Co-operation that from that time on all action by the League's Intellectual Co-operation Committee, "with a view to the better use of broadcasting to foster mutual understanding among the nations, should be primarily directed to supporting the efforts already being made by the National Broadcasting Companies," and that "close co-operation with the International Broadcasting Union would be one of the most effective means of achieving this end."[11]

International Amateur Radio Union

In the same year that the *IBU* was organized (1925), the International Amateur Radio Union was established at Paris. It brought together the radio pioneers from thirty countries. Its objects are:

> The promotion and coordination of two-way radio communication between the amateurs of the various countries of the world; the effecting of

cooperative agreements between the national amateur radio societies of the various countries of the world on matters of common welfare, the advancement of the radio art; the representation of two-way amateur radio communication interests in international communication conferences; the encouragement of international fraternalism; and the promotion of such additional activities as may be allied thereto.[12]

How these amateurs have contributed to the progress of radio, how they have influenced and are recognized in the official regulation of radio has been described by Keith Clark, in his book on *International Communications*, as follows:

> The recognition in the Convention of Washington [1927], a convention between governments, of the status of the amateur, an individual, is one of the most interesting achievements in international legislation. It was however just; to the development of no other art, in the experimentations of no other science, has the amateur contributed so much. . . . [Amateurs] proved the value of the short wave length. . . . It is the amateur who has spanned the seas and connected remote continents. . . . These international amateurs [members of the International Amateur Radio Union] led in the campaign to secure recognition in the Convention of Washington.
>
> The amateur is recognized, in the latest international legislation on the subject under the term "private experimental station," to be "a duly authorised person interested in radio technique solely with a personal aim and without pecuniary interest" (Gen. Regs., Art. I). All the general rules of the convention and the regulations apply to the amateur. . . . The administration of a member state assigns frequencies to amateur stations out of the international allocation chart.

Mr. Clark also points out that bilateral treaties have been concluded in the interests of the amateur, as, for example, in an agreement between the United States and Canada.[13]

International Maritime Radio Committee

To improve maritime radio services, The International Maritime Radio Committee was organized in 1928 with headquarters at Brussels. Its members in 1938 were fourteen Maritime Radio Companies (representing about 60 per cent of all merchant ships equipped with wireless) including the Marconi International Maritime Communication Company, Ltd., and the Radiomarine Corporation of America.

In the prewar years much had already been accomplished by this Committee. In about a hundred ports the members were jointly managing the control of maritime radio depots, which have repair experts and temporary operators available for emergencies. Agreements on the calculation of the costs of these services, on the standards required of the operators, and on the exchange of experience for mutual benefit, have been successfully worked out. Also through its efforts, technical standards for apparatus have been improved, particularly in relation to installation and methods of tuning; and technical advice is given to operators. In addition, through its Scientific Centre measurements of ship radios frequently are taken so that errors (which would cause interference with other stations) are corrected. Advice on new equipment and other information is made available to the members.

The Committee defends the interests of maritime radio in official conferences and is especially concerned that the frequencies assigned for the use of ship stations should be adequate.[14]

INGO's CONCERNED WITH TRANSPORT

SURFACE TRANSPORT

In this field, as already indicated, a great deal has been accomplished by the International Railway Congress Association and the International Union of Railways. Since their membership is so largely composed of administrations representing government-owned and -operated railways we cannot consider the contributions of these groups as coming from private international organizations, even though they come within the technical definition of an *INGO*. The Union, which has been concerned with "the unification and improvement of the conditions for the construction and operation of railways for European international traffic,"[15] has worked on technical standardization; created an international Clearing Office; drawn up model international passenger and goods tariffs; issued model regulations on many subjects; and has maintained a number of information services including the publication of a monthly *Bulletin* and annual volumes on international railway statistics.[16] The Railway Congress, on the other hand, has had a world-wide membership, and its chief function has been the bringing together of experts from both governmental and administrative circles for a discussion of technical problems.[17]

International Union of Tramways, Light Railways and Motor Omnibuses

This Union has recently changed its name to the International Public Transport Union. Here too it should be noted that as public transport comes more and more to be government-owned and -operated, the Union, which was once almost entirely private, becomes more and more official.

The Union, which includes firms, group associations, and individuals such as directors, managers and engineers connected with the industries indicated in its title, has been in existence since 1885, with headquarters at Brussels, and has dealt with almost every problem connected with local transportation enterprise, from the care and feeding of horses and their capacity for work to such modern questions as "the advent of the Diesel engine in road passenger transport service," "the use of light metals in the construction of rolling stock," "the influence of the world crises on the exploitation of public transport in the great cities and their suburbs." At least 125 such studies were prepared from 1922 to 1938 alone.

The Union has made it possible for its members, which are entirely European, to benefit from each other's experiences and technical knowledge and therefore to increase the efficiency of their services and to effect important savings. The Union claims credit for "most of the improvements made in urban and interurban public transport" in Europe, and its constantly increasing membership indicates that it has been of real service to the industries it serves.[18]

SHIPPING

Baltic and International Maritime Conference

With headquarters at Copenhagen, the Baltic and International Maritime Conference, whose present-day field of interest is wider than its name indicates, is composed of shipowners, brokers and shipping associations. In 1938 its members, from twenty-two countries (all but one were European) were operating nearly ten million short tons of sea tramp shipping, only 25 per cent of which was connected with the Baltic and the White Sea.[19] It was organized in 1905 when "shipowners from various countries interested in the coal trade and the timber trade to and from the Baltic and the White Sea met together to discuss the exigencies of the freight market, which for a number of years had been badly depressed" due to cut-throat competition. It was the first organ to bring shipping interests together and "the value of cooperation was quickly discovered at a time when organization in general and concerted action by parties with common interests was more or less in its infancy."[20] The reasons for its establishment, as described by the organization itself, indicate the need for initiating international action:

> Not only were freight rates depressed during the early days of the Conference, but conditions in general in the shipping industry were far from satisfactory. Chartering conditions were more or less left to chance, and standard documents and systems had been organised in only a few trades. Agents, stevedores, and port authorities meted out arbitrary treatment to vessels in the various ports, and each individual owner had to go through a hard experience and to suffer disappointment and disillusionment without support.[21]

In the beginning the Conference "found a wide field of operation" in correcting these abuses, and although it has continued such activities during the years, in order to serve the interests of its members it has had to extend its operations "to deeper waters" and "to questions of wider interest to the shipping industry." After World War I the Conference increased its activities "to matters of general regulation such as private maritime law, tonnage measurement, labour conditions and flag discrimination," and served "as a kind of Information Bureau for Scandinavian and other shipowners in regard to market conditions in various trades. In this respect its functions resembled those of a trade association."[22] Today, as in 1938, it is ready to take action on any question affecting the interests of its members.

International Shipping Conference[23]

Established at London in 1921, the International Shipping Conference at the outbreak of World War II represented the merchant shipping industry of the leading maritime countries. At that time its membership consisted of shipowners' associations (such as the Baltic Conference) from twenty-six countries, six of which were non-European. Its objects are:

> To coordinate the views of the Shipping Industry internationally, and by means of friendly association and consultation to develop and organise cooperation amongst shipowners of the various maritime countries, with a view to the attainment of uniformity in practice, either on a voluntary basis or by means of International conventions, and/or legislation in the various maritime states.[24]

The Conference has been concerned with "the regulatory side of shipping" dealing with such varied problems as "trade barriers, flag discrimination, safety of life at sea, maritime law, shipping documents, international sanitary regulations, load line, radio, tonnage measurement, passenger insurance and helm orders."[25] It has cooperated with other private organizations interested in commerce, and has worked closely, for example, with the International Chamber of Commerce, as may be seen by reading *ICC* publications. It was a member of the League of Nations Maritime Committee, and has been represented at a number of official conferences.

International Shipping Conferences

Charles Hodges in his 1931 study, *The Background of International Relations*, pointed out that passenger and freight carrying trade has been long controlled on a world-wide basis through private organizations, the shipping companies concerned having organized several hundred *INGO's* known as "Conferences." The first such conferences came into being in the late nineteenth century (the North Atlantic Passenger Conference in 1868 and the Calcutta Conference in 1875). He wrote:

> The shipping conferences cover all the important steamship services so

that practically every trade route is self-regulated by the participating companies. The highest organization is found in the North Atlantic services, where the luxuriant "ocean ferry" traffic has been so controlled by the passenger line conference that rivalry ceases to be one of price-cutting and becomes that of accommodations and speed. Even the freight services, though hampered by the "tramp" tonnage which moves wherever cargo is offered, have gone far toward effecting similar stabilization.

Each conference represents a regional carrying trade—passenger or freight—with a permanent organization. The spokesman of the lines concerned meet periodically to adjust conditions in the light of current developments. This cooperative control may stipulate the minimum tariff charged for passengers or freight; provide for alternate sailings between lines to provide the maximum service; establish a rough classification for commodities; impose penalties for evasion; defend the conference system when jeopardized by outsiders; and even allocate traffic, in addition to providing rebates for shippers constantly using conference ships, among the lines in a given trade.

The conference organization goes far toward constituting literal government in the shipping world. It points to the lengths to which highly specialized business enterprise, international in operation however national its properties may seem, can go in establishing "autonomous" control over its own sphere. The shipping trades are significant for the way the conference system occupies the no-man's land of jurisdiction which lies "between" the nations of the world. Here the ship operators, themselves highly organized national units, have built up their own international administration where no single state alone can reach.[26]

To illustrate their organization let us glance at the conferences which have controlled passenger traffic between Europe and the United States. The North Atlantic Passenger Conference, founded in 1868, was concerned with the sailings to and from British ports, while the Atlantic Conference, itself in turn composed of several conferences, dealt with travel between Europe and North America generally. At the outbreak of World War II this conference included the Belgian, British, Dutch, French, German, Norwegian, Polish, Swedish and U. S. lines. Before World War I, the members pooled third-class reservations, each member receiving a quota; those who fell below this were compensated. After the war an arrangement controlling rates and conditions was substituted. Set fares were determined by the conferences on the basis of an elaborate classification which took into consideration the size and speed of the vessel and the type of accommodation.[27]

It is interesting to note that some of the conferences, like cartels, utilized a system of sanctions in order to ensure observance of the conference agreements, demanding "a very substantial cash deposit" from each member. If, through arbitration, failure to comply with an agreement was "confirmed," "a member could be made to forfeit up to that amount by way of fine."[28]

International Shipping Federation

Representing thirteen countries in 1938, the International Shipping Federation, organized at London in 1909, is chiefly concerned with labor questions affecting shipping. When such questions arise in the International Labour Organization, the Federation represents the interests of shippers. In this limited field it has performed a service similar to that of the International Organization of Industrial Employers, whose activities have already been discussed, in the general field of labor problems. This Federation has controlled the organization of the shipowners' group at the special maritime conferences of the *ILO*, and therefore, also, the election of shipowner delegates to the Joint Maritime Commission of the *ILO*.

AIR TRANSPORT

Authorities in this field agree that the *INGO's* have been responsible for at least the first steps in rising above nationalism in the increasingly important field of air transport. As early as 1930, Kenneth W. Colegrove expressed this opinion most strongly in his *International Control of Aviation* when he stated:

> . . . It may be said that the development of the governmental regulation of the air would be retarded if the support, encouragement, expert collaboration and even driving force of private organizations were withdrawn. Democratic Governments of today largely act at the behest of popular demand of the prodding of energetic citizens; and the orderliness of the development of international control of aviation is partly due to the intelligent labors of private organizations.[29]

Certainly, without the spadework of the *INGO's* the establishment of the United Nations International Civil Aviation Organization would have been unlikely. Undoubtedly the most important *INGO* which has been directly concerned with air transport questions is the International Air Traffic Association which, as we have already seen, has worked closely with the International Chamber of Commerce, their action regarding air mail having already been described.

International Air Traffic Association (*IATA*)

IATA (now reorganized as the International Air Transport Association) was founded in 1919, and before World War II was composed of twenty-nine air transport companies, most of which were European. Virtually all Europe's air transport companies were represented, and it should be noted, as Lawrence C. Tombs in his study on *International Organization in European Air Transport* pointed out, that these companies relied "in varying degrees" on national governments "for sustenance."[30] Legal, Postal, Technical and Radiotelegraphic Committees and a Committee for Traffic Questions assisted the Central Office located at The Hague (now at Montreal) in carrying out the objectives of the Association, which were:

> (a) to receive proposals from or to make proposals to any contracting States for the modification or amendment of the provisions of the [official] Convention [of 1919 regulating aerial navigation] and to notify changes adopted;
> (b) to carry out the duties imposed upon it by the Convention;
> (c) to collect and communicate to the contracting States information of every kind concerning international air navigation;
> (d) to collect and communicate to the contracting States all information relating to wireless telegraphy, meterorology and medical science which may be of interest to air navigation;
> (e) to ensure the publication of maps for air navigation;
> (f) to give its opinion on questions which the States may submit for examination.[31]

The Association has served its members in many ways. It has made possible the necessary cooperation between the transport companies in order to achieve such aims as "the publication of a monthly timetable for air lines . . .; the establishment of an international bill of lading, together with an international passenger ticket (1927); combined air-rail transport."[32] Annually, it has brought together the technical managers of its member companies for a discussion of such questions as the classification of causes of accidents, standardization of gasoline, electric tensions, running lights on planes, ice formation, atmospheric electricity, standardization of a mooring, towing and hoisting system for seaplanes. It has published technical and informational reports on such questions as standardization of pilot cockpits, gasoline characteristics and the quick filling of tanks, marine airports, and prevention of fire on commercial aircraft. Its Radiotelegraphic Committee has studied many technical questions; typical are the use of adcock in ground stations, radiogoniometer with visual indicator for planes, night effects on radiogoniometric bearings, suitable means for avoiding collisions between aircraft, radio-electric infrastructure, and radio beacons.[33]

IATA has had a great influence in the development of both public and private international air law. In the field of public air law a close collaboration existed between *IATA* and the official International Commission for Air Navigation (known as *CINA*, the initials of its title in French). Since the early years the Secretary General of *CINA* has attended the meetings of this *INGO* in order to assure that in the sessions of *CINA* due regard will be paid to the exigencies of the air traffic companies. To give some idea of the efficacy of their collaboration, an example is given here.

Annex H of the 1919 Convention lays down general provisions regarding customs, and point six of these provisions requires a customs declaration for the goods which are to be carried. As the drawing up of this document offered, in practice, difficulties, when a new text for Annex H was being drawn up, *IATA* appealed to *CINA* requesting that this provision be altered and that instead of a customs declaration being required, the declaration be replaced by two copies of the air consignment note. The Special Custom Committee of *CINA* accepted the proposals of *IATA*. Thereupon, *IATA* requested its members to urge their governments to accept the new Annex H in its revised form, as approved by the *CINA* Committee. This procedure was successful, and in May, 1935, at Brussels, the plenary meeting of *CINA* accepted the decision of its Committee that the customs declaration be replaced by two copies of the air consignment note.[34]

In the field of private air law, *IATA* has worked closely with the official International Technical Committee of Legal Experts on Air Matters (*CITEJA*). This Committee, whose members are appointed by governments, at the time of the war was composed of legal experts from thirty-three countries charged with preparing draft conventions on private air law to be submitted before intergovernmental conferences for action. Frequently, it has examined drafts for such conventions submitted by *IATA* and the International Chamber of Commerce.[35]

The members of *CITEJA* are mostly lawyers and, therefore, need the advice of airline operators when drawing up rules affecting air navigation. When *CITEJA* draws up final drafts to be referred to an International Conference on Private Air Law, *IATA* examines these drafts and makes suggestions. If it is too late for these suggestions to be put into *CITEJA's* draft, *IATA* charges its members to inform the government delegates participating in the International Conference on Private Air Law of *IATA's* objections to *CITEJA's* draft. This method was followed in regard to the Warsaw Convention, which incorporated many of *IATA's* wishes. Should a Convention be signed which does not recognize the interests of the airline operators, *IATA* asks its members to urge their governments to delay ratification until a new Conference on Private Air Law has re-examined the Convention. This procedure was followed as regards the Rome Convention for the unification of certain rules relating to damage caused by aircraft to third parties on the surface. The steps taken by *IATA* were successful and the Governments of Denmark, Finland, Great Britain, Norway, Netherlands, Switzerland, and Czechoslovakia decided not to ratify the Rome Convention before article 14b was amended.[36]

It was rather startling to learn that this *INGO* was able to put into effect an official international convention in countries which had not yet ratified it. Lawrence C. Tombs reported:

> The air transport companies which were members of the International Air Traffic Association had unanimously decided to apply the "general conditions for the transport of passengers and baggage and of goods," which are based on the Warsaw Convention, from the date of the entry of the latter into force, even in states which had not ratified the Convention. This important decision of the *IATA* means that, for practical purposes, the Warsaw Convention is already in effect between the points in the various countries, both European and extra-European, served by air transport companies which are members of the *IATA*.[37]

IATA applied this Convention to internal as well as international traffic. This action, which called for certain additional liabilities on the part of the air transport companies themselves, led to changes in the laws of a number of states. This was explained by the headquarters of *IATA* as follows:

> As regards the Warsaw Convention, attention should be drawn to the general conditions of carriage for passengers and goods accepted by the *IATA* in 1932. . . . When accepting these conditions the *IATA* decided to apply them not only to international carriage coming under the Warsaw Convention, but also to international carriage falling outside the scope of the Convention and further to internal carriage.
>
> By virtue of these conditions and in conformity with the Warsaw Convention, the carrier is liable in the case of death or wounding of a passenger and in the case of loss or damage to goods, unless he proves that he has taken the necessary measures to avoid the damage.
>
> Notwithstanding the fact that the national laws of several countries in which Companies members of the *IATA* resided permitted the carrier to exonerate himself completely of his liability, all members of the *IATA* were willing to carry under the mentioned conditions, though in certain cases this involved the acceptance of a liability which was not imposed on them by law. The reason why the Conference unanimously accepted the conditions was that the advantage of uniform rules for all carriage was considered to outbalance completely the disadvantage of accepting a certain liability.
>
> The influence of the *IATA* deciding to apply the rules of the Warsaw Convention to internal carriage has been far-reaching. Seven countries, viz, Italy, Belgium, Holland, Denmark, Finland, Norway and Sweden, already have passed laws by which the rules of the Warsaw Convention are made applicable to internal carriage. According to information received from official sources, the internal legislation of Argentina, Brazil, Denmark, Esthonia, Finland, France, Germany, Hungary, Norway, Poland, Rumania,

Sweden, and Switzerland will in the near future be harmonised with the rules of the Warsaw Convention. The *IATA* has decided to approach the Governments of those countries which have not yet taken steps to put their national legislation in harmony with the Warsaw Convention, and to draw their attention to the interest that lies in applying the rules of the Warsaw Convention to all carriage by air without exception.[38]

To illustrate further the type of services the *IATA* performs, here is summarized the work it did to develop combined air-rail transport of passengers and goods. Often, to effect "delivery" to a point of destination it is necessary to combine both air and rail travel; to make possible an orderly system many problems of an international scope had to be solved. This achievement has been described by the *IATA* as follows:

> In 1926 the *IATA* and the International Railway Union began to study the possibility of introducing a system of combined carriage for passengers and baggage. In 1930 a form of contract regarding the carriage by rail of passengers unable to continue their journey by air owing to the flight being broken for one or another reason, was approved by the *IATA* and the *IRU*. By reason of the form of contract, the *IATA* elaborated an agreement containing provisions concerning the legal relation between the air Companies themselves. This agreement came into force on 1st March for all the members of the *IATA* having at that time signed the agreement and concluded the contract adopted by the *IATA* and the *IRU*.
>
> In March 1933 an agreement concerning air-mail goods traffic was made between the *IATA* and the *IRU*. This agreement applies to all international air-rail carriage of goods. General conditions of carriage are annexed to the agreement, by virtue of which the principles of the Warsaw Convention are applied to air-rail carriage. The only transport document applicable to the carriage is the consignment note provided for under the conditions of carriage. This consignment note is very similar to the air-consignment note of the *IATA*. The only differences are supplementary remarks which are considered necessary by the *IRU*.[39]

International Association of Registers

Known as the *AIR,* the International Association of Registers represented aviation surveyors and underwriting interests.[40] It was concerned with a study of "the unification of statistics on accidents, principles of rules regarding aircraft performances, length of serviceability of aircraft, test flights, load capacity of aircraft, and periods of aircraft inspection" with a view to establishing common regulations and a common measuring-stick for the use of insurance companies.[41] Regarding airfields in Europe, for example, *AIR* drew up rules on behalf of European air insurance companies which "provide means of classifying aerodromes according to the degree of their compliance with the requirements laid down in order to establish a uniform system of assessing risks. The companies represented on *AIR* may issue certificates specifying the classification of a particular aerodrome under this scheme as far as any effective classification exists."[42]

INGO's CONCERNED WITH TRAVEL

Quite a number of *INGO's,* although not directly concerned with travel, are interested in the promotion of international travel as a means of education or of advancing international friendship. Some, like the Inter-Allied Federation of Ex-Service Men before the war, even maintain "tourist" services for their members, helping them to make their travel arrangements. Others, like the Hotel Associations, are interested in international travel from a business point of view. Many assist their members in making contacts while they are traveling. Still others, like the Apostolatus Maris Internationale Concilium, founded for Catholic sailors, or the International Transport Workers Federation, are concerned with the spiritual or material welfare of those who travel for a living, while some, like the International Social Service (formerly the International Migration Service), help migrants. In a way, all *INGO's* are indirectly concerned with international travel, for it makes possible the execution of their activities; in fact, makes possible their very existence. Here, however, we shall examine the role of those *INGO's* which were directly concerned prior to the war either in making travel arrangements, or in securing from governments facilities for travel, or in supplying travel information for the international tourist.

Commission for International Relations and Travel

In 1924, the International Confederation of Students,* believing strongly in travel as an educational force and as a means of promoting international understanding, founded the Commission for International Relations and Travel. This Commission, composed of the national student travel offices in thirty countries (1934), had from the beginning the following comprehensive aims:

> To act as a coordinating link between organizations interested in promoting student travel and student exchanges and to provide a forum for the discussion of new schemes and methods of work.
> To encourage the organisation of group tours between the continents and to arrange international centres.
> To secure reductions on the cost of travel and other facilities so as to bring foreign travel within the reach of as many students as possible.
> To ensure that students visiting or studying in a foreign country are hospitably received.[43]

* See p. 127. The Confederation was disbanded before World War II.

From a report published in 1934 reviewing its accomplishments to that date, we find that the Commission did much within the first ten years of its existence to achieve those aims.

The Commission established a General Tours Department and an American Travel Department which together served "as the clearing house for the regular exchange of groups between South Africa, the United States, Canada and Europe," and organized special holiday camps and social centres at Paris and Geneva. Its Report states that in the years 1928–30 alone its departments "had charge of some 430 students traveling on itineraries that lasted on an average seven weeks and covered at least five countries," and that about a thousand students took advantage of the camps and social centres at Paris and Geneva.

Annual meetings, often supplemented by informal half-yearly conferences at its headquarters at London, were held to discuss common methods and policy on tours, exchanges, hospitality, etc. In addition, special meetings were held "to study particular problems of policy and technique, such for instance as those involved in the system of Exchange and Tuition (*au pair*) Visits; services to the individual student traveller; and training of student guides."

Each national travel office provided a corps of "hosts and guides" for foreign students visiting within its borders, and arranged tours for the students of its own country. Details on these tours were submitted three times a year to the Commission which studied "the direction of new movements and the cost of accommodation and fares" to ensure that the existing facilities were being "used to the fullest advantage and extended where most necessary."

In all its work the Commission kept in close contact with the Institute of Intellectual Co-operation of the League of Nations, and was able to secure special concessions for student travelers. In the words of the Report:

> The fifth Assembly of the League of Nations adopted a resolution requesting the Governments and the Railway Companies to grant reductions and all possible facilities to students travelling. This resolution has formed the basis of the Commission's work in this field.
>
> It was essential to provide a means of identification which would establish the *bona fides* of the holder as a registered student at a University. For this purpose the Commission devised the International Student Identity Card which received the approval of the League of Nations Committee for Intellectual Co-operation in 1926. The card serves (a) as a proof of student status; (b) as a letter of introduction to student organisations and University authorities; (c) as a basis for special reductions and facilities. These facilities include Government recognition; reductions in visa charges; reductions in steamship, railway and airway fares; hotel and restaurant

tariffs; museum and art gallery fees; and a number of miscellaneous concessions such as reduced admission charges to theatres and cinemas in certain countries.

To spread word of these concessions as well as information on the services of the national offices, so that students everywhere would avail themselves of the benefits in planning their travel, the Commission published a *Handbook of Student Travel* containing information on almost every country in Europe.

International Youth Hostel Association

In the student field, the International Youth Hostel Association, which is coordinating the work of a rapidly growing movement, should also be mentioned. Founded in 1932, with national associations in eighteen European countries and the United States, it has done much from its headquarters at Amsterdam to make inexpensive travel possible for young people wishing to go abroad.

International Association of Recognized Automobile Clubs (*AIACR*) and
International Touring Alliance (*AIT*)

These two groups are being considered together, since it is almost impossible for an outsider to determine to which organization credit should go for certain achievements in the field of international touring; they advance conflicting claims.

The International Association of Recognized Automobile Clubs, now known as the International Automobile Federation, was founded at Paris in 1904 and before World War II represented the national automobile clubs of forty-two countries. Established at Brussels in 1898, and now located at Geneva, the International Touring Alliance, reaching out to sixty-two countries, had as members national touring associations as well as forty-five national automobile clubs, thirteen of which were also members of the Automobile Federation.[44] Both *INGO's* have similar interests to a very great degree. However, the Automobile Federation has been interested in tourist and travel questions from a motoring point of view while the Touring Alliance has concerned itself with international travel of every kind. Both study ways to facilitate touring and try to bring about improvements through international action. Each is concerned with customs and administrative barriers to frontier crossings, with the Automobile Federation, through its International Traffic and Customs Committee, probably having concentrated more attention than the Alliance on this aspect of the work. Both published detailed information for tourists. Before World War II, the *Annuaire Officiel* of the Touring Alliance, a volume of about eight hundred pages, contained material on the organization itself as well as information from the sixty-two member countries relating to passports, customs, taxes, hotels, money, etc. This *Annuaire* contained much the same information as the *Recueil de Renseignements de Tourisme* of the Automobile Federation. Published each year, the *Recueil,* of over fourteen hundred pages, furnished more complete information on motoring conditions in a greater number of countries, providing details for 110 countries on passports and visas, the documents necessary for bringing in a car, taxes, customs duties, price of gasoline, laws regulating driving, maps and tourist guides, hotels, climatic conditions, etc., etc. The Federation issued also a road map of Europe which was considered "certainly the most complete and exact of all maps published so far" and "the only road map of Europe worthy of the name." Its national clubs provided their members with a "presentation card" which entitled the motorist on the road to avail himself of the services of the auto clubs in all affiliated countries.[45]

These two groups have had a direct influence in securing governmental action on an international scale which has facilitated automobile touring. Undoubtedly both are responsible (although the Automobile Federation reserves sole credit for itself—a claim loudly challenged by the Touring Alliance) for the existence since 1909 of the international permits which, since they have received world-wide recognition, remove for the tourist the necessity of obtaining a driving permit as well as an automobile license in every country whose frontiers he crosses.[46] Probably both (although each claims sole credit), through the efforts of their national clubs, are responsible for the prewar acceptance in all European countries of the "triptyque," a document meeting the customs requirements of a country for the admission, for touring purposes, of a foreign registered automobile. There is a separate triptyque for each country. The Touring Alliance, it seems, acknowledges that the Automobile Federation is responsible for the introduction in 1913 of the then new document called "Carnet de Passages en Douanes" which from that time brought together "in a single document the numerous triptyques that were necessary for foreign travel by automobile" and by 1936 was "accepted in forty-five countries of Europe, Asia, Africa and America."[47]

Undisputed credit can be given to each for particular achievements. The Automobile Federation has long been interested in promoting common traffic laws, and played an important part in the League of Nations Conference of March 1931 which considered the question of traffic signs, and adopted the system which the Federation had been advocating for many years, a system "based on the geometrical form of the sign . . . triangle for danger; circle for an obligatory police regulation; rectangle for other information."[48] It has also been concerned with the regulation of international auto races and the establishment of world's records, so decidedly a sport interest that this aspect of its work will be discussed in the chapter on Sports.

On the other hand, the *AIT* performed a very active role in promoting the London-Istanbul automobile route. At its request, the Hungarian Government called an international conference of governments in 1935 to consider this question. Ten governments officially participated. The representatives of the *AIT* and of the clubs especially concerned were included in the Conference "on a footing of complete equality." The Conference adopted a number of conclusions of a technical nature relating to such matters as road widths, the radius of curves, etc. Resolutions regarding customs formalities and other matters were also passed, and the decision taken to set up a permanent committee, constituted by governments, which would supervise the progress of the route.[49]

In April 1937 representatives of both organizations cooperated in drawing up a proposed "Gentlemen's Agreement" to regulate the relations between the two organizations, and in 1938 a rapprochement seemed to be under way. This rapprochement took place after World War II, when the two organizations established a "Central Office" in London. In November 1950 the *FIA*, the *AIT* and their "Central Office" were dissolved and a new *INGO*, the World Touring and Automobile Organization, was set up to replace them.

Central Council of International Touring

The Central Council of International Touring, organized in 1925 with headquarters at Paris, should be of particular interest to the student of international organization for its mixed membership. Before the war it included government departments of twenty-four countries, tourist associations of twenty-six countries, and nine international organizations, five of which were distinctly private.[50] Its object is:

> the joint study of all questions concerning (1) the improvement of the general organisation of international tourist traffic, and also the lines to be followed in concerted action; (2) cooperation between tourist associations and representatives of Government departments, and, where necessary, commercial and industrial groups which are directly interested in travel for its own sake with no ulterior object.[51]

In an interview, the author was informed that at the Council's meetings each country represented in its membership is allowed one vote, the governmental and organizational representatives voting as a group. Each international organization votes as part of the group from the country in which its headquarters is located. The delegation from any country might include more private persons than government representatives or vice versa. How each delegation decides to vote, and whether or not the wishes of the government representatives override the desires of the private delegates is not known by the Secretariat officials nor is it of any concern to the Council.

The League of Nations *Handbook* reports that the Council "refrains from any action that might compete with the activities of national associations or international groups of such associations, all of which retain their complete independence and full powers."[52]

The Council publishes the *Calendrier Touristique International* which gives the date, place and other pertinent information on all sorts of events which might be of interest to tourists.

3 LABOR[1]

PRIOR TO World War I, labor had already made considerable progress in cutting across international boundaries to deal with questions affecting its welfare. International trade union organizations were functioning. At labor's initiative, the first steps toward regulating labor conditions through international agreement on an official level had been taken, and the demand for an international labor office had already been advanced.[2] The war almost shattered this international structure for, within the countries at war, national labor groups, like other segments of society, supported their nation's policy. However, during the war, labor found a new strength at home and did what it could to preserve its prewar international ties. It is generally agreed that labor's wartime demands directly contributed to the establishment of the International Labour Organization (*ILO*)—not to its structure, for that was a contribution of the Peace Conference itself, but to its purpose, scope and aspirations.[3] The program of two wartime labor meetings, the Leeds congress of 1916 and the Berne congress of 1919, had much influence on the Commission on International Labor Legislation of the Versailles Conference.[4] The Leeds conference was under the auspices of the Inter-Allied Trade Union Congress, a temporary international non-governmental organization, which included representatives of trade unions from four of the warring countries (Belgium, France, Italy, the United Kingdom), while the Berne meeting was a joint conference of the International Federation of Trade Unions and the Labor and Socialist International.

After the war, labor in its rising strength quickly reconstituted and expanded its international structure. The reorganized *IFTU* soon became the most prominent *INGO* in the labor field, and for political purposes the Labor and Socialist International and the Communist International came into being, both playing a leading role in the advancement of their respective political theories during the years between the two wars. During this period, also, we find that the labor *INGO's,* linking a large element of the world's population, were an effective segment of international life. Their influence was felt in the grave economic and political questions which faced the statesmen of the world, during crisis after crisis. A major part of the support given to the League of Nations and the *ILO* came from them. They performed an important educational task in promoting an understanding not only of labor questions but also of the concept of the interdependence of the world and the meaning of international solidarity. Quite naturally, they were also responsible for much of the progress achieved in international labor legislation.

International Association for Labor Legislation

The creation of the International Association for Labor Legislation, organized in 1900, has been called the "highest point" in the development of international labor administration prior to the establishment of the official International Labour Organization.[5] This Association was directly responsible for the official action taken before 1919 in the field of international labor legislation. At its request, the Swiss Government was the first to convene an official conference on labor legislation, bringing the question of international action, which had been discussed previously at private congresses, from a private to an official level.[6] Although this conference, held in 1890, failed "to produce tangible results in the form of a treaty,"[7] it was "the decisive step in the establishment of the principle of the regulation of labor conditions by international agreement, which later received its full development in the creation of the International Labour Organization."[8]

At its Brussels Conference in 1897, the first steps were taken which led in 1900 to the creation of its international labor office at Basel, Switzerland. Its Governing Body consisted of two delegates from each national committee "together with the representatives of governments which desired to take part in the enterprise." The office began its work in 1901, when its first conference was held, at which four governments were represented. In 1902, eight governments participated. Its work led to three official conferences at Berne, 1905, 1906, 1913, which adopted the first international labor conventions. These conventions, based on proposals submitted by the Association,[9] dealt with the limitation of night work for women in industry, the prohibition of white phosphorous in the match industry, the limitation of the maximum daily working hours for women, and the prohibition of the employment of young persons in industry at night. Sir Malcolm Delevingne, in his chapter on "Pre-War History of International Legislation" in the comprehensive study on *The Origins of the International Labour Organization,* states that "the experience of these conferences had an important influence on the proposals for the constitution of an international labor organization which were laid before the Labor Commission of the Peace Conference in 1919."[10]

This Association also brought about a number of bilateral treaties for the protection of workers, based on reports and information it had gathered. The first of such international agreements was the Franco-Italian treaty of 1904."[11]

The labor office of the Association was supported "partly by the contributions of national sections but more largely by subscriptions of governments." Even with this official backing it failed to achieve the official action it strove for. Paul S. Reinsch in his study on *Public International Unions* points out that the governments were reluctant "to commit themselves to any definite policy of uniformity" on labor questions, while Delevingne explains the following defects in the work of the Association:

> In its investigations into industrial questions, it could not command the information necessary. Its inquiries were carried out partly through the national sections, partly by the Office at Basel, with no access to official sources of information apart from the official publications. Under such conditions, the information on which the Association based its recommendations for international conventions was necessarily incomplete. Moreover, the reports, being compiled by persons with a particular view to promote, tended to be one-sided in the treatment of the subject. The result necessarily was that the memoranda or recommendations issued by the Association could not be accepted by governments as authoritative. . . .
>
> [The Association attempted too much and] tended to dissipate its energies over a vast field.
>
> The Association had done notable pioneer work (with which the names of Millerand, Fontaine, Mahaim, Frey, and others must always be associated), but it was attempting a task which no unofficial body could fulfill, and the movement toward international action in labor matters was destined to develop, and could only develop, on other lines.[12]

The next step proved to be the International Labour Organization, and as C. Howard-Ellis points out in his study on the League of Nations, "So well recognized is the role of the International Labour Office as heir to the old International Labour Association that the latter has been dissolved and the personnel and library of its office at Bâle formed the nucleus of the office of the new organization at Geneva."[13]

International Federation of Trade Unions[14]

Before World War II, the International Federation of Trade Unions, organized in 1901 and reconstituted in 1919, was the most important private international organization concerned with labor. Of all the international trade union organizations in existence in 1936, Alexandre Berenstein in his *Les Organisations Ouvrières, Leurs Compétences et Leur Rôle dans la Société des Nations,* judged it to be "without doubt numerically the strongest and in other ways the most representative," adding furthermore that the *IFTU* was the only one of the great international trade union organizations which accepted "the workers of all nations, of all faith and of all political opinions" and, therefore, could "claim to represent the workers' movement as a whole."[15] Even though its membership represented varying political views and included such unions as the American Federation of Labor, most of its member unions were socialist (the British trade unions, for example, constituted the greatest support of the British Labour Party). On the whole, it can be said that the *IFTU* looked forward to the peaceful and gradual replacement of capitalism by socialism. It maintained very close relations with the Labor and Socialist International, shortly to be discussed.

Its objectives were to unite labor internationally by bringing about closer relations between the trade unions of all countries; to promote the organization of workers on an occupational basis (miners, textile workers, etc.); to foster the trade union movement in all countries, nationally and internationally; to develop international social legislation; to encourage workers' education; and to avert war and combat reaction.

In 1938, it was composed of trade unions with a total membership of more than seventeen million in twenty-five countries, and in addition some thirty International Trade Secretariats were closely related to it, among them the International Transport Workers' Federation, the International Miners' Federation, the International Metal Workers' Federation, the International Union of Building Workers, the International Union of Wood Workers, and the International Federation of Textile Workers Associations. Often referred to as the "Amsterdam International" or simply "Amsterdam," during the time when its secretariat was located there, the *IFTU* had an important history, carrying on many activities, which Lewis L. Lorwin in his study on *Labor and Internationalism* classified under six headings: educational, organizational, financial, militant, legislative, and political, a classification which we shall utilize here.

Its educational activities were numerous: it maintained an information bureau, published a *Weekly Bulletin,* a periodical, *The International Trade Union Movement,* a *Yearbook* of labor statistics which was issued every three years, triennial reports of the *Activities of the International Federation of Trade Unions,* and special reports on political, economic and social questions as well as on trade union problems. One of these reports, "The *IFTU* Demands for Economic Planning," indicates the interest of the *IFTU* in economic planning which undoubtedly influenced and stimulated the action of various national trade unions in this respect, not only from the information received about other countries but also from their personal contacts with *IFTU* leaders.

Organizationally, we have already mentioned its international trade secretariats. In addition, it supported trade unions where they were weak, as in the Balkans; it helped to organize mixed committees to protect foreign workers in areas where immigration complicated the "task of trade unions," as in "the industrial frontier districts of France, Belgium, Italy and Luxembourg"; it gave assistance to union leaders in helping to organize, when faced with governmental opposition.[16]

Financially and otherwise, it came to the aid of workers in many countries. It collected and distributed relief funds for many purposes, for example, for Russian famine relief (1921–23), for the textile workers in India (1925), for the 1926 British General Strike, and throughout the Spanish Civil War, relief for the Republican workers.[17] Also, as Lorwin reported, its policy was to prevent strike breaking by outside interference and to apply embargoes against countries where big strikes were under way, provided that the workers in those countries would do "everything in their own power to stop the import and export of specified goods to and from their respective countries."[18] Typical of its militant policy to aid the labor movement of individual countries, and a striking example of how at times *INGO's* have taken direct action against governments, are the boycotts which the *IFTU* undertook. Of these, the effect of its famous international boycott proclaimed against Hungary in 1920 and the results of its action in organizing the refusal of workers to transport munitions to Poland during the attack on Russia in the same year are well known. The boycott of Hungary, "Labour's answer to the atrocities perpetrated by the White Terror in Hungary, especially against the workers," is considered the "first international trade union action of real importance" and, although of limited success, did cut off Budapest from the rest of the world and did bring about on the part of the Hungarian Government a "somewhat modified" attitude toward the trade unions. Against Poland, the *IFTU* urged the workers "to refuse all transport of goods for war purposes," and called upon the national federations to enforce this decision "if necessary by mass action or by a General Strike." The *IFTU* has stated that this action, falling short of its ultimate aim, did however prevent any government from giving aid to Poland against Russia, "in view of the attitude of the trade unions."[19]

The legislative and political actions of the *IFTU* have been perhaps the most important. As Lorwin pointed out, it attached great importance to "the promotion of social legislation—of protective labor laws, of laws extending the rights and powers of trade unions, and of social insurance," and toward this end took an active part in the International Labour Organization. In executing its legislative program, Lorwin adds that the *IFTU* trod "upon the precincts of politics," and became "entirely political in character, when concerned with general economic and political objectives." This was the case concerning its action on such international questions as the occupation of the Ruhr, reparations, etc., and in its relations with the League of Nations and its organs, the *IFTU* having demanded "special representation at all official gatherings dealing with world problems and on official international commissions or committees."[20]

Concerning the occupation of the Ruhr:

> In the years 1920–1921 the threatened military occupation of the Ruhr District played a fateful and disturbing part in European politics.
>
> After receiving the report of the commission sent by the Federation of the Ruhr District, the London Congress declared that the organised workers were prepared *to use all and every means to oppose such measures and to prevent a military dictatorship over the workers in the Ruhr District.*
>
> It is an open secret that this decision was very largely responsible for causing the constantly threatened occupation of the Ruhr at the end of 1920 to be abandoned; and furthermore in causing the exclusion of the Ruhr District from the application of the Sanctions which were so severely condemned by the International Federation of Trade Unions. The trade unions had no need to take any subsequent action in this matter.[21]

In discussing the role of private organizations in bringing about a successful solution to the problem of reparations, the action of the *IFTU* needs to be mentioned. In its *Report on Activities* for 1924–1926 we find the following statement:

> Under these circumstances [the occupation of the Ruhr] the *IFTU* could not do otherwise than again point to the fatal results of the policy of sanctions (which were quite without practical results), and urge strongly a final settlement of the reparations. A comprehensive memorial sent to the Fourth Assembly of the League of Nations in September, 1923, again set forth the policy of the *IFTU*. In the memorial . . . it was declared that if it was desired to fix the capacity of Germany to pay, and the total amount of her liabilities, this could not be done by one side only, namely, by the creditor: Germany must take her full part in the discussions. The demands laid down in the memorial were emphasized still further by a Conference of the *IFTU* with the *LSI* [Labor and Socialist International], which took place in 1923 at Brussels. . . . The settlement outlined by [the Reparations] Commission (known as the Dawes Plan), which fixes definitely the specific amounts to be paid by Germany every year for reparations purposes, was in 1924 finally accepted by the governments concerned including that of Germany. The *IFTU* approved the adoption of this settlement, which was entirely in harmony with the policy it had pursued for years.[22]

The *IFTU* had great influence in the work of the League of Nations. For example, it participated in the 1927 Economic Conference and in the Commissions on trade, industry and agriculture created by this Conference. In this respect, Léon Jouhaux said before the *IFTU's* Fourth International Congress, "We may recall here that the scheme for an economic conference arose out of ideas which I myself expressed when I spoke in the Third Commission of the League Assembly, in September 1924, not only as a member of the French delegation to Geneva, but also, and explicitly, in the name of the Labour Movement."[23] The *IFTU* presented, and offered widespread support to, proposals for disarmament at the Extraordinary Session of the Disarmament Conference in Geneva in 1932. Also, the *IFTU* evidently played an important part in the establishment of the League of Nations High Commission for Refugees. In the *IFTU's* 1933–35 Report we find the following statement:

> As will be remembered, Comrades Kupers, Mertens, Jouhaux, and Schurch submitted a resolution to the International Labour Office, immediately after the breakdown in Germany, which demanded that the refugees should, through an international agreement, be granted the rights of citizenship of those countries which had taken them in. The International Labour Conference adopted this resolution with slight amendments in June, 1933, and transmitted it to the League, and it is mainly due to this initiative that the League Council decided to set up a High Commission for Refugees (Jewish and Other) coming from Germany, and appointed Prof. James McDonald to the post of High Commissioner at the beginning of November, 1933.
>
> In agreement with the Management Committee of the International Matteotti Fund, the General Secretary of the *IFTU* at once got into touch with the High Commissioner, with the result that the workers' organisations seat was given to the *IFTU*, as being the most representative organization of the workers. . . .[24]

It is no exaggeration to state that without the support of the *IFTU* it is doubtful whether the International Labour Organization would have been able to function successfully in the period before the war, for the *IFTU* played a vital role not only in the actual workings of the *ILO* but in supplying the support and pressure needed to secure national ratifications of its conventions. From the very first days of the *ILO's* existence, the *IFTU* exercised tremendous influence. It was responsible for the early admission of Germany and Austria into the *ILO*, forcing this decision before the trade unions would agree to participate in the Organization. Without their participation, the Washington Conference, the first *ILO* Conference, could not have been held, and this forced the Allied Supreme Council to accede to the wishes of the *IFTU*.[25]

From early days on, the *IFTU* had almost complete control over the election of workers' delegates and workers' policy in both the Conferences of the *ILO* and in its Governing Body.* Constantly it was engaged in a study of the problems before the *ILO*, and secured agreement among its

---

* For structure of the *ILO* Conferences and Governing Body, see p. 257.

members well in advance of the *ILO* Conferences as to the policy they would follow there. When the workers' group was organized just before each Conference met, the *IFTU* was in control. Usually an official of the *IFTU* was chosen as secretary of the workers' group.

Berenstein in his study refers to the "remarkable cohesion and discipline always shown" by labor at *ILO* Conferences, and points out that it is freely consented to since nothing obliges the members of the workers' group to conform to the decisions which are made.[26]

Within the *ILO,* the attitude of the *IFTU* toward Fascist workers, representatives of the Christian trade unions and of other international associations needs to be summarized, for the *IFTU* was able to have its way to a considerable extent. The *IFTU*-controlled workers' delegates repeatedly challenged the credentials of the Italian workers' delegate to the Conference "because of the failure of Italy to respect the freedom of association which is stated so clearly in the Peace Treaties." They also "kept the Italian workers' delegate from committee memberships, out of the Governing Body, and consequently from the committees of the latter." The Christian trade unions of Europe, shortly to be discussed, also were excluded by the *IFTU* from Conference committees, and from membership in the Governing Body,[27] "though not with the same rigor as the Fascists." For two years, the *IFTU* allowed the International Federation of Christian Trade Unions to have one substitute delegate on the *ILO* Governing Body, but soon discontinued this practice. As far as the *ILO* is concerned, the main difference of policy between the Christian and Socialist (*IFTU*) trade union representatives was their attitude regarding the acceptance of the credentials of the workers' representatives from the USSR. The Christians protested against acceptance, while the Socialists reluctantly accepted. The *IFTU* even tried to prevent members of the Christian Trade Unions from being appointed as advisers on the national delegations to *ILO* Conferences. Francis G. Wilson in his study on *Labor in the League System* reports that this attitude of the *IFTU* toward the Christian Trade Unions was finally brought before the World Court for an opinion.

The Court in its first advisory opinion (1922), "sustained in fact the thesis of the Christians and weaker unions of the Netherlands . . . that when article 389 of the Treaty [*ILO* Constitution] speaks of appointing the workers' delegate from the most representative body of the workers, it does not mean that one organization, the one with the greatest membership, shall be consulted exclusively by the government."[28]

With the rise of Fascism in Germany, the credentials of the Fascist workers' representatives were also challenged. Here, Wilson reports, the result was "the withdrawal of the entire German delegation from the Labor

LABOR 83

Conference in 1933," and this "motivated, no doubt," the German Government to withdraw from the *ILO* in 1933, when it withdrew also from the League.[29] Wilson also reported on the attitude of the *IFTU* toward other international organizations:

> It must be said for the *IFTU* that it has not adopted a wholly niggardly policy as to other workers. Its representatives have defended the interests of professional and intellectual workers when they have been before the Organization, as they have likewise supported the claims of agricultural workers and salaried employees. While organizations of disabled war veterans have sought recognition by the Organization, just as have the cooperatives, the workers' representatives have, in general, been opposed to formal recognition of either the veterans' organizations or the cooperatives. They have felt a fundamental distrust of the cooperatives, and the general view has been that any problems of the veterans should be settled by national collective agreements rather than by international action.[30]

These groups, he reports, owing to *IFTU* domination, were able to secure representation in the *ILO* only through "the appointment of their representatives to committees of experts" which are set up by the *ILO* office to assist it in research on special labor problems.[31]

This control by the *IFTU* naturally determined to a great extent the type of labor questions which became the subjects of *ILO* Conventions, and determined, therefore, the direction which international labor legislation took in the years before World War II. The *IFTU* was concerned not only with the drawing up of *ILO* Conventions, but also with their ratification by governments, and upon ratification, equally concerned with their enforcement in the individual countries. The *IFTU* made a conscientious effort to collect, from its national members as well as from unaffiliated trade union groups, detailed information on the application of conventions within their countries, which it made available to *ILO* Conferences. From a reading of the verbatim reports of these Conferences it is evident that the government and employers' representatives "delegated" criticism of the application of *ILO* Conventions to the workers' delegates. This, of course, had important political significance. First, it prevented the need for one government to criticize the action of another, and secondly, as Jean Zarras points out in his study on *Le Contrôle de l'Application des Conventions Internationales du Travail*:

> The degree of trade union liberty existing in the defaulting country may not be such as to permit the workers to freely criticize their government. Thus it sometimes happens that the workers' delegates from a country having an authoritative government do not have the courage to speak freely to the Conference. But even in this case, other qualified representatives of the workers' group, duly warned and fully documented, denounce as far as

necessary the illegal policies of these states by speaking in the Commissions or from the tribune of the Conference. Thus governments, when this happens, are obliged to recognize the right of the workers' delegates, even those belonging to another state, to make public charges against themselves (the states) regarding the way in which they observe their international obligations.[32]

Politically, also the *IFTU*, as already indicated, fought Fascism, and its attitude toward communism was equally adamant. Strongly opposed to the theory of a "dictatorship" of any type, it carried on a strenuous fight against the Communist trade unions; its opposition to communism is reviewed below.

International Federation of Christian Trade Unions

The International Federation of Christian Trade Unions, together with its Trade Secretariats, came into being after World War I; it was founded in 1920 with headquarters at Utrecht. Its membership, completely European until after World War II (in 1938, Austria, Belgium, Czechoslovakia, France, Hungary, Luxembourg, Netherlands, Yugoslavia), has never been large; in 1938 its membership totaled about one-tenth of that of the *IFTU*. Some twelve trade secretariats are affiliated with it, such as the International Federation of Christian Trade Unions of Railway and Tramway Men, the International Federation of Christian Workers in the Building Trade and of Wood-workers, and the International Federation of Christian Factory and Transport Workers' Syndicates. Its objectives prior to World War II were "to spread the ideas of Christian trade unionism in all countries," especially in those in which the movement is not represented; to defend "the social and economic interests" of workers within the League of Nations and the *ILO;* and "to exert its influence in international economic and social life."[33] Due to its limited membership, both in numbers and in area, its influence has been considerably less than the *IFTU* or the Labor and Socialist International.

Labor and Socialist International

The Labor and Socialist International (*LSI*) represented in the prewar years the labor and political parties which accepted as their goal "the economic emancipation of the workers from capitalist domination and the establishment of the Socialist Commonwealth," and which believed in "the class struggle which finds its expression in the independent political and industrial action of the workers' organisations" as the means for attaining their objectives.[34] At the height of its influence, in 1931, forty-six socialist parties of thirty-five countries were members.[35] Founded at Brussels in 1923, as the postwar successor to the Second International, discussed below, it soon rose to prominence, particularly when the Labor Party in England was in power; at that time the *LSI* was quite influential in European affairs. In the thirties, however, because of the rise of Fascism and the decline in strength of the British Labour Party, its influence started to wane. During these years, it lost some of its most important members and unlike the *IFTU* and many other international labor organizations it was unable to make up this loss in membership, particularly since the American and Canadian union groups, then growing in numbers, were politically to the right of socialism. Before the outbreak of World War II, needless to point out, it was impossible to judge what the strength or role of this *INGO* would become, for at that time the future of socialist political parties seemed to depend on whether or not Fascism continued to grow.

Its influence was mainly of a propagandist or educational nature. It assisted its members by various publications and the furnishing of information. It endeavored to promote its ideals through the press and by holding large international congresses and smaller conferences. Its last printed *Reports and Proceedings,* of more than nine hundred pages, was for its 1931 congress. One of the most important services it performed was the opportunity it offered to socialist leaders of the different countries to meet and discuss common problems. It assisted the weaker parties and, financially and otherwise, went to the aid of the victims of political persecution. C. Howard-Ellis, in his 1928 study of the League of Nations, pointed out that a number of the government delegates to the League Assemblies were members of the *LSI,* and they tended "to form a group at the meetings of the Assembly for the purpose of exerting joint pressure on their delegations" on questions where there existed "an agreed Socialist policy in many countries."[36]

It cooperated closely with the International Federation of Trade Unions and with such socialist organizations as the Socialist Youth International, the Socialist Workers' Sport International, the International Commission for Resistance to Fascism, and the International Alliance of Socialist Lawyers. As is well known, socialist organizations carried on a continuous fight against Communism until the late prewar years, when the menace of Fascism made a "United Front" seem necessary. They showed as bitter antagonism toward Communism as toward Fascism, and were suspicious of the "United Front" appeals of the Communists. For example, in the 1931 Report of the *LSI,* it is stated:

> During the period under review, as in previous periods, there has been no intercourse of any kind with the Communist International and its auxiliary institutions. The attempts at a "United Front Manoeuvre" were less frequent than in the past. They are rendered more difficult at a time when

the Communist International is carrying on the fight against Social-Democracy under the shameful slogan of "Social-Fascism."[37]

Also, in the reports of the *IFTU*, whose membership was predominantly socialistic and anti-communist, we find this attitude toward the United Front Policy:

> The harnessing together of democratically-minded Socialists with dictatorially-minded Communists does not mean—and this avowal must be made courageously!—any strengthening, but a weakening, of the fight against Fascism. It means a weakening because the principle of democracy comes to be questioned even among the supporters of democracy themselves; because the unequivocal democratic creeds, both within our ranks and beyond them, become sullied with the suspicion that concessions at least are being made to dictatorship; because finally a working class front of a purely proletarian character inevitably loses the support of all the other sections of society whose cooperation, as we know, is essential for the defeat of Fascism and the creation of a new economic and social order.
>
> It should be particularly emphasized here that the abhorrence of the dictatorship methods of violence and terror aroused among all sections of the populace and not least among the workers (who have been most affected by it), does not even in the Fascist countries offer the slightest chance of success to, and indeed deprives of all its point, the slogan of a counter-dictatorship of the workers. We believe that it is just in the Fascist countries that our deeply-rooted aversion to any kind of dictatorship must be most clearly and plainly expressed, not least because a successful fight can only be waged in the Fascist countries with the help of the peasants, craftsmen, middle classes, etc., who cannot be won over to the idea of any kind of dictatorship whatsoever. We can reach these sections of the people if we place in the forefront the ideals of human dignity, democracy, self-determination and freedom, which have wrongly been brought into discredit. . . .
>
> No one can accuse us of trying to prevent or of not desiring the formation of a really sincere United Front of the workers, aiming at a common purpose, but the very importance of unity itself makes it essential at the same time that this unity shall not be established at the price of automatically isolating us from the other classes of the people—the peasants, craftsmen, the middle class, non-manual workers and officials, etc. The political United Front, even if it is not clear as to its ultimate aim, must inevitably bring with it such isolation for our movement, and not only isolation, but it will actually alienate the other sections of the population instead of making them rally to our ideals.[38]

Communist Internationals

The part played by an *INGO* in the origin of the famous Communist Manifesto of 1848 is described by Alexandre Berenstein in his comprehensive study on labor organizations:

Let us recall the circumstances under which the Manifesto was drawn up. In 1837 a little "Federation of Communists" . . . held two Congresses at London. It was composed internationally, but the Germans were in the majority. Karl Marx . . . became very quickly the most influential. The second Congress which had adopted, after ten days of debates, the principles on which the program of the federation was to be based, charged Marx and his friend Engels to draw up a manifesto to the workers of the whole world. At the beginning of 1848, the Communist Manifesto made its appearance at London.[39]

The history of the "First International" is briefly described by Carlton J. H. Hayes in his *Political and Cultural History of Modern Europe:*

The particular organization which Marx himself founded and directed was not very strong or influential. Formally established in 1864 [at London] as the "International Workingmen's Association," and usually referred to as the "First International," it comprised groups (or sections) of workers in various countries of Europe (and in the United States) and held several international congresses. It did spread a knowledge of "Marxism" and it did alarm the governments of the time. Its membership, however, was small and poor; and, despite the strenuous efforts of Marx and Engels, it suffered from the passions attendant upon the Franco-Prussian War, from the disillusionment following the suppression of the Paris Commune in 1871, and from internal dissensions arising from the expulsion of anarchist members who criticized Marx. The last real congress of the Association was held at Geneva in 1873, and its dissolution was decreed by a few of the faithful assembled at Philadelphia in 1876. [Its headquarters by then had been transferred to New York.][40]

The Second International functioned from 1889–1914 and, according to Lenin, under the leadership of Karl Kautsky it "adulterated" the revolutionary aspects of Marxism and instead tried to fight capitalism through parliamentary means. When war broke out in 1914 and it failed to live up to its threat of "war against war," it came to an abrupt end.[41] After the war, in 1923, it was reconstituted as the Labor and Socialist International.

Following the Russian Revolution, under the leadership of Lenin the Third International held its first congress at Moscow in 1919. This Third International, called the Communist International and known also as the Komintern, was composed of Communist political parties of various countries and, unlike its predecessors, was interested in the formulation of basic international policy. Many have felt that this International could not be classified as an *INGO* on the grounds that since its beginning days its policies in all countries seemed to be determined or directed by the government of the USSR, regardless of the fact that Russian officials disclaimed any responsibility for or control over its actions. Whatever its status, its great influence, even in leading countries like France and China, must be recognized.

At its second congress in 1920 it founded the Red International of Labor Unions (*RIUL*) which met for the first time at Moscow, the seat of its headquarters, in 1921, for at this congress it was decided that the *IFTU* "because of its programme and tactics" could not "secure the victory of the proletarian masses in all countries," and therefore a new trade union movement was needed:

> It is the duty of the working class to gather together all trade union organised forces with a powerful revolutionary class association, which, working shoulder to shoulder with the political organisation of the Communist International of the proletariat and in closest contact with this organisation, would be able to develop all its forces for the general victory of the social revolution, and the establishment of a world Soviet Republic.[42]

The *RIUL* had very little influence in the years before World War II. Although it claimed an affiliated membership of nineteen million, over ten million were from the USSR; of the remainder, it claimed over a hundred thousand members in Cuba, Australia, Czechoslovakia, United States; over five hundred thousand in France and Great Britain; one million in Germany and three million in China. "These figures include the membership of minority groups within trade unions which are affiliated to the *IFTU*. It will be seen that no national trade union body representing the whole of the organized workers of any country, apart from Russia and certain small countries where trade unionism is an ineffective force, has associated itself with the *RIUL*, and that outside Russia its chief support comes entirely from individual trade unions and minority groups, though Losovsky is at pains to point out that the figures of membership of the *IFTU* are swollen by the adherents of the *RIUL*."[43]

How the *IFTU* felt toward the *RIUL* is well recorded in its 1933 Report: "Another cause for congratulation is the complete decay of the Communist disruptive organization in every country except Russia. Trade union work cannot possibly be done by means of empty phrases and slogans; it must be practical, and the results obtained must be in harmony with the demands put forward. In view of this, Communist trade union work is foredoomed to failure. In fact, the whole of the Red International of Trade Unions, which was started in 1920 on purpose to oust the hated 'Amsterdam International,' is now defeated and prostrate. In name, it is true, it is still in existence, and now and then it launches an appeal in order to remind the world that it is still there. In reality, however, it is now little more than an International Propaganda Committee of the Russian Trade Union Movement. Its complete insignificance is, indeed, so obvious to all eyes that it is not worth while to waste more time on it."[44]

4 AGRICULTURE

ON THE international level, agriculture, in sharp contrast to the business and labor worlds, has not been organized highly nor has so much been accomplished. The failure until recently to develop strong national organizations of farmers in most countries is undoubtedly a major cause; this failure has been due partly to the lack of the means essential for organizing—transportation, money, etc.—and partly to the fact that farmers have a tendency to be rather "isolationist," an attitude which is rapidly changing. Yet, there have been important international non-governmental organizations (*INGO's*) established and significant achievements in this field. We have already seen something of the work of the steadily increasing cooperative movement among agricultural producers. There are also the international associations of producers in particular fields, such as the World's Poultry Science Association (1912), International Goat-Breeding Federation (1925), International Federation of European Beet Growers (1932), International Federation of Olive-Growers (1934). These *INGO's* represent and promote the interests of their members internationally; organize congresses; encourage scientific research and practical experiments to improve methods of production; promote educational programs toward this end, including the sponsorship of demonstrations; maintain informational services on economic as well as technical questions; undertake campaigns to promote greater consumption, and to suppress fraud in the marketing of products. Before World War II there was, however, only one overall *INGO,* the International Commission of Agriculture.*

The first steps to cope internationally with common agricultural problems were the results of private initiative. F. Houillier in his *L'Organisation Internationale de l'Agriculture* states that the first international convention relating to agriculture was the 1878 convention concerning phylloxera. He points out:

> [The] wine-growers, victims of the parasite, met first at Montpellier in 1874 and a second time in 1877 at Lausanne. They succeeded, the following year, in securing the signature, at the diplomatic conference convoked at Berne, of a convention laying down international measures of protection against the phylloxera.

* Since the war there has been established an International Federation of Agricultural Producers.

This convention, modified in 1881, is still in force. It was, according to Houillier, successful in meeting the problem and demonstrated that international agricultural problems exist and are susceptible to solution by international action. He goes on to say:

> ... it is not to states that we owe the origin of the international agricultural movement. We saw that meetings of wine-growers preceded the convention on phylloxera; when the French government tried in 1878 to organize international agricultural statistics it was by request of an international congress of statistics; and finally, when, at the congress of 1889 it was thought of having regular international agricultural congresses, and when two years later the International Commission of Agriculture was created, it was from private groups and personalities of the agricultural world that support was sought.[1]

International Commission of Agriculture (*ICA*)

Founded in 1891, as Houillier points out, primarily to organize regular international congresses, the International Commission of Agriculture, known also as the International Confederation of Agriculture, was reorganized in 1926 and 1928 to serve as an international union of agricultural associations. Its membership has embraced both national and international groups interested in the advancement of agriculture, including forestry, viticulture, animal husbandry, and other branches of agriculture; in 1938, eighty-six associations from twenty-three countries were members. Among the international organizations represented were those organized in particular industries, such as the beet-growers, the International Federation of Technical Agriculturalists, the International Agrarian Bureau (composed then of political parties in sixteen European countries), and the International Secretariat of Women's Rural Associations.[2]

The *ICA* has been a center of documentation; its congresses, "true meetings of international agriculture," have been convened every two years and have had real influence. First, they have dealt with every significant problem of international interest in agriculture, and the reports prepared for these meetings have been of value in advancing basic knowledge of the various problems in agriculture. The congresses have dealt with "agricultural policy and rural social economics; training and propaganda in agriculture; agricultural cooperation; production of vegetables; viticulture; animal husbandry, with frequent sub-sections on pisciculture; farm industries; women in the agricultural economy." Second, the resolutions adopted at these meetings have given influential backing to the aims of individual organizations representing particular agricultural interests. Owing, undoubtedly, to the lack of highly organized national units, the recommendations of these *INGO's* have not met with quick success; Houillier states:

> It does not seem that governments pay much attention to the resolutions which are sent to them by these associations; their result is, therefore, so to speak, invisible. It is sometimes only by the repetition of the same desires and at the end of many years that the ideas of such meetings come to be carried out. Thus the protection of birds desired in 1884 by the ornithological congress at Vienna, became a reality only on the 19th of March, 1902. Likewise the problem of the adulteration of food stuffs, of seed, of poultry-food [engrais], reached a solution only in 1912.

The *ICA* has helped in supplying the needed pressure to bring problems of concern to its member organizations to governmental attention. Third, the congresses of the *ICA* have formulated significant programs of action, as the recommendations of its Berlin 1933 meeting illustrate.[3]

At this meeting, the *ICA* made preparations for the 1933 International Economic Conference at London. The memorandum it drew up for submission to this Conference was based upon certain principles which were later adopted by the Economic Commission of the Conference. The *ICA's* memorandum emphasized that if chaos in agriculture was to be overcome, both the production and export of agricultural products had to be organized. This would require national and, then, international agreements among particular industries. These agreements (both bilateral and multilateral) would have to provide for reciprocity of both obligations and advantages, and the *ICA* stressed that they would prove effective only if limited to one product, or to a group of allied products. The Economic Commission incorporated these principles in its resolutions concerning the possible coordination in the sale of dairy products, sugar, wine, wood, coffee, cocoa, rubber, coal, copper and tin. The *ICA's* Berlin resolutions had other repercussions in a number of bilateral treaties concerning the export and import of agricultural products, conforming with these principles; for example, the 1934 arrangement between Poland and Germany, and the 1935 agreement between France and Poland, which resulted also in the establishment of a "Chambre" for the development of the exchange of agricultural products between the two countries.[4]

Its relationship with governmental organizations has not been always most cordial. In the beginning much was expected from the International Institute of Agriculture at Rome.[5] Paisant reports that M. Louis Dop, Vice-President of the Institute, at its 1909 general assembly expressed himself as follows on article nine of the 1905 convention establishing the Institute:

> By recommending that the Institute be inspired by the wishes expressed by the [private] International Congresses, when it presents to Governments

the measures that it judges favorable to the interests of agriculture, the convention of 1905 confided to it a mission of considerable theoretical importance; it constitutes an implicit recognition by the creators of the Institute, of the present and future usefulness of the [private] International Congresses and a justification of the Commission [the *ICA*] charged to ensure their continuation. Practically it solves the problem of how to use the efforts put forth by private initiative.

Paisant adds: ". . . the representatives of the Institute always have a place reserved for them in the Congresses; . . . the heads of the agricultural associations who meet each other in the International Commission of Agriculture usually take part also in the Government delegations to the General Assemblies of the Institute; they meet again in the Permanent International Commission of Agricultural Associations . . . [of the Institute]."[6]

However, Houillier says that "the reorganization of the International Commission of Agriculture may be interpreted as a reaction against the centralizing and absorbing tendencies of the International Institute of Agriculture." Adding that one cause of the "feebleness" of the official Institute was lack of money, he continues:

> Another cause of weakness is to be found in the tendency of the Institute to regard itself as alone qualified to treat agricultural questions. For example, it committed, in a certain sense, the blundering action of creating consultative organs such as the *P.I.C.A.* (Permanent International Commission of Agricultural Associations)[7] and the *I.S.A.C.* (International Scientific Agricultural Council). It would have done better to make use of the existing organizations: for example, a good number of the commissions of the *I.S.A.C.* only duplicate the pre-existing international scientific institutions [olive-growers, wine-growers, etc.]; it is true, on every side, one often encounters the same experts. But what is one to think of an institution which proclaims in creating the *C.I.C.A.* [International Agricultural Co-ordination Commission][8] that it wishes to eliminate "all over-lapping of work, all loss of time and energy" and which, itself, gives the example of this overlapping.[9]

Little can be said of *ICA's* relations with the League of Nations, for agricultural work was largely lacking from the League's activities. It was, however, represented on the Economic Consultative Committee (1927–1930) set up by the Economic Conference of 1927. Paisant states:

> The Economic Consultative Commission asked in May 1929 that agricultural experts be associated in a permanent manner with the work of the Economic Committee of the League of Nations. Conforming to this wish, supported by a resolution of the International Commission of Agriculture . . . a Committee of Agricultural Experts was constituted at the end of the year, but it met only twice, in January 1930 and January 1931.

The absence of agricultural experts in the Economic Committee of the League of Nations was keenly felt, notably in that it deprived its resolutions of all credit in the agricultural world, and the International Commission of Agriculture had occasion in its meeting at Brussels, in 1935, . . . to criticize the report on agricultural protection presented by the Economic Committee. On this occasion . . . the International Commission of Agriculture expressed the desire that the Economic Committee of the League of Nations should henceforth examine agricultural problems in close contact with agricultural groups, and by that secure for itself, as it had already done in the past, the assistance of qualified agricultural experts.[10]

Its relations with the *ILO*, since both organizations desired collaboration, have been close. On the International Committee of Inter-Cooperative Relations, for which the *ILO* performed secretariat services, both the International Commission of Agriculture and the International Cooperative Alliance were members; this committee has already been described in connection with the latter.

5 THE ARTS AND SCIENCES

THE RESEARCH worker in the natural sciences fully appreciates the meaning of interdependence, for his interests do not allow his work to be confined within the boundaries of any one political entity. Perhaps in no other field is cooperation so essential. Merely to embark upon, let alone accomplish, a particular research task almost always calls for the contribution of men and women from other parts of the world. It is easily understandable, then, why international non-governmental organizations (*INGO's*) are useful in this field.

Within the social sciences this same awareness of the worth of organized cooperation has become apparent only recently. Perhaps no one has better expressed the value of *INGO's* in this area of knowledge than J. B. Condliffe in a speech in which he drew upon his experiences as Research Secretary of the Institute of Pacific Relations. Dr. Condliffe mentions advantages which are inherent in *INGO's* in all the sciences—cooperative planning, pooling of resources, interchange, joint discussion and comparison of results, and beyond these, other values—"the building up of research prestige and resources in hitherto backward countries, the linking of research scientists and men of affairs, and, in the long run most important of all, the cultivation of an international fraternity of scholarship with a common interest in constructive thought for cooperative and peaceful international relations." Dr. Condliffe, moreover, mentions certain values which are of special significance in the social sciences. He states that "the research worker, particularly in the social sciences, needs to have the opportunity occasionally of meeting his fellow-workers. If he does not, it is difficult for him to retain his sense of the utility of his work and his standards of workmanship." This contact is achieved through international conferences, and from these there develops a greater possibility of interchange of workers. These conferences, he points out, "besides revealing the existence of competent workers and new points of view in the remoter countries to the more established workers in older lands . . . give greater confidence and keenness to the isolated research men. Not only their academic self-respect but their confidence in regard to practical affairs also is buttressed by contact with others competent to appreciate their work." He mentions one other significant contribution, namely that *INGO's* make possible the comparative study of international problems, a method of work which is helping to develop a scientific approach in the study of social science problems:

> The importance of the method lies in the fact that it offers a partial substitute for the experimental verification of results which is so fruitful in the natural sciences, but which is almost wholly denied to the social sciences. There are as yet few workers in the social disciplines, and more of them are engaged in teaching than in research. There is no army of workers continuously engaged in measuring, testing, and experimenting. The original workers on economic and social problems are surprisingly few. There is more need therefore for them to be brought into touch, and to check their methods and results. One way to do so is to have men working in different countries upon a common problem. . . . The combined consideration of . . . studies is very fruitful, particularly in checking generalizations from limited experience. The young specialist who studies the sociological problems of Samoa is apt to be skeptical of the dogmatic theories which are only too apt to be universalized from the limited range of urban life in industrial America. In such a major economic problem as that of the recent [1929] cyclical depression, important new angles of vision come from the experiences of such countries as China or Australia.[1]

We need to add still another value to those in Dr. Condliffe's summary, an advantage of organized private efforts over governmental action in this field, as pointed out in the following statement:

> International social science associations . . . bring leaders of social thought into close friendly and cooperative contacts across international boundaries. A number of inter-American child welfare, medical, psychiatric, sociological, etc., congresses have been held in various of the American countries and have had a marked influence in stimulating the investigation of common social problems. It is of the utmost importance, however, that these congresses should be nowise official, otherwise they cannot escape the suspicion and the fact of making propaganda and of exercising political pressures.[2]

Considering these functions, one can readily understand why in the arts, which recognize no national language, and in the sciences, there are more *INGO's* in existence than in any other field except business, religion and social welfare.[3] In the following pages we will attempt to give some idea of what has been done in this great field of international activity. We will show how private international cooperation has developed in these fields; how organized institutions, whose aim it is to promote cultural interchange and intellectual cooperation, have assisted knowledge and wisdom to pass over the frontiers in this world which is steadily becoming a cultural unit. But more than interchange of what has been learned is involved; essential as that is, international cooperation organized to discover new knowledge may become even more important.

INGO'S CONCERNED WITH NATURAL AND EXACT SCIENCES[4]

ENGINEERING

World Power Conference

The World Power Conference, whose purpose "is to consider how the sources of heat and power may be adjusted nationally and internationally," has been one of the truly important *INGO's* ever since its establishment, at London, in 1924. Its national committees in all the important countries of the world (in 1938, United Kingdom, China, France, Germany, Indian Empire, Italy, Japan, U.S.S.R., U.S.A. and thirty-four other countries) include men of the highest standing in all branches of the power industry and frequently top-ranking government officials as well as leading professional and trade organizations concerned with power from a scientific, professional, business, or governmental point of view. A few names from the membership of the American National Committee in 1936 will well illustrate this point: Chairman, Harold L. Ickes, Secretary of the Interior; Chairman, Executive Committee, Morris L. Cooke, Administrator, Rural Electrification Administration; Owen D. Young, Chairman of the Board, General Electric Co.; Karl T. Compton, President, Massachusetts Institute of Technology. Such organizations as the American Institute of Electrical Engineers and the National Electrical Manufacturers Association were also members.

Its Constitution outlines the means by which it has worked to fulfill its objectives:

> By considering the potential resources of each country in hydroelectric power, coal, oil and other fuels, and minerals.
>
> By comparing experiences in the development of scientific agriculture, irrigation, and transportation by land, air, and water.
>
> By conferences of engineers, technical experts and fuel experts, and authorities on scientific and industrial research.
>
> By consultations of the consumers of fuel and power and the manufacturers of the instruments of production of power.
>
> By conferences on technical education to review the educational methods in different countries, and to consider means by which the existing facilities may be improved.
>
> By discussion on the financial and economic aspects of industry, nationally and internationally.
>
> By conferences on the possibility of establishing a permanent World Bureau for the collection of data, the preparation of inventories of the

world's resources, and the exchange of industrial and scientific information through appointed representatives in the various countries.

The international gatherings of power experts held by the Conference every three years were among the greatest of the prewar meetings. For example, 3,891 delegates from thirty-four countries attended the 1930 Berlin Conference, while 3,000 from fifty-four countries were present at its third (1936) conference. This was its last prewar congress and was held at Washington, D.C., by invitation of the President under authorization of Congress, which appropriated seventy-five thousand dollars for the expenses of the conference. The Secretary of State pointed out that this conference "would bring to the United States from foreign countries the leaders in public and private administration of power development," and that through the exchange of information both our own engineers, industrialists and public officials would benefit as would those who would become acquainted with the "character" and "extent" of our power development.[5] Smaller "Sectional Meetings" were also held from time to time. Literally hundreds of papers on power problems were especially prepared for presentation at these meetings, contributing to the pool of technical knowledge and the greater exchange of national experiences in this field.[6] For example, although the Conference is concerned primarily with purely technical problems, it decided that the Washington Conference should "devote its discussions to the more fundamental, and in many respects more important, problems of the relations of power resources, their development and use to the social and economic interests of the nation." This congress was planned to appeal to the layman as well as the expert, and dealt with the question of a nation's power economy in terms "of the economic and social consequences of what the engineer has done, and of the problems in organization, planning, management, and control arising therefrom." Such aspects as the organization of utilities, public regulation, national and regional planning, conservation of fuel and water resources, and national policies concerning power and resources were considered. Each National Committee was asked to prepare eighteen papers, covering these aspects from its own experience and policy, and the Conference outlined the information it desired for each of these papers, requesting a most detailed and complete approach.[7]

Besides publishing the transactions of its conferences, the World Power Conference has issued a *Statistical Yearbook of the World Power Conference,* making available in a comprehensive and comparable manner statistics on power resources, development, and utilization for about sixty countries, as well as special reports and surveys, such as its 1936 *Survey of the Present Organization of Standardization—National and International.* This study was the "first authoritative compilation of facts regarding national organization of standardization in thirty-two countries," while the international section described in detail the organization, constitution, procedure and field of work of the two international standardizing bodies, the International Electrotechnical Commission and the International Federation of the National Standardizing Associations, and notes were included on the International Commission for Testing Materials and the International Commission for Testing Electric Installation and Wiring Equipment. In its leading article of November 20th, 1936, the *London Financial Times* said:

> The fact that the Conference has been able to assemble this information emphasizes its usefulness as a clearing house for the completed results of standardization research. Twenty-five of its member countries are affiliated to the International Electrotechnical Commission and nineteen to the National Standardizing Associations. As its total membership includes forty-nine countries in all, it is clearly in a position to persuade the remainder to come into line as regards establishing their national standards association.

Among the many technical problems under its purview has been the question of transport and transit of electric power across international frontiers. As a result of a speech before the Second World Power Conference (Berlin, 1930), the Belgian Government took up this problem with the League of Nations Commission of Inquiry for European Union. At the request of this Commission, the Council of the League asked its Communications and Transit Organization to study the question, and the World Power Conference was approached by the Secretary of the League of Nations Permanent Committee on Electric Questions for assistance "in regard to legislation in the European States affecting the transport, transit, export and import of electric power." In the meantime, however, the International Union of Producers and Distributors of Electric Power had decided to collect "as complete a documentation as possible regarding the international exchanges of power already existing, and regarding the legislation of the different countries on this subject." Upon learning of this project, the World Power Conference, in order to avoid any unnecessary overlapping, decided to send to the Union, as well as the League of Nations, copies of all the material it had received on the legal aspect of the matter. Later an expression of appreciation was received to the effect that, owing to the help of both *INGO's*, the League of Nations had ample and satisfactory documentation for its study. Further information was collected and studies continued, but in 1938 it was recognized that the European political situation at the time made any important action unlikely. However, the research part of the task was well along, and it was conceded that when action would again become possible, it could be undertaken in the light of a thorough investigation.[8]

International Union of Producers and Distributors of Electric Power

and

International Conference of the Principal High-Tension Electrical Systems

These two *INGO's* are the most important organizations in the field of production and distribution of electric power. The Union, organized in Paris in 1925, has naturally been interested in all questions affecting its field of interest; professional unions, firms and individuals are members, and in 1938 fifteen European countries were represented on its governing body. An information office was established which furnishes to the members the results of research and experience in the various countries, and provides documentation, especially on legislation, rates, and statistics. International conferences are held which have been attended by a constantly increasing number of participants. Special Commissions have been established to deal with particular problems, such as its Commission on questions concerning broadcasting and aviation, and its Commission charged with the study of a plan for a European network. Statistics on world production and distribution of electricity have been gathered. A map of generating plants and electric lines in Europe was prepared in collaboration with the Conference of High-Tension Systems. A bimonthly circular has been published for the members, containing general and technical information of interest to producers and distributors of electrical energy, statistics, data on production and sales, etc. Close cooperation has been maintained with the Conference, the International Electrotechnical Commission and the World Power Conference to avoid overlapping work.[9]

Founded in 1921, at Paris, mainly by private initiative but with some governmental participation, the International Conference of the Principal High-Tension Electrical Systems came into being primarily "to provide the means necessary for organizing" the series of periodical congresses (known by the same name as the organization) which have been held under the auspices of the International Electrotechnical Commission since that time. Further, its object has been:

> To facilitate international studies relating to (a) the building and maintenance of power-houses, sub-stations and transformer stations; (b) the erection, insulation and maintenance of electrical power lines; (c) the management, protection and linking-up of electrical power systems.

These questions have been the subject of its periodic congresses. Also, it has striven "to create and maintain friendly technical relations between competent organizations in all countries," and it has maintained close collaboration with other *INGO's* whose interests fall in this field. In 1938 individuals as well as "most governments and important electro-technical associations" were included in its membership.[10]

The participants at its congresses, which are held every two years, have increased each time one has been held. At its last prewar congress in 1937, 1175 persons were present from forty-one countries. Twenty-nine governments were also represented, an increase from six which participated in the first (1921) conference.[11] At the congresses, the fullest cooperation prevails between the private and official members, and all votes have been unanimous. The chief results of its work have been that the best methods are determined, made known, and adopted through the mutual sharing of experiences.

The Conference, contrary to the usual procedure of *INGO's* of meeting in different cities, has always held its congresses in Paris and in the same building. It is felt that this practice has certain very desirable advantages: first, less time is lost by the delegates in familiarizing themselves with the meeting place; secondly, language difficulties are reduced by the practice of sending French speaking delegates rather than changing delegates according to the language of the city where a conference is held; and third, continuity in the work is promoted by the tendency to send the same persons year after year.

International Association for Testing Materials

The International Association for Testing Materials, whose primary object has been to promote "international cooperation, exchange of views, experience and knowledge in regard to all matters and problems connected with the testing of materials," was founded in 1927 at Zurich. In 1938 twenty-seven countries were represented in its membership, which included, on its Permanent Committee, individuals, private companies and corporations from sixteen European countries and the United States, and corresponding members in eleven countries, five of which were non-European. Through the years, it has been concerned "with more than the mere testing of materials for use; it [has] also considered the behavior of materials and their nature, and its work [has] ranged from the purest science to the most empirical tests." It held several international congresses concerned with the technical aspects of a wide range of subjects; its last prewar conference was held in London in April 1937 and brought together over nine hundred delegates from thirty-three countries. More than two hundred technical papers were presented dealing with such questions as "Testing High-endurance Oxidation-resistant Alloys," "Preparation of Specimens for Macro- and Mico-examination," "Experiments on the Abrasion of Metals," "Methods of Testing Cements for Large Dams," "The Behavior of Textiles under the Herzog-Geiger Wearing Tests," etc., etc.[12]

INGO'S CONCERNED WITH THE PURE SCIENCES
International Council of Scientific Unions

In the field of pure, rather than applied sciences, the International Council of Scientific Unions has occupied a predominant place. Organized in 1919 at London, by 1938 it consisted of scientific societies representing forty-two countries (in some cases the governments themselves) and seven international scientific unions which were founded at its initiative: International Astronomical Union, International Union of Geodesy and Geophysics, International Union of Pure and Applied Chemistry, International Union of Scientific Radio-Telegraphy, International Union of Pure and Applied Physics, International Geographical Union and the International Union for Biological Sciences.[13] All these unions are composed of national scientific societies. The Council's object has been:

> To establish liaison between the national member organisations, on the one hand, and the various international unions, on the other; to guide international scientific work in fields where no competent associations exist; through the medium of the national member organisations, to secure contact with the Governments of the member countries with a view to recommending action favorable to the scientific development of those countries.[14]

The Council, except through its member unions, has not attempted to organize cooperative research in the various fields of science; instead, its method of work has been "to bring the Unions into active cooperation and to initiate studies involving the joint efforts of many specialists" from varied but related fields. For this purpose, it has set up a number of special committees; for example, its Committee on Solar and Terrestrial Relationships is composed of members appointed by its Unions of Astronomy, Scientific-Radio, and Geodesy and Geophysics together with several members at large.[15] Its main task is that of coordination, which it has undertaken with some degree of success. In 1934 its President, George Hale, said: "In most of the special branches of science, effective international cooperation, leading to results not attainable by individual or local effort, is not difficult to accomplish. No one who has read the valuable publications of our more active Unions can doubt this statement."[16] Undoubtedly, the growing dependence of scientists on each other's work and the fact that it is in the frontier regions of the unknown where two or more sciences meet that the most important discoveries are made today, makes the coordinating work of the Council of increasing importance.

On July 9, 1937, the International Institute of Intellectual Cooperation of the League of Nations entered into an agreement with the Council under which the Council would act as an advisory body to the Institute. The latter undertook to consult the Council on the scientific problems submitted to it, while the Council agreed to consult with the Institute "on all international questions concerning the organization of scientific work."[17] It was said at the time:

> It would seem, therefore, that an elastic and practical procedure has been devised. The sole great international organisation concerned with science, whose members are representatives of national learned societies and of international unions founded for the benefit of research workers in the same field, is eminently qualified for the task of making known the requirements of science. Thanks to the machinery at the disposal of the Intellectual Cooperation Organisation, the secretariat of the Council of Scientific Unions will be usefully reinforced for the carrying-out of a programme of work to be undertaken by the two institutions in collaboration. The Institute will, more particularly, provide the secretariat for the committees responsible for the study and execution of this programme. Its negotiations will be greatly facilitated by the new contacts offered to it in the scientific world and by the position of authority occupied by the members of the Council of Scientific Unions and by the bureaux of the Unions themselves.
>
> If this new work develops in the same way as the other efforts of the Intellectual Cooperation Organisation in the field of coordination, a notable step will have been made towards dispelling the hesitation that has arisen in the past regarding the choice of subjects to be studied in connection with the sciences and towards removing all possibility of overlapping.[18]

In December, 1937, the Institute organized a study meeting on the "Determination of molecular and atomic weights of gases by physicochemical methods" in collaboration with the Council and two of its member unions, the Union of Chemistry and the Union of Physics.[19] Various meetings were planned for the future—but war intervened.

Now we will consider some of the special fields of activity represented by the member Unions of the Council.

ASTRONOMY

The International Astronomical Union coordinates the activities of many observatories throughout the world. In 1938 it was working through thirty-one commissions, each dealing with a special problem; the work of several of these commissions is discussed in the following summary taken from the Union's 1938 report on its activities. This report points out the vast amount of coordination which has been achieved under the guidance of the Union, and the important service it has been performing as a clearing house of information on the latest available data in the field:

> The necessity for cooperation in astronomy arises [from the fact] that a thousand million stars might be photographed . . . while the number of stellar systems of extra-galactic nebulae observable must be near fifty mil-

lion. It is evident that of such an overwhelming material only relatively small specimens can be satisfactorily studied, and even that only by large-scale cooperation.[20]

The largest cooperative astronomical enterprise is that of the Carte du Ciel, started by French astronomers in 1887, [now being carried on by the] commission on the Carte du Ciel of the International Astronomical Union] and intended to furnish as complete a representation of the entire heavens as practicable with present means. The results are published in the form of a catalogue of positions and rough magnitudes which, when completed, will contain these data for perhaps five million stars, and for a much greater number of fainter stars in the form of charts. The catalogue and more especially the Chart will form a document of the greatest value for astronomers in the future, when a sufficiently long time interval will permit the derivation of accurate motions for the faint stars concerned. Though the work was distributed over twenty observatories, each furnished with a similar instrument constructed for this purpose, the completion of the Carte du Ciel has taken a very long time, and is not nearly finished today. . . .

Another extensive scheme in which cooperation is indispensable and for which a commission, with headquarters at Groningen, has been nominated by our Union is the so-called "Plan of Selected Areas." . . . It is evidently impossible to collect data for all stars down to a considerably fainter limit than that of the Carte du Ciel; even for those contained in that Catalogue it appears impracticable with present means to furnish the accurate information required for actual statistical investigations of our stellar system. The "Plan of Selected Areas" is a project for collecting such data by the concentration of observations upon 206 small standard regions distributed regularly, as well as upon forty-six special areas selected in particularly interesting regions of the sky. The magnitudes as well as colors, spectral classes and motions of objects in these regions were to be measured down to the faintest limits which for each of these characteristics could be reached by large instruments. Most of the measures of brightness which were projected have been published and have already proved of great use: extensive series of observations dealing with spectra, proper motions and colors have also been finished. About fifteen observatories are at present engaged in observations of some phase of the work; the Plan thus appears to play an important part in coordinating efforts for obtaining an insight into the general structural features of our galactic system.

A third extensive project which should be mentioned in this connection is that of the determination of the apparent motions of all stars contained in the Catalogue of the "Astronomische Gesellschaft," a catalogue of accurate positions of about a hundred thousand stars brighter than 9.5 visual magnitude observed by means of meridian circles in the last decennia of the nineteenth century. The catalogue is now being reobserved by photographic methods supplemented with meridian observations of standard stars. This photographic repetition of the Astronomische Gesellschaft Catalogue had been commenced by Professor Schlesinger at the Allegheny and Yale Observatories. German and Russian observatories are now repeating the entire northern hemisphere under the auspices of the Astronomische Gesellschaft, while the southern sky is being taken care of by the Yale Observatory station at Johannesburg and the Royal Observatory at the Cape of Good Hope. Again a sub-commission of the Union deals with the problems for which mutual discussion is desired.

The three large projects which were described in order to illustrate the extent to which general cooperation has been practised in astronomy were organised long before the Union came into existence, but the commissions of the Union now form a very desirable medium for the discussion of further coordination of the work.

In conclusion, reference may be made to the triennial publication of reports of the presidents of the specialist commissions, which contain full reviews of progress made as well as of the programs in execution, and which must doubtlessly be counted among the most useful phases of the Union's work.[21]

GEODESY AND GEOPHYSICS

The International Union of Geodesy and Geophysics has carried on its work through seven international Associations, the Associations of Geodesy, of Seismology, of Meteorology, of Terrestrial Magnetism and Electricity, of Physical Oceanography, of Scientific Hydrology, and of Vulcanology.

Geodesy is the science of determining the form and dimensions of the earth. In this science the principle of triangulation, which need not be explained here, is used. The Association of Geodesy is particularly interested in the establishment of a number of triangulations which require international cooperation, and in the use of internationally accepted standards and methods. The determination of the intensity of gravity in different places also requires the collective effort of "reference stations" of various countries, and the Association has taken the initiative in many cases in bringing about such cooperation. At times it has sought the cooperation of governments in this work, as well as scientific societies. For example, it was able to persuade the American, Italian, and French governments to use their submarines for measuring the intensity of the earth's gravity at various times. The Association has also prepared many publications of which we may mention the international bibliography on geodesy.[22]

The Union's Association of Seismology, which has also issued many publications, is particularly interested in the development of telegraphic and radio communication of information on earthquakes.[23]

Its Association of Meteorology has worked closely with the International Meteorological Organization,[24] the two groups having agreed on a division of work; the Organization deals with the practical aspects of the field, particularly the exploitation of national weather reporting networks, while the Association is concerned with academic or purely scientific problems. It has planned its international assemblies around a few scientific themes in order to concentrate efforts; this method, it is felt, has given very satisfactory results.[25]

The Union's Association of Terrestrial Magnetism and Electricity has had ten special committees dealing with different aspects of this field. Only a few of its many activities will be mentioned here, for purposes of illustration. The Association itself organizes special research, such as its study of sudden commencements of magnetic storms, a question it undertook from the early days of its establishment as "the investigation of which could be based upon international cooperation only." At the same time, it has stimulated other projects in its field of interest; for instance, certain projects of the Department of Terrestrial Magnetism of the Carnegie Institution of Washington were "done largely under the stimulus offered by the Association." This work included extensive electric surveys of oceanic areas which were made on the yacht *Carnegie*, the development of instruments both for ocean and land work, and the establishment of atmospheric-electric observations conducted regularly at three widely placed observatories. Also, the Association has cooperated in research with a number of organizations, in particular with the Polar Year Commission of the International Meteorological Organization, which has an International Commission on Terrestrial Magnetism and Atmospheric Electricity. In this work, outlined below, the Association has played an indispensable role. In addition, certain methods and standards have been supported by the Association, and financial and moral support has been given to many undertakings in this field.[26]

The Association of Physical Oceanography of the Union of Geodesy and Geophysics has not been, perhaps, so important as some of its other Associations. Its Associations of Scientific Hydrology and of Vulcanology coordinate the work in their respective fields and have published many scientific studies.[27]

CHEMISTRY

The Council's International Union of Chemistry is performing an important function in this field of research together with the governmental organizations, the International Chemistry Office and the Permanent Bureau of Analytical Chemistry. Its task has been:

> To organize permanent cooperation between the chemical associations of the member countries; to coordinate their scientific and technical means of action; to contribute towards the advancement of chemistry in its most

comprehensive aspect, more particularly by means of conferences and congresses.[28]

Perhaps its most important contribution has been in the development of international uniformity in the nomenclature of chemistry. Commissions for different branches of chemistry have been set up to promote this work. The publication of constants has been carried on under its patronage by the International Committee for the publication of Annual Tables of Chemical, Physical, Biological and Technological Constants. An International Bureau for Physico-Chemical Standards was founded under its auspices as a center "for the study of the methods of preparation and [of?] physical constants of very pure materials; to form a collection of standard materials." The Bureau has furnished standard substances to many important scientists throughout the world, and has undertaken the European distribution of standard products prepared by the Bureau of Standards at Washington, D. C.[29]

The report of the president of the Union of Chemistry at the 1936 Conference showed the tendency of those concerned with chemical problems to look to the Union for support and leadership, and it pointed out the fact that the Union has been playing a constantly greater role in international technical work.[30]

International Committee for the Polar Year, 1932–33

The International Committee for the Polar Year, 1932–33, conducted one of the most interesting and important examples of international cooperation for scientific purposes. The first Polar Year had been held fifty years before, and it is planned to repeat them every half century.

The organizations represented in the Committee are the International Meteorological Organization, the Permanent Council for the Exploration of the Sea, and two of the International Council's scientific unions—the Union of Geodesy and Geophysics and the Union of Scientific Radiotelegraphy. Important financial support for this undertaking was given by the Rockefeller Foundation.[31]

The following statement by Dr. D. la Cour, Director of the Meteorological Service, Copenhagen, explains the purpose of the undertaking, and the reasons for the extensive cooperation on the part of the various branches of science:

> The observations made during the Polar Year involved the study of widely differing phenomena and the interaction of these phenomena. In the domain of meteorology it was desired to gather the information necessary for the study of the working of the great heating machine that the Atmosphere is. Observations of solar radiation, of air currents and of temperature and humidity to great heights was for the same purpose. The polar aurora

borealis was observed with the special purpose of determining the position in space, the extent, and the relations with the conducting layers of the upper atmosphere, but also in order to study the relationship to solar phenomena, to terrestrial magnetism, cosmic radiation, and the propagation of radio waves. Magnetic observations were predestined to play a predominent role in the work of the Polar Year because of the close relationship between magnetism, solar phenomena, and atmospheric electricity. . . . Contributions to the study of the variation of the earth's magnetic field and the gathering of the facts necessary for making complete magnetic maps for the benefit of science and maritime and aerial navigation were desired. The study of periodic and aperiodic magnetic disturbances, their distribution, their propagation and their dependence on solar phenomena was also to be sought. An effort was made to study the structure of magnetic storms and their sudden beginnings over the whole earth. The radio-electric researches during the Polar Year were especially concerned with the occurrence of conducting layers and the determination of their height and the density of ions, but also with the study of the relation between the factors just mentioned and the propagation of waves of different lengths.[32]

To carry out these objectives, not only was use made of the observation stations which were already in existence but many new ones were especially established. The enormous amount of information collected still serves as the basis for research and will continue to do so for many years. Some idea of this may be drawn from the fact that the observations taken of the aurora borealis at one station in the Canadian arctic will require about nine thousand hours of mathematical work.

As a result of the Polar Year, certain stations established especially for this project have been maintained ever since; better instruments have been made available to institutions and observatories, and certain instruments were greatly improved; also, the basis for continued international collaboration was greatly improved.[33]

International Institute of Statistics

Often the trend is from private to official organization. However, in the case of the International Institute of Statistics we find the opposite to be true, for the Institute succeeded the official International Congress of Statistics. Although the Congress in its twenty-three years of existence (1853-1876) contributed much to the development of statistics,[34] in the end, its official backing proved to be a drawback to its successful functioning. According to Friedrich Zahn in his history of the private Institute, "During a quarter of a century, the important organizational defects of the Congress were more and more felt. . . . eminent statisticians became determined adversaries of the Congress. Its more or less official character left it too easily open to political influences. . . . Close official relationships with the governments . . . often prevented any free discussion and influenced the decisions in the direction desired by these governments.

"The prestige of the Congress suffered very much and accordingly, in spite of its claim to an official standing, it was not able to assure the practical realization of its decisions."[35]

A few years after the end of the Congress, the need for international statistical conferences became quite apparent and efforts were begun to establish a new organization. Neumann-Spallart, a pioneer in international statistics, in drawing up a plan of organization tried to avoid the faults of the International Congress of Statistics. "That is why," says Friedrich Zahn, "he preferred the principle of a free scientific association rather than a purely official organization of governments, or a semi-official meeting of official statisticians and representatives of statistical institutes and associations. After what had happened, these forms of organization had little chance of adoption." The plan suggested that the heads of official statistical organizations be members, but only in a private capacity and not as the representatives of governments. The International Institute of Statistics was established at The Hague in accordance with these ideas at a meeting held in London in 1885.[36] Its membership has been completely on an individual basis; in 1938, 180 experts, the world's greatest statisticians, from twenty-five European and eleven non-European countries were members.

Since its creation, the Institute has been most concerned with the international comparability of scientific and administrative statistics. It is obvious that, for example, the statistics relating to unemployment, the cost of living, or any other subject in different countries cannot be compared unless they are collected with a similar degree of accuracy and in accordance with definitions internationally accepted and understood. Statisticians feel that the international comparability of statistics is one of the most important requirements for the development of their science and for its usefulness. Friedrich Zahn, President of the Institute, has said:

> In fact, the efforts related to the local, national, and finally international comparability touch the very essence of statistics. With the progress and development of statistics, with the increase of intensity of international relations in the most diverse domains, due in particular to the increasing complexity of political economic life, international comparability of statistics has become an increasing necessity. It is the hypothesis at the basis of research on demographic, economic, cultural, and social phenomena, and the laws which govern them.[37]

The success the Institute has had in this very difficult field of endeavor is all the more impressive when we consider that progress is dependent to a great extent on the will of governments, and is hampered by technical obstacles occasioned by varying climates, conditions of work, manners, customs, and traditions. The Institute has nevertheless carried on a great and varied activity and has made important contributions to the advancement of statistics both as a science and as a practical tool. It has studied every or almost every important statistical subject of international interest, and its publications have advanced the results of the studies. Its work has influenced many national statistical services to adopt better methods, and its cooperation with other international organizations has had significant results.

It has published a *Review* (which superseded the Institute's *Bulletin* after twenty-eight volumes had appeared) devoted to scientific studies and the deliberations of the Institute on various statistical problems, as well as yearbooks of international statistics and special surveys which have made possible a scientific basis for action on vital international problems. For example, it brought together in its yearbooks (*Annuaire International de Statistique* 1916, '17, '19, '20, '21, and *Annexes* 1920) *and* in its demographic surveys (*Aperçu de la démographie des divers pays du monde*, 1922, '25, '27, '29, '31) what is said to be the "most complete set of numerical documents dealing with international population movements" of the prewar period.[38]

Only a statistician could fully appreciate the scientific or practical value of the Institute's work on such subjects as: the nomenclature of professions, statistics on forests, industrial statistics, railroad statistics, statistics on money and precious metals, indexes on the cost of living, public finance, social insurance, national incomes, statistics on crime, teaching of statistics, election statistics—to mention only a few among many.

How it has gone about to secure progress in national methods is implicit in the following remarks of Friedrich Zahn:

> The organization, methods, operations and results of the [national] labor statistical offices were described by a number of monographs on different countries. . . . Without any doubt, the proper organization of labor statistics, the knowledge of the most fruitful methods and, finally, the publication of the results, have contributed greatly toward the progress of labor statistics. The continued documentation furnished by the members of the Institute on the progress of this branch of statistics in different countries . . . has certainly aided the diffusion and application of the best methods, and by that facilitated gradual international standardization.[39]

Through its cooperation with many governmental and private international organizations, its influence has been multiplied, and it is acknowledged that the establishment of numerous statistical publications, yearbooks, etc., has been due to the indirect influence of the Institute. It has had a number of joint committees with other *INGO's*. For example, the Institute cooperated with the International Association for the Fight against Unemployment beginning in 1911; it set up a committee with the International Chamber of Commerce to study the problems of automobile transport statistics, and had a joint commission with the International Union of Local Authorities. Likewise, it has worked closely with governmental organizations, having had joint commissions for the study of international statistics with the International Labour Office, the International Institute of Agriculture, the Health Organization and the Communications and Transit Organization of the League of Nations and with the International Penal and Penitentiary Commission.[40] Its relationship with the League of Nations was quite close.

In 1920, at a conference convened by the Council of the League of Nations, a proposal to establish a Statistical Section in the League Secretariat was brought up. The President of the Institute, who had been elected as president of the conference, and others objected to this proposal and put forward a counter-suggestion to the effect that the Institute should be made the advisory body in statistical matters for the League of Nations. This was adopted and the recommendation sent to the League's Council. The final result was a resolution of the Assembly that the League of Nations would make use of the statistics obtainable from already existing international statistical organizations without affecting their autonomy.[41] If the Institute had not been in existence at that time, it seems altogether likely that a Statistical Section would have been established in the League Secretariat.

Later, a Study Committee on the Unification of International Statistical Methods, composed of members of the Institute, the Economic Committee of the League and the *ILO* Office was set up. Its reports served as a basis for the deliberations of the Institute in 1923, 1925 and 1927, and the Institute's findings were transmitted to the League which, "after a new examination, presented the results of the research to the governments in the form of recommendations for the improvement of their statistical work. The fact that the League of Nations accepted the reports and decisions of the Institute in great part word for word and also gave them its approval should be appreciated as a recognition of the scientific competence of the Institute." Furthermore, "all the recommendations on economic matters sent by the Institute to the League of Nations were . . . transmitted to the governments as a basis for a convention." In December 1928, a diplomatic conference was held and a convention concluded, based on the propositions submitted by the Institute, which was later ratified by nearly all countries. Later, in its report to the Council, the Economic Committee of the League stated that throughout the Conference it was "struck" with the value of this cooperation with the Institute. The Institute's attitude toward the convention was that although it laid down only a minimum program, nevertheless it marked "a considerable progress for the development and unification of international economic statistics."[42]

The Institute did the technical preparatory work for the conferences of government delegates called by the French Government from time to time for the revision of the international nomenclature of the causes of death; the fourth revision took place in 1929, at Paris. For this revision, preparatory work was also done by a joint committee including four members of the Health Section of the League. The text accepted by this Committee (which adopted the decisions of the Institute reached at its Cairo Conference) was approved by the governmental conference with slight modifications, and the proposed international nomenclature has been adopted by many States.[43]

A Study Committee on the statistics of foreign commerce was set up by the Institute and the League, and its resolutions, with slight modifications by the General Assembly of the Institute, were the basis of the official International Statistical Conference held at Geneva in 1928. At this Conference, the International Chamber of Commerce, the Economic Committee of the League of Nations, the Committee of Experts for the Unification of Customs Nomenclature, and the Communications and Transit Organization of the League were represented. As a result of the convention adopted, "the represented States engaged themselves to furnish annual or monthly information on the quantities of imports and exports, and annual and, if possible, trimonthly or monthly information on the net tonnage of the products of all countries, of interest to foreign commerce, arrived in a port of the reporting country, or leaving one of its ports." In regard to this, "A detailed annex deals with the methods which the contracting states adopt for the preparation of the statistics of foreign commerce. They are, on the whole, in conformity with the principles fixed by the preceding resolutions of the Institute."[44]

The Institute and the *ILO* set up a joint Committee to study the resolutions of the first two Conferences on Labor Statistics, which were held at Geneva in 1923 and 1925. The conclusion was reached that the problem of the international comparison of real wages, their determination, and the value of conclusions drawn from such comparisons required further study. The Institute thereupon set up a special committee for this purpose. The decision to set up a joint committee of the Institute and the *ILO* for the purpose of developing the statistics on migration was taken at the diplomatic conference on migration called by the *ILO* in 1932. Still another joint committee of the Institute and the *ILO* was set up to study the statistics of unemployment.[45]

The Institute also established a joint committee with another of the League's organs, the International Institute of Intellectual Co-operation, to deal with the international statistics of intellectual life.[46]

INGO'S CONCERNED WITH THE SOCIAL SCIENCES

Numerous *INGO's* are concerned with the social sciences; this section, however, will include only those whose work is devoted to the theoretical or learned aspects of this field.[47] The important contributions to this field made by other *INGO's* which are carrying on field work or are concerned with the practical aspects of the social sciences are discussed in other chapters; for example, in economics, there is the work done by the International Chamber of Commerce, the trade associations, the International Co-operative Alliance, the International Federation of Trade Unions and other similar associations; in sociology, the contributions of religious groups, such as the International Missionary Council, as well as the work of many *INGO's* primarily concerned with social welfare activities.

International Academic Union

Organized in 1919 at Brussels, the International Academic Union has as its object:

> To establish, maintain and strengthen corporate and personal relations between men of learning who are working in the humanities, by means of regular correspondence, interchange of communications and periodic scientific congresses; to inaugurate, encourage and direct such research work and publications as would appear best to further the progress of archaeology, history, philosophy, the moral, political and social sciences and which necessitate or deserve a high degree of cooperation.[48]

It has brought together scholars representing learned Academies and scientific institutions (in 1938, from twenty countries) and has carried out its enterprises through special Commissions set up for the purpose of cooperative research or publication, such as those on: Corpus Vasorum Antiquorum, which has promoted the publication of pictures and other information on ancient vases from many of the greatest collections of the world, and on the Catalogue of Alchemical Manuscripts, which in its various volumes fills 3,371 pages and was prepared by a number of scholars of different countries. Its other Commissions have been concerned with: Oeuvres de Grotius, Droit coutumier d'Indonésie, Dictionnaire du Latin médiéval, Forma Orbis Romani et Compléments aux Corpus d'inscriptions, Corpus des Mosaiques de Grèce, Catalogue des Bibliographies courantes, Unification des méthodes à suivre et des signes conventionnels à employer dans les éditions savantes, Corpus Philosophorum Medii Aevi,

Codices Latini antiquiores, Concordance et Index de la Tradition musulmane.[49]

In addition to organizing these cooperative research tasks, the Union has contributed financially to many of them; the publications have been issued either by the Union or under its patronage.

International Institute of Administrative Sciences,
International Union of Local Authorities, and
International Federation for Housing and Town Planning

These three organizations, each concerned with the field of public administration,[50] established common offices before World War II in the Shell Building at Brussels and, while avoiding duplication of research, cooperated closely in maintaining common services such as "a joint reference library, a common secretarial and stenographic service, a collaborative research division, a common division of publications and publicity, a joint reference service, a collaborative division for the administration of conferences and the conducting of external affairs, and a joint accounting service."[51] At present their headquarters are respectively in The Hague, Brussels, and London. Cooperation between them is, however, still close. Each has intimate connections with governments.

The International Institute of Administrative Sciences, organized in 1930, has been concerned with:

> Comparative examination of administrative experience in the different countries; working out of rational administrative methods, affirmation and spreading of general principles; generally speaking, all studies, investigations, schemes and agreements for improving administrative law and practice.[52]

In 1938 fourteen states were "officially represented" at the Institute, as well as many private groups; it had national sections in twenty countries, two non-European.

Congresses have been held every three years; its last prewar meeting was in 1936, at which it considered such topics as the "Guarantees of the Rights of Administrative Persons in Procedure and in the Exercise of Administrative Jurisdiction," "Rationalization in Administration and in State and City Enterprises," "The Chief Executive and his Auxiliary Organs."[53]

The Institute maintains informational services for its members, sponsors research, and publishes *La Revue Internationale des Sciences Administratives*.[54]

The International Union of Local Authorities has a membership, consisting of Unions of towns and municipalities in twenty-eight countries in 1938, which is official in character. It is not, however, based on an intergovernmental agreement and, therefore, is considered to be an *INGO*. It has been concerned, since its foundation in 1913, with "the establishment and development of intermunicipal relations through national relations between local authorities in each country and international relations between the national unions." It has organized international congresses and research studies in its field of interest, and has served as a center for documentary material on local administration questions. It issued *Local Government Administration* as well as special publications.

The Institute and the Union have jointly published *Tablettes Documentaires à l'usage des Administrations Publiques* (monthly). The issue for January-February 1938, in addition to many short articles, contains numerous citations of then current writings on housing and town planning, including such subjects as public swimming pools, transportation, water supply, lighting, etc.

An illustration of the benefit of collaboration between the Union and the Institute is the use the latter makes of research experiences of the Union on questions in the field of administration in which it has not itself specialized. When, for example, the Institute receives from one of its members a question concerning local government the answer is prepared by the Union, but the reply is sent by the Institute "so as to preserve its prestige in the mind of the member concerned." (This idea was adopted from a practice of the Public Administration Clearing House of Chicago.)[55] In fact, the three organizations helped each other in this manner, thereby increasing their efficiency.

When the Institute and Union started their collaboration, their first joint effort was the preparation and publication of a "Directory of International Organizations in the Field of Public Administration." This project was undertaken as a preliminary step in their study of increased cooperation on the part of international organizations in the field of public administration:

> Frequently through ignorance of the existence of other organisations the same problems were investigated by several bodies whilst other urgent problems were left completely unexplored. The existence of the directory would enable this multiplication of research to be avoided, and provide a basis for future cooperation, thus leaving each organisation free to concentrate upon its own particular specialty.[56]

In 1937 the two organizations brought together the representatives of six other international associations,[57] whose work was more or less closely related to public administration, for the purpose of promoting a closer cooperation, and various methods of doing this were discussed.[58]

THE ARTS AND SCIENCES

The third group at this Brussels center for public administration was the International Federation for Housing and Town Planning (now at London). This Federation, whose membership is both private and official, including "societies engaged in technical, educational, scientific or propaganda work in the field," as well as such public agencies as "ministries, municipal housing departments, public boards, commissions, etc., concerned with housing and town planning affairs," had had as its aim:

> to advance the knowledge of and secure improvements in the practice of the following matters: Housing for all Classes; Housing Costs; Financing of Working Class Housing; Rural Housing; Abolition of Slums; Housing for special Groups, such as single or aged persons; the Use of Land; Town and Country Planning; Traffic Problems in Relation to Planning; Garden Cities; Decentralisation of Industry; City redevelopment; and the preservation of Rural Amenities, and beautiful or historic Buildings.[59]

Its governing body (Council) which is composed of representatives from both its private and official members has at times a majority of official representatives and at other times a majority of private representatives.

Its activities have included congresses, study tours, publication of a *Bulletin* and special reports as well as the supplying of information. The Federation keeps "full records of housing and town planning activities, etc., all over the world. This enables persons in all countries to obtain reliable information as to the methods and conditions in other countries and to estimate the applicability to their own conditions of the various solutions of a given problem." For example, a particular city decides to build tenements for workers, and desires information on successful three-story buildings for workers; the Federation collects this information for it, culling the material from various countries. Or, a certain city decides to draw up a new housing code. The Federation supplies it with information on the laws in other cities; this helps to avoid the omission of essential provisions and helps generally to make the laws better.[60]

International Institute of African Languages and Cultures

The Institute, now called the International African Institute, was founded in 1926 at London:

> To act as a coordinating agency, a central bureau and a clearinghouse for information regarding research in African linguistics, anthropology and sociology; and to bring about a closer association between scientific research and the practical problems with which administrators, educators, missionaries, those engaged in industry and commerce and the leaders of the African race have to deal.[61]

Its membership includes a considerable number of educational institutions (Cambridge, Oxford, Yale, etc.), scientific associations such as the

American Anthropological Association and the Société des Africanistes (France), groups such as the International Missionary Council, several museums, etc. Its prewar income reached as high as £10,058 (1936), with substantial contributions from the Rockefeller Foundation, the Carnegie Corporation, and various governments.[62]

The Institute's official journal is *Africa* (quarterly). Before the war it had published about twenty books and over a dozen "Memoranda." A few of its titles are: *Practical Phonetics for Students of African Languages, The African Labourer, The Food and Nutrition of African Natives.*

In its anthropological research, the Institute has concentrated on the problem: "What is happening to the structure of African society under the pressure of Western civilization," a hitherto neglected subject. Financial aid in the form of studentships, fellowships and grants have been extended to more than forty persons to enable them to carry on research.

The Institute has also served as an information center, and at times has rendered technical assistance to governments. For example, the governments of the Gold Coast, the Sudan, Kenya, Uganda, Nigeria, and Sierra Leone called the Institute's Director, Dr. D. Westermann, into consultation on language problems in 1927–29. The recommendations of the Institute were adopted in several of these colonies.[63]

In regard to its work in linguistics, we may quote the following:

> To produce a satisfactory script for an unwritten language is not an easy task. It is therefore not surprising that many of the older alphabets used in African languages should be felt to be inappropriate; nor that there should be a great variety of alphabets, so that often several languages spoken in the same area are written in different ways. Here it was natural that a desire for unification should be heard. Then there was the question of languages which were reduced to writing for the first time: which script were they to have? Enquiries referring to matters like these were so frequently addressed to the Institute that it seemed imperative to decide upon a definite policy, and this was done by the publication of the *Memorandum on Practical Orthography for African Languages*. It has had a wide distribution in Africa. A special edition in simplified form is now in preparation, mainly intended for Africans, many of whom take an increasing interest in the writing and literary use of their mother tongue. The Memorandum was later supplemented by a book on *Practical Phonetics for Students of African Languages*. Europeans who have to acquire a practical knowledge of a language will also find help in Dr. Ward's memorandum, *Practical Suggestions for the learning of an African Language in the Field*. For a first recording of new languages or dialects a *Short Linguistic Guide* was published; it has been used by many and has been instrumental in producing much valuable linguistic material, some of which is being prepared for publication.[64]

The Institute's alphabet is in practical use in more than forty African languages, and every year adds to their number.

The Institute makes the convincing claim that the indirect influence which it has exerted "in awakening and fostering an interest in the scientific study of African problems has been far-reaching." It is interesting to note that its work is of such a nature that governments, educational and scientific institutions, religious and racial groups—Catholics, Protestants, whites and negroes—of many different countries can and do cooperate.

International Institute of Documentation

Many *INGO's*, as we have already shown, have been concerned with the organization of documentation in their respective fields, and some, like the International Library Association and the International Chamber of Commerce, have made significant contributions. Governmental agencies, such as the *ILO* and the International Office of Chemistry, have also made contributions by establishing specialized documentary centers, and, of course, the problem in all its aspects was of interest to the League of Nations Institute of Intellectual Co-operation. At its initiative, in 1937, a conference on documentation was held, for which an International Committee of Documentation—"a sort of Estates-General of Documentation" —was set up. The International Institute of Documentation was represented on it. About thirty *INGO's* as well as a number of official organs participated. The Conference was held since, despite the progress achieved in this field, much remained, and still remains, to be done. At the time, the Institute of Intellectual Co-operation said: "coordination, cooperation, concerted and unified measures are still slow in coming, while scholars and practical men demand from every side more efficiency in what should serve everyone as an intellectual tool." The conference tried to secure an over-all picture of "existing conditions, a comparison of principles, programs and methods, as well as an exchange of opinions on the results obtained" and aimed "to establish a minimum plan of work and service" which would be feasible to achieve.[65]

The International Institute of Documentation has been the pioneer in this field, having been organized in 1895. "By contributing to the elaboration of the technique of documentation, in all its aspects," the Institute of Intellectual Co-operation of the League of Nations said of its work, "it has opened the way for world-wide cooperation." From its headquarters in Brussels, it has worked to bring about international methods and rules regarding classification, including development of the decimal system. It has maintained the Universal Bibliographical Repertory, a world-wide listing of over fourteen million entries (1938), according to subject and author; it cooperated with the International Library, the International

Press Museum, the International Encylopaedical Museum in compiling the *Encyclopédie documentaire* on filing, concerning both texts and illustrations; among its various publications is its *Manuel* of bibliography, of over two thousand pages, containing the Decimal Classification.[66]

INGO'S CONCERNED WITH THE ARTS

The *INGO's* in the arts pursue a variety of purposes including the organization of conferences for the exchange of ideas, the promotion of particular opinions or methods (such as the promotion of modern architecture), the defense of the professional interests of their members and of their copyright and other property rights in their artistic creations, as well as the development of friendly international relations among those interested in the arts. These *INGO's* have held numerous conferences, issued many publications, and have often brought together the leaders in their respective fields. In many respects the results of their work are largely intangible.

Among the *INGO's* in the arts are: the Permanent International Committee of Architects, the International Congress on Modern Architecture, the Permanent Council for International Co-operation between Composers, the International Concert Federation, the International Society for Contemporary Music, the International Federation of Dramatic and Musical Criticism, the International Bureau of Musicians, the International Society of Musicology, the Universal Theatre Society, the International Committee on the History of Art, the International Federation of Arts, Letters and Sciences, the International Federation of Professional Societies of Men of Letters, and *PEN*—a World Association of Writers. Two organizations whose work is related to many of the arts are the International Confederation of Authors' and Composers' Societies and the International Publishers' Congress.

International Confederation of Authors' and Composers' Societies

The International Confederation of Authors' and Composers' Societies, organized in Paris in 1926, has been primarily concerned with the protection of rights. Composed, in 1938, of fifty authors' and composers' societies in twenty-eight countries, its object has been:

> To improve and as far as possible to standardise the organisation of the various member societies with the special purpose of ensuring more effectual protection for the moral and material rights of authors and composers, under the laws at present in force; to work, in concert with the other associations interested, to secure recognition for literary and artistic copyright in all countries in which it is not yet recognised or protected and to improve the various national laws and international legislation regarding literary and artistic copyright, the moral and material rights of authors and composers,

and works of which the copyright has expired; to establish a documentation, information and control centre enabling the various member societies to provide their members with effective guarantee as regards the performance, execution, translation, circulation and adaptation of their works abroad; in general, to make a joint study of all problems affecting the drama, poetry and music in their different forms, and the collection and payment of royalties.[67]

It has tried in a number of ways to help its members protect their rights; it has drawn up model contracts, including several on the granting of rights for translation, adaptation, and presentation of dramatic works; it worked out an agreement with the International Federation of the Phonographic Industry; and at times has intervened on the national level. When for example, in 1933, Germany issued a decree very unfavorable to foreign authors, the Confederation sent a delegation to see Dr. Goebbels, and after the visit the law was modified. Again, in 1936, the Confederation secured the understanding that Italy, which was then engaged in many counteractions against the sanctions invoked by the League of Nations, would not interfere with international intellectual exchanges nor the rights of authors.[68]

The Confederation has been interested in seeing established one over-all universal convention on the rights of authors, to replace the Berne and Havana conventions. When the League of Nations Institute of Intellectual Co-operation and the International Institute at Rome for the Unification of Private Law (intergovernmental) set up a committee of experts to draft a project for such a convention the Confederation was asked to appoint two representatives.[69]

The Confederation is another *INGO* which has established Rules of Arbitration for the settlement of disputes among its members; the arbitrators are chosen from a list published by the Confederation. In a number of cases, the Confederation itself through its conciliatory efforts has brought about the signing of an agreement.[70]

International Publishers' Congress

The Permanent Bureau of the International Publishers' Congress was founded in 1896 at Geneva and has been concerned with many different problems; in 1938 it had national member societies in Canada, the United States and seventeen European countries. It has issued a technical publishers' vocabulary in seven languages, as well as other material, including a regular *Bulletin;* it has been interested in the protection of authors' rights and exerted some influence in securing ratifications to the Berne Copyright Convention, particularly in the case of Holland; its action concerning the arrangements for translations under Spanish law is typical of the services based on special research which it renders to its members. Under Spanish law, contracts granting translation rights to Spanish companies must be registered. This requirement had caused considerable difficulty, for some publishers were ignorant of the law while others objected to having to register private agreements with a foreign country. The Federation had a special report on the subject prepared, and on the basis of its findings voted in 1936 to recommend to its members "that when publishers make arrangements for translations with their Spanish colleagues they should comply with such formalities as are required by Spanish law, that is to say that they should have contracts dealing with the translation rights registered by the Spanish consulate in their country." This brought an end to the difficulties. It has also been concerned with customs prohibitions; for example, in 1936 its Permanent Bureau successfully took steps to head off a proposed 25 per cent customs duty on books which was scheduled to come before the legislature of a certain unnamed country.[71]

As early as 1912, it established "Rules for international arbitration in case of disputes between publishers of different nationalities," under which the cases may be submitted to the Executive Committee of the Congress for settlement.[72]

6 PRESS

ROBERT W. DESMOND in his *The Press and World Affairs* (New York, London, 1937) made a number of interesting statements on the function of international non-governmental organizations (*INGO's*) in the field of journalism. He pointed out that newspapermen "in organizing to advance their own interests and work" as a consequence have helped the entire press. Among the organizations he specifically credits are: the International Association of Journalists Accredited to the League of Nations, the Anglo-American Press Association in Paris, the Foreign Press Association in London, and the Association of Foreign Correspondents in the United States. "Some of these groups," he stated, "have worked to raise journalistic standards, have dealt with local government officials, and have won their cooperation in simplifying news-gathering problems or clearing news channels."[1] We will see to some extent what the influence of *INGO's* has been in the press world, but no attempt has yet been made by anyone to evaluate them fully.

International Association of Journalists Accredited to the League of Nations

The newspapermen themselves formed, in 1921, the International Association of Journalists Accredited to the League of Nations, so that a better job of reporting League activities could be done. Approximately two hundred, or about half of the maximum number of correspondents accredited to the League, were members of the Association, with twenty-nine countries represented. Desmond wrote:

> Through this organization, the journalists arrange with the League's Information Section as far as necessary, for services of news transmission and for prompt and accurate preparation of documents and other data that they require.[2]

This experience undoubtedly proved helpful in organizing the Press and Publication Bureau of the United Nations.

World League of Press Associations

Desmond reports that before the war there existed for the exchange of news "an unofficial but effective World League of Press Associations" which included the "thirty principal news agencies in as many countries." He states:

> The original membership included Reuters (Great Britain), Havas (France), Associated Press (United States), Wolff (Germany), Westnik (Russia), Kokusai (Japan), Stefani (Italy), Fabra (Spain), and others. Westnik or the Petrograd News Agency became known as Rosta and later as the Tass agency under the Soviets. Kokusai in 1926 was transformed into the Rengo agency and in 1936 it was known as the Domei agency. Wolff became known in 1933 as the Deutsches Nachrichten Büro.[3]

The private character of this League is doubtful, for of the thirty members in 1937, nine were official, nine quasi-official, six private, and the status of the remaining six is unknown to the author.[4]

Desmond discusses the arrangements covering the international sale of news services:

> Although each of the agencies forming the "world league" originally was restricted, by mutual agreement, to the sale of news entirely in its own country or in well defined territories, that arrangement was "liberalized" at a London meeting in 1932, between the heads of Reuters, the Associated Press, Havas, and the Wolff agency. By this agreement any one of the agencies was permitted to sell its service independently to any newspaper or other clients wanting it in a country normally served by one of the other member agencies.
>
> In practice, the four biggest agencies have arranged coverage of most of the world in the following way, with an exchange of news among them:
>
> Associated Press—Covers the United States, Central America, and cooperates with Havas to cover South America.
>
> Havas—Covers France, the French colonies, Romanic countries of Europe, and cooperates with the Associated Press to cover South America, and with Reuters to cover the Near East.
>
> Reuters—Covers Great Britain and the British Empire, the Netherlands, the Far East, and cooperates with Havas to cover the Near East.
>
> DNB—Covers Germany and Austria.*

Desmond states that the United Press (United States) and the British United Press (Great Britain and Canada), which were not members of the League, formed "a smaller and quite new affiliation" together with the Agence Télégraphique Radio (France) which is allied to Havas, and with Tass (Russia). Both Havas and Tass were in the "world league."[6]

Press Congress of the World

The prewar Press Congress of the World, with a membership reaching out to seventy-five countries, was organized in 1915 with headquarters at

* Paul F. Douglass and Karl Bömer, "The Press as a Factor in International Relations," *Annals of the American Academy of Political and Social Science* (July, 1932), Chapter 2, "The International Combination of News Agencies," pp. 265–68. This was before the Wolff agency had been reorganized as *DNB*.[5]

the famous School of Journalism, University of Missouri, Columbia, Missouri, from which it probably received its greatest support. It held three world conferences and one regional meeting for discussion of newspaper problems. The following statement of its activities is taken from one of its own publicity leaflets:

> The briefest sort of a resumé of what the Press Congress has accomplished shows that it has done much by bringing journalists of all countries together for discussion of their problems, by aiding in the reduction of press cable and wireless tolls, by securing the liberation from prison and [the] fair trial of several newspaper men in countries where the press is still far from free, by promoting journalistic education, by increasing the flow of international news, by fostering the exchange of journalists among newspapers and schools of journalism in various countries, by working toward an international press identification card which will be officially recognized as both a passport and press card, and by other activities.

7 EDUCATION

FROM ONE point of view all international organizations have an educational function, for whenever and wherever men cooperate in dealing with common problems, the increase of knowledge and of understanding is inevitable. This "educational" influence no doubt has been very great, but in this chapter we are concerned with education in its more formal aspects. International non-governmental organizations (*INGO's*) within this area can be classified under five general headings, although there exists some overlapping of interests and activities: (1) *INGO's* devoted to promoting education for particular groups; (2) those concerned with a specific teaching method or attitude; (3) those almost in the nature of professional or trade associations, either of teachers or schools; (4) those of or for students; and, (5) those concerned with education in general. Only a few of these *INGO's* have done useful or important work; on the whole it must be said that the influence of private international organizations in the field of education has not been extensive. One gains the definite impression that their contribution has been insignificant in comparison with the achievements of *INGO's* in the fields of business, labor, social welfare, religion, etc.

EDUCATION FOR PARTICULAR GROUPS

Prior to the last war, among the *INGO's* dealing with education for special groups were the International Association for Business Education, the International Commission of Congresses for Family Education, the International Bureau for Technical Training, the International Centre for Workers' Education. The one organization devoted to adult education in general was the World Association for Adult Education, which was dissolved shortly after the end of World War II.

World Association for Adult Education

Organized in 1918, the World Association for Adult Education helped to bring together those interested in education for adults, and assisted many who desired to study the adult education methods of other countries. It maintained a Bureau of Information on Adult Education which performed very useful work in this respect, as indicated in the following quotation from its 1936–37 report:

EDUCATION   125

Visitors from twenty-six countries were received, but correspondents represented a much wider area. The following are a few examples of inquiries dealt with: . . . A French Judge was supplied with material on Adult Education in prisons, organisation of prison visitors, etc.; . . . facilities for the study of all Government regulations pertaining to Adult Education in England since the inception of the movement were provided for a Canadian organiser; an Indian student of Illiteracy was put in touch with the Mass Education movement in Egypt, China, Russia and Turkey; . . . information with regard to continuation schools and other forms of post-primary education in the United States, Scotland, Ireland and Canada was prepared for a Parliamentary Committee in Finland.[1]

The Association conducted varied investigations—workers' education, education in prisons, university extramural and extension work, etc.; published a number of reports in addition to a regular *Bulletin;* and was responsible for the establishment of several institutions, including the American Association for Adult Education (founded as a result of a memorandum presented to the Carnegie Corporation of New York by the World Association), the British Institute of Adult Education, the Seafarers Education Service in England and a similar Service in Norway. At the time of the author's visit to the Association's headquarters in London in 1938, it was endeavoring to organize an International Advisory Committee on the Welfare of Seamen, in the hope that the idea of special services for seamen could be extended to other countries.

SPECIAL EDUCATIONAL METHODS AND ATTITUDES

The *INGO's* promoting special teaching methods or attitudes were the International Commission on the Educational Use of Films and Broadcasting, the International Montessori Association which has aimed to advance the progressive Montessori system of training and instruction for pre-school age children, and the New Education Fellowship devoted to "progressive" education.

New Education Fellowship

This international association, organized in 1915, groups those who desire to see education reformed along progressive lines, under the belief that "each child has a natural eagerness to learn and to perfect his innate capacities;" that education should "provide an environment in which this eagerness can find full expression" and that "Education should work for the gradual attainment of the discipline of freedom in place of the external discipline of compulsion." Responsibility to the community in both its narrower and world-wide aspect is emphasized. From its headquarters at London it has organized international conferences, conducted investigations, maintained publications, etc. Its international conferences have been attended by as many as two thousand persons and its regional meetings by up to nine thousand individuals.[2] It has performed a three-fold task, summarized as follows:

> First, through its international and regional conferences, its thirty-one national sections and groups and twenty-one magazines in fifteen languages, it acts as a permanent working laboratory in which new developments in educational thought and practice in different lands, can be exhibited and discussed throughout the world. Secondly, it maintains friendly personal contacts between educational thinkers and practitioners in different countries and thus contributes notably to the feeling of human solidarity among those engaged in education. And lastly, owing to its national organisations and international outlook and character, it is helping educators to understand the differences in social attitude and custom which characterise different classes and different countries and constitute one of the most fruitful causes of misunderstanding and conflict in the modern world.[3]

PROFESSIONAL TRADE ASSOCIATIONS

A number of *INGO's* represent teachers and are concerned with their professional opportunities, rights and privileges as well as with education itself. Only two examples will be briefly described here, for although established to perform an essential function little seems to have been accomplished up to 1939 by these *INGO's*. Organized on an institutional basis, the International Committee of Schools for Social Work has functioned with more success.

International Federation of Teachers' Associations

The International Federation of Teachers' Associations was organized in 1926 at Paris; in 1937 it had national associations in Australia, Bolivia, Brazil, Netherlands Indies, New Zealand, Porto Rico, San Domingo, and eighteen European countries, with a total membership of 547,500. It has sought "to raise the standard of popular education, to improve methods of teaching, to raise the level of the general and professional training of teachers and to protect their material and moral interests."[4]

International Federation of Secondary School Teachers

With federations in twenty European countries, the International Federation of Secondary School Teachers, organized in 1912 at Charleroi, Belgium, has had as its aim:

> To cultivate friendship and international unity between all its members; to promote the progress of secondary education; to study means of enabling young persons who have to live abroad to continue their studies there without loss or delay; to endeavour to improve the material and moral situation

of teaching staff; to collaborate with general official or private associations pursuing the same objects.[5]

International Committee of Schools for Social Work

The International Committee of Schools for Social Work was founded in 1929 at Brussels; in 1938 its membership consisted of seventy-eight schools in seventeen countries. In its field it has helped the international exchange of views and information as well as the exchange of teachers and students. It has maintained a document service, and has organized international courses on social work. Its congresses have served to bring together from the various countries leaders with vastly different experiences and have helped them to get to know each other and to compare methods. The Committee served the *ILO* library as a center for information concerning the programs and activities of schools for social work.

INGO'S CONCERNED WITH STUDENTS

Some of the student groups, such as the World's Student Christian Federation and "Pax Romana"—International Secretariat of National Federations of Catholic Students (now called "Pax Romana—International Movement of Catholic Students") have a religious aim as their primary function; these are discussed under religion. Omitted are those *INGO's* with specialized functions, such as the international associations of blind students, of Jewish students, etc.; several whose principal aim is to promote better international relations are to be found in the section, *Pursuit of Peace.* Included, however, are some *INGO's,* like the International Student Service and the International Federation of University Women, which although concerned with other interests have devoted an important share of their activities to education; only this aspect of their work is discussed in this section.

International Confederation of Students

The International Confederation of Students, organized in 1919, was the largest student organization functioning in the prewar years; it was completely disbanded before the outbreak of World War II. In 1937, its "titular" or full members comprised the student unions of twenty-five countries with a total individual membership of 759,785; in addition, its "free members," "cooperating" student unions, etc., from nine countries, brought 134,160 more students within the membership of the Confederation. Its purpose was:

> To create bonds of esteem and friendship between students throughout the world, to establish a permanent liaison between their organisations and

to coordinate their activities in the sphere of university life; to study international questions concerning higher education and the moral and material needs of students, and thus to contribute to intellectual expansion.[6]

In addition to its Central Office at Brussels, it maintained a number of permanent committees and offices: "committees for intellectual and scientific cooperation; international office for cooperation between students and industry; international office for training in scientific agriculture; international committee of law students; international secretariat of university presses; committee for traveling and international relationships; office of statistics and social information; international office of university sports."[7] These provided information and endeavored to secure international cooperation. One of the most successful activities of the Confederation, the promotion of student travel, has already been described (see pp. 69). Also successful was its work in organizing international university sports. However, in some areas of its interests, its "offices" did nothing, and the *Annuaire* of the Confederation itself admitted that in the field of intellectual cooperation little had been accomplished.[8]

The Confederation suffered from internal political difficulties which to a considerable extent were reflections of antagonistic national feelings. Its structure was severely criticized in 1931 and six of the strongest national unions resigned when their proposals for reform were refused. Following a constitutional change, some of these members returned, including the National Students Federation of the United States with 425,000 members.[9]

That it was able to secure a certain degree of cooperation is all to its credit, but the great possibilities inherent in the Confederation were never fully realized.

Committee of the International Students' Associations

The Committee of the International Students' Associations was composed of seven *INGO's:* the International Federation of University Women, the Pax Romana—International Secretariat of National Federations of Catholic Students—the International Confederation of Students, the World's Student Christian Federation, the International University Federation for the League of Nations, the International Student Service, and the World Union of Jewish Students. The moving spirit in the formation of this Committee was Conrad Hoffmann, Secretary-General of the International Student Service, who proposed its establishment before the Sub-Commission on University Relations of the League of Nations Institute of Intellectual Co-operation in July, 1925. The creation of six or seven new student *INGO's* from 1920 and the growing danger of duplication of effort made it desirable, he argued, to bring about a more effective coordination of their work. From this came the decision to constitute the Committee under the auspices of the Institute. The Committee worked closely with the Institute which furnished secretarial aid, headquarters space, and paid the travelling expenses of the chief delegate of each organization to the annual plenary sessions. The Institute also published information on the activities of the member organizations as well as the reports of the plenary sessions of the Committee, and other special material.[10]

Certain resolutions of the Committee were incorporated in the resolutions of the League's International Committee on Intellectual Co-operation and were thus brought to the official attention of governments.[11]

The Committee enabled each organization to keep in close touch with the work of the others and with the work of the Institute itself. Particular care was given to avoiding conflicting dates for international conferences in order to enable the various student groups to be represented at each other's sessions.

The Committee was also concerned with the international exchange of students, the conditions of life for students studying outside their own country, and questions concerning university study in general. It was felt that:

> Since the Committee is primarily a coordinating organ, it is natural that the results of its activity are to be found principally in the life of its affiliated organisations. There is no doubt but that the reciprocal knowledge of the activity of each of its members and the emulation resulting therefrom constitute a favorable factor in the development of these organizations; that this same emulation will not degenerate into ruinous competition is precisely one of the great merits of the Committee. It is certainly thanks to it that the encouragement of intellectual cooperation occupies today such an eminent place in the activities of the students' organizations. . . .[12]

International Federation of University Women

The International Federation of University Women (graduates) is an important *INGO* whose contribution cannot be considered under education alone. Organized in 1919 at London, its membership, which was about fifty-five thousand in 1933, increased to 65,456 during the crisis years in spite of the loss of the national units in Germany, Italy and Portugal. In 1938 it had national units in the Union of South Africa, Australia, Brazil, Canada, Egypt, India, Mexico, New Zealand, Palestine, the United States, and twenty-four European countries. Its object has been:

> To promote understanding and friendship between university women in all countries of the world and thereby to further their interests and develop between their countries sympathy and mutual helpfulness.[13]

Along educational lines, it has awarded international Fellowships for Research and grants-in-aid amounting by 1937 to fifteen thousand pounds; it has promoted the international exchange of teachers; it has issued a number of useful publications including "A List of International Fellowships for Research." Before the outbreak of World War II, it was in the process of preparing an "International Dictionary of Academic Terms."

International Student Service

The International Student Service (*ISS*) was founded in 1920 by the World's Student Christian Federation under the name of European Student Relief; in 1925 it became an independent organization under its present name.[14] Between 1920 and 1924 European Student Relief raised about five hundred thousand pounds "for the benefit of starving and destitute students and professors in Central Europe and Russia." Not only money but "hundreds of tons of fuel, meal, potatoes, chocolate and clothing" were distributed; "but what proved to be still more important for many of the universities in the years to follow was that students were organized to help themselves, and thus through cooperative action the relief contributions from abroad were greatly enhanced in value, and a self-help movement started which has since reached enormous dimensions in the universities of many countries."[15] John R. Mott, in discussing the value of this work, pointed out that in addition to having helped in "the meeting of crying physical needs and economic necessities, and the preservation from decadence of the imperiled intellectual life of so many centres of learning and influence," great indirect results were also achieved. Referring to those who were helped, he said, "The preservation of their highest ideals, the safeguarding of the springs of their faith and spiritual vitality, and the maintenance of their confidence in the integrity and unselfishness of their comrades of other lands constitute assets that, though imponderable, are simply priceless"; and, referring to the students who helped in the work, "a training ground has been afforded for preparing a generation to deal . . . with industrial, international, and interracial relations."[16]

The purpose of the *ISS* has been:

> To encourage all efforts made by students, professors, etc., with a view to developing universities and establishments of higher education, true centers of national culture, which remain in close contact with international, economic and social realities of the modern world.[17]

It has been concerned with all types of university questions, sponsoring research, publications, conferences. Prior to the last war it served not only as a "study centre" for economic and social problems of university life, undertaking special inquiries on such questions as graduate unemployment and overcrowding in universities, but also as an "experimental centre for the improvement of student life in all its forms, by encouraging the formation of centres, cooperative clubs, the organisation of work-camps, etc. The *ISS* [had] a monopoly of student exchanges between camps in different countries."[18] Its important contributions to student relief and its activities in connection with international relations are described elsewhere (see p. 240–241); here, we are concerned with the more purely educational aspects of its work.

In 1932, the *ISS* initiated an important international inquiry into unemployment in the learned professions. The inquiry, carried out under Dr. Walter Kotschnig, who had previously been General Secretary of the *ISS*, attracted a great deal of attention, and a number of other international organizations—the Committee of International Student Organizations, the Advisory Committee of Intellectual Workers of the *ILO*, the International Confederation of Intellectual Workers, the League of Nations Committee on Intellectual Co-operation, etc.—took up the problem, "to a large extent using the results of the research initiated by *ISS*." Also, national organizations were stimulated to make investigations "of a more detailed nature," and it was said that the inquiry "greatly assisted" universities in making needed reforms. In 1937, Dr. Kotschnig's report was published under the title *Unemployment in the Learned Professions* (Oxford University Press), and some of the most important educational leaders of various countries were brought together in Paris to consider its findings.[19]

In his book Dr. Kotschnig noted the need for some international body to serve as a "clearing centre" which would "collect information on the methods of 'planning'" utilized by national agencies and which would "publish that information . . . together with essential results attained by these methods." He stated, "The work of the International Student Service has proved conclusively how much an international agency of this kind can do to stimulate national efforts. The various conferences it has held, which have brought together experts from many lands, have furthermore undoubtedly helped to improve existing methods of predicting occupational opportunities in the professions." It is obvious from Dr. Kotschnig's report that the *ISS* inquiry influenced official thinking, for he continues:

> It is encouraging to note that both the International Labour Office and the International Institute of Intellectual Co-operation, which have supported these [*ISS*] efforts consider pursuing them on a larger scale. The International Committee on Intellectual Co-operation in its 1936 session, commended the steps already taken by the Institute of Intellectual Co-operation in Paris to obtain information on the unemployment in the professions and the ways of meeting it, and asked that these efforts be continued. After recommending that the greatest possible number of countries should

form "university information and intelligence bureau," it decided that "the results of the permanent inquiry which might be set on foot and conducted by the Institute with the assistance of the International Labour Office, the Joint Committee of the Major Associations, the International Student Organizations, and the National Committees on Intellectual Co-operation might be published in the bulletin *La Coopération intellectuelle,* in order to provide documentary material which could be consulted by all parties concerned."[20]

The *ISS* issued many other publications including monographs on student health, loan funds, hostels, work camps. A large number of its international conferences were designed to meet particular problems in the university world, such as overcrowding, with an eye to concrete action, while others brought together university people for study and discussion of general international problems in the hope of promoting better international understanding. Its Geneva office served as an information center for all sorts of university matters.

EDUCATION IN GENERAL

World Federation of Education Associations

Established in 1923 at Washington, D.C., the World Federation of Education Associations in 1938 had national member associations in seventeen countries; its purpose has been: "To develop international goodwill through education; to promote the cause of education and to elevate the character of teaching throughout the world."[21] There is a feeling among some who have come into contact with the Federation that it has not accomplished much. It has not always given evidence of good management. However, it has had perhaps a certain value in spreading a rather vague concept of "international goodwill." It has been superseded by the recently established World Organization of the Teaching Profession.

8 RELIGION

THE SPREAD of Christianity has created in all countries groups of men and women who have certain fundamental beliefs and practices in common. Throughout most of its history this great movement of Christianization was motivated almost exclusively by the desire to save souls, with little thought of international problems. The Churches were frequently nationalistic, even chauvinistic, and were, in fact, too often the servants or the tools of militaristic states. However, in recent decades, it has become increasingly clear to Christians that such attitudes are un-Christian, since love of all men lies at the very heart of their religion. Christian organizations now constantly reassert the supra-national character of their faith. The Christian dream of the "Kingdom of God" on earth is that all men will live in love for one another in obedience to divine authority. This is international or world organization carried to its highest degree.

Religion has been extremely important in the development of international organization, not only in the creation and expansion of purely religious associations but also in the establishment of international non-governmental organizations (*INGO's*) for moral, humanitarian, labor, educational, health and social matters, and, of course, for the pursuit of peace. It is a matter of opinion whether the religious or the economic motive has played in the past or will play in the future the greater role in the development of international organization.

Whether we take the period before 1914 or that between the World Wars, we find that the religious, humanitarian and moral organizations are the most numerous, and even today are being created at a more rapid rate than those of any other type. They are, in general, the oldest of existing international organizations, even if one leaves out the Roman Catholic Church and its world-wide monastic orders such as the Benedictines, Dominicans, Franciscans, and Jesuits, which are centuries older than other international organizations. The Church claims to be an official supra-national organization. The existence of the Vatican State with the Pope as its temporal ruler, and the acceptance of its diplomatic representatives by many nations constitute evidence of this status and recognition of it. The Catholic Church as a world organization occupies an unusual, even unique, position. However, it is certainly not an international union of states, and falls more readily into the classification of an *INGO,* since the Catholic churches in the various countries are generally in the same position as the Protestant churches, that of private organizations. In any case, the Catholic Church will not be described in this book, for the great role it has played in world history for many centuries is well known. It is undoubtedly the most important international or world organization. Its relations with the various Catholic *INGO's,* of which there are many, is very close.

While some of the Catholic *INGO's* are extremely old, it is the impression of the author that the Protestant groups have been more active in the great movement for international organization which began about the middle of the last century. However, in more recent years, influenced perhaps by these Protestant associations and by the creation of international labor organizations by socialists as well as by other factors, Catholics have set up *INGO's* for many purposes. In the years immediately preceding World War II, both Catholics and Protestants were among the most active groups in the creation and development of international organization. With increasing realization of the fact that human needs can be more fully met through international organization, they were uniting more and more in all sorts of social service organizations. The study of their own faith has increasingly led them to the realization that unless they do so they deny the very basis of their religion. Recognizing the essence of Fascism and Communism as anti-Christian, conscious of the widespread indifference to Christian concepts, appalled by the onrushing possibility of a second world war, Christian leaders considered the challenge they faced as greater than any since the days of Constantine, and the need for a "united front" became more and more evident.

Although lacking the participation of the Roman Catholic Church, the oecumenical movement—the movement toward Christian unity—is one of the most significant developments in international organization and will undoubtedly take an important place in world history. On the international level the agencies of this movement have been the World Conference on Faith and Order, the Universal Christian Council for Life and Work, the International Missionary Council,[1] the World's Alliance for International Friendship Through the Churches,[2] the youth organizations—the World's Student Christian Federation, the World Alliance of *YMCA's* and the World's *YWCA*—and more recently the World Council of Churches.

> The total sum of these approaches, along with varied lines, toward a common faith and common action among Christian people, and between organised Churches, has come to be known as the "Oecumenical Movement." This is a loose phrase open to misconception, but it stands for "the expression within history of the given unity of the Church of Christ."[3]

The motivating forces of this movement have been and are still powerful. How strong they are may be judged by this statement made in 1935 by the well known oecumenical leader, John R. Mott:

> The materialistic philosophy of the day, the violence of the destructive communistic activity, the powers of paganism and of faiths and systems contrary to the teachings of Christ, the reactionary attitude of so many governments with reference to religious liberty, the perilous subordination of religion to serve the political ends of the totalitarian conception of the state, and the necessity of recasting the prevailing industrial and commercial system so that it will not negate the principles of Christian love and brotherhood nor conduce to international war—all present a challenge to Christ's followers which has never been surpassed in gravity and urgency. In truth we are facing stupendous changes in the whole make-up of the world, changes as revolutionary as any in the history of mankind. . . .
>
> At such a time any failure to coordinate our scattered efforts and to present a united front cannot be in accord with the divine will. The great central motivating fact must be emphasized, as never before, that the governing consideration for undertaking this larger and more vital cooperation is not the present unprecedented crisis, or the still grave economic conditions, but the conviction that Christ wills such larger and closer cooperation for His Church in our day. Of this the convincing evidence is His high-priestly prayer. In praying that His followers across the ages "might be one," the very least He could have meant is that in our conception and practice with reference to the spread of His Kingdom and reign, we might be so at one in our thinking, our fellowship, our planning, our action, and our intercession, that the keenest critic could receive no other impression than that we are presenting a united front to the world-wide need and task of bringing all mankind into vital relation to Him. Thus cooperation must be insisted upon, not on grounds of expediency, but on grounds of unshakable conviction that this is good, and is God's will for His servants.[4]

The year 1937 marked the greatest prewar manifestation of the oecumenical movement, when the Oxford Conference on Church, Community and State and the Edinburgh Conference on Faith and Order were held within one week of each other. These meetings were more representative and involved more cooperative planning than any previous attempt. The eight organizations mentioned were associated in a consultative body under the chairmanship of the Archbishop of York, and they set up "a Committee of thirty-five representative Christians of different countries and Churches" who considered the future of the oecumenical movement as a whole and reported to both Conferences, at Oxford and at Edinburgh. Dr. Walter W. Gethman has said of these eight bodies, "through their continuous emphasis on the universal aspects of Christianity and their increasing affirmation through studies, literature, and conferences of the Eternal Values . . . [they] are exerting what may prove the most telling integrating force in the world today."[5] Of the Conferences, Henry Smith Leiper stated, "For those in every land who desire to know what the best Christian thought of the age has to say about the fundamental relationships of society and the duties of the individual who would play his part in building a better world, the conferences have provided a store of wisdom not likely soon to be surpassed either in soundness or in relevance to life."[6]

We will first examine the steps leading to the establishment of a World Council of Churches, which will give us a general understanding of the oecumenical movement, before proceeding to a discussion of other religious associations.

International Missionary Council

The steps leading to the establishment of the International Missionary Council (New York and London) need to be mentioned, for they represent the seeds of the oecumenical movement:

> After one of the meetings of the Alliance [of Reformed Churches Throughout the World Holding the Presbyterian System], the Foreign Missions boards of the American Churches of the Alliance, finding such conferences so helpful, called a meeting of the Foreign Mission boards of Alliance. This proved so successful that they issued a call for a larger meeting of all the Foreign Mission Boards of the Protestant churches of America. This organised itself into the "Conference of Foreign Mission Boards of America." Out of this grew the great World Missionary Conferences of 1900 and 1910.[7]

The 1910 conference, held at Edinburgh, was concerned with the Church's collective responsibility for spreading the gospel, and its Continuation and Emergency Committees were able (1) "to preserve the work of the German [missionary] societies, to deal with Government regarding it, and to enlist the help of missionary bodies in Great Britain, North America and the Continent of Europe" in maintaining it intact, and (2) to advance, even during the War, freedom for missionary work. As a result of their efforts, missionary freedom was recognized in the peace treaties and in the mandate system of the League of Nations, thus ensuring "for the future this vital principle with the cordial assent of the authorities concerned."[8]

The most important result of the 1910 conference, however, was the establishment in 1920 of the International Missionary Council, after which "there developed a degree of unity in this great field of Christian activity such as had not been dreamed of when the process was begun."[9] National missionary bodies in more than twenty-five countries were members of the Council (1938); in India, China and Japan, with the help of the Council, national Christian councils were built up "on the basis of representation of missionary organisations and of indigenous Churches," with the Council serving "as a link between them and the different organisation of missionary bodies in the Western world":

> . . . the missionary societies or churches which enter into cooperation through the International Missionary Council do not surrender control of their policy to it. . . . The task of the International Missionary Council is rather to focus attention on the greater issues which face all sections of the Church in its missionary work. It endeavors to promote study, thought and action on such matters in different countries, and in particular to help in the vital process of bringing together the outlook and experience of many different countries for their mutual enrichment.

The 1928 Congress of the Council, at Jerusalem, is a landmark in the history of missions, carrying "forward the missionary task envisaged at Edinburgh." Among the issues discussed were "the relation of the Christian message to non-Christian systems," "the improvement of religious education," "the mutual understanding of the older and younger Churches of the East and West," "race and industry," and "rural needs." This conference helped to establish the understanding that there was missionary need at home as well as abroad. This significant influence of the conference is pointed up in the 1931 Report of the World's Committee of the *YMCA:*

> The central point in these discussions, namely that the typical characteristic of modern civilization as compared with older civilisations is that modern civilisation tends to reject religion as a basis for its life, is by no means new. But what is new, is that it is now being approached as a world problem. This is largely due to the Jerusalem Conference of the International Missionary Council in 1928 . . . there is a growing realization on the part of Christians all over the world, that there is no longer any room for a distinction between the situation of Christianity in so-called Christian countries and the situation in "missionary lands," for the essential question to be faced everywhere is the relation of Christianity to an increasingly unified and increasingly secularised world-civilization.[10]

While discussing the movement for cooperation in the missionary field, John R. Mott delineates the significant role of the Council:

> The first stage [of cooperation] was the period preceding the World Missionary Conference at Edinburgh in 1910—the period when experiments were initiated which were ultimately multiplied into a large and increasing number of detached pieces of cooperative effort scattered all over the world. The second stage embraced the years between the Edinburgh conference and the meeting of the International Missionary Council at Jerusalem in 1928—the period which had as its distinctive characteristic

the creation and development in many parts of the world of national and international agencies, or councils, for the express purpose of inaugurating and fostering interdenominational, international, and interracial cooperation. Moreover, during this second period cooperative or union projects, largely local or regional in scope, though at times also national, continued to multiply at an almost geometrical rate. The third stage, upon which we entered at Jerusalem in 1928, is the one in which the Christian forces related to the missionary enterprise pool not only knowledge and experience but also plans *in the making,* personalities, funds, names, and, increasingly, administration. It is thus the period in which the implications of cooperation are taken, generally speaking, much more seriously than ever before.[11]

Among the outstanding achievements of the Council is its work in Africa:

> The officers of the . . . Council and notably Mr. Oldham, have been intimately associated with the Governments and also with educational commissions sent out by the Phelps Stokes Fund in the whole great task of organising African education on sound lines. Close as has been in India the cooperation of missions with Government in the conduct of education, there can be no doubt that the cooperation between missions and Government in Africa in the same sphere is closer. The Advisory Committee of the Colonial Office on Native Education in Tropical Africa comprises members who are definitely chosen to represent the interests of missionary education, so that the point of view of the Christian educator is taken into account not merely in the carrying out of policy, but, what is more important, in the framing of it.[12]

In 1932, the Council set up an "Africa Industrialization Study" for which the Carnegie Corporation of New York furnished all but five hundred of the twenty-three thousand dollars spent for the project. Its report was published in a 350-page volume, *Modern Industry and the African* (London, 1933); the Council, in 1935, said of this report:

> As the first comprehensive study of the whole position of the primitive African under the impact of European Civilization, the report was received with interest by colonial governments, great industrialists, educators, and anthropologists as well as by mission groups and students of many aspects of native African culture. The book was reviewed by over two hundred journals and papers in twenty countries and eleven languages. Conferences of mission executives for studying the report with a view to acting upon its findings have been held in New York, London, Hartford and N'dola, Northern Rhodesia. In line with the recommendations of the report, a committee has been formed in Northern Rhodesia for the purpose of pooling inter-mission activities upon the Copper Belt, and steps are being taken not only in this great new mining area, but in the adjacent Copper Belt of Katanga, to reinforce the present missionary staff with workers

trained in social welfare methods. The demands of the situation in this part of Africa for union missionary evangelistic effort and for missionaries equipped with anthropological training and experience in rural community work are stressed by the report.

One of the economc findings of the Commission has been put into action by the Northern Rhodesia Government, viz., the introduction of the penny as a smaller medium of exchange to assist the purchasing power of the natives.

Although it is for others to estimate the value of the Commission's report, it is clear that the favor with which it has been received is partly due to its objectivity and fairness in giving credit where credit is due, and in pointing out the elements of harmony as well as of conflict in the aims and policies of Government, Industry and Missions, together with practical steps for coordinating the programs of these three forces that are revolutionizing African native society.[13]

The Council also undertook "The Bantu Educational Cinema Experiment," for which it received fifty-five thousand dollars from the Carnegie Corporation. Its 1935 report states:

> This project has met with remarkable response from the principal British and international groups who are interested from various angles in the development of native African life. The Committee on International Intellectual Co-operation of the League of Nations, the International Educational Cinematograph Institute of Rome and the International Institute of African Languages and Cultures have all offered assistance. The British Colonial Office has been helpful from the beginning. The Governments of Northern Rhodesia, Nyasaland, Tanganyika and Kenya have vied with one another in providing facilities for furthering the experiment. A glance at the membership of the British Advisory Council of the project will show the scope and influence of the groups represented. Lord Lugard, dean of British colonial administrators and member for Great Britain of the Mandates Commission of the League of Nations, is Chairman of the Advisory Council.
>
> In the opening meeting of the Council, Lord Lugard said that the Bantu Educational Cinema Experiment might prove to be one of the most important steps yet taken for the advancement of native African life. It is planned that a permanent producing organization, yet to be created, will take over the results of the Experiment and provide suitable films upon a large scale for the use of African natives.[14]

Universal Christian Council on Life and Work

Representing the Anglican, Protestant and Orthodox Christian Churches, the Universal Christian Council, at Geneva, came into being in 1925 when, at the initiative of Archbishop Nathan Söderblom of Sweden, there convened at Stockholm the "most widely representative conference and the first to bring the great Eastern Orthodox communion into touch with the Anglican and Reformed (Protestant) world in general . . . after nine earlier attempts of the same sort had failed." This Conference "was concerned with unity in Christian life and work, the practical side of cooperation being considered more than the philosophical, theological or organizational sides."[15] The nature of its 1937 Conference at Oxford, which dealt with the attitude of the church toward political, social and international problems, was explained by J. H. Oldham as follows:

> Apart from these two main exceptions [The Church of Rome and the German Evangelical Church] the Conference was representative of present-day Christianity throughout the world. It is true that, as has been stated in some reports of the Conference, certain traditions and types of Christian thought were more largely represented than others. But when due allowance has been made for this, the range of Christian tradition and experience represented is remarkable. Delegates were present from forty different countries. Of the four hundred and twenty-five members of the Conference three hundred were appointed officially by the different Churches. . . . Delegates were sent by all the principal Churches in the United States of America, in Great Britain, in the British Dominions, and on the continent of Europe. The Eastern Orthodox Churches were represented by some of their leading patriarchs, bishops, and scholars. Representatives of the Old Catholics took part in the proceedings. There were delegates also from the younger Churches in Japan, China, India, Africa, and South America.
>
> In addition to the delegates appointed by the Churches there were one hundred members of the Conference appointed by the Universal Christian Council. . . . The object of this provision was to ensure that the membership of the Conference should include a sufficient proportion of Christian laity, representing other departments of knowledge besides theology and possessing practical experience of public affairs.[16]

The Conference's findings have been published in a series of seven volumes entitled, *The Christian Understanding of Man; The Kingdom of God and History; The Christian Faith and the Common Life; Church and Community; Church, Community and State; Church, Community and State in Relation to Education; The Universal Church and the World of Nations*. These findings are all the more significant when one considers that at the conference:

> At least three or four hundred persons, including some of the ablest minds in the Church, took part in this interchange of thought. They represented the most diverse theological traditions and the widest differences of view on social and political questions.[17]

In discussing the results of the Conference, Bishop Oldham stated:

> The common thought and prayer with the representatives of so many different nations and races was a new, and for many a unique, experience

of the reality of the universal fellowship of the Christian Church. The measure of agreement reached by those coming together from such diverse backgrounds was greater than most had dared to hope. . . . It is hardly possible to overestimate the educative value of this oecumenical interchange of thought for those who participated in it. . . . The major importance of the Oxford Conference may lie less in the value of the conclusions which it reached on the subjects with which it dealt than in the fact that it did something to awaken the mind of the Church to their significance and urgency, and attempted to lay foundations for the continued study of them in the years to come. . . .

The clue to an understanding of the reports is to realize that they aim primarily at doing two things. The first is to define the points in the contemporary situation at which the specifically Christian understanding of life is crucially involved. The second is to define the right Christian attitude on these issues, taking account both of the measure of agreement which at present exists among Christians and equally of the differences of view which now divide them. . . .

World Conference on Faith and Order

With headquarters at Winchester and New York, the World Conference on Faith and Order is composed of delegates designated by "those Trinitarian Churches in Christendom which have responded to the invitation to appoint representatives," which in 1938 included the "Anglican, Armenian, Baptist, Congregational, Czechoslovak Disciples, Eastern Orthodox, Friends, German Evangelical, Lutheran, Methodist, Moravian, Old Catholic, Presbyterian, Reformed and United" Churches.[18] On the "Foreword" of the program of the 1937 conference at Edinburgh, we base the following summary of its work.

This *INGO* came into being at Lausanne in 1927 when, at the initiative of Bishop Brent of the United States and other Christian leaders, the first conference on faith and order—which Leiper describes as "the most official conference" of the early oecumenical meetings[19]—convened. It was planned in order to bring together "the Churches in a spirit of earnest desire to understand one another, to discover how far they are kept apart by genuine differences of conviction which made unity impossible, and how far their growth in isolation from one another had concealed fundamental agreements under different habits of thought and language." Over four hundred delegates representing more than a hundred Churches—"which accept our Lord Jesus Christ as God and Saviour"—attended for "consideration of questions pertaining to the Faith and Order of the Church of Christ."

> They sat for nearly three weeks, and produced a Report recording agreements and disagreements reached in the course of their discussions. The

Conference ordered this Report to be referred to the various Churches, with a request that they should consider it and express their judgment upon it. There was also appointed a Continuation Committee to receive and consider the responses of the Churches to the Report, and to take such further action as it should think fit to further the cause for which the Conference stood.

The Report was circulated. The responses of the Churches began to come in. Steps were taken to promote the joint study of outstanding matters of disagreement by theologians representing different Churches. And in 1931 the Continuation Committee unanimously resolved to call a second World Conference to meet in 1937, and adopted a provisional programme for it. Then came the work of programme-building for 1937. . . . The Continuation Committee established for itself a two-fold task: First, it has attempted to discover as accurately as possible what each Church stands for, how each Church views its own confession of faith by which it lives, through which it is in vital contact with Christ. This has been done by the collection of the responses of the Churches to the 1927 Report, and their publication in 1934 in the volume *Convictions*. Secondly, it has called on theologians from different Churches to come together in Commissions and begin the work of digging down through those confessions in patient search for some underlying ground of unity.[20]

The reports of these Commissions on *The Church and the Word,* the *Church's Ministry and Sacraments,* and *The Church's Unity in Life and Worship* was submitted to the 1937 Edinburgh Conference. For this conference, as for Oxford, "attempts were made to secure the cooperation of the Roman Catholic Church."

Although in the view of the leaders of that communion it was not possible for them to take part directly in either conference, the state of the Church throughout the world and the growth of a more Christianlike attitude toward their "separated brethren" did lead them to cooperate in certain invisible ways with the Oxford Conference studies and to address a significant message, couched in terms of warm friendliness, to the Edinburgh Conference.[21]

This conference, as in 1927, dealt with the theological or doctrinal questions upon which agreement must be reached before organic unity can be achieved. Both meetings have helped to make clear exactly where there is agreement and where disagreement, thus defining the problem of doctrinal unity. This in itself is a real achievement, and a necessary preliminary step to further unity. Of course, in the doctrinal field agreement is more difficult to achieve and progress is slower than in either the missionary or "Life and Work" movements.

The studies prepared for the Edinburgh Conference pointed out several important facts:

(1) That many of the existing divisions among Christians correspond to no important differences either of faith or order, but owe their existence to cultural or political causes independent of the nature of the Church.

(2) That there is a growing conviction among Christians that such divisions are not only administratively wasteful, but if continued after their real origin and nature have been exposed may become morally wrong. This has led to a determined and on the whole not unsuccessful effort to overcome them. . . .

(3) That the motive which leads Christians to desire corporate or institutional union is strongest in the foreign field where conditions most closely approximate those of primitive Christianity.

(4) That one of the greatest obstacles to the success of such efforts (apart from the natural inertia which is satisfied with the *status quo*) is the dependence of the bodies to be united upon larger units with different history and tradition, many of whose members do not feel the urge to unite with the same insistence and are not therefore prepared to approve the concessions which must be made.

(5) That the line between those who regard corporate union as essential and those who do not is not to be identified with the contrast between Catholics and Protestants, but that in each major division of Christians there are to be found a High Church party determined, or at least desirous, to make acceptance of their own view of the divine constitution of the Church the condition of fellowship with other Christians, and a Low Church party who feel the existing spiritual unity so important that they are willing to recognize Christians of other order and polity on equal terms.

(6) That apart from the efforts to achieve institutional union in either of the forms mentioned above there have been developed a number of organizations, largely federative in character, through which it is possible for communions, while maintaining their legal independence, to combine with others for purposes of common witness, common worship and common service. The bearing of these federations upon our matter of corporate union is differently interpreted, some regarding them as an obstacle to corporate union, others thinking of them as a step toward such union, still others believing that they may suggest one among other possible forms which ultimate union may take.

(7) That a factor of growing importance in the movement for unity is the recognition that in circles not consciously affiliated with the Church or even actively opposed to it we find ideal elements dominant and motives operating which are essentially Christian in quality. With these, too, every lover of unity must desire to make contact, that he may appropriate for the Church whatever of truth and of goodness they have to impart.

(8) That besides the more formal approaches to church union, either by the merger of different denominations or through federation for the purposes of common action, we find a number of experiments in the way of closer union taking place in unofficial ways. Some of these take the form of meetings for common worship, others for religious education, others for

joint evangelism, still others for social service. Christians are found working with their fellow Christians, together with persons of other faiths, in undenominational or interdenominational societies or in specific projects of transient or temporary character.

(9) That from these must be distinguished a number of attempts to overcome the existing obstacles to union by temporary devices, either with or without ecclesiastical sanction. Examples of the first are the practice of admitting communicants of other Churches to sacraments administered by Episcopally ordained ministers, or the partaking of the sacraments by Episcopalians at the hands of ministers non-Episcopally ordained. To the same class belong the various efforts to regularize the ministry of other communions for special purposes by means of a Concordat such as that proposed for the Congregationalists and Episcopalians in 1919, or for the Presbyterians and Episcopalians by the overture of the Presbytery of Santa Barbara in 1935. To a different category belong the cases of occasional inter-communion between Episcopalians and members of other Churches, when that practice runs counter to the law, or at least custom, of the diocese in which the act of inter-communion takes place. These cases raise the question whether the experiment deemed desirable must in every case wait upon ecclesiastical action or whether there are cases where action should precede legal authorization, its wisdom being justified by its fruits.

(10) That not the least important of our tasks in our movement towards unity is to bring about some effective correlation of the various agencies that are working for unity. . . .[22]

This last task was considered by both Oxford and Edinburgh, resulting in steps for the establishment of a World Council of Churches, shortly to be discussed.

World Alliance for International Friendship Through the Churches[23]

With headquarters at Geneva, the World Alliance for International Friendship through the Churches, founded on the first day of World War I (August 1, 1914), had national member councils in thirty-seven countries, "whose duty," explained Lord Dickinson, its President, was "to persuade Christian people that the promotion of goodwill between the nations should be an essential part of their religion. The growth of this idea," he stated, "has been slow." However, there has been much progress toward acceptance of this responsibility as contrasted with the period before 1914, when, according to Lord Dickinson, "The work of the Hague Conference of 1907 . . . was being carried on by diplomatists and jurists. The Churches as organized bodies were standing aside, as if the promotion of peace was no concern of theirs."[24]

The Alliance, one of the important pre-World War II peace organizations, promoted its aims by "Regional Conferences" where church leaders met to discuss the difficulties affecting their countries, by supporting such movements as those for disarmament, arbitration, etc., by supporting the work of the League of Nations, and through its activities with children and young people.[25] Two illustrations of the manner in which the Alliance functioned are given here in order to demonstrate how effective its work was.

The Alliance was concerned with the question of minorities, "primarily from the religious and moral standpoint," and it set up a Minorities Commission which sponsored several regional conferences, bringing together representatives from various churches. These conferences achieved some important practical results and helped to promote the application of Christian principles in the treatment of minorities.[26] Discussing this work, Charles S. Macfarland, then General Secretary of the Federal Council of Churches of Christ in America, wrote in 1924:

> Since the meetings of the representatives of the churches in the Balkan states, where the whole subject of Religious Minorities was thoroughly debated, there have been held various local meetings of these same representatives which never could have been arranged had it not been for the first meeting of these representatives with one another in the presence of their friends from the Great Powers at such meetings as these in Geneva and Copenhagen. Whatever improvement there has been in the treatment of Religious Minorities in the Balkans is largely due to the bringing together of these leaders of the churches from these countries. The prestige and scope of these National Councils [of the Alliance] have been steadily increasing every year since the war until today most of them are centers of goodwill, really felt throughout the length and breadth of their own countries.[27]

The second illustration concerns the cessation of bad feeling between Bulgaria and Yugoslavia and the resulting Pact of Friendship between the two countries.[28] After World War I some territory was separated from Bulgaria and added to Yugoslavia. The Bulgarians felt this was intolerable and according to Professor Stefan Zankow, International Secretary of the Alliance for the Orthodox East, "the worst was to be feared between the two countries." The Bulgarian Council of the World Alliance presented the matter to the 1929 meeting of the Alliance where, through the agency of the Alliance, discussions were held with the Yugoslavian delegates. It was agreed that the two National Councils should meet in conference to examine the whole question and endeavor to arrive at a peaceable solution. The meeting took place in 1933 and the two national councils resolved that they regarded it to be "the imperious and urgently pressing duty of the Holy Churches and of the two nations, the Serbian and the Bulgarian, professing the same faith, to set in motion all possible activities for the creation of a new spirit in their relations to one another."

They then energetically set to work, approaching government officials, the Churches and the people. It is said that "the whole atmosphere of the relations between the two nations, churches and states was soon changed for the better." One result was the exchange of visits between the heads of the governments and later between King Alexander of Yugoslavia and King Boris of Bulgaria.[29]

The Secretary of the World Alliance told the writer that it was both difficult and dangerous for the state churches to go against their governments, that the leaders had met nevertheless, and that King Alexander, in spite of the attitude of his own government, decided to back up this effort of the churches and therefore decided to visit King Boris, which led to the Pact of Friendship.[30]

World's Alliance of *YMCA's*
and
World's *YWCA*

Both the World's Alliance of *YMCA's* and the World's *YWCA* have made important contributions to many social, political, and international questions. They have encouraged and fully participated in united action on such problems, advancing a Christian approach to their solution; they have lent their influence in dealing with official agencies, and their national committees spread throughout the world have done yeoman service. Their activities in these realms must be taken into consideration in any estimate of their inffuence. Both organizations have tried to preserve a balance between the two chief aspects of religious life, that is, the personal relationship in the worship of God as contrasted with action regarding human welfare.

The World's Alliance of *YMCA's,* being one of the oldest *INGO's,* has played a considerable part in the creation of other international associations, including the World's *YWCA*, the World's Student Christian Federation, and the Institute of Pacific Relations. It was interest in *YMCA* work which led the pioneer internationalist, Henry Dunant—a founder of the World's Alliance and of the Red Cross—into international activities.

Through great world conferences and numerous smaller international meetings, through international camps and travel tours, field visits, interchange of workers, study visits of national secretaries to the international headquarters, through extensive publications and research work, financial aid, organized international correspondence, these two *INGO's* have stimulated and inspired their member associations and thousands if not millions of individuals in the course of many years. Bringing together in common activities Christians of many different denominations within

RELIGION

nearly all nations and uniting them in a single fellowship, the *YMCA* since 1855 and the *YWCA* since 1894 have helped to spread the ideal and practice of Christian unity throughout the world. Their influence on the oecumenical movement has been considerable, particularly that of the *YMCA*. It is an interesting fact that:

> The founders of the . . . [*YMCA*] Movement in England, France, Belgium, and Switzerland were not consciously attempting to create interdenominational Youth societies, and some time had to elapse before this characteristic of the Associations was fully realized. The Associations in the United States on the contrary, after having seen this principle in action in the London Association, gave it a central place in their basic policy. . . . Each World's Conference since then has been more or less marked by this spirit. It is interesting to note, however, that it becomes somewhat less evident after 1881 when times were difficult for the World's Evangelical Alliance, which was then devoting its energies especially to the defense of liberty of conscience. But if less was being said about Christian Unity, it would seem that it was being all the more put into practice, and without perhaps being fully aware of it the Associations were influencing the whole thought of the Churches in that direction.[31]

World's *YWCA*

With headquarters at Geneva, the *YWCA* in 1938 had affiliated organizations in forty-five countries. Its object, since 1894, has been:

> To organise, develop and unite national associations which, accepting its basis or one in conformity with it, endeavor to extend the Kingdom of God according to its principles, and to bring young women to such knowledge of Jesus Christ as Lord and Savior as shall manifest itself in character and conduct. It also calls all national associations to promote Christian principles of social and international conduct by encouraging the development of a right public conscience such as shall strengthen all those forces which are working for the promotion of peace and better understanding between classes, nations, and races; believing that the world social order can only be made Christian through individuals devoted to the single purpose of doing God's will, and that through obedience to the law of Christ there shall follow the extension of His Kingdom, in which the principles of justice, love and the equal value of every human life shall apply to national and international as well as to personal relations.[32]

World's Alliance of *YMCA's*

Also located at Geneva, the World's Alliance in 1938 had national units in thirty-six countries; movements existed in twenty-six other countries or colonies, but they were not officially affiliated with the Alliance. The task of its World Committee has been:

1. The coordination of Association activities throughout the world. It is the clearing house of the movement.

2. The survey of the Association movement throughout the world encouraging fidelity to its central purpose of winning young men and boys to Christ and His service.

3. The extension of work to unoccupied fields.

4. The summoning and organizing of World Conferences.

5. The summoning of the whole Association movement to the observance of one special week in each year for special prayer.

6. The promotion of understanding, reconciliation and cooperation among the youth of the world.

7. Careful and continued research and study of world conditions and tendencies as they affect the extension of the Kingdom of God among men and boys. The provision of material for the study of the problems of industrialism, racialism and internationalism in relation to the welfare of youth and the furthering of world peace and understanding.

8. Cooperation in the development of a comprehensive programme in all lands for the spiritual, social, physical and intellectual welfare of young men and boys.

9. The undertaking of work for certain classes of men and boys which, through the nature of the case, can only be done by an international organization.

10. The production or promotion of Christian literature.[33]

We shall not say as much about the efforts of the International Committee of *YMCA's* of the United States and Canada as we would if it were representative of a larger number of countries; it is to a very great extent representative of the U. S. alone. Since 1889 this Committee has provided secretarial and financial assistance to many countries, helping to build up largely self-sustaining national movements. One of its policies

> has been emphasis upon the growth of indigenous secretarial leadership. From a handful of men in the early '90s, North American personnel abroad increased to a peak of 227 secretaries in 1925. A rapid decrease to the present [1936] staff of fifty-one men followed in the next ten years, due partly to economic conditions. Within the same countries, on the other hand, the number of nationals on secretarial rosters has followed a continually rising curve to the present peak of 737 serving in 1936.

Between 1890 and 1930, this committee sent out 529 secretaries; thirty countries received secretarial and financial assistance; over seven and a half million dollars was given for buildings[34]—in recent years about half a million dollars has been given yearly.[35]

Great influence was exerted in China especially, where at one time seven out of ten cabinet ministers under President Chiang Kai-shek "were either former secretaries of the *Y.M.C.A.* or officers and directors of local associations. . . ." According to Lord Willingdon, at one time Viceroy of India, "The one organization in India that is making a serious effort to introduce the Indian to the Englishman and the Englishman to the Indian, is the *Y.M.C.A.*" Bishop Fred F. Fisher estimated the value of its work in these terms, "The Foreign Work of the Young Men's Christian Association, since its inception, has been a most potent agency for the incoming tide of new world consciousness,—the most potent missionary influence since the Civil War. It has lifted other missionary activities by magnetism from above."[36] A summary judgment on its work was given by an independent "International Survey Committee" in these terms:

> But on the whole, it is fair to say that the work being carried on abroad with the aid of the North American Associations has a marked degree of vitality, shows a large measure of resourcefulness, has courageous and sacrificial leadership, has a recognized genius for discovering social needs and mobilizing resources for meeting them, has a superior strategy in dealing with inter-racial, international and interreligious problems, and is, at its best, in line with the major world trends of the present day.[37]

World's Student Christian Federation

Founded forty years after the *YMCA* movement, the World's Student Christian Federation, Geneva, has played a very significant role in promoting student religious life and it has exerted a real influence on the oecumenical movement. Immediately following the meeting at which the Federation was founded (1895), its General Secretary, John R. Mott —today an outstanding leader of the oecumenical movement—was sent on a twenty-month tour of Europe and Asia.

> In the pathway of this, the first world-wide student ministry of Mott, seventy new Student Christian Associations were organized and scores of already existing societies were reorganized and revitalized. Five new national student Christian movements were formed and became affiliated with the World's Student Christian Federation.[38]

This immediate response "to the idea of a student Christian international" typifies the general awakening of the new spirit of internationalism at the time. Within the first five years Christian Associations increased from nine hundred to fourteen hundred, with a jump in individual membership from forty-five thousand to sixty-five thousand; paid secretaries increased from thirty-eight to one hundred one; the value of buildings owned rose from eighty thousand pounds to two hundred thousand pounds; and five new national movements were established.[39] Twenty years later, John R. Mott pointed out:

> The Federation has made possible the beginnings of what may well be called a science of the moral and religious culture of students. Not until

there had been established such a world-wide organization was it possible to make accessible the facts and experiences involved in the cultivation of the moral and religious life of the students of all lands.

The handicaps of isolation have been overcome, so that now the most distant branch of any national movement, for example, in Australia, has been brought into near communion with kindred societies in other lands. It is possible for each movement to send its influence throughout the world. Its ideals, ideas, trials and triumphs are made known and accessible to all.[40]

To summarize its functions, we quote Tissington Tatlow, for many years Secretary of the Student Christian Movement of Great Britain:

The most important work of the Federation is pioneering in lands where there is no Student Christian Movement, or helping in countries where it is small and weak. This it does through visitations by its secretaries and special workers, arranging conferences and providing special literature. . . .

The Federation, in addition to its pioneering work, has led the thought of the national Movements along three lines in particular since the world war [1914], in addition to helping them in their regular work in university and college branches.

First, it has enabled them to come into contact with Churches not represented in their own country, and thus caused them to become more deeply concerned with the question of Christian unity. In Great Britain we owe our present contact with members of the Russian and Bulgarian Orthodox Churches and several Lutheran Churches to the Federation. Thus the Federation has helped us to enrich our life as a Movement as well as to teach us to look for the unity of all the Churches of Christ.

The Oecumenical Commission of the Federation has for some years brought together from time to time Anglicans, Calvinists, Lutherans, Orthodox and Roman Catholics for frank discussion and interchange of spiritual experience. This is proving valuable pioneer work in the cause of reunion.

Second, the Federation has stimulated national movements to "lead students to realize that the principles of Christ should rule in international relationships" by affording opportunities for Christian fellowship in cases where nations and races are in danger of being estranged from each other. Those whom the Federation has brought together have not been denationalized people, but students who will become leaders in their own countries, and who have been eager to discuss with the nationals of countries with which their people were in a state of tension those questions, however difficult, which were producing the tension. Over and above this, the Federation has done much to arouse students to definite action for disarmament and international reconciliation. . . .

In the third place, the Federation has given time and energy to the international discussion of the Christian Gospel and its presentation to students today. At a time when great divergencies in tendencies of thought threaten to make the Christian witness ineffective, and when only a common

Christian message can hope to deal with the forces of the modern world, this work . . . is of special importance for the future, not only of the Federation but also of the Christian Church.

The Federation provides a medium of exchange between Christian students the world over. The knowledge of ideas and methods that arise in one Movement pass with extraordinary rapidity all over the world. Also students migrate in large numbers from one country to another, and this has been a means of extending the influence of the Movement.

It is remarkable the degree in which students of one Movement feel at home with members of another. . . . Not least important are the ties that bind us Occidentals to Oriental friends. The Easterner and the Westerner in the main have not learned how to make friends. These unaffected and deep personal friendships between East and West have really been a new thing in the world. . . . No words can express the strength of the tie that binds men and women in all lands who have entered at all deeply into the life of a national Student Christian Movement, and through such into the fellowship of the World's Student Christian Federation.[41]

Its spirit of evangelism has been strong; we quote W. A. Visser't Hooft, as General Secretary of the Federation, whose statement is also indicative of the way in which international organization serves religious ends:

The story of the recent spread of evangelism in our Movement can be told only in outline. But even so it may serve the purpose of showing how the spark of evangelism has travelled along the wires of Federation contacts from one country to another, and how many of our Movements have been affected and vitalised by it.

For example, by contacts from England to Paris to Geneva to Lausanne to Neuchatel the Student Christian Movement in French Switzerland was reborn.

The most obvious service which the Federation can render and has rendered in this connection is to ensure that the network of communications which it establishes between the national Movements should be the means of transmitting conviction and experience. The very fact that—humanly speaking—many of the recent Missions [evangelistic meetings] owe their origin to inspiration received from other national Movements shows that the existence of the Federation is a significant factor in the growth of evangelism in recent years.[42]

And, to summarize its influence on the oecumenical movement, we quote from one of the publications of the Federation:

The world is waiting for the manifestation of a United Christianity which will do away with the scandal of division and disintegration among Christians. Among the Christians themselves the postwar [1914] period has given rise to great movements for collaboration and reunion of the Churches. But the great goal of effective unity can only be realised if a new generation appears which not only believes in the fundamental unity of those whose faith is in Christ, but which is actually realising that unity in fellowship with their contemporaries of other denominations and confessions.

From its earliest days the Federation has been a pioneer of this unity. At a time when none of the great oecumenical movements existed, the Federation gathered students from all denominations and gave them a consciousness of oneness in faith and action. Soon the fellowship was widened. Even before the war,[43] Eastern Orthodox and Roman Catholic students began to join some of the national Movements. More recently, especially through the close contracts between Russian and Western European students, and through the awakening of interest in the cause of unity, the inter-confessional problem of relations between the great historic branches of the Christian Church has become one of the great issues in Federation life. The problem would be relatively easy if the Federation would cease to believe in the divine mission of the Church. It could then form a sort of substitute for the Church, and overlook all important differences. But if it did it would neither be true to its own mission nor would it be realistic. It can no more disregard the Church-loyalty of its members than it can disregard their national loyalties. The job of the Federation is therefore not to replace the Church but to pioneer on behalf of the Church in realms where the Church can only move slowly or not at all. The best pioneering work is in the providing of close contacts between the students of different confessions, which make them respect or even love each other's Churches. The growth of the sense of common cause, and of cooperative work between leaders of the Student Christian Movement in the United States and leaders of the many denominations working with students, is one evidence of the importance of this work. What it means when in the South Eastern European Leaders' Conference students of Eastern Orthodox, Calvinist, Lutheran and Roman Catholic convictions meet on equal footing and discuss very frankly, only those can understand who know something about the depth of confessional misunderstanding in that as well as other parts of the world. No less far-reaching are the Anglo-Orthodox meetings where Russian and Anglican come to an interchange of spiritual riches which during a thousand years of separation between Eastern and Western Christianity has been impossible. At Oecumenical Retreats and at the annual European Theological Student Conferences the younger generation of theologians learn to think in "oecumenical" terms and become inspired with a desire to serve the cause of Christian Unity. It is not astonishing that the three men who, as it were, incarnate the three great so-called "oecumenical" movements (Life and Work—Stockholm, Faith and Order—Lausanne, and the International Missionary Council), Archbishop Söderblom, William Temple, Archbishop of York, and John R. Mott, all owe their vision of unity to the contacts with other confessions established in Federation conferences.[44]

World Council of Churches

In coping with the problem of how to effect closer cooperation between the seven organizations just described, it was a logical decision to establish a World Council of Churches; such action was approved at both the Oxford and Edinburgh Conferences. In a preparatory document for the latter conference, the problem was thoroughly analyzed, and it was pointed out that:

> Any general plan for the future of the oecumenical movement must face or raise four major questions:
> (1) How to provide for some symbolic act by which from time to time the unity of the Christian movement can be brought visibly before the imagination of the Church and of the world.
> (2) How to provide for some continuing executive body which would correlate the work of education and research . . . and would act for the Churches in matters of common concern (e.g., disarmament, the fight against opium, calendar reform, etc.) when such action seems desirable and practicable.
> (3) How to provide for some freer and less official agency, recognized and approved though not controlled by the Churches, through which contact might be had with persons and groups not now in touch with the Church, experiments tried for which the Church as a whole is not yet ready, and lessons learned which, so far as approved, might later be included in the regular educational program of the Church.
> (4) Finally, how to guard against the danger of letting the pressure of present need weaken our interest in the more distant goal of a completely reunited Church.[45]

The preliminary plan of organization for such a World Council was described as follows by Leiper, in his discussion of the achievements of both Oxford and Edinburgh:

> It contemplates a World Council of Churches functioning through a general assembly of approximately two hundred representatives appointed directly by the cooperating churches and meeting every five years. There would also be a central committee, of approximately sixty members, likewise representative of the churches, meeting annually as the executive of the general assembly. The council would have "no power to legislate for the churches or to commit them to action without their consent." Its functions, as provisionally defined, would include the following:
> "To carry on the work of the Faith and Order and the Life and Work movements; to make it easier for the churches to act together; to promote cooperation in study; to further the growth of ecumenical consciousness in the churches; to call world conferences on specific subjects as occasion requires."
> There would be two special commissions, one for the further study of

Faith and Order subjects, the other for the study of Life and Work subjects.[46]

The Council was provisionally established at the Conference of Utrecht in 1938 and a Provisional Committee was set up.[47] In July 1939 this Committee convened at Geneva an "international conference of lay experts and ecumenical leaders" to consider "the action open to churches and individual Christians 'with a view to checking the drift towards war and to leading us nearer to the establishment of an effective international order.' " This conference drew up a statement of principles as "clear applications of the Christian message," which included among the points: no denial of "essential rights to human beings on the ground of their race or religion or culture or any such distinguishing characteristic"; *"some form of international organization which will provide the machinery of confidence and cooperation";* an acceptance on the part of nations "of the responsibility for maintaining good order in the international community. The full discharge of this responsibility will require that the collective will of the community shall be used to *secure the necessary changes in the interests of justice, to the same extent that it is used to secure the protection of nations against violence*. As to the use of force in this connection we are not agreed"; and a colonial administration, based on specific principles, with control transferred to an international body.[48] This statement of the World Council foreshadowed the position of the religious organizations in regard to the establishment of the United Nations.

World Congress of Faiths

Although not a part of the oecumenical movement, the World Congress of Faiths, established at London in 1936 "to promote a spirit of fellowship and to awaken and develop a world loyalty through religion," may well be considered in connection with it. The oecumenical movement is confined to Christian bodies and hopes to unify them; the World Congress is organized to promote a spirit of fellowship among mankind through bringing together representatives of all religions—Buddhists, Confucianists, Moslems, Hindus, Christians and others—with no attempt to obtain unity of belief. In 1938 it had affiliated societies and individual members in Africa, Burma, Ceylon, China, Egypt, India, Japan, Palestine, the United States and ten European countries;[49] among its members were Russian and other refugees. Its membership, although only a few hundred, included some very eminent individuals.

Its Chairman, Sir Francis Younghusband, in 1937, explained:

> We think not only nationally but internationally, not only in terms of one religion but of all religions. Together with others working on similar lines

we seek to build a new world-order based on religion and aiming at the highest happiness for all mankind.

We would get men to realize the importance of religion and of religious individuals in promoting the peace and happiness of mankind. It is being recognized now that war is not an effective instrument of policy nor the sole means of obtaining political and economic security. In place of war we would put religion. The prescription we would recommend for peace is religion—religion rightly understood and duly practiced. . . .

As Lord Samuel said at the Oxford Congress, we recognize the influence of the existing faiths and seek to work through them, using the influence of each faith on its own devotees to bring about true cooperation in relief of the present dangerous situation. We afford opportunities for mutual understanding. And while recognizing differences we seek to transcend those which divide.[50]

OTHER RELIGIOUS INGO'S

European Central Office for Inter-Church Aid

This office was set up in 1922 at Geneva to provide "information about the general Church situation and aid to suffering Churches, institutions, Faculties, theological students and religious minorities." Composed of Church Federations of Europe and America, including representatives of Churches in South Africa and Australia, by 1938 it had "brought aid to churches and institutions in sixteen European countries and to old Christian minorities in the Near East. It developed a leadership programme with bursaries for future ministers, and helped Christian refugees in various countries."[51] Its work, while of very real value, has been limited in scope. For example, in 1936 it spent more than eighty thousand dollars for its relief aid; however, most of the relief money raised by churches and other religious organizations was not sent through the Central Office, for the amount raised from such sources in 1936 totaled about eight hundred thousand dollars. The Office founded the International Protestant Loan Association "which was able to save a considerable number of Protestant institutions in seven countries."[52]

World's Sunday School Association*

The World's Sunday School Association (*WSSA*), representing in 1937 forty-eight national and international bodies with thirty-eight million members, has done much since its founding in 1889 to promote a religious education throughout the world. Perhaps the best brief description of its work is as follows:

1. The *WSSA* seeks the cooperation of all the Christian forces within

---

* Recently adopted a new name, the World Council for Christian Education.

a nation or other natural areas that are concerned with the work of Christian education; such cooperation has been achieved in fifty nations.

2. The *WSSA* federates these national cooperative agencies in a world-wide fellowship that is interdenominational, international and interracial. It has been designated "the greatest voluntary movement in the world, working for the spiritual education of the rising generation."

3. The *WSSA* has pioneered the way in behalf of Christian education in many lands by sending Sunday School missionaries, religious educational specialists and deputations to many fields, and by assisting in the support of national Sunday School organizations in the work of planting and fostering Sunday schools, daily vacation Bible schools, young people's conferences and similar agencies.

4. The *WSSA* is now making appropriations to assist the work of Christian education in the following forty-eight fields: . . . [names of countries follow].

5. The *WSSA* is leading an approach in Christian fellowship to the eastern orthodox churches that has resulted in a remarkable awakening within these ancient churches and in their adoption of modern programs of Christian education.

6. The *WSSA* serves as a clearing house for the workers of all lands in the distribution of materials in many languages, a service designed to stimulate and encourage the securing of indigenous leadership and the creation of indigenous materials and methods for the work of Christian education.

7. The *WSSA* gathers quadrennially the Sunday School statistics of the world; in 1936 reports were gathered from 129 countries which gave a total Sunday School enrollment for the world of 37,285,519, a gain of almost a million in the four years, 1932–1936.

8. The *WSSA* since 1889 has held twelve World Sunday School Conventions, each widely representative of the nations, in such centers as London, St. Louis, Jerusalem, Rome, Washington, Zurich, Tokyo, Glasgow, Los Angeles, Rio de Janeiro and Oslo. The Thirteenth World's Convention will be held in South Africa in 1940.[53]

The average number of delegates to the Conventions held after World War I was more than three thousand. Its annual budget has been about a hundred thousand dollars; its headquarters have recently been moved from New York City to Geneva.[54]

Salvation Army

The religious and social work of the Salvation Army is known throughout the world. Its activities may be summarized as follows:

> Conferences, meetings, visitation and propaganda, spiritual and social (humanitarian); the foundation of homes for men, women and children; rescue homes for women, industrial homes, schools; homes for soldiers

and sailors; re-education; agricultural colonies and various institutions; 26,877 [correction for 1938] officers of the Salvation Army are working in ninety-five countries and colonies. The Gospel is preached in a hundred different languages.[55]

Established in 1865, it constitutes not a federation of national associations cooperating in one international organization, but rather one worldwide association, organized on a quasi-military basis. Commanders and other officers are responsible to the General, who exercises an almost unlimited control over the whole organization. He may not appoint his successor, who is chosen by the *High Council* of the Army; he may be removed from office by the High Council or by vote of the *full Commissioners;* he does not handle certain financial matters which are under the direction of various *trustee companies*. However, the members of the High Council and the trustee companies are all appointed by the General, and he has the power to dismiss them or any other officer of the Army. Before 1931 there were not even these restrictions on his power.[56] The Territorial Commanders may be transferred from one country to another and in a number of states (not only in backward countries) are not citizens of the country where they are stationed. This unusual structure is mentioned to show that it may be quite incorrect to speak of "national" Salvation Army work. It may very well be argued that anything done by the Army anywhere is the work of the local agents of an international (or world) organization. In what we say here, however, we will try to emphasize those things which are either due entirely to its international character or which have been definitely influenced by it.

The International Headquarters in London has employed more than 150 ranking officers and about the same number of nonranking employees, or a total of about three hundred. During the prewar years this was probably the largest number of employees in the international headquarters of any organization except the Catholic Church, the League of Nations and the *ILO*. In addition, in 1938, throughout the world close to twenty-seven thousand officers and ten thousand persons without rank were employed on a full-scale basis, and there were more than 285,000 voluntary helpers. One hundred twenty-six periodicals were being published with 1,550,422 total copies per issue. Also, an international training course was being maintained.[57]

Concerning its work of instruction to young people:

> In its dealings with youth, singular, almost unique advantages are afforded by The Army's internationalism, as well as by its special methods and its coordinated machinery. Take the teaching for children . . . for example, as contained in "The International Company Orders." This volume of . . . Sunday lessons . . . is issued yearly from International

Headquarters as the authorized handbook for every Army "Sunday-school" teacher . . . in the world. Overseas Territories . . . translate the book and re-issue it in the tongue of their own people. West and East, all the world over, the same lessons are taught. . . . So at the beginning, uniform ideals and standards are inculcated. . . .

Perhaps even Salvationists themselves do not entirely realize what our world coordinated machinery does in fostering worthy competition and emulation among the Army's youth. Officers in charge seldom stay longer than two years in one Corps; their coming and going means the constant carrying of fresh ideas to new districts. . . . In larger fields, the same effect follows the changing, about every five years, of Territorial leaders—a change involving at times distances literally as wide as "from China to Peru." And it is up to the special Young People's Officers set apart in every Territory—and also constantly changing—to keep their young people as nearly as possible abreast with the rest. . . .

"Understudying" for Salvation Army Officership . . . is done in a youth organization, especially designed for the purpose—the Corps Cadets' Training Brigade . . . it is youth at this fluctuating stage of adolescence, and upward to the age of eighteen, whom The Army, with far-sighted faith and patience, enrolls in its Corps Cadet Brigades; and their success is unquestioned. Of these student-Salvationists, the Training Colleges in every Territory later receive a large proportion; and others become leaders in the local Corps. All over the world the system—again ordered and regulated from International Headquarters—is carried out.[58]

Another important aspect of Salvation Army work, which is very definitely connected with its international character, is its almost continual extension to new lands ever since 1878. Its International Secretary, Commissioner Arthur R. Blowers, writes (1938):

The Army's entry into previously untouched fields sometimes follows the trail of isolated Salvationists, who may have found Christ in some Salvation Army Meeting far from their native land; or it may be in response to urgent pleas from groups of men and women concerned for the spiritual welfare of their people; or, again, it may be the outcome of a recognition by The Army's leaders of the great needs of a land or community.

Within the past five years no fewer than eleven countries or colonies have been newly "occupied" by our international Movement. Such an expansion in so short a period is the more remarkable as it has been made in face of universal financial and economic difficulties. Every advance into new fields requires an adventure of faith—but our faith has never been disappointed.[59]

It may also be said that the local workers in all countries where the Army is engaged are inspired and helped by the activities of the International Headquarters, by visits of officers, by the international publications, and by the knowledge that they belong to a world-wide movement. It seems

RELIGION

clear that if Salvation Army work had been organized as entirely separate national undertakings without international connections it would not have spread as it has and its work would not have been nearly so effective. Therefore, much of what the Salvation Army has accomplished in raising the religious, moral, and social environment in many countries must be credited to its international character and organization.

DENOMINATIONAL INGO'S

Alliance of Reformed Churches Throughout the World Holding the Presbyterian System

This Alliance (Edinburgh), founded in 1877, whose influence we have already seen in the establishment of the International Missionary Council, has fulfilled a pioneer role of value to the oecumenical movement. Writing in 1924, Charles S. Macfarland, then General Secretary of the Federal Council of Churches of Christ in America, said:

> The first result of the influence and activity of the Alliance was acquaintance. Many of its Churches were located so far apart they knew little of each other. The day of religious internationalism had not yet come and most of the Churches had lived mainly for themselves alone. Often Churches that were nearest to each other were far apart in spirit. Sometimes there were standing quarrels and controversies between neighboring denominations. The Alliance brought them together, they learned to know each other, to understand each other, to love each other and thus to work together. In doing this, the Alliance performed a great work in preparing the Church for the recent great movements of international religious cooperation. But for Alliances like this, the world would not have become ripe in our day for the present world-movement in religion.
>
> The Alliance exerted a large influence by making the home churches so well acquainted with each other that they readily allowed their missions in foreign lands to unite with other churches of our order in forming foreign churches. Not only in mission fields but also in South Africa, Australia and New Zealand the different Presbyterian bodies were led to form a single church.[60]

Baptist World Alliance

For the various churches of its denomination, representing over 11,300,000 members, the Baptist World Alliance, founded in 1905, has performed a task similar to the Presbyterian Alliance. From headquarters at London, its officers have visited many of the local churches, and the Alliance feels that, "It is impossible to exaggerate the strengthening and inspiring effects of [this] contact with the 'rank and file' of the churches."[61] The function which its conferences, both regional and world, have performed is implicit in the statement of J. H. Rushbrooke, first Baptist

Commissioner for Europe, and afterwards, Eastern and General Secretary of the Alliance, reporting on the Fifth Baptist World Congress held at Berlin in 1934:

> . . . the spirit of this Congress in Berlin will be felt in Argentina, in South Africa, in China and in New Zealand, in India and Burma and Australia, as well as in every part of Europe. We who come from Britain or from the United States, where conferences abound, where hundreds of thousands of fellow-believers satisfy our craving for comradeship, and where the home work is on a vast scale, can scarcely realize the glowing, quivering interest stirred by the brother who goes from this city to tell a small group, feeling its loneliness amid the darkness of paganism, or striving to hold aloft the banner of the Cross amid superstition and indifference and contempt, that he has companied with those who represent millions of fellow believers, and has heard stories that have brought home to him the world-wide range of his Christian fellowship. Our Congress means something very great to our weak and isolated groups: even an Elijah is cheered by learning of the seven thousand![62]

Its 1920 Conference at London, which initiated organized relief for Baptists and others in Europe amounting to about one million dollars within four years, produced some important religious results:

> . . . their effect has been to link the stronger mission boards of the U.S.A., Canada, Britain, and some other lands, with the needier countries of Europe, marking out fields of cooperation so as to avoid overlapping. The results exceeded all hopes. The struggling communities were heartened and encouraged . . . a great increase of membership was reported within a few years—in most lands 50 per cent or more, whilst in some countries, Rumania being the most conspicuous example, the numerical strength of the Baptist communion multiplied several times over. The scheme of cooperation . . . emphasized the need of adequate training for preachers; and since the year 1920, thanks to the aid of American, Canadian, and British Baptists, no fewer than ten new preachers' schools have been set up in as many countries.
>
> These new relations of cooperation and material assistance are, as already noted, sustained by the mission boards, but it was the union of these in the Alliance which enabled the conference of 1920 to be summoned. Indeed, the contacts already made by the Alliance before the War counted as a powerful influence in healing the wounds of Europe.[63]

The following statement by Rushbrooke indicates a function that many *INGO's* have performed—that of achieving strength through organization:

> From 1920 onwards the writer as Commissioner for Europe and as General Secretary of the Alliance has maintained a continuous watch upon

RELIGION

conditions which menaced or violated religious liberty and, apart from the U.S.S.R. and Rumania, has had to protest and appeal to Ministers of State in some half-dozen other lands. In most instances there was no need to initiate public agitation. The fact that the Alliance was in existence, and that its representatives voiced the mind of a Christian world-communion, gave moral weight to our plea, and usually brought prompt redress. Three examples may be given. The Baptists of Czechoslovakia were in the early "twenties" subjected to unequal treatment in certain matters of taxation as compared with Roman Catholics. An interview with President Masaryk led to an immediate change and the abandonment of an attitude which was quite opposed to his spirit and that of his Government. In Hungary proceedings were taken against an active Baptist preacher; a judge issued an order for his expulsion from the country, on the technical ground that he had not acquired Hungarian nationality. I record to the honour of the Hungarian Minister of Cults (who was in fact a Roman Catholic priest) that he at once accepted a protest which in the name of the Alliance I personally made to him, and the order was annulled. It is also worthy of record that in the case of an Italian pastor sentenced to some years' banishment on charges whose real basis was religious prejudice (he had spoken rashly, though not criminally, and had thus given an opportunity to his theological opponents), an appeal to Signor Mussolini through the Italian Minister in London led to the quashing of the sentence within a few days. In general, we may assert that where Baptists are few, poor, and weak, and administrators are inclined to ride roughshod over them, it makes all the difference when Governments realise that the handful of feeble folk represents a fellowship of millions throughout the earth.[64]

International Eucharistic Congress Movement

In 1938, with members in thirty-three countries, the International Eucharistic Congress Movement (London) had held thirty-four Congresses since 1881, the date of its founding.[65] These Congresses ("to proclaim and honour throughout the world the Holy Sacrament of the Eucharist")[66] have been "the mightiest demonstrations of public faith the Christian world affords." For the Budapest Congress of 1938 about twenty-five thousand pilgrims went to Hungary from other countries; hundreds of thousands of persons took part; a Mass for a hundred thousand children was held, while a million persons watched the procession of ten vessels on the Danube in another ceremony. Many important addresses were given; several thousand masses were celebrated.[67] The religious effect upon the participants and those with whom they came into contact could hardly fail to be significant.

Christian Young Workers

The Christian Young Workers (better known as the Jeunesse Ouvrière

Chrétienne—*JOC;* and known also as the Christian Working Youth) is a Catholic movement which:

> . . . intends to group all the working class young men and women into a powerful organisation, directed entirely by the young workers themselves, in order that it may:
>
> (1) Be for them a means of mutual religious, moral, intellectual, and social betterment.
> (2) Help them especially to lead an essentially Christian life and show them their divine vocation and destiny.
> (3) Make them aware of their dignity as men and women and as children of God.
> (4) Raise the moral and social life of the whole working class.
> (5) Above all, defend their interests whenever or wherever it may be necessary.

Among its demands:

> (1) A professional as well as general education, in order that they may learn a particular trade and thus earn a livelihood.
> (2) Healthy environment for their work where moral and religious convictions are respected.
> (3) A reasonable wage, increasing according to individual needs, to enable them to save and, in due course, set up a good home.
> (4) Suitable time and place for recreation.[68]

It will be seen that *JOC* has been concerned with working conditions and the general social and moral environment of young workers (fourteen to twenty-five years of age) as well as with purely religious matters. Its methods, which emphasize the responsibility of Christian workers themselves to convert other workers and to insist on the improvement of their environment in every way, have proven effective. Internationally the movement is not very old; its first world congress was held in 1935, the year it was founded, at Brussels. However before the outbreak of war it had already extended to all parts of the world. We can agree with the claim that, "This world-wide extension of the *CYW* in such a short time is a significant indication of the real value of its activities."[69]

During the first years, in Belgium particularly, some very real improvements in wages of young workers and in moral conditions in factories had been secured. A great deal of information concerning the low wages being paid to young workers and the bad moral conditions in factories was obtained and a public campaign started, which had immediate results. The idea and methods which came from this work in Belgium were then applied in other countries. Through such work, its various publications, and the bringing of young workers into contact with priests, the *CYW* has helped to strengthen the religious life of many thousands of young workers and has converted others to the Catholic faith and a more religious life.

International Union of Catholic Women's Leagues

Founded in 1910, the International Union of Catholic Women's Leagues had as members in 1937 four international Catholic woman's organizations and national Catholic women's leagues or associations in thirty-one countries, grouping thirty million Catholic women and girls. At that time its Youth Section had two million members. This Union is concerned not only with purely religious matters but also with many moral, social, political and international problems.[70] The Pope names its president and the Union acts, needless to say, in close cooperation with the Catholic Church.[71]

Its International Council meets every four years.

> Each International Council fixes the subject to be studied during the four following years. The Study Commissions, each of which has its own president and correspondents in all member countries, studies a special aspect of the general subject, and prepares conclusions for the next Council. Two years before the meeting a "study week" is held to discuss the work already done and the study yet to be done.[72]

In latter years, emphasis was placed on the question of Catholic women in the contemporary world, with eight study committees considering various aspects of the subject—religion, morals and health, the family, education, civic life, the problems of intellectual, working, and agricultural life.[73]

Its international headquarters, at Utrecht, has assisted the member organizations in many ways and has even "played a part in the forming of more than one League in countries where none existed."[74]

In one of its publications it is said that:

> ... the International Union of Catholic Women's Leagues is the most extensive and strongest international women's organization, because it alone unites women of all nationalities having only a single Faith, all professing the same principles, and all looking to the same end and ideals: Give the world to Christ and Christ to the world![75]

Apostolatus Maris Internationale Concilium

The *AMIC* (Apostleship of the Sea), organized in 1922, "is a society for the spiritual and moral welfare of Catholic seafarers throughout the world,"[76] which has helped to carry out Pope Pius XI's mandate "that Catholic sailors should be trained to be apostles to their fellow seamen."[77] With headquarters at London, in 1938 it had members in the Union of

South Africa, Argentina, Australia, Brazil, Canada, India, New Zealand, United States and thirteen European countries.

It began as an international body and has proved to be a very effective instrument for the extension of Catholic work among seamen, as the following statement shows:

> Catholics form more than a half of the world's seafarers. Despite the progress shown in the following statistics, hardly a quarter of the world's sailor service is yet being done by Catholics. There are more than five hundred non-Catholic Seamen's Institutes of various types in the world; hundreds of Seamen's Chaplains and port missionaries. [These are operated in almost all, if not all, cases on a national rather than an international basis.]

	1920	1938
Catholic Seamen's Institutes	11	58
Whole-time Port Chaplains	—	18
Hon. Port Chaplains	10	260
Hon. lay workers at ports	100	1,550
Ports "adopted" for Prayers by Religious Communities	—	390

These figures show how effectively the Apostleship of the Sea is carrying out The Holy Father's Mandate to spread its organisation *more and more along the seacoasts of the two hemispheres*.[78]

It has received the support of the highest authorities of the Catholic Church.[79] It has published special literature for Catholic seamen and provides them with Catholic and secular periodicals and other reading matter. Sailors are visited on board ship, "homes" are provided in port cities, and sailors are organized to help themselves. The international secretary particularly emphasized this last point, stating that the *AMIC* is not an "uplift" movement; it is designed to induce sailors to improve their own spiritual, social and moral conditions. Its system of organizing

> is built up on voluntary work by the sailors, clergy, and many secretarial helpers, supplied with organising directions (eight languages are employed) and various types of organising material. In the course of *AMIC* work over 350 different organising instructions have been drafted—each one adding something to the machinery which drives this international Apostolate.

Contact is maintained with 390 ports, "212 of which depend *directly* on Headquarters for all organizing directions and supplies."[80]

Other Religious *INGO's*

In this chapter no attempt has been made to include all religious *INGO's*. The following organizations may, however, be briefly mentioned:

The International Federation of Calvinists has held Congresses every two years, at which theological questions have been discussed. The Bahai Cause, "to re-awaken humanity to spiritual truths," has attracted some attention. It is claimed that the founder, Báha'u'lláh, ". . . laid the foundations of a New World Order giving a solution of racial, social and economic problems for this Age." It draws much of its inspiration from a number of the older religions and seems to be a synthesis of various elements taken from them.[81] The World's Christian Endeavor Union (and its division, the European Christian Endeavor Union) is evidently an important organization represented in many countries.[82] The International Service of the Society of Friends (Quakers) is recognized to have achieved much. However, as it is not organized on an "international basis," it constitutes "a national organization having international activity." More exactly, there are two such organizations—the American Friends' Service (Philadelphia) and the Council of the Friends' Service (London)—which cooperated but which before the war had set up no common organization. Recently there has been established a Friends World Committee for Consultation. The World's Evangelical Alliance, founded in 1846, is another organization which cannot be classified as international. Its "members" throughout the world have no vote; the organization is controlled by the "World's Evangelical Alliance (British Organization)"; the "members" merely agree to its principles, make a donation and receive its publications. Finally, we may mention the World Union of Freethinkers, which aims "to free humanity from religious prejudices."[83] In all his reading of the literature of religious *INGO's,* the writer can remember no reference to it. It apparently has had little influence.

Since most of the Jewish organizations seem to be chiefly concerned with social, humanitarian, and peace work, or with Palestine, rather than the promotion of the Jewish faith, these are considered in other chapters. For similar reasons discussion of many of the Christian *INGO's,* both Protestant and Catholic, are also found elsewhere. Here we have tried to see what has been the influence of international religious work concerned in widening the circle of converts, strengthening the faith of followers, or in determining the meaning of Christianity in relation to specific problems. How to measure influence is as yet an undetermined technique, but there is in these pages some evidence that the influence of international religious organizations has been important.

9 SOCIAL WELFARE

HEALTH

THE CONTRIBUTIONS of international non-governmental organizations (*INGO's*) in this sphere are impressive. They have worked successfully for the improvement of health conditions in the world through health education, scientific investigation, cooperation with governments and official organs, and through their efforts in behalf of children, war wounded, refugees and others in need of assistance. Their contribution has ranged from the promotion of sports to the actual operation of health services. A score of other *INGO's* have contributed their share, although technically they cannot be considered "health" associations. For example, among its many activities the Associated Countrywomen of the World has on several occasions conducted inquiries on problems related to health. It undertook an inquiry into the consumption of milk in rural households for the League of Nations' study on nutrition.[1] A report on *Midwifery Services in Rural Areas*, based on information collected from many countries, was prepared. This report pointed out a number of ways in which rural women's organizations could aid the "country mother." A review in the *Medical Officer* said of it:

> The report is extremely well drawn up and in the course of 20 [pages?] gives information which must have taken much time and research to get together and much journalistic ability to reduce to readable form. Its main object was to collect and contrast and compare the various systems of midwifery in different countries with a view, not to establish a standard system, but to enable each and every system to learn from the others and perhaps in them discover solutions of difficulties which its own system does not cover.[2]

On the other hand, the Jewish Agency for Palestine has made a contribution of a vastly different nature. In Palestine, death and disease rates fell greatly during the Thirties and health standards were exceptionally high compared with neighboring countries as a result, both directly and indirectly, of the Agency's work in promoting the establishment of a National Home for the Jewish People in Palestine. Its large-scale drainage works helped greatly to reduce malaria and it made important financial contributions to the Jewish Health Services whose prewar annual budget of £250,000 was considerably greater than the health expenditures of the government (£166,000).[3] The great contribution of the International

Red Cross to the health of the world is described below under "Social and Humanitarian Activity." When we couple such efforts with the activities of *INGO's* functioning directly in the field of health, we see that these organizations have made a significant contribution to world health.[4]

HOSPITALS

International Hospital Association

The International Hospital Association, composed, in 1938, of the national hospital associations of seventeen countries, official representatives of sixteen countries, as well as individual members, has organized the study of hospital problems and the exchange of information thereon. It has published *Nosokomeion* quarterly. It is acknowledged that the Association since its founding in 1931 (Lucerne) has contributed to the improvement of hospitals the world over.

NURSING

Florence Nightingale International Foundation

The Florence Nightingale International Foundation, London, was established in 1934, by the joint action of the League of Red Cross Societies and the International Council of Nurses, to continue the international nursing courses established by the League in 1920. By 1934 more than 250 nurses from forty-four countries had taken these international courses in London and the success of the program indicated the need for continuing and expanding the work, for, it was said, these nurses already occupied

> in almost every European country, in China, in Japan, in South Africa and New Zealand, leading posts in the nursing profession . . . and their achievements everywhere had shown how immense a contribution able women, backed by such training, could make. In many countries they had been instrumental in raising the status of the nursing profession; in some they had shown themselves successful pioneers of modern methods and modern technique in the public health field; in almost all they had proved towers of strength to their national Red Cross Societies, and attained positions of leadership in the campaign for the improvement of health and the prevention of disease.

National Florence Nightingale Memorial Committees have been established in many countries for the selection of students.[5]

International Council of Nurses

The International Council of Nurses, established in 1899, stands for:

> self-government by nurses in their associations, with the aim of raising the standards of education, professional ethics and public usefulness of its members. The International Council of Nurses stands also for that full development of the human being and citizen in every nurse, which shall

best enable her to bring her professional knowledge and skill to the many-sided service that modern society demands of her.[6]

The Council's activities have included the exchange of ideas, the study of various questions related to nursing, and the service of its headquarters at London as a center of information. It has published *The International Nursing Review* containing articles on nursing, public health work, history of nursing, descriptions of hospitals, articles on the work of the Council itself, and other pertinent information. It has had a number of international committees engaged in making investigations, whose work has had a marked influence. For example, its Committee on Education, then composed of representatives of nearly thirty countries with "corresponding members" from ten countries, undertook a study designed "to focus attention on the need for well-organized educational programs in nursing and to make available to nursing schools in all countries the best ideas which this representative group could bring together from their varied experience and common deliberations." Through the assistance of the Nursing Advisory Committee of the League of Red Cross Societies the first draft of the Report of this study was distributed to a large number of interested persons in various countries for criticisms and suggestions, and it was carefully considered by many other groups. The chairman of the Council's Committee was given a travel grant from the Rockefeller Foundation. The Report was published in 1934 under the title, *The Educational Program of the School of Nursing*. It was said of the Report:

> The ideas and suggestions incorporated into this Report are drawn from a great many sources and have been tested out by leading schools in different countries. According to the opinion of the members of this Committee, they represent the best present practice in nursing schools of the better type and also indicate the newer trends. . . . If these are applied intelligently and consistently with due regard for national and individual differences and the changing conditions of social life, the Committee is confident that a marked improvement will result in the work of nursing schools and in the type of nurse they produce.[7]

Its international congresses have dealt with a wide variety of subjects; its 1937 Congress, for instance, considered many aspects of nursing education, the organization and administration of the nursing profession, public health, and specific nursing problems.

MEDICAL AND DENTAL ASSOCIATIONS

International Professional Association of Medical Practitioners

The *APIM* (initials of its name in French) has been chiefly concerned

SOCIAL WELFARE

with the relations of the physician with government authorities and other physicians. Purely scientific matters are outside the scope of its action. Organized in Paris, in 1926, its membership in 1938 consisted of national professional associations in Cuba, Palestine, Peru, Uruguay and twenty-two European countries. Its purpose has been to

> constitute an international center for inquiries, information, and liaison among the national groups of physicians in order that each of them may profit from the experience of others in the study of the many problems of a professional nature which concern the individual and social life of the physician.[8]

The problems with which it dealt may be grouped as follows:

> (a) *Relations of the physician with the government and the great enterprises in the medical-social organization:* sickness-insurance, invalidism, medicine in mining, railroads, factories and all the great establishments of industry, commerce and agriculture—with the study of the free choice of the physician by the patient, the illegal practice of medicine, the method of payment for medical services, the role and utility of the group in the control of medicine by the profession itself, in view of maintaining the high moral qualities of the physician, etc.
>
> (b) *Relations of the physician with the government or the great enterprises of Social Hygiene* in regard to contagious diseases and epidemics or in the fight against the social scourges: tuberculosis, syphilis, cancer . . . and the situation of the doctor in relation to dispensaries, sanatoria, hospitals, with the questions of instruction directly related thereto, etc. . . .
>
> (c) *Relations of the physicians among themselves;* various professional groups; assistance to elderly doctors without means of support, and to their widows and orphans; insurance against severe or chronic illness and the invalidism of the physician himself; pensions; insurance of the physician against the risks of professional responsibility, the bad faith of clients and, in general, all the professional risks [ennuis] of daily practice, etc. . . .[9]

The Association has published a *Revue Internationale de Médecine Professionnelle* in which the results of about thirty international investigations had been published by 1937. The following discussion as to why an international association is needed to cope with such problems will be of interest:

> But some will object asking why an international association is needed for the study of all these varied problems. Cannot each national medical association just as well examine these questions by itself and are they not fully able to defend their rights without having need of the assistance of foreign medical associations?
>
> Those may reason so who have not yet had to fight against certain social forces, already internationalized, in private associations and even in the

official international circles of Geneva. These forces are dangerous to the future and the independence of the practicing physician.

One example will suffice. Since 1926 there has existed the "International Conference of National Unions of Mutual Benefit Societies" . . . [It is especially concerned with sickness insurance.] Now those who have had occasion (as is the case almost everywhere in Europe) to become acquainted with the aims, the actions and influence of the sickness insurance societies have recognized for a long time the need for the medical profession to oppose our association to this other, thus putting up "bloc against bloc."[10]

International Dental Federation

Besides the usual activities one would expect, the International Dental Federation, with headquarters at Brussels, has been much concerned with the maintenance of a documentary center for dental information. For this purpose it entered into an agreement with the Dental Documentary Foundation, located in the Eastman Institute at Brussels, which provides that:

> In as much as the *F.D.I.* [the Federation] cannot at the moment obtain any legal standing which would permit internationally of its possessing and keeping any material assets, whilst it is recognized to be essential that it should have some place for the safekeeping of the archives and collections of the International Centre, and a civil authority capable of defending its rights.
>
> The *F.D.I.* confides to the Foundation the safekeeping of its documents, their cataloguing . . .[11]

The Foundation has been engaged in "collecting, classifying, and making available for future study with the minimum research, any paper on any branch of dentistry." More than 150 periodicals, many thousands of articles as well as numerous books, pamphlets, etc., are received each year. Fees are charged for the gathering of information but the Foundation is not a profit-making organization.[12]

The international Congresses of the Dental Federation have been attended by from four to twelve thousand dentists, including the best known men in dentistry. Smaller "General Meetings" are held annually. Its Commissions are concerned with dental legislation and documentation, dental education and terminology, scientific research, oral hygiene, and public dental service. The Federation, founded in 1900, is supported by the leading dental associations of the world; in 1938, its membership represented about a hundred thousand practitioners in forty-five countries.[13]

INGO'S *COMBATING PARTICULAR DISEASES*

Among the associations organized to deal with particular diseases are the

SOCIAL WELFARE

International Union Against Tuberculosis, the International Association for Prevention of Blindness, the International Union Against Cancer, the International League Against Epilepsy, the International Leprosy Association, the International League Against Rheumatism, the International League for the Campaign Against Trachoma, and the International Union for Combating Veneral Diseases (also called International Union Against the Venereal Diseases). They all conduct scientific inquiries, collect information and spread knowledge, hold international conferences, publish reports, encourage the use of the best methods, etc. A number of them have maintained close official connections, governments sometimes being members. Perhaps the most important of the organizations are those dealing with blindness, tuberculosis, venereal disease, and cancer. A few carry on rather extensive activities,[14] and many are responsible for the establishment of strong national units. For example, before the foundation of the International Association for Prevention of Blindness there existed national societies in the United States and England. Following its establishment, on the initiative of its Chairman, Professor de Lapersonne, national committees were created in Algeria, Argentina, Belgium, Brazil, Bulgaria, Egypt, France, Hungary, Italy, the Netherlands, Poland, Portugal, Spain.[15]

The International Association for Preventive Pediatrics (which functioned as the Medical Section of the "Save the Children" International Union) held annual conferences for the study of children's diseases. Such subjects as malaria, rickets, the means of preventing the spread of diseases in children's hospitals, and tuberculosis have been considered. The conferences have provided the opportunity for specialists, chiefly of European countries, to discuss their common problems and to learn the best methods.[16]

OCCUPATIONAL DISEASES AND ACCIDENTS

Among the first attempts to cope internationally with the problem of industrial diseases was the work of the International Association for Labor Legislation, founded in Paris in 1900, and the International Committee on Industrial Medicine, which came into existence in 1906 at Geneva. Their attempts preceding the outbreak of World War I helped to prepare the way for the occupational diseases activities of the *ILO*. These efforts have been described by an official of the *ILO* in a report on the activities of the International Health Service of the *ILO:*

> . . . medical specialists from different countries gradually formed contacts, and so there came into being the International Committee on Industrial Medicine which before the War organized International Congresses on Industrial Diseases, the first in Milan in 1908, and subsequent meetings in Brussels in 1910, and Vienna in 1914 . . .[17]

> The year 1900 saw the foundation at Paris of the International Association for . . . [Labor Legislation], with headquarters at Basle, which represented the first attempt to make an international collection of legislative measures relating to industry, and which arranged for the holding of meetings where problems of hygiene and pathology were discussed resulting in the drawing up of Conventions, such as the Berne Convention relative to the prohibition of the use of phosphorus in the making of matches (1908).
>
> Such tentative suggestions and efforts paved the way for the post-war creation of the International Labour Organization. . . .[18]

Of course, much has been done in this field by the international trade unions, particularly, the International Federation of Trade Unions. Their role is typified, perhaps, by the action regarding silicosis, which is summarized in a report of the International Secretariat of Stone Workers of the *IFTU*:

> One vital question for the stoneworkers has been solved in the period under review. This was to get silicosis recognized internationally as a compensatable industrial disease. . . . we put forward our case in 1921, proving that the disease which attacks stonecutters is not tuberculosis. . . . We stated, therefore, that silicosis should be recognized as an industrial disease and we then set to work to get it recognized as such, with the continuous assistance of the International Labour Office, and particularly of Albert Thomas. The fight was a long and difficult one, especially against the medical authorities and the employers, but in 1933 we had advanced so far that the workers' delegates on the Governing Body of the International Labour Office in the 61st Session, at our request, got the question of silicosis as an industrial disease put on the agenda of the 1934 International Labour Conference in Geneva.
>
> Then began the fight of the stone and mining trusts against us. Tremendous sums were spent, and various doctors worked against us, especially in Belgium and France. All this did not prevent our expressing our certain convictions in many meetings of the special committee with the government representatives and the professors and specialists in industrial disease. By 104 votes to 11 it was decided to extend the schedule of compensatable industrial diseases and to include silicosis in this list [which was included in the revised Convention on Occupational Diseases]. All the government representatives voted in favour.
>
> When it is remembered that this decision not only applies to the stoneworkers, but also to the miners in particular, and to metal workers, factory workers, pottery workers, etc., the full success of our years of fighting will be seen in its proper light.[19]

Among the associations concerned with occupational diseases and accidents, the following should be mentioned: the Permanent International Committee for the Study of Industrial Accidents, the Permanent International Commission on Acetylene and Autogenous Welding, the International Association of Industrial Accident Boards and Commissions (U. S. and Canada only, may be quite official in character), the International Technical Fire Committee, the International Conference for the Prevention of Accidents (first meeting in April, 1937), the International Association for Life-Saving and First Aid to the Injured (mainly official in character), the International Electro-technical Commission, the International Federation of National Standardizing Associations, the International Railway Union and the International Railway Congress Association (both mainly official).

HEALTH OF SEAMEN

Before the war a number of *INGO's* cooperated in sponsoring several conferences on the health and welfare of seamen, the third of which was convened in 1936 by the League of Red Cross Societies, the International Association of Mercantile Marine Officers, the International Transport Workers' Federation, and the International Union Against Venereal Disease. The International Labour Office cooperated closely. Other international associations which participated were the Apostolatus Maris Internationale Concilium, the International Council of Women, the International Committee of the Red Cross, and the League of Nations. The work of this conference was closely related to that of the *ILO,* as it was devoted to a study of the *ILO's* "Draft Recommendation Concerning the Promotion of Seamen's Welfare in Ports." Suggested modifications were submitted to the *ILO* Conference of 1936, which examined the proposals submitted; a study of the definitive text adopted by the *ILO* Conference shows that of the eighteen proposed modifications five were incorporated.[20]

To act between these jointly sponsored conferences, a Standing Committee on the Health and Welfare of Seamen was established in 1927, upon the request of the Norwegian Red Cross and the League of Red Cross Societies, from whose headquarters, then at Paris, the Committee functioned. Before the war this Standing Committee was composed of representatives of the League of Red Cross Societies, the Health Organization of the League of Nations, the International Health Bureau, L'Office International d'Hygiène Publique, the International Association of Mercantile Marine Officers, and six Red Cross Societies in maritime countries. The private element has been in control. This Committee has published *Hygiène et Médecine à bord,* which has been translated into several languages. It has been working to establish an international standard medicine chest, so that the giving of medical advice by wireless can be greatly facilitated.[21]

SOCIAL AND HUMANITARIAN ACTIVITY

This section is closely related to the preceding chapter which deals with the work of the international religious associations. Overlapping is inevitable, for one aspect of religion is its interest in social and humanitarian services, while, on the other hand, it is certainly true that the religious motive is very strong in many of the *INGO's* to be described here, even though most of them do not consider themselves to be religious organizations.

We find *INGO's* concerned with every aspect of social and humanitarian work. Among them are some of the most important private organizations in existence, the most outstanding being the International Red Cross. Some of them are true international pioneers, for among the earliest *INGO's* were those engaged in social welfare activities. Since their contribution has been so extensive, it was not an easy decision to determine what phases should be presented here; the activities of the *INGO's* have ranged from the moral censorship of the International Catholic Film Bureau,[22] which carries on internationally the same type of work which the National Legion of Decency does in the United States (the Legion is a member of the Bureau), to the "humanitarian" efforts of the International Game-Shooting Council, which secured the cooperation of the French government, the Ligue Internationale Aéronautique, the diplomatic representatives of various governments at Paris and the press in securing the protection of elephants against shooting from the air.[23]

SOCIAL SERVICE

Permanent Committee of the International Conferences on Social Work

Composed of both public and private bodies in forty-three countries (1938), this Committee, beginning in 1928, arranged world Conferences every four years, the fourth of which was to have been held in 1940:

> The foundation of the International Conferences on Social Work is due to Dr. René Sand, Technical Counsellor of the League of Red Cross Societies, who was aware of the valuable contribution to the progress of public and private welfare made by the National Conferences on Social Work in North America and also of the results of the European International Conferences (from 1856 onwards) on Charity and Welfare.
>
> His project was favourably received by the American National Conference and Association of Social Workers, by the Russell Sage, Millbank, Laura Spelman Rockefeller, the Commonwealth Foundations, and by the European centre of the Carnegie Endowment for International Peace, and the League of Red Cross Societies. The Foundations provided the greater part of the funds, and contributions from certain national sources were also received. An international organization committee was set up under

the chairmanship of Dr. Alice Masarykova and National Committees were formed.

The First International Conference on Social Work was held in Paris from July 8th–13th, 1928, in conjunction with other international congresses. Two thousand four hundred and eighty-one delegates, representing forty-two countries, attended. . . .

The Second Conference was held at Frankfort-on-Main in 1932. . . . Twelve hundred delegates from thirty-four countries registered as members. The general theme was Social Work and the Family. . . .

The Third International Conference on Social Work took place in London, from . . . July 12th, to . . . July 18th, 1936. About fourteen hundred members were registered; these represented thirty different countries. The . . . theme of the Conference was Social Work and the Community. Preliminary studies of the subject had been carried on for two or three years before the Conference in many of the countries participating. To assist these a handbook was issued by the Executive Board under the title "Social Work and the Community."[24]

At the close of the 1936 conference, Dr. René Sand, as president, passed judgment on its work. Among its shortcomings, he mentioned "failure to obtain an adequate representation from far-away countries," and expressed the regret that there were among the members "too few doctors, judges, teachers, and, generally speaking, too few men." The conference discussion, he felt, did not achieve "as complete an exchange between the various countries as could have been desired." Among the half-successes he counted the effect the conference had "in awakening a spirit of curiosity, in fostering a real open-mindedness," and in supporting "the spirit of cooperation" while depreciating "any tendency to particularism among social agencies." Among the full achievements he included "the prominence given to social research" and the progress made toward "a solution of the ever-recurring discussion about public and private work":

> The experience of every country, from Japan to Europe and the United States, has proved beyond doubt that if a service has to be provided on a permanent and general basis, the public authorities only will have the material resources and the power to maintain it in the long run. But it has, at the same time, been demonstrated that even under a State system, private agencies have not only their place, but render services which no official administration could secure. Thus, in every country, the problem is how to use best the existing opportunities in order to develop and harmonize public as well as private social work.

Among the achievements, also, was the fact that the conference "approached a settlement on the vexed question of specialization versus generalization."

> It has become quite clear that neither of these two systems can be dispensed with. To choose between them, or, better, to combine them is merely a question of the circumstances. The importance of training has been again emphasized; it has been recognized even for the volunteers. . . .

Other results of the conference were:

> Our attention has been fixed on the community, especially on the local community—the definite limited unit in which social work and, indeed, our whole life takes place.
> The relation of social services of all types to the community, and their influence on the community have been examined.
> An agreement has been reached on the principle that social work must not be administered from outside the local community, which should have a great share in the working of social services.
> The means of developing closer relations between urban and rural communities have been considered.
> The existence of large urban areas where community life is weak has been admitted, and methods to revive it have been presented.

Dr. Sand then referred to the useful work achieved by the Conference's five Commissions, and by the special meetings on Medical Social Work, on the Volunteer, "and the preliminary meeting on the Progress of Social Work throughout the World, which M. Thélin, of the I. L. Office, has so vividly presented."[25]

What this Permanent Committee has achieved since its founding in 1928 was summarized in a note, dated January 4, 1939, sent to the author by the Secretary-General:

> The most obvious achievements of the International Conferences on Social Work have been the establishment of a permanent Conference organization with National Committees and Correspondents in a large number of countries, and the publication of the printed Conference Reports. The latter will undoubtedly have some permanent value as works of reference, and may, indeed, be found in the future to give in a more handy form than any other publication a conspectus of the development of social work throughout the world in the periods that they cover.
> The influence of the Conferences has, however, made itself felt in other ways, which may be summarized as follows: (1) They have given occasion for, and have developed contact between social workers from many different countries and from all branches of the profession. These contacts have had much intellectual value and some of them have ripened into close friendships. (2) The Conferences have given an impetus to the organization of social workers within national limits. National Conferences of Social Work have in some cases been organized to deal with the subjects set down for discussion at the International Conferences, while in other cases the idea of a free discussion on social problems has been communicated from

the Conferences to national groups. Further, association with the International Conferences has strengthened the activities of newer national groupings of social workers. (3) The Conference discussions have led to a recognition that social problems everywhere today are to a large extent similar. At the same time, the differences arising from differing conditions in the various countries have been recognized and their importance has been made clear. (4) Opportunities have been given for a discussion of the relations between individual or voluntary social services and State social services. These discussions have never been conclusive, but they have served to bring out the value and continuing function of both types of service. (5) Further, the Conferences have given some opportunities of discussing social service problems that are international in character, e.g., the problems of providing adequate services for aliens.

International Migration Service

The International Migration Service, which recently changed its name to International Social Service, owes its creation to the World's *YWCA,* which had after several years of work built up a service for migrants, "connecting the more important ports and centres through which migrants pass as they journey from continent to continent."

> Relations were also established with other international organizations interested in the same problem. In the course of 1923, after a careful study of the work and future development of this service, it was realised that its best interests would be met by separating it from the work of the World's *YWCA*, and this action was taken by the Executive Committee with a due sense of its responsibility towards the experiment which it had had the privilege of initiating. The new organization, known as the International Migration Service, began in temporary headquarters at the office of the World's *YWCA*, and continued to look to it for a measure of financial support until its complete independence was secured in 1925.[26]

The reasons for creating a permanent organization were pressing, and no existing organ, private or official, was coping with the need:

> [An inquiry into migration undertaken in 1921] revealed the inexperience and helplessness of the majority of emigrants, the absence of governmental protection, the conflict between the naturalization and residence laws of different countries, the lack of clarity in official regulations which are often difficult to apply. . . . In many cases, these poor people were the prey of exploiters and often found themselves in the worst difficulties. The deplorable physical, economic and moral consequences of this state of things were harmful not only to the emigrants but also to the societies in which they occurred. An immense ignorance and a total incapacity to remedy this situation was revealed as much among government officials as among representatives of public or private social institutions. The following conclusions were presented to the Committee [of the World's *YWCA*]:

> Most cases concerned the family and the community as much as the woman and the young girl in particular.
>
> In a great number of cases, the solution of a single family problem necessitated combined action in several countries.
>
> Although one could hope for a certain amelioration of local aid to emigrants, no effective measure was envisaged for the solution of problems demanding international action. The existing international organizations (including the League of Nations and the International Labor Office) were not even going to undertake this task.
>
> It was then decided that as soon as circumstances permitted, an international organization, independent, nonsectarian . . . should be created. It is thus that the International Migration Service was born. . . .[27]

Since its establishment in 1925, the *IMS* has endeavored:

> To render service through cooperative effort to individuals who have, as a consequence of migration, been involved in difficulties the solution of which involves action in more than one country; to study, from an international standpoint, the conditions and consequences of migration in their effect on individual, family and social life.[28]

In 1938, it had branch bureaus in Czechoslovakia, France, Germany, Greece, Poland, Switzerland and the United States, organized cooperation with bodies in Canada and six European countries, and individual correspondents in other countries.

Up to 1934 the *IMS* had dealt with difficulties of twenty thousand families. In some cases correspondence had been kept up for several years in an endeavor to find a solution.[29] Its influence on American social case work with immigrants has been described by Porter Lee, Director of the New York School of Social Work, as follows:

> [There] has been a slowly changing attitude in American social workers toward the immigrant. Social case workers in America who are dealing constantly with immigrant families have discovered that satisfying relationships with immigrants require as much adaptation on the part of American institutions, habits and practices as on the part of immigrants themselves. Such adaptation cannot be made without the understanding of the cultural backgrounds from which the immigrant members of the American nation have come. Good social case work . . . requires the knowledge and ability to interpret the cultural setting of immigrant clients. This point of view is not yet widespread in American social work but it is gaining ground. Evidence of its extension is found in the presence of an increasing number of courses in training schools for social work whose purpose is the interpretation of other national cultures.
>
> The strongest persistent influence in this direction upon American social case work at the present time is probably provided by the International Migration Service. In its organisation it has provided for skillful interna-

tional leadership conscious of the delicate balancing and adjusting required between its own branches by the differing philosophies and methods of social work in the different countries. Experience has taught that mere coordination of local efforts is inadequate to deal with the complex problems presented in the lives of migrants.[30]

Catholic International Union for Social Service

The Catholic International Union for Social Service, established in 1925 at Brussels, has had as its object:

    1. Developing Social Service on the basis of Catholic doctrine and Christian charity;
    2. Studying in common, in the light of Catholic principles, the doctrinal, scientific and practical questions connected with Social Service;
    3. Facilitating intercourse between Catholic Social Schools;
    4. Uniting and supporting the activities of groups of Catholic trained social workers;
    5. Promoting the foundation of Catholic Social Schools and Associations of trained Catholic Social Workers in every country.[31]

In 1938, its members consisted of schools of social service and associations of social workers in Brazil, Canada, Chile, the United States and eight European countries.

The results of the activity of the Union are: (1) in many Catholic social service schools more care is given to teaching Catholic doctrine in relation to social work; (2) the Union has taken up some subjects given little consideration before, such as the Catholic attitude regarding "professional secrets in social work"; the results of such studies are used in the schools and by Catholic social workers; (3) the Union has arranged international study tours; (4) it has promoted the development of Catholic principles in social service work; (5) owing to its efforts, schools of social work were established in five South American countries and also at Lisbon and Budapest.[32]

Information from many sources is collected and published by the Union, for from experience it knows that "the example of what is done in one country can often be a stimulant and a precious help to others."[33]

STATUS OF WOMEN

Quite a number of international women's organizations have worked for the advancement of women's rights, and some have been particularly concerned with nationality rights. Among those functioning before the war, we may mention the International Alliance of Women for Suffrage and Equal Citizenship (now called the International Alliance of Women —Equal Rights, Equal Responsibilities), the World's *YWCA,* St. Joan's

Social and Political Alliance, the International Council of Women, the Equal Rights International, the International Union of Catholic Women's Leagues, the International Federation of Business and Professional Women, the Consultative Committee of Women on Nationality, composed of the International Council of Women, the Women's International League for Peace and Freedom, the Inter-American Commission of Women (intergovernmental), the Equal Rights International, and the All-Asian Conference of Women.[34] Perhaps the *INGO* which best symbolizes this movement is the International Alliance of Women for Suffrage and Equal Citizenship, which since its foundation in 1904 has witnessed the fulfillment of many of its demands. Also to be taken into account is the general work of many of the women's *INGO's* which have helped to prepare women to take a more constructive role as citizens of the world, and to illustrate this phase of international activity, we will consider the work of the Associated Country Women of the World.

International Alliance of Women for Suffrage and Equal Citizenship

The International Alliance, located at London, had in 1938 affiliated societies in Argentina, Australia, Bermuda, Brazil, Ceylon, Egypt, India, Japan, Netherlands Indies, New Zealand, Palestine, Syria, the United States, Uruguay, and twenty-three European countries. In nearly all countries, before the outbreak of war, where agitation was permitted, most of what the suffrage movement had struggled for had already been won. On the whole it can be said that such inequality as then existed was in most countries a social or economic inequality enforced not by law but rather by custom and prejudice. Thus, the Alliance found itself in the peculiar position that where its work was most needed it was not permitted to function, and where it was permitted relatively little remained to be done. To attempt to measure the influence exerted by the International Alliance itself, in distinction to that exerted by its national member associations, in bringing about this great stride in women's rights, is quite impossible.

Concerning nationality rights, the Alliance is said to have originated, in 1923, the demand that an international conference of governments should be called to deal with the question. The Swedish government, having been approached both by the Alliance and by the Swedish national society belonging to it, brought the matter before the League of Nations.[35] At the time of the First Codification Conference of the League of Nations (1930) the International Council of Women together with the Alliance held a joint demonstration in favor of giving women "the same right as a man to retain or to change her nationality." This demonstration was supported by ten other international organizations and many national groups.

SOCIAL WELFARE   181

The Convention adopted by the Codification Conference was unsatisfactory to the demonstrators.[36] The fight for equal nationality rights has not yet been won.

Associated Country Women of the World

Established in 1929 at London, the Associated Country Women of the World has endeavored "to help the world's country women to help themselves, so that they can improve their homes and their communities through their societies."[37] It has assisted in forming and developing country women's organizations in many parts of the world; in 1938 it had associations in East Africa, Union of South Africa, Australia, Canada, Ceylon, India, New Zealand, Nyasaland, Palestine, Southern Rhodesia, United States, and sixteen European countries.

> No one who knows the country can fail to know how country women's societies have aided women in their own homes; how they have conquered the feeling of isolation and beaten down suspicion; how they have built up good fellowship and civic consciousness. By the interchange of practical information, the ACWW has intensified the value of this work and ensured the sharing of good ideas among a sisterhood of a million or more women.[38]

The organization performs this service by means of conferences, meetings, publications, etc. The 1936 Conference held in Washington, D.C., was attended by two hundred delegates from twenty-three countries and over seven thousand American farm women visitors. The U.S. Government made a grant of ten thousand dollars.[39] It has published a monthly review, *The Countrywoman,* and several books, for example, *Food in the Country Home.* The results of its work are here expressed in the words of the organization itself:

> (1) Through the country women's organizations much unexpected talent has been discovered and developed among rural women, talent not only for public speaking, but also of great executive ability.
> (2) Belonging to a society provided moral support to women who previously had been trying to solve home problems alone.
> (3) The women found that they had now more to talk about at home, gossip about people was going out of fashion and talk about the society's activities was coming into fashion.
> (4) Good citizenship was coming to be considered a duty.
> (5) In many of the outlying areas of the sparsely populated countries, membership of a country women's association had not only been a source of enjoyment and a means of education, but had saved the sanity of many women living in isolated places.[40]

INGO's from many fields have taken a prominent part in the efforts to prevent the traffic in women for immoral purposes which is carried on by criminal international organizations. Many of the women's organizations, such as the World's *YWCA,* the International Alliance of Women, and the International Catholic Association of Girls' Friendly Societies (the latter an offshoot from the International Federation for Aid to Young Women), worked to secure the support of public opinion for action against white slave traffic and in support of the work that the League of Nations was undertaking in the field; some *INGO's* were represented on the League of Nations Advisory Committee on the traffic in women and children. True, the greatest strides in suppressing the traffic have been achieved by official action, but the impetus for this action has come since early times from private sources. Paul S. Reinsch in his book on *Public International Unions* says, "The matter of coming to an understanding was first taken up by private international congresses," and that the most important were those called by the International Bureau for the Suppression of Traffic in Women and Children.[41]

Many of the private organizations, like the International Federation for Aid to Young Women and the Jewish Association for the Protection of Girls, Women and Children, which has maintained representatives in many countries to meet migrants on their arrival and thus endeavor to protect them, have been concerned with preventive measures, while the International Abolitionist Federation, founded in 1875 at Geneva, carried on a propaganda fight to abolish licensed or tolerated prostitution in all countries, an approach to the problem which the League of Nations later became convinced was more effective than attempting to repress the traffic.[42]

International Bureau for the Suppression of Traffic in Women and Children

Founded in London in 1899, its early conferences "worked out definite principles and methods for the purpose of preventing the traffic in question,"[43] and its Congress at Paris in 1902 led to the signature of the International Agreement of 1904 by European governments and the United States. In addition to its conferences, the Bureau has undertaken many enquiries, has carried on port and railway station work, and has maintained close cooperation with police and governmental officials. It was represented on the League of Nations Permanent Advisory Committee for the Suppression of Traffic in Women and Children. In 1938, it had national committees in most of the countries of Europe, in Canada, Egypt, India and the United States.

International Federation for Aid to Young Women

This organization, now known as the International Federation of Friends of Young Women, began as an international association by the spontaneous adhesion of individuals from seven different countries in 1877. Located at Neuchatel, in 1938 it had committees in twenty-four countries and corresponding members in twenty-two other countries, representing an individual membership of twenty thousand. In a letter from its President, dated December 15, 1937, the purpose of the Federation and the results obtained were explained as follows:

> Its purpose is to establish an international protection by centralizing and coordinating the efforts being made to form a network of protection around every young woman who has to leave her home to search elsewhere for her living, and, so far as possible, every young woman who is isolated or in a bad environment whatever be her nationality, religion, or occupation.
>
> The action of our Federation being *preventive* it is very difficult to prove by statistics all the results of its action relating to the three hundred thousand to four hundred thousand young women that we aid each year. They are protected in their travels by our agents in railroad stations and seaports, sheltered in our homes, placed in employment by our offices, brought together in our clubs, informed by our posters, our lists of addresses, and by our international information service, visited where they work, in hospitals, etc. Sometimes we learn that suspected individuals have ceased to frequent such a railroad station since our agents have been stationed there and that they return when they believe that the vigilance of the agents has relaxed. We know also that our offices, among the thousands of notices of employment offered received each year, find a great number of undesirable ones—as high as 20 and 30 per cent in certain countries. But it is impossible in spite of these figures to say how many young women have been protected from danger, from falling into sin or even from moral ruin.
>
> Independently of its practical activity, the Federation has played a certain part in the formation of public opinion. Since 1902 at the diplomatic Conference of Paris for the Suppression of the Traffic in Women, the attention of diplomats has been drawn to the methods of action of our association and the necessity of surveillance of stations, ports, and employment agencies. It has held forth the preventive aspect of the problem in the national organization of the battle against the white slave trade and in the drawing up of international Conventions relative to it. Its influence on public opinion is also exercised . . . by means of reports presented to the international conferences of our association and other organizations.
>
> During the World War [1914] our international office and several national committees acted as a center of information between belligerents [receiving and transmitting tens of thousands of letters and messages into occupied territories] and enabled hundreds of young women to be repatriated.[44]

Concerning its relationship with the League of Nations:

> Since 1922, the Federation . . . has had an assessor's seat in the permanent

Consultative Committee for the Protection of Children and Young People of the League of Nations. During these sixteen years of collaboration with the government delegates, our association, like other international organizations, has placed its practical experience at the service of the Committee and has always tried to make abolitionist principles prevail. This Committee which, at the beginning, was favorable to the regulation of vice has so changed its point of view that the last international convention that it drew up to deal with the exploitation of the prostitution of others is strictly abolitionist.

CHILD WELFARE[45]

"Save the Children" International Union*

This Union has had a great record of constructive activity for child welfare, and was one of the most important of the prewar international humanitarian associations. Located at Geneva, its membership in 1938 consisted of thirty-four member organizations and thirteen affiliated organizations in thirty-one countries. Its motivating purpose was "to make of the normal child an agent of social reconstruction and a herald of a better humanity." It firmly believed in preventive measures,[46] which "by creating healthy surroundings and proper conditions of life and work, *prevent* the child from falling sick, from being underfed, uneducated, untrained, and from becoming delinquent." It concerned itself with "the most urgent problems of the normal child" and aimed "to secure the carrying out of a general and systematic welfare programme." It sought the support of other organizations, and two guiding principles were to enlist "the services of highly qualified and well-trained executives" and to adopt and put "into practice the considered opinion of the foremost experts in Child Welfare."[47] The work of the Union may be considered under two headings—relief and the development of child welfare.

After World War I, various organizations endeavored to care for the starving children of Europe and the Near East. The Union was founded in January 1920 to prevent overlapping and to coordinate the work. It raised over one hundred million gold francs (about twenty-five million dollars), provided clothing and fuel and two hundred million free meals. It did much for refugee children of the period between the two World Wars:

> After the Smyrna disaster and the expulsion of the Greeks from Asia Minor, the *S.C.I.U.* fed forty-five thousand refugee children and adults in Greece. In Bulgaria, the *S.C.I.U.* distributed food, erected a model

---

*In September 1946, this Union amalgamated with the International Association for the Promotion of Child Welfare, adopting a new title, International Union for Child Welfare.

SOCIAL WELFARE

village in which numbers of Bulgarian refugees were able to settle permanently, and organized child welfare work. In Albania, refugee villages were built.

The work of the *S.C.I.U.* on behalf of exiled Russian refugee children is also of a constructive kind. Besides giving individual relief, the *S.C.I.U.* supports schools, orphanages and other institutions founded in many countries for this class of children. It gives support also to large numbers of Armenian refugees in Syria.

At the present hour [1934], the *S.C.I.U.* is making great efforts to supply urgent relief to the children of German refugees.

It constantly endeavored to secure a general recognition of the duties which men, women, and governments owe to children. These duties were stated in its "Declaration of Geneva," which was formally adopted by the League of Nations, and the Union tried to secure universal application of these principles. The text of the Geneva Declaration reads

I. THE CHILD must be given the means requisite for its normal development, both materially and spiritually.
II. THE CHILD that is hungry must be fed; the child that is sick must be nursed; the child that is backward must be helped; the delinquent child must be reclaimed; and the orphan and the waif must be sheltered and succoured.
III. THE CHILD must be the first to receive relief in times of distress.
IV. THE CHILD must be put in a position to earn a livelihood and must be protected against every form of exploitation.
V. THE CHILD must be brought up in the consciousness that its talents must be devoted to the service of its fellowmen.

The Union introduced the now-famous "Adoption" plan for saving children under which a person's financial contribution ensures food and clothing for a child for one year. In 1934 one thousand children of fifteen nationalities were being helped in this manner. Also, the Union secured aid for children in cases of natural catastrophe and economic depression, and helped the children of both sides during the Spanish Civil War.

In its general child welfare work, the Union carried on many activities; one of the most interesting was its "Missions":

Missions.—The delegates of the *S.C.I.U.*, by regular visits, and by stopping for longer or shorter periods in different regions, have helped many countries to organize and develop their system of child welfare. The most outstanding instance is that of Bulgaria where a mission remained in permanence from 1925 to 1929, establishing and building up various institutions, today taken over, and their scope widened, by the Bulgarian Child Welfare Union with the co-operation of the public authorities.

This work in Bulgaria started when Bulgarians present at the First International Child Welfare Congress, held by the Union in Geneva in 1925, asked for a survey of the situation in their country and advice on how to begin child welfare work. At that time there was no legislation for child welfare in Bulgaria, and practically nothing was being done even by private institutions. As a result of the Union's help, a great deal was accomplished to remedy the situation—community committees, playgrounds, hospitals, kindergartens and a national "Children's Day" are examples.

The conferences of the Union were important gatherings. Over a thousand workers in the field attended the first Congress. In 1930 the International Conference for African Children considered problems of stillbirth and infant mortality, education and labor. In 1936 at Athens, the First Balkan Child Welfare Conference was held. And, annually, beginning in 1931, "the medical section of the *SCIU,* the International Association for Preventive Pediatrics, has met, and studied questions concerning the prophylaxy of children's diseases."

The Union served in its field, also, as a center of information; the organization itself issued many publications.[48]

International Association for the Promotion of Child Welfare

The International Association for the Promotion of Child Welfare was primarily concerned with legislation for child welfare, scientific study, and the collection of information. Founded in 1921 at Brussels, it had members in thirty-nine countries in 1938. Conferences were held annually; the 1937 Conference was divided into four sections: Medical (nutrition, infantile convulsions), Pedagogic (punishments in education), Legal (regulation of motion pictures, proposal for the establishment of special tribunals to deal with all questions concerning children), Social (family grants, effect of slums). It published a number of documents on such subjects as child welfare in Romania, the rights of children in the Swiss Civil Code as compared with other countries, public health in the United States, delinquent children, etc., as well as the reports presented to its conferences, which were prepared by authorities of various countries.

The results of the Association's efforts have been the improvement of child welfare legislation, the creation of new institutions (children's courts, benevolent institutions), various actions to protect children from dangerous working conditions, and from harmful influences of some motion pictures and infractions against morality, the promotion of health, intellectual and professional training, and public and private assistance. Some particular instances are: the Association collaborated in the preparation of two international conventions proposed by the child welfare committee of the League of Nations; in Portugal the establishment of a children's court resulted from a Conference of the Association; the Association collaborated

SOCIAL WELFARE

indirectly in securing the passage of an Italian law setting up a national child welfare institution. In general, however, it is difficult to specify exactly what the influence of the Association has been. Besides having helped to promote social, moral, pedagogic, and juridical activity which otherwise would have been slower or would not have existed at all, it induced qualified people to inquire, investigate, compare and study the problems of child welfare. The Association feels that a study of the legislation of various countries would convince anyone of its influence.[49]

International Association of Children's Court Judges

Since its establishment in 1930, the International Association of Children's Court Judges, located at Brussels, has worked to secure general acceptance of the idea that delinquent children should be helped rather than punished. It has studied the problems of juvenile crime, and has brought together children's judges from various countries. In 1938, its membership included children's judges in seventeen countries. Its international organization makes easier the solution of legal difficulties of alien children "by expediting enquiries or researches about families, or by providing documents about deeds and procedure."

At its conferences reports on such questions as the effect of the depression on children or the results of the employment of women police at Paris are given, and visits are made to various institutions dealing with children.

The Association followed the child welfare work of the League of Nations closely.

Its General Secretary in her report for the years 1920–35 stated that the practical utility of the Association was to be found in its support and diffusion of the idea that there should be a special jurisdiction based on the principle of education and protection for minors who have violated the law.[50]

RELIEF

International Red Cross[51]

It is not necessary to point out the general importance of the International Red Cross which has behind it not only a tremendous popular support but the backing of governments. It has indeed served as "one of the most powerful promoters of goodwill, peace and understanding between the peoples of the world."[52] However, certain facts are worth noting. The International Committee of the Red Cross, whose task it is to coordinate the war-time activities of the national Red Cross Societies, was founded in 1863 at Geneva, among the first *INGO's* established. A year later the governments of the world, through the Geneva Convention of 1864, agreed to respect and protect its work. The formation of the League of Red Cross Societies in 1919 and the consequent broadening of the program of the Red Cross to include the relief of suffering in peace as well as in war led to a more general acceptance of the Red Cross idea throughout the world, especially in South America. From 1919 to 1938 the number of national Red Cross Societies increased by about thirty. National societies in practically every country of the world represented in 1937 a total membership of over thirty million. The Junior Red Cross represented the largest and most widespread international youth organization, reaching out (1937) to fifty-three countries with a membership of nearly eighteen million young people.[53]

In addition to its widespread war work and almost instantaneous relief of the suffering due to natural disasters, the International Red Cross, in the judgment of the present writer, has done more for health education than any other international organization, governmental or not, and it is quite possible that its influence on the world's health has also been first in importance.[54] In reviewing its work prior to World War II, we shall first consider this health activity of the Red Cross before discussing its other welfare work.

The League of Red Cross Societies, through its international secretariat, conferences, publications, visits to national societies, etc., has stimulated and aided the development of health activities of its national member societies. Its Secretary General wrote that:

> In nearly all countries the Red Cross has organized first aid and home-nursing classes, health lectures, and has participated in efforts to meet the special problems of each country by establishing child welfare centres, anti-malarial and anti-tuberculosis dispensaries and sanatoria, and a great variety of special institutions. . . . Most of these activities were undertaken as a result of direct or indirect stimulation of the League and often with the assistance of its Secretariat.
>
> In nearly all Red Cross work the indispensable factor is the nurse. . . . Nursing training has been initiated by the Red Cross in countries formerly without proper schools, improvements have been made in existing schools, and the training and activities of public health nurses inaugurated. In Eastern Europe, in the Far East, and in Latin America, the Red Cross Societies have been the chief factor in nursing development. . . .
>
> The League has aided the national Societies, not only with technical advice and guidance, but by supplying competent staffs for new schools, by facilitating full training abroad for promising students, and by keeping in constant touch with the problems and needs of each country.[55]

International nursing courses were established by the League in 1920. Its work in this field is described in connection with the Florence Nightingale International Foundation.[56]

SOCIAL WELFARE

The League is constantly supplying its national societies with popular health information and in later years has been particularly concerned with nutrition, rural hygiene, tropical hygiene, mental hygiene, and blood transfusion services.[57]

The League has been responsible for the establishment of several important *INGO's* in the field of health. Its action in the founding of the Standing Committee on the Health and Welfare of Seamen and the Florence Nightingale International Foundation have already been noted in this chapter under the earlier discussion of health. The League was also largely responsible for the establishment of the International Union for Combating Venereal Diseases, for which it is a Technical Adviser, the International Union against Tuberculosis, for which it provided the secretariat for ten years, and the International Association for the Prevention of Blindness. It has cooperated with a great many other international organizations in the field of health, and is constantly being consulted by other groups. It maintained relationships with the Child Welfare and Health Committee of the League of Nations, the International Hospital Association, the International Guild of Hospital Librarians, the International Congress of Public Health Work, the Organizing Committee of the Second International Mental Hygiene Congress, and the Permanent Committee of the International Congresses of Open-Air Schools, the Standing Committee of the International Conferences on Social Work. Such relations are maintained through the intermediary of a Technical Counsellor, who for many years has been Dr. René Sand. He said of this relationship:

> ... They provide the League with firsthand, up-to-date data on a wide range of subjects, which are extremely useful in the compilation of articles, notes and brochures on topics of interest to the National Red Cross Societies, such as rural hygiene, maternal and child welfare, hospital administration, social welfare, etc.
>
> This collaboration also gives to the Red Cross the place to which its initiatives entitle it in the fields concerned and which might not receive full recognition were a representative of the League not associated with the work of the organizations in question.[58]

The Junior Red Cross has done its share "to improve health, to prevent disease and to mitigate suffering." The juniors are trained in general hygiene and health, care of the sick, and in first aid. They maintain and support "summer colonies, convalescent homes, sanatoriums and preventoriums, hospitals, clinics, dispensaries, hospital beds, open-air and seaside schools, school baths and showers, school canteens (milk and fruit), libraries and swimming pools"; they "adopt sick children, orphans, poor families and children, war invalids, old people"; they provide "treatment for delicate, sick and crippled children"; they undertake "campaigns against tuberculosis, malaria, flies, rats, alcoholic drinks"; they grow and gather medicinal plants and provide "safe drinking water in villages."[59]

The great wartime work of the Red Cross can be grouped under three headings: care of the wounded, relief, and activity on behalf of prisoners of war. What its contribution has been in caring for war wounded is too well known to require much discussion here. The International Committee of the Red Cross has played the leading part in securing international agreements to respect Red Cross workers and the wounded during wartime. It has closely watched the carrying out of these agreements, has acted as the center to which complaints of violations have been sent, and has communicated these complaints to the national Red Cross Society of the country accused, asking for an inquiry.[60] During the Spanish Civil War, as in previous wars, the Committee provided great amounts of medical supplies; by October 1937 it had collected $225,000 for Spain, for both sides.[61] Its experience in this field proved of immeasurable value in World War II.

In its war relief, the Committee has facilitated the efforts of those engaged in feeding civilians, but ordinarily, before the last War, had refrained from taking a direct part in the work. By exception, up to fifteen hundred tins of milk per day were distributed to children in Madrid.[62]

Also, the Committee has helped families to keep in contact when separated by war or political upheaval, and with the assistance of national Red Cross Societies and other organizations it has carried out investigations for the purpose of reuniting families so separated. It also secures and transmits documents necessary for migrants and refugees. In 1937 requests for news received by the exchange-of-news service for Spain grew from 174,528 in March to 514,908 in October; the number of replies grew from 63,966 to 311,748. Moreover, the Committee supervised the rescue of 1,100 persons from Madrid to Valencia by the middle of October, 1937.[63]

The work of the Committee for prisoners of World War I constitutes one of the greatest humanitarian enterprises ever undertaken. Again, the value of this experience in World War II can hardly be overestimated. During the first World War, it maintained an "International Prisoners of War Agency" at Geneva:

> It obtained information concerning hundreds of thousands of missing men, of prisoners and of civilians; it furthered the exchange of severely wounded men, of the ambulance and medical corps, as well as of fathers of families. It contributed to the organizing of the internment, in Switzerland and other neutral countries, of sick and wounded prisoners. It organized an office for the transmission of news to relatives in occupied areas.

As many as twelve hundred assistants were employed at a time and up to twenty thousand letters a day were handled. The number "of index cards of prisoners reached the enormous figure of eleven millions; nearly two million prisoners were identified or aided."

> During the whole of the war, delegates from the International Red Cross Committee visited the prisoners' camps in Algeria, Asia Minor, Austria, Bulgaria, France, Germany, Great Britain, Greece, Japan, India, Italy, Morocco, Roumania, Russia, Serbia, Siberia, Tunis, Turkey, and other countries. These visits not only did much towards improving the material and moral condition of the prisoners, they also gave assurance and comfort to their relatives who were in the deepest anxiety.

And, throughout the war, "the International Red Cross Committee urged the belligerent countries to adopt measures calculated to lessen the terrible consequences of the war."[64]

When the War ended, hundreds of thousands of prisoners needed to be returned to their own countries. The Committee began this work soon after the Armistice. As early as January 3, 1919, the French government placed five hundred thousand francs to the credit of the Committee. However, it was not until 1920 that repatriation actually began, and in May of that year cooperation with the League of Nations High Commissioner for Repatriation of Prisoners, Dr. Fridtjof Nansen, began.[65] The General Report for 1921–23 states that:

> [Various difficulties prevented the return of prisoners, especially of Central European prisoners in Russia and of Russian prisoners in Germany. Finally in March, 1920, the Conference of Ambassadors agreed] to the proposal repeatedly put forth by the International Committee, and finally authorized the return to Europe of Central prisoners in Siberia. The actual work of repatriation could therefore only begin in the spring of 1920.
>
> In February 1920, the German Government applied to the International Committee for its collaboration in their negotiations with the Baltic States, with a view to obtaining permission for the unhindered passage of prisoners of war to and from Russia. The German Government at the same time proposed that the Committee should organize a special mission for the inspection of the camps where Russian prisoners were interned pending their repatriation. Several other Governments subsequently took similar steps and asked the International Committee to negotiate with the Baltic States with a view to the free passage of their nationals. The negotiations of the Committee's representatives with the Governments of Esthonia, Finland, Lithuania were rapidly successful, and transit camps were established first in Esthonia and Finland. On May 12th, 1920, the first detachment of Russian prisoners was brought to Narva and was there exchanged against the first convoy of Central prisoners coming from Moscow.

Almost simultaneously, Dr. Nansen accepted the invitation of the Council of the League of Nations to undertake the work of repatriation; the appointment as High Commissioner of this well known personality had the happy result of greatly facilitating the carrying out of the Committee's vast undertaking. A first conference was held at Berlin on May 18th and 19th, 1920, which was attended not only by Dr. Nansen and representatives of the International Committee, but also by delegates of the German, Austrian, Hungarian and Russian Governments. This Conference led to complete understanding as to the methods to be employed, and laid the foundations of a mutual *entente* without which the work of repatriation could never have been carried out so rapidly. Thanks to support given by the League of Nations, the funds to meet the expenses of hiring shipping were quickly found, by means of special arrangements made with the International Committee for Relief Credits in Paris. From that instant, the International Committee, strengthened by the financial and diplomatic support of the League of Nations, could take in hand the systematic development of its organization. In March, 1921, the Committee was able to announce that already more than three hundred thousand prisoners of war had been repatriated in both directions.

At the present day the total number repatriated amounts roughly to 425,000 men, women and children.[66]

The account of the repatriation of the prisoners and of the aid to Russian prisoners in Germany to be found in this Report of the Committee is an amazing story of hardships, of negotiations with governments, and of difficulties overcome. Anyone who reads it will greatly admire these accomplishments of the Committee, which was coping with a problem which, at that time, was unsurpassed in history. In 1937 the Committee was still carrying on researches and investigations regarding ex-prisoners of war.[67]

During the Spanish Civil War delegates of the Committee visited many thousands of prisoners, arranged exchanges of prisoners and performed other services.[68]

Still another activity for which the Red Cross is noted is disaster relief, but the burden of this activity falls mainly on the national societies of the League which have aided each other on occasion with money and goods. The American Red Cross has given the most. The League has assisted the national societies in the development of their relief plans, organization and equipment. The League has strongly supported the idea that there should be international action to deal with such disasters, wherever they may occur, and was largely responsible for the setting up of the intergovernmental International Relief Union.

When the League of Red Cross Societies was founded in 1919 certainly no one could foresee the need for the widespread relief which the economic crises of the Thirties demanded. The establishment of the League itself, which gave a great stimulus to the development of Red Cross work, proved at the time a significant factor, for national societies in many countries were built up to a point where they were able to render effective service in dealing with the effects of the depression. A secretariat official of the League said:

> Since the crisis began it has been realized that the experience which the Red Cross had gained during the previous ten years, through the extension of its programme after the end of the World War and the foundation of the League, was a vital factor in enabling the responsible heads of the Red Cross everywhere to shoulder unlooked-for responsibilities and to carry unexpectedly heavy loads."[69]

International Voluntary Service for Peace

Among the aims of the International Voluntary Service for Peace (which now uses only its French title, "Service Civil Internationale"), organized in 1920 at Berne, has been the recruiting of "men and women from all countries who will give practical help in time of natural catastrophes and will carry out voluntarily works of general utility." Its other objectives were: "to obtain in countries in which military service is compulsory, the recognition of civilian service as equivalent to military service, on conscientious grounds; to set up an international voluntary service for peace, if possible under the control of the League of Nations."[70]

From 1920 to 1934 close to twenty-five hundred persons volunteered for more than twenty projects, each of which generally lasted about fifty to ninety days. The projects included clearing up after floods, avalanches, landslides, storms, and earthquakes in a number of European countries and in India. In these projects all European countries, Mexico, India, and Iceland were represented.[71]

MIGRANTS AND REFUGEES[72]

HIAS-JCA Emigration Association ("HICEM")*

HICEM was founded in 1927 to provide:

> Legal, moral and material assistance to Jewish emigrants in countries of emigration, transit and immigration. Co-ordination of the efforts of the different organizations of assistance to Jewish emigrants.[73]

In 1938, it had affiliated committees in fifty-three countries and correspondents in twenty-five other nations. The headquarters office at Paris was paying from 50 to 100 per cent of the expenses of these national committees and it controlled their work. Financial assistance

---

HIAS stands for Hebrew Sheltering and Immigrant Aid Society of New York, while *JCA* stands for the Jewish Colonization Association of London, which were the founding organizations.

generally has not been given to individuals. *HICEM* has endeavored to secure financial aid from relatives; forty million dollars was thus raised during 1920–1938. *HICEM* has often been able to secure better terms for transportation, etc., than individuals could obtain for themselves. The emigrants are assisted in securing passports and other documents; agents to help at ports are provided; legal assistance is made available; emigrants are protected against fraud. In 1937 the committees in six countries of emigration (Poland, Romania, Latvia, Lithuania, France and Manchuria) received and sent over two hundred thousand letters, secured 5,942 passports at reduced rates, searched for and found 5,135 relatives, sent on 6,356 emigrants, and saved them a total of forty-eight thousand dollars. No charge was made for these services. During the years 1933–37, *HICEM* helped 17,405 refugees from Germany, and loans were made to many of them.

In its work it has been able to influence governments; for example, in 1936 Paraguay postponed the expulsion from its capital of the then recently arrived Jews following the intervention of a "special delegate" of *HICEM*.[74]

In the prewar period, the yearly expenses of the headquarters and grants to national committees amounted to $145,000; starting in 1936 an additional $50,000 yearly was spent for joining families.

James G. MacDonald as League of Nations High Commissioner for Refugees from Germany said at the time, "The *HICEM* has not only done a remarkable work, but it still offers the best means of advancing the great work of caring for refugees."[75]

Permanent International Conference of Private Organizations for the Protection of Migrants

This Conference, composed of about forty international as well as national associations, was organized in 1924 at Geneva. It has done little since 1932. Its activities were largely directed toward influencing governmental action.[76]

In addition to the relief work of the organizations already discussed, we should note international trade union relief, relief contributed by religious organizations, and by cooperatives; also, aid to migrants, and aid to refugees, such as that given by the International Student Service. Also to be mentioned is the work of the Near East Association, which became international in 1923, grouping about fifteen national associations for the purpose of providing relief for the people of the Near East. By 1927 it had spent a hundred million dollars in this work. The Association was dissolved in 1928, and was succeeded by the Golden Rule Foundation of New York.[77]

MINORITIES

Congress of European Nationalities

Organized in 1925 at Vienna, this Congress in 1938 had as members organized groups of minorities in many European countries;[78] it claimed to represent about forty million people. The Congress enabled minorities to exchange ideas and to cooperate in presenting their requests to the League of Nations and to governments. Many of the leaders of these minorities were elected to their national Parliaments and thus were able to exert some influence.[79]

In 1930, a letter to the author from the General Secretary stated:

> The results of our activity are of various kinds. Above all we have without question stimulated the whole treatment of the minority problem in the League of Nations; indeed without us the whole clarification and development of the law of minorities would lack its most essential basis. Thanks to our yearly resolutions which touch the most varied fields of the rights of nationalities we have become in a certain way pioneers for the case of the rights of nationalities and of conciliation. Also, as concerns the scientific clarification of the problem, we provide, to a certain extent, the stimulus and the platform for the treatment of new ideas with regard to this. . . . Further, it is extraordinarily important that the members of our Congress can work in an official way with the state in which they are located to the end that the government of the latter will help the situation of the minority concerned.

After 1930, it is very doubtful that the Congress was able to accomplish much. It did not survive World War II.

World Jewish Congress

The World Jewish Congress was organized in 1936; its activities have since become very important, but come after the period covered by this book. The Congress which established it was attended by delegates representing organized Jewry of thirty-two countries. With headquarters at Geneva, Paris, and New York, it grouped a large number of Jewish organizations of many countries in order to deal with political, economic, and social problems affecting Jews and especially to defend their rights in all countries. It superseded the Committee of Jewish Delegations which was active at the Paris Peace Conference, and which later influenced the League of Nations and various governments. The Committee brought together much material relating to Jewish problems. This turned out to be very useful at the famous judicial process on the Protocols of the Elders of Zion at Berne in 1934, and in other cases.[80]

In this connection, in addition to the organizations described more fully above, the work of the World Alliance for International Friendship

Through the Churches and other religious organizations on behalf of religious minorities needs mentioning, as well as the activities of a number of peace groups such as the International Federation of League of Nations Societies.

ANTIALCOHOL MOVEMENT[81]

The international associations especially devoted to fighting the use of intoxicating drinks include the following: the International Bureau Against Alcoholism (thirteen governments and twenty-nine national societies), the International Catholic League Against Alcoholism, the International League Against Alcoholism, the World Student Federation Against Alcoholism, the International Federation of the Blue Cross Temperance Societies, the International Order of Good Templars, the World Prohibition Federation, the World's Women's Christian Temperance Union.[82]

These organizations have opposed the use of alcohol by all the methods which might be expected. The Good Templars, with a membership in 1938 of five hundred thousand throughout the world, and the World's *WCTU* (which in 1931 had 670,765 members) are, perhaps, the most important. The prohibition movement seems, however, to have been confined largely to Anglo-Saxon–Scandinavian peoples, and has made little headway elsewhere.

The associations mentioned have stimulated the creation of antialcohol societies in many countries, but it cannot be said that as international associations they have had much influence. Probably the most important effect of their work has been to encourage and assist small groups of people working against the use of alcohol in countries where the national sentiment as a whole is indifferent or even decidedly in opposition to their point of view.

PENAL LAW

International Bureau for the Unification of Penal Law

The Bureau, founded in 1928 with headquarters at The Hague (now at Geneva), is concerned with the unification of penal law and the codification of international penal law. Before the war the Bureau was composed of delegates appointed by forty-eight states and representatives of the six other organizations which are named below. It is not, however, based on an intergovernmental agreement and, therefore, is an *INGO,* although largely official in character. In 1932 the League of Nations called into consultation the Bureau, the International Association of Penal Law, the International Penal and Penitentiary Commission (an *IGO*), the International Criminal Police Commission, the Howard League for Penal Reform (a national organization), the International Law Association and the International Union of Penal Law. Such a meeting had never been held before and important resolutions were adopted pointing out what action could be taken by the League of Nations. It was agreed that the six organizations should be represented in the Bureau. In 1933 the League called on the Bureau to assist in the elaboration of conventions on penal matters. The Bureau accordingly endeavored to reduce the divergencies in national laws which prevented States from cooperating in the fight against crime and to propose texts which could be adopted into national legislation in order to standardize the definitions in national laws of unlawful acts which affect the interests of different peoples, as for example: counterfeiting, traffic in women, trade in narcotic drugs, slavery, piracy, the circulation of obscene publications, terrorism, family abandonment, and falsification of valuable papers and passports.

The Bureau also considered how penal law might be used to promote international peace as, for example, by making war propaganda illegal. The question of setting up international regulations to provide for a right of reply and of correction for false statements in the press was studied. The Bureau influenced the terms of the international conventions on counterfeiting of April 20, 1929, on terrorism and an international penal court of November 16, 1937, on traffic in women of October 11, 1933, and on the drug traffic of June 26, 1936. In all these and in other ways the Bureau played an important role in the development of international penal law.[83]

10 SPORTS

THERE IS an international nongovernmental organization (*INGO*) for almost every sport—even for roller-skating. One of the most interesting aspects of these associations is their legislative and enforcing power. They determine the regulations under which individuals or national athletic organizations are permitted to participate in international competition. They determine whether violations of these regulations have occurred and they can invoke sanctions against violators. For example, Paavo Nurmi, claimed by sport critics to be the "greatest footracer of all times," was excluded from all international athletic meets by the International Amateur Athletic Federation.[1] Thus, in a certain sense, for that aspect of life under their control, these *INGO's* have assumed the functions of governments—they lay down the law, judge the accused, and administer punishment to the guilty. They are also the accrediting authorities for international or world's records. They determine what conditions must be fulfilled before a claim for a world's record will be considered and they judge the validity of each claim.

To illustrate these functions of the individual sport organizations let us take the International Association of Recognized Automobile Clubs (now called the International Automobile Federation, whose work for international travel has already been discussed), which governs international automobile competitions and the establishment of world's records in racing events; then, we will examine the work of the organizations governing the Olympic Games and amateur field and track athletics.

International Association of Recognized Automobile Clubs

An article in its *Revue Internationale de l'Automobile* described its functions in the world of sports as follows:

> In the domain of sport, the *IARAC* is the international sporting authority which establishes and enforces the regulations provided to encourage and to govern sporting events and automobile records. It is the international court of last appeal charged with judging the disputes which may arise between National Automobile Clubs regarding the application of these regulations. These regulations are brought together in the "International Sporting Code," which is the charter for automobile sport and is applied in every country in the world. Whether a record be established at Montlhéry, in the U. S., or in any other part of the world, the same conditions of execution,

of timing . . . are applied and the results obtained are comparable everywhere.

The *IARAC,* after having verified the sincerity and the rigorous precision of these records, records them officially, dividing them into two categories: world's records, which are the best performances by automobiles, without regard to their weight or the dimensions of their motors, and international records, which are the best performances of automobiles in the different categories of automobiles classified according to the displacement of their cylinders. As concerns automobile races, their organization and execution are controlled by general rules for the purpose of assuring integrity and determining the rights and duties of the competitors and the drivers. Finally the *IARAC* does not forget that the purpose of races is to develop the technique of automobile construction. Since the beginning it has endeavoured to impose on the manufacturers "requirements" for racing vehicles taking part in the great international competitions. It is incontestable that the efforts and the ingenuity shown by the constructors in solving the problems presented by these "requirements" has been one of the principal causes of automobile progress.[2]

The *IARAC,* like the sport associations, has the authority to enforce its regulations. By 1938 it had disqualified seven competitors and suspended fifty-four. It once suspended a certain make of automobile from international competition for a period of six months. It has maintained close cooperation with the International Association of Automobile Manufacturers, which, for violations, has the power to exclude a member from international automobile shows.

International Olympic Committee

Established in 1894, at Lausanne, the International Olympic Committee, "creator of the Olympic Games," is "the supreme authority concerning them."[3] It draws up the rules and the general program, determines the qualifications of the athletes chosen to participate, and decides where each Olympiad is to be held. Its Executive Committee acts as the "Jury of Honor" for the games.[4]

The *IOC* is perhaps a unique example of an international organization which selects its own members not as representatives of any outside association and not because of their individual status, but as its representatives to national organizations. The Statutes say:

> The members of the International Olympic Committee must consider themselves as delegates of the International Olympic Committee to the Federations and Sports Associations of their respective countries. They must not accept from these Associations any mandate which will in any way bind them as members of the Committee or interfere with the independence of their vote.[5]

Each National Olympic Committee must include the "members of the *IOC* of that country."[6]

The *IOC* convenes and manages an Olympic Congress to which the members of the *IOC*, the delegates of the various national Olympic Committees, and the delegates of the international sporting federations belong.[7] This Congress regulates all questions submitted to it by the *IOC*, the sporting federations or the national Olympic committees, unless they have been previously decided by the *IOC* itself.[8]

The role of the international sporting federations in the Olympic Games has been officially described as follows:

> The International Federations, whose technical rules are in force, decide the number of events for each sport after agreement with the Executive Committee of the International Olympic Committee; fix, each in their own sport, the number of entrants for each event, keeping within the limits of the General Rules. They have the control of all sporting equipment and the technical control of the events. They choose the Ground Judges and the Judges of Appeal. They shall deal finally with all complaints.
>
> The International Olympic Committee will leave to the International Federations all the technical side of the Games, dealing itself only with the instructional and moral side.[9]

International Amateur Athletic Federation

Composed, in 1938, of amateur athletic associations in fifty-one countries, the International Amateur Athletic Federation, founded in 1912 at Norrköping, Sweden, establishes the rules and regulations for international amateur field and track competitions, supervises this part of the Olympic Games, passes upon and registers world's amateur records, and generally coordinates the national field and track associations.[10] Similar activities are carried on by about thirty other international sports organizations.

II INTERNATIONAL LAW AND THE LEGAL SETTLEMENT OF DISPUTES

IT HAS become more and more an accepted practice for international nongovernmental organizations (*INGO's*) to establish procedures and machinery to facilitate the settlement of disputes arising between their members, or between individuals or firms closely identified with their work. Disputes of a business or commercial nature are the most common of these, but in all fields, from sports on, there is need for such arrangements. Also, among *INGO's* there are personal quarrels, organizational disputes over policy and other matters, and at times, disagreements between member associations of one country. We have already shown that *INGO's* have contributed much to the organization necessary for the settlement of these private disputes. We have seen their action at three distinct levels. First, the unorganized settlement of disputes brought about through the conciliatory efforts of an *INGO*, which prove successful due to the prestige of the organization or the prominence of its officers. Second, we have seen *INGO's* in many varied fields establish rules of arbitration binding on their members; at times reference is made to the rules already established by another *INGO*. At this same level, we have seen provision made for clauses to be inserted into contracts, making obligatory the settlement of a dispute arising under them by means of conciliation or arbitration. The third stage involves the establishment, not only of these contract clauses or rules of procedure, but also the setting up of an international organ to deal with the disputes. The most outstanding institution of this kind is the Court of Arbitration of the International Chamber of Commerce, which was discussed in some detail earlier (see p. 29).

The work of *INGO's* in advancing the principles of conciliation, arbitration and judicial settlement has not been limited to the private field only; their action, since the early days of the Hague Peace Conferences, has been a powerful force behind the movement for the peaceful settlement of disputes between nations by legal methods.[1] They have also contributed greatly to the movement for the codification of international law.

In numerous places we have shown the influence of *INGO's* on international treaties or conventions and on the creation of intergovernmental organizations, all of which affects international law in the broad sense.

William Martin, well known as the editor of *Le Journal de Genève,* claims for the Red Cross a three-fold influence on the development of international law: "(1) in influencing the movement for the codification of international law; (2) in causing the humanitarian ideas and moral aims which inspired the Geneva Convention to enter the law of war; (3) in influencing the movement toward the organization of international life."[2]

Many other examples could be cited of the incidental influence of *INGO's* on international law. Here, however, we wish to consider the work of those which devote themselves more specifically to international law as such.

Institute of International Law

Foremost among these *INGO's* is the Institute of International Law, which was founded in 1873 at Brussels and is composed of the leading international lawyers of the world (membership is limited to 120 individuals, *i.e.,* sixty members and sixty associates). The purpose of the Institute is to promote the progress of international law:

> 1. By endeavouring to formulate the general principles of the science in a way which will respond to the juridical conscience of the civilized world;
> 2. By giving its assistance to every serious attempt at the gradual and progressive codification of international law;
> 3. By urging the official adoption of the principles which shall have been recognized as being in harmony with the needs of modern society;
> 4. By contributing, within the limits of its competence, to the maintenance of peace and the observation of the laws of war;
> 5. By examining the difficulties which arise in the interpretation or application of the law and by pronouncing reasoned legal opinions, when needed, in doubtful or controversial cases;
> 6. By contributing by means of publications, public instruction and other means, to the triumph of the principles of justice and humanity which ought to regulate the relations of all peoples among themselves.[3]

Its Study Commissions cover practically every aspect of the law,[4] and its work since its beginning days has been acknowledged as indispensable. James Brown Scott, writing on the work of the Institute, in 1916 stated its influence in the following terms:

> An examination of almost any treatise on international law published since the organization of the Institute would show the dependence of teachers and students upon its resolutions. But men of affairs, too, have referred to the resolutions and have accepted them as authority and pressed their acceptance upon foreign governments in international controversies. From many examples, one will suffice. In the correspondence with Guatemala concerning the expulsion of Mr. Hollander, an American citizen, Mr.

Richard Olney, then Secretary of State of the United States, quoted and relied upon the resolutions of the Institute of International Law concerning the right of a government to expel aliens from its midst and the conditions to which such expulsion should be subjected.

In international arbitrations, the resolutions of the Institute have been invoked and relied upon by arbitrators in reaching decisions and have been quoted extensively as authorities in their awards. A single instance of this must suffice; and in view of the many, the award of Ralston, umpire, in the Buffalo case, may be cited, in which that distinguished jurist based his judgment upon the resolutions of the Institute of International Law.

But it is not alone in treatises on international law, in the diplomatic correspondence of nations, and in the adjustment of controversies by arbitration that the resolutions of the Institute have been used as authorities. A distinguished American statesman [Elihu Root] . . . has repeatedly referred to the resolutions of the Institute as furnishing the framework of various conventions of the First and Second Hague Peace Conferences. And of these many references one alone can be quoted, to the effect that "in practice the work of the unofficial members of the Institute of International Law has made possible the success of the official conferences at The Hague, by preparing their work beforehand and agreeing upon conclusions which the official conferences could accept."[5]

Earlier we quoted part of Elihu Root's acknowledgment of the importance of the Institute's work to the success of the first Hague Conference (which owed its very inception to an *INGO*, the Inter-Parliamentary Union) when he said, "I think it is not generally understood that the first conference at The Hague would have been a complete failure if it had not been for the accomplished work of the *Institut de droit international.*" In this speech before the American Society of International Law in 1915, he added:

> Here was a conference called by this great Power about to meet, and something had to be done, so they took the accomplished work of the *Institut de droit international,* which had been threshed out through the labors and discussions of the most learned international lawyers of Europe, including most of the technical advisers of the foreign offices of Europe meeting in their private capacity, and embodied it in the conventions of the First Hague Conference. It would have been impossible for the Hague Conference to do that work or one tithe of it if they had not had the material already provided.[6]

George A. Finch, then Assistant Director of the Division of International Law of the Carnegie Endowment for International Peace, stated in 1937:

> The project for international arbitral procedure adopted by the Institute of International Law constituted an important basis for the Hague Con-

ventions for the Pacific Settlement of International Disputes. So, too, the Institute's Oxford Manual of Laws and Customs of War on Land was of no small aid to the framers of the Hague conventions on that subject.[7]

The proceedings of the Hague Conference of 1899 support Mr. Finch's statement. For example, the report to the Conference from the Commission on the pacific settlement of international disputes stated that the Institute "has, for a long time, led the way" in working out rules for arbitration. In regard to the law of war, we find the following in the report to the Conference from the Commission on the laws and customs of war: "The subcommission consequently adopted . . . a more precise wording which closely follows the text of Article 22 of the manual of the laws on land of the Institute of International Law."[8]

The work of the Institute as a technical basis for the Second Hague Conference is apparent in such matters as the Conventions on opening of hostilities, on conversion of merchant ships into war-ships, on sea-mines, on bombardment by naval forces, on the right of capture in naval warfare, on the creation of an International Prize Court, and on the rights and duties of neutral Powers in naval war.[9]

Weighing its influence in the in-between years, James Brown Scott, again discussing the work of the Institute, in 1929 stated:

> The Institute of International Law beginning with its first session has had a greater influence than any individual author of our time writing on international law. . . . Its resolutions on different aspects of international law and on the conflict of laws have had more influence, since its foundation, than all the writers who have written on these subjects. . . . Unconsciously, thanks to the Institute of International Law, the principle of codification has been accepted by the scoffers and by the incredulous, and the prophecy or rather the dream of Lieber has been fully realized.[10]

In view of the recent adoption by the United Nations of the "Universal Declaration of Human Rights," it is interesting to note that in 1929 the Institute, meeting at Briarcliff, New York, formulated what is generally believed to be the first draft of such a declaration.[11] The Institute's declaration, however, apparently had little influence and no further action was taken until after World War II had begun.

American Institute of International Law

In the Pan-American world the American Institute of International Law, founded in 1912 (inaugural session, Washington, D. C., 1915), composed of eminent lawyers of North and South America, played an important role before World War II in relation to the codification of international law. Its projects of conventions, said by James Brown Scott to be the first ever prepared by a private organization on the official request of governments,[12] were considered at intergovernmental conferences and served as the basis of conventions adopted by the Sixth International Conference of American States, Havana, 1928 (the conventions on status of aliens, duties and rights of states in the event of civil strife, treaties, diplomatic officers, consular agents, maritime neutrality, and asylum) and as the basis of conventions adopted by the Seventh Pan-American Conference, Montevideo, 1933 (on rights and duties of states, nationality, extradition, and political asylum).[13] J. S. Reeves, writing in the *American Journal of International Law*, has stated, "It is not too much to say whatever has been accomplished in the way of the codification of international law under the auspices of official Pan-Americanism has been due to the activities of the American Institute."[14]

Stevan Tchirkovitch in his *l'Institut Américain de Droit International* (Paris, 1926) discussing the Institute's projects of conventions, said:

> [It] has then accomplished a work, which was considered until now, with or without reason, as impossible: *it has codified international public law.* . . .
>
> This very fact that a scientific body, supremely qualified for the study of international law, has just codified, *on the official request of the Governments of 21 Republics,* all or almost all of the international public law of peace, is without doubt, not only momentous, but a new factor.[15]

He states that an immediate result of this work was to cause the League of Nations (by an Assembly Resolution of September 22, 1924) to take up again its work for the progressive codification of international law. There may also have been some influence in relation to the offer of the Italian Government to found the International Institute at Rome for the Unification of Private Law, which was subsequently established in 1928.[16]

Writing about the famous "Declaration of the Rights and Duties of Nations" proposed by the Institute in 1916, Tchirkovitch states:

> Some of these principles, and more particularly the spirit which filled this Declaration, exercised a considerable and immediate influence on the American Continent. The entrance of the United States into the war was greatly advanced. Afterward, taken up by two Leagues, by "The League of the Free Nations" and by "The League to Enforce Peace" and from it by President Wilson, the principles of the American Institute exercised a worldwide influence. The principle of nationality became, in the words of President Wilson, the famous right of self-determination, which spread out in its turn and influenced, as we know, very great movements of thought on international affairs in the entire world.
>
> But from a theoretical point of view, it is above all in the period after the war, that the Declaration . . . became the object of very lively discussions in which the European scientific bodies having the greatest competence in international law took part.[17]

International Maritime Committee

The International Maritime Committee, composed of the leading maritime lawyers of the world, has performed very important services in the maritime world. Repeatedly, since its establishment in 1897 at Antwerp, its work has been recognized officially and incorporated into international conventions. Manley O. Hudson, writing in 1928 on "The Development of International Law Since the War," said of this body:

> Another fruitful agency whose labors have resulted in international legislation in recent years is the *Comité Maritime International*. This is not an official body, but its work forms the basis of the deliberations of diplomatic conferences held at Brussels from time to time for the adoption of international legislation relating to the maritime law of peace. The sixth of these conferences was held in 1926. Their recent labors have produced four important conventions, relating to the limitation of shipowners' liability, bills of lading, maritime liens and mortgages, and immunities of state-owned ships.[18]

The Committee prepared the draft conventions which were adopted by the Brussels Conferences of 1909, 1910, 1922, 1923 and 1926; in addition to the conventions mentioned by Manley O. Hudson, there were the conventions concerned with collisions at sea and salvage and assistance at sea; several of these through ratification have become the "law of the nations." It also took part in the drafting of the International Convention of January 20th, 1914, for safeguarding human life at sea, and at its 1937 conference at Paris it prepared preliminary draft conventions on criminal jurisdiction, civil jurisdiction and the attachment of vessels.[19]

International Legal Committee on Aviation

Another group of legal experts which is concerned with a particular area of law is the International Legal Committee on Aviation (Comité Juridique Internationale de l'Aviation). Kenneth W. Colegrove in his *International Control of Aviation* says of this Committee:

> It is difficult to estimate the exact influence of this rather remarkable private body of jurists. The French Government has highly valued its collaboration. Likewise the Comité International Technique d'Experts Juridiques Aériens [International Committee of Legal Experts on Technical Air Matters which prepares draft conventions for consideration at diplomatic conferences] seeks its services. Indeed, many of the experts appointed by Governments to serve on C.I.T.E.J.A. are members of this private organization not only in France but also in their respective countries. The Comité was invited to collaborate with C.I.T.E.J.A. in the drafting of the convention on liability of shippers in international traffic and many members consulted with the official organization for this purpose in the Madrid Session of May, 1928.

The Comité has rendered an outstanding service to the science of air law by supporting the publication of a periodical, the *Revue Juridique Internationale de la Locomotion Aérienne*. Some other excellent journals have been published in the field of air law. . . . But the *Revue* was the pioneer.[20]

International Law Association

The International Law Association, with a membership in 1938 of about two thousand individuals, who in many cases have founded national branches, was established in 1873 at Brussels. Its biennial conferences have been devoted to the study of international law, and the following summary of its activities, from the report of its 39th Conference in 1936 at Paris, points out its widespread influence in the development of international legislation governing many varied aspects of international life:

> In 1877, after only four years of existence, this Association achieved at our Antwerp Conference the great triumph of the unification of the Rules of General Average [referring to the sacrifice of property at sea for the common benefit of all, as when part of a cargo is thrown overboard to save the ship], which almost immediately came into general use as the York-Antwerp Rules of General Average. They were once more revised by our Association in 1890, and at Stockholm in 1924, and are today incorporated into bills of lading and charter-parties all over the world.
> The Rules on Bills of Exchange adopted in 1908, at Budapest, have served as a basis for the public discussion of the subject both in Great Britain and at The Hague Conference of 1910 on Bills of Exchange. The earlier Rules, framed at Bremen in 1876, formed substantially the foundation of the Scandinavian Bills of Exchange Law passed soon afterwards.
> The Reports of the different Conferences contain a mine of information on a vast number of subjects, and while not always immediately resulting in draft Laws, Conventions, Rules or Treaties, have been and are in wide use by all intelligent workers in the same field.
> Since the Great War the following more outstanding matters have been discussed and finished so far as an unofficial body can finish anything: in 1921, at The Hague, the Regulations for the Treatment of Prisoners of War were passed and have since been adopted in substance by the British Government; The Hague Rules of Affreightment were passed and, slightly modified in drafting, are in general use and in some Statutes. At Stockholm, in 1924, Nationality, Statelessness and Expatriation were discussed and embodied in a Model Statute; Rules for the Enforcement of Foreign Judgments were drafted. At Vienna, in 1926, the Conference adopted a draft Convention of Maritime Jurisdiction in Time of Peace, the Statutes of a proposed International Penal Court,[21] and Rules relating to the Protection of Minorities and of Private Property. . . .
> At Warsaw, 1928, Conventions were adopted on Extradition, on Maritime Neutrality and Rules for the Governance of Occupied Territories. At

New York, 1930, there were passed a Convention on the Legalisation of Documents and Rules on Effect of War on Contracts. At Oxford, 1932, Conventions were adopted on the Sale of Goods and the Protection of Private Property of Foreigners and a general Form of C.I.F. Contract. At Budapest, 1934, were passed Articles of Interpretation of the Briand-Kellogg Pact of Paris. At Paris, 1936, much progress was made in several current subjects.

At its successive Conferences, now numbering thirty-nine, the Association has been presided over by many distinguished men, and has discussed many important subjects affecting international relations. As the result of these discussions, resolutions have been adopted, or model rules of law or practice have been drafted, which have undoubtedly in some cases exercised an important influence on legislation in the various States: whilst other of the reforms desired by the Association still await execution, whether by international treaty, by State legislation, or by business contracts.[22]

The success of its efforts in drawing up the Hague Rules for uniform bills of lading under which most of the world's tonnage now operates, has already been told (see p. 23). The story of the York-Antwerp Rules, which the Association developed and which today are universally accepted, illustrates how *INGO's* have been able to secure the general adoption of complicated rules and principles in particular fields, thereby establishing world-wide law without the action of any government. In this case it is done by inserting in bills of lading and in other forms of contracts a simple clause to the effect that the York-Antwerp Rules shall apply. Such action by *INGO's* is an approach to international government in the specific field in which the *INGO's* are functioning; in this story the area is one of commercial law.

The history and development of the York-Antwerp Rules are fully discussed in George Rupert Rudolf's book, *The York-Antwerp Rules, Their History and Development, with Comments on the Rules of 1924* (London, 1926) from which the following summary is given to illustrate the effective pooling of efforts of *INGO's* to attain international uniformity in this field of commercial law.

From early times, it has been an accepted rule that if at sea one suffers a loss of property sacrificed for the common benefit, such as throwing part of a cargo overboard to save the ship, the owner shall be recompensed by those whose property has been saved. This principle has been adopted into the law of all maritime countries.

> But of necessity the exact losses which must be regarded as General Average, their methods of calculation and the manner in which they shall be borne, vary considerably with the law of the country concerned. At the present time [1926] there are some twenty commercial codes in existence,

very few of which agree in detail on the subject of General Average, and many differ vitally, in addition to which the law in this country [England] and in the United States of America, the two greatest commercial nations in the world, can only be ascertained by a careful study of the numerous decisions given in their Courts. Thus, on this important subject which affects, and constantly affects, those engaged in overseas commerce, it is unsafe to hazard an opinion, even as to what constitutes a General Average sacrifice or loss, let alone the correct method of dealing with it, without reference to the pages of voluminous text-books or the intricate sections of a foreign code.

It is not surprising, therefore, that attempts have been made from time to time to bring about some common international agreement on the subject of General Average. . . .

In 1860, through the National Association for the Promotion of Social Science, an appeal was sent out by British commercial and shipping interests to commercial bodies in other countries, asking them to send representatives to a Conference at Glasgow, convening on September 24. The appeal set forth in striking terms the evils resulting from lack of uniformity and uncertainty in the law, stating, "It is not of so much importance how the disputed points of General Average are settled, as that they should be settled."

This meeting was held, and another followed in 1862 at the Guildhall, London, at which an International General Average Committee was set up to work on the problem. A Third International General Average Conference met at York, England, September 26, 1864. However, various difficulties having been encountered at these meetings, little or nothing was done until the matter was brought up again in the 1875 and 1876 Congresses of the International Law Association, then called the Association for the Reform and Codification of the Law of Nations. As a result, another meeting was held at Antwerp in August 1877, where the York Rules were approved with certain modifications. By 1881 they had been almost universally adopted by the action of shipowners, merchants and underwriters inserting a clause to that effect in bills of lading, charter-parties and in insurance policies.

In 1890 the International Law Association took up the matter of revision at its Liverpool Congress. The resulting group of eighteen rules received the title, the York-Antwerp Rules 1890.

> The York-Antwerp Rules of 1890 fully justified the labours of the previous thirty years in the direction of international uniformity. Not only were they well-nigh universally adopted in all maritime states, in itself a notable achievement, but in some countries where the law of the subject of General Average was not fully developed, the rules have undoubtedly aided in forming practice among adjusters in conformity with the rules, and sup-

plemented, if indeed they have not to some extent supplanted, the existing law on the subject.

But the movement for international uniformity did not end in 1890, for the Rules grew out of date due to changing conditions, and points arose in practice for which no provision had been made. The International Law Association concerned itself with the matter from time to time, and its 1910 conference at London was the occasion of an important milestone in the development toward uniformity. An international committee was appointed whose task it was to prepare a summary of the existing law of a number of countries. In 1912, the Association enlarged this committee and placed upon it an additional duty of preparing a model form of the law of General Average. The Committee drew up a Draft International Code which was circulated in the spring of 1914. This Code was not as a whole favorably received, and the outbreak of war prevented further action until 1922 when the International Law Association revived the matter. At its Extraordinary General Meeting of October, 1923, it set up a special committee to consider the draft Code.

> Before they had actively started on their labours, however, an invitation to each of the individual members of the committee was issued by the International Law Association to a meeting to be held at Gray's Inn on the 16th of January, 1924, for the purpose of considering the best means of procedure to be adopted to attain some practical result which would commend itself to the mercantile community.

The special committee, as a result of this meeting, devoted itself to the task of reviewing the York-Antwerp Rules. Their report as to desirable changes was unanimously adopted at the General Meeting of the International Law Association in May 1924.

> In his presidential address . . . the writer . . . expressed the belief that if the commercial interests desired it there did not appear to be any good reason why codification or at least the embodiment of some definitions of principle in the existing rules should not be successfully undertaken, pointing out that until some such step was taken, no real uniformity of practice could be looked for in view of the infinite variety of cases which may arise, many of which are totally unprovided for by the 1890 Rules.

This point of view was backed up by a resolution of the International Conference of Shipowners held in London in May 1924. Meanwhile a committee of the French Branch of the International Law Association issued a report which attempted "for the first time to embody a definition of the main principles of General Average."

The meeting of the General Average Committee of the International Law Association at Gray's Inn in June, 1924, resolved:

That it is desirable that a draft be prepared for consideration of the Conference at Stockholm, embodying: (1) A revision of the York-Antwerp Rules, and therein (2) A declaration of the general principles applicable to General Average. . . .

A drafting committee was appointed to carry out this resolution. The final stage in the movement for uniformity, which started in 1860, occurred when the 33rd conference of the International Law Association convened on the 8th of September, 1924. The report of the drafting committee was considered, and new rules under the title of the York-Antwerp Rules 1924 were adopted to replace those of 1890.

The new rules were immediately published in the Press and were also circulated shortly after to the leading mercantile bodies throughout the world, and it was soon evident that they met with a very general measure of approval. No serious criticism of their provisions was raised, except in the United States . . . and the business community as a whole appears to have accepted the rules as a satisfactory solution of their demand for revision which would provide a greater degree of uniformity in all cases of General Average, whether under modern or future conditions of commerce.

Although the new Rules were unanimously approved by the Sea Transport Committee of the International Chamber of Commerce, the United States Chamber of Commerce was not too favorable toward them, and it seemed at the time as if the Rules, as drafted at Stockholm, would not be adopted by U. S. commercial interests "to anything like the same extent as they have been in other countries, and this breach in what otherwise appeared to be almost universal approval" could "only be regretted in the interests of uniformity in this important branch of maritime law."[23] However, today they are almost universally applied.

Academy of International Law

Performing an important educational task for many students of international affairs, the Academy of International Law, whose administrative council is composed of members of different nationalities, was founded in 1923 at The Hague as a center for the study of international law; the published collection of its courses or lectures through 1939 alone fills sixty-nine volumes.[24]

International Association of Penal Law

The Association, which was founded in Paris in 1924, is composed of criminologists of many countries who have come together to study crime, its causes and remedies, and to promote the progress of international criminal law. It led the way in proposing ideas which when later adopted by the United Nations led not only to the conviction of Goering, von Ribbentrop, Hess, and other top Nazis by the Nuremberg Tribunal, but also of thousands of other war criminals both in Europe and Asia.

This action was far different from that which had taken place after World War I; the Kaiser was never punished since there was no international law against aggressive war and, with few exceptions, all others accused of war crimes escaped without punishment. Even so, official circles were reluctant to support the idea of an international penal justice; the Assembly of the League of Nations, for example, in considering the matter in 1920, decided that the problem was premature and should first be studied by the *INGO's*. In 1924 Professor V. V. Pella presented to the Inter-Parliamentary Union a plan for an international penal court to try both individuals and states which committed offenses against international peace. It was, however, the International Association of Penal Law, of which Professor Pella is now President, which took the lead between World Wars I and II in the effort to develop an international penal law.

For more than ten years the leading problems in the field were given careful consideration by the Association and a number of progressive proposals were adopted. In 1926 at its first Congress the Association adopted a resolution proposing, among other things, that the Permanent Court of International Justice should have international criminal jurisdiction and that individuals should be considered responsible for acts of aggressive war, for crimes connected therewith, and for all violations of international law during either peace or war. In 1929 the Association adopted another resolution, in which, considering that the Pact of Paris of 1928 had outlawed war, it called upon the competent authorities, including the League of Nations, to take the Association's 1926 resolution into consideration. In the same year the Association decided to draw up an International Criminal Statute. The Inter-Parliamentary Union had decided in 1925 to elaborate a criminal code of nations. The International Law Association entrusted Professor Pella with drawing up a "Plan for a World Criminal Code," which was published by the International Association for Penal Law in 1935. In this and in other ways the Association took the lead in putting forth the ideas later adopted as the basis for the Nuremberg and other war crime trials.[25]

12 PURSUIT OF PEACE

ESTABLISHED IN 1888, the Inter-Parliamentary Union, together with the International Peace Bureau, founded in 1892, led the general movement for peace before 1914, which stressed the pacific settlement of disputes and the codification of international law as the keys to peace. With the success of the Hague Peace Conferences of 1899 and 1907, the belief that mankind was on the threshold of a warless world was fairly widely accepted. World War I, as unexpected as it was horrible, came as a great shock. The terror of modern war and the determination that "it" must never happen again, gave birth during the war and in the years immediately following to a number of international non-governmental organizations (*INGO's*) dedicated to the pursuit of peace. The demand for a permanent league of nations surged during the war, with collective security as the new slogan of the peace movement. There is no question that the wartime efforts of *INGO's* influenced the policy of Wilson and crystallized in the establishment of the League of Nations, which received the overwhelming support of the *INGO's*. Soon pacifism became the dominant spirit, promoted to a great extent by the work of the peace societies and the religious groups, and the keys to peace, even as the rumbles of war were being heard from the Pacific, were believed to be disarmament and the outlawry of war. In the face of aggression, the peace societies pressed for action short of war; collective security was supported in its preliminary stages—investigation, conciliatory efforts, economic sanctions—but at no time did the peace movement raise a united voice to proclaim that force should be met with force. In the 'Thirties, the years of economic disaster, plans for organizing economic cooperation were advanced to meet the problems of reparations, monetary stabilization, and the organization of international trade. As the effects of the world crisis deepened and when the challenge of Fascism was not successfully answered by the League of Nations, the international peace movement had to fight the cynicism and apathy that became all too prevalent.

Practically every *INGO* discussed in this book has been concerned with international relations, and many, as we have already seen, contributed considerably to the efforts for peace—in advancing unity, supporting measures to improve the economic and social conditions of life, and in promoting international friendship and understanding. Every kind of *INGO* from the Universal Esperanto Association to sport groups has shared in the movement. The work of religious groups, during the last few decades, deserves special mention. The efforts of the *INGO's* ranged from international radio programs, such as those sponsored by the International Broadcasting Union, to successful conciliatory efforts at an official level. The value of their conferences as a force for peace needs no added statement here, but perhaps it will be worthwhile to mention some facts concerning their number which Herbert R. Shenton brought out in his *Cosmopolitan Conversation,* the *Language Problems of International Conferences* (New York, 1933). Drawing on the *Annuaire de la vie internationale,* 1908 to 1909 and 1910 to 1911, published by the *Office Centrale des Institutions Internationales* at Brussels, he points out that there were 2,699 international conferences from 1840 to World War I. After the war until 1932 there were 2,018 conferences. Shenton states, "There have been, therefore, in less than a century, a total of 4,717 international conferences," and adds, "We are now entering the last decade of a century of international conferences. In less than ninety years the average number of such convocations has moved from one to over three hundred per annum," the majority of which were private.[1]

In this section, we will consider the contribution of those *INGO's* which are generally classified as peace organizations, some engaged, primarily, in propaganda and popular education, others in research and study. We will look also at the efforts of other *INGO's* which have accepted the advancement of peace as a major objective.

Perhaps the best tribute we can pay to these advocates of peace is to offer evidence to the fact that their aims, at times spurned as impractical dreams of idealists, later became the accepted aims of world statesmen.

PEACE SOCIETIES

International Peace Bureau

From 1843 on, several peace congresses were held at various times, but no permanent organization was set up; in 1892, the International Peace Bureau, Geneva, was founded to continue these meetings, and its annual "Universal Peace Congresses" attracted much attention and developed support for the idea that international problems should be settled peacefully. A. C. F. Beales in his *History of Peace* lists the "salient lines of advance" of the international conferences both of the Bureau and of the Inter-Parliamentary Union:

> First and foremost, both series of conferences gained enormously in respect. Already ministers [*i.e.,* members of cabinets] had been known to attend their sittings. After 1900 ministers invariably did so. . . .
> Secondly, the gatherings no longer avoided, as of old, discussing current

political problems. They realized by now that their task had reference to a present as well as to a future. . . .

Thirdly, themes already familiar were gone over time and again with increasing definition and assurance. . . .

Fourthly, there were many innovations. Some were stillborn, by reason of inherent weaknesses. . . . Others were of wide significance for the future: in particular a letter from Andrew Carnegie, read at the Universal Peace Congress at Boston in 1904, proposing a union of the Great Powers to declare that there would be no more war and to *enforce* the declaration. Eleven years later this paradoxical idea took shape in America as the League to Enforce Peace. . . .

But the most arresting decision of the whole period was a lengthy document which did, in effect, what a fusion of the Kellogg Pact and the League of Nations Covenant will do at the present moment; that is, at once outlaw private war completely and buttress the outlawry with sanctions: abolishing private war, but consecrating the punishment of an outlaw State by the rest of the world. The document was drawn up in 1902 by the Universal Peace Congress at Monaco.[2]

After the end of World War I, the Bureau continued its work, but its influence was weak; other organizations took the lead in the international peace movement.

Inter-Parliamentary Union

Composed of National Groups[3] all of whose members either were or had been members of the national parliament or legislature of their respective countries, the Inter-Parliamentary Union has been a leader in the peace movement since its establishment in 1888 at Brussels. In 1938 the membership totaled about five thousand from thirty-one nations. The purpose of the Union has been to secure the cooperation of States for international peace and to "study all questions of an international character suitable for settlement by parliamentary action."[4] In 1930, its ultimate purpose was stated as follows:

> Although an unofficial and as yet incomplete representation of the Parliaments, it aims at becoming an international legislative assembly. In improving its Statutes, it does not merely seek to better its constitution, but it also prepares the way towards the future creation of a World Parliament, or of a House of Commons of the League of Nations.[5]

Before 1888, treaties of arbitration between States were extremely rare. Neither the United States nor a single European country was a party to such a treaty; only a few South American States had made such agreements. In its first years of existence, the Union devoted itself primarily to the study and promotion of arbitration treaties and a permanent arbitration court, in order that it would not be necessary to organize a special court for each dispute.[6]

Following up its declaration of the year previous, in 1895 the Union communicated to Governments a draft Convention for the establishment of a permanent international court. The note of John Hay, Secretary of State of the United States, proposing a Second Hague Conference stated:

> Among the movements which prepared the minds of governments for an accord in the direction of assured peace among men, a high place may fittingly be given to that set on foot by the Inter-Parliamentary Union. . . . Its annual conferences have notably advanced the high purposes it sought to realize. Not only have many international treaties of arbitration been concluded, but, in the conference held in Holland in 1894, the memorable declaration in favor of a permanent court of arbitration was a forerunner of the most important achievement of the Peace Conference of the Hague in 1899 [that is, the establishment of the Permanent Court of Arbitration].[7]

The very decision on the part of Nicholas II to call the Hague Conference of 1899 was due to the Union. In an interview with William T. Stead the Russian Czar acknowledged this fact.[8] The details have been given by Christian L. Lange as follows:

> In 1898 the Russian War Minister learned of a very important order of the Austrian Government for artillery. He demanded, for Russia, cannons of the same kind which would have cost several millions. The Minister of Finance, Witte, objected strenuously to this proposal because the work of financial reconstruction to which he was devoted would have been endangered. He suggested that negotiations be opened with the Austrian Government in order that the two countries might agree not to increase their artillery. However, the Russian cabinet considered that such a request would be a confession of weakness and no decision was reached. At this juncture a young attache in the Ministry of Foreign Affairs, Priklonsky, called the attention of his superiors to the movement against increasing armaments and for peace, and particularly to the work of the Inter-Parliamentary Union. He had attended . . . the Seventh Inter-Parliamentary Conference at Budapest in 1896. . . . He had written, at that time, a report for his Ministry on the Conference and on the importance of peace work in general. He now proposed that an appeal to the Governments be launched on the basis of these ideas which seemed to be gaining more and more influential support.[9]

It was not strange that Priklonsky's proposal was adopted. It had the great merit of pointing out how the dilemma, arising from the alternative of embarrassing expenditures or a "confession of weakness," could be avoided in a manner calculated to increase the prestige of the Czar and his Government.

The Union was also largely responsible for the convocation of the 1907 Hague Conference, taking the initiative at its 1904 meeting where it passed a resolution requesting the President of the United States to call a second Conference. President Roosevelt, having been properly prepared by the President of the Union, received its delegation and acceded to its request. Through his Secretary of State, John Hay, he very soon took preliminary steps. However, when the Czar intimated that he wished to have the honor of calling the second Conference as well as the first, President Roosevelt agreed.[10]

At the Hague Conference of 1907 the most important matter considered and the one which led to the most prolonged discussion was the Model Arbitration Treaty submitted by the Portuguese delegation. Prepared by the Inter-Parliamentary Union, this Model Treaty included the principle of compulsory arbitration. The Treaty gained favor until thirty-two out of the forty-four States represented voted for it. However, unanimous acceptance was required. This could not be secured for the Treaty, but it was obtained for a declaration in favor of the principle of obligatory arbitration, especially for disputes "concerning the interpretation and application of international conventions."[11]

Following the Conference, the Inter-Parliamentary Union carried on strenuous efforts to hasten the ratification of the Hague Conventions and the Naval Declaration of London (1909), carefully studied the subjects discussed at the Conferences, and published *L'arbitrage obligatore en 1913,* a study of all treaty stipulations of this kind in force in 1913, by Christian L. Lange, its Secretary-General. The Union's attention was focussed also on disarmament and it published in 1914 *La Limitation des Armaments* by Hans Wehberg, covering all known schemes on this subject; this was a result of the Union's committee on disarmament, for the Union was planning to take up the problem of disarmament at its 1915 conference, and it was endeavoring by this to prepare the way for a Third Hague Conference, to have been held in 1915 or 1916.[12]

In 1912, the Union created "a Committee to study the question of the institution and composition of a 'permanent body' for the Hague Conferences," and this "problem engaged the attention of the Union more than any other on the eve of war." During the war its efforts were directed toward the establishment of a lasting peace. Both its studies and work helped to pave "the way for the creation of the League of Nations and its permanent Secretariat."[13] During the war,

> Special efforts were made by the Groups of the three Scandinavian countries in particular—Denmark, Norway, and Sweden—in order to obtain that the peace treaty which would end the war should lay the foundations of a really lasting peace. Their delegates, meeting in yearly assembly,

adopted important agenda on the subject, based on the ideas which had inspired Inter-Parliamentary work and aiming at a permanent organization of the international community of States—already called the League of Nations—the creation of an international judiciary, also permanent, and reduction of armaments. Other Groups, in particular those of certain other neutral countries, expressed their support of these recommendations, and similar resolutions were also adopted by the American and British Groups.

The Inter-Parliamentary Bureau meanwhile did everything in its power to make these efforts known to all the Groups of the Union. This it did by means both of steady correspondence and annual reports, and of personal visits from the Secretary General to most of the Groups in Europe during the war itself.

Finally, the Bureau published two books during the war, one on "The American Peace Treaties," being a collection of the treaties known as the "Bryan Treaties," with a commentary, and the other a Statement of the work of the Union during recent years, as seen in the light of the declarations made by statesmen on both sides of the trenches, and of the "Programmes for a lasting Peace" drawn up by the organisations created during the war. . . . Many prominent members of the Union had taken an active part in the work of the most important of those organizations: the *Organisation centrale [pour une paix durable]*, whose seat was at the Hague. . . .

These various endeavours no doubt had a decisive influence, more particularly on the policy of President Wilson. . . .[14]

And,

The formation of the League of Nations in 1919 was the point of crystallization of all the influences at work, of which the efforts of the Union was only one, to bring about the sway of justice in international affairs. The Interparliamentary Union may at any rate claim the honor of having, throughout the whole of its career, played the part of pioneer to this permanent organization of international relations between Governments.[15]

After the war, beginning in 1921, the Union gave almost continuous attention to disarmament, supporting the League of Nations, insisting on action, and preparing various technical plans. All this work carried much weight (particularly in view of the disarmament conference of 1932), coming as it did from an organization composed of members of the parliaments of some thirty-one states.[16]

Lange credits the Inter-Parliamentary Union with having played a part in the creation of the Permanent Court of International Justice. He states:

The organization of the Court was in some very important respects based on the draft elaborated in 1914 by an Inter-Parliamentary Committee, under the chairmanship of Henri La Fontaine, which was to be laid before the Stockholm Conference in 1914 whose meeting was prevented by the World War.[17]

Central Organization for a Durable Peace

In November 1914, a Dutch society, the Anti-Oorlog Raad (Anti-War Council) issued a "Minimum Program" which was, according to A. C. Beales in his *History of Peace*, "the most widely discussed of all plans thrown up by the War." In April 1915, together with other national peace groups it convened an international meeting at The Hague which took up the Minimum Program and developed from it a "Manifesto and Minimum Program" of five points, and created the Central Organization for a Durable Peace "to serve as a link between national organizations and individuals in sympathy with the plan." The Central Organization, composed of representatives of forty nations, with many of the outstanding men of the times participating in its work, advanced this program internationally, which Beales states was "the earliest of the plans which influenced Wilson in propounding the "Fourteen Points." This Manifesto of the Central Organization demanded: (1) self-determination for peoples, and equality of treatment for minorities within States; (2) "liberty of commerce or at least equal treatment for all nations" within colonies and spheres of influence; (3) a permanent Society of Nations, with a Permanent Court of International Justice and a permanent international Council of Investigation and Conciliation established, with States assuming the obligation to submit all disputes to peaceful settlement, and to join in sanctions, diplomatic, economic or military, in case any nation resorts to force; (4) disarmament, and freedom of the seas; (5) foreign policy under the control of "the parliaments of the respective nations," and secret treaties considered void.[18]

Women's International League for Peace and Freedom

Another organization born during the war, the Women's International League for Peace and Freedom, was to have considerably more influence on Wilson's policy. Beales writes:

> But despite the disruption of almost every link that bound the [peace] movement together, there emerged within twelve months of the outbreak an organization which . . . surmounted difficulties of travel and prohibitions by Governments. . . . It began with no more than a score of people, all women, and in three short months it had reached the ear of President Wilson. Its influence on the Fourteen Points is undoubted.
>
> The women, Belgian, Dutch, German, and British, met in the spring of 1915 . . . for the purpose of organizing an International League of Women for Peace and Liberty [now the Women's International League for Peace and Freedom]. The Congress in which the League was launched, on 18th April 1915, at the Hague, numbered over eleven hundred women from twelve countries. Many of the delegates—the British in particular—attended

in spite of definite prohibition by their Governments. . . . The League's programme is important as one of the earliest to be evolved during the War. Its terms were made known to all the Governments of Europe and America by the proven method of special deputations. And in this wise Jane Addams, who had presided at the opening congress, heard from Wilson's own lips three months later that, "I have studied these resolutions, and I consider them the best proposals that have been formulated by any association."*
There is at all events a marked coincidence of emphasis between the League's recommendations and the Fourteen Points: a concentration on the right of peoples to dispose of themselves, on democratic control of foreign policy, on the freedom of the seas, on open diplomacy, on State monopoly of munitions of war as the first step towards disarmament, and on a League of Nations "based on a constructive peace."[19]

In 1938, with headquarters at Geneva, the *WILPF* had national sections as well as individual members in Australia, Canada, Haiti, Japan, Mexico, New Zealand, Tunisia, the United States, and nineteen European countries. It also had corresponding members in twenty-two countries. Throughout the years the dominant goal of the *WILPF* has been disarmament and the reigning spirit, pacifism. As early as 1915 and 1919, the *WILPF* passed resolutions against the munitions industry, attacking profits from war or the preparation for war, and in 1919 proposed an international commission to conduct an investigation of the munitions industry. Miss Dorothy Detzer, Secretary of the U. S. section of the *WILPF*, was responsible to a large extent for the famous Nye Inquiry into the munitions industry undertaken by the U. S. Senate in 1934.[20] In a letter to the writer Miss Detzer stated, "I think our Section was influenced in part by the original action of our International organization in 1919 when it passed a resolution calling for an international investigation of the munitions industry."[21]

International Federation of League of Nations Societies[22]

The International Federation of League of Nations Societies, Geneva, was founded in 1919 for the purpose of "promoting the understanding, approval and application of the principles imbodied in the Covenant of the League of Nations." The membership of its national societies mirrored to a great extent the feeling of national governments toward the League system. For example, in 1930, before the League was challenged by any major aggression, there were 841,208 members in Great Britain, 500,000 in Czechoslovakia, 19,341 in the United States, 19,200 in Germany, and 12,303 in Japan.[23] In a number of countries, notably Great Britain, the officers of the national societies were the leading statesmen

---

* Page 66, International Peace Bureau, Annuaire, 1924.

of their countries. Many of the official delegates to the Assemblies of the League of Nations were members of the Federation societies.

It maintained a number of "Permanent Commissions" on education, national minorities, International Labour Organization, economic and social questions, legal and political questions. In these Commissions and in its annual Assemblies the work of the League of Nations was closely followed and resolutions on problems facing the League were adopted. The resolutions adopted by its annual Assembly were communicated each year to the General Committee of the League of Nations Assembly.

The Federation endeavoured to enlighten public opinion about the work of the League, tried "to facilitate that work itself by studying those questions which the League . . . [might] in its turn be called upon to study and to solve, and [drew] the attention of the League frankly and firmly to those questions in which the world [looked] to it for a lead and for efficacious action." The Federation existed not only to defend the League, but also to help it do its work and to prod it into activity when that was necessary. The Federation kept its members "regularly informed of the educational methods employed and the results obtained by the most active among them," and thus helped to make more effective their efforts at peace education, particularly the efforts in support of the League. In 1926 the Federation organized at Geneva an annual Summer School on the League of Nations, conducted in German, French and English, which in the years following was attended by hundreds of students from many countries. One of its policies was to reach the rising generation. In 1936 it organized the First World Youth Congress for the promotion of peace, which brought to Geneva 750 delegates and observers from thirty-five countries. The Congress set up an autonomous continuation committee.[24]

Another example of its influence is to be found in the work of its Commission on National Minorities. When complaints were brought before the Federation, its policy was:

> . . . before taking any other action, to bring face to face the representatives of the Majority and of the Minority, and to invite these to explain the situation freely before the Commission. The relations existing between Majorities and Minorities have never been envenomed as a result of those dialogues, and in more than one instance they have been improved. The Commission has sometimes seen the complaints submitted by a Minority evaporate before the explanations furnished by the delegates of the Majority. Often enough still more striking results have been obtained. Majorities and Minorities, who had till then indulged in more or less acrimonious expression of their views in Parliament and in the press, have undertaken, in the presence of the Commission, to study their difficulties among themselves and to make an effort to smooth them out. Sometimes, too, the representatives of two countries, of which the Majority in one is of the

same nationality as the Minority in the other, have undertaken to approach their respective Governments in order to obtain a more attentive and more liberal application of the Minorities Treaties. In this respect a most satisfactory result was secured in the case of the treatment of Danish Minorities in Germany and German Minorities in Denmark.[25]

The direct negotiations between the Danish and German associations of the Federation led to negotiations between the respective governments and to the granting of new rights to the minority in 1926. Representatives of both associations reported on this to the Federation. It may be said that their membership in a common organization facilitated the negotiations.[26]

The Federation also influenced discussions on minorities in the Assembly of the League of Nations, but it cannot be said that very important results followed.

A fair judgment on the over-all influence of the Federation is the following statement made by Professor Ruyssen when he was its Secretary General in 1930:

> Can the League of Nations Societies boast of having had any influence upon international relations, and upon the development of the League of Nations itself? Such a question must be answered with circumspection. Between the resolutions of purely nonofficial organizations and the influence they exert on political life, it is no doubt arbitrary to trace a too direct line of cause and effect, for we are dealing here with *imponderabilia* which should neither be over-estimated nor ignored.
>
> Yet one need only run through the resolutions adopted by the Plenary Congress of the Federation to see that many of these have been carried out. If on the one hand it would be extravagant to attribute those results expressly to the effort of the Federation, it would be quite as unjust to deny that the Federation has carried out the characteristic task it has set for itself, namely, to enlighten public opinion and to pave the way towards solutions which the League of Nations itself must reach in its effort to fulfill the continuous demands of the present day.[27]

Examples given by Ruyssen show that official action frequently followed the lines laid down in resolutions of the Federation.

An interesting criticism of the Federation was made by Felix Morley, who claimed that an increasing conservatism was evident in the Federation in the direction of merely supporting the decisions of the League, rather than in urging action in new ways. He explained this development as being due to the fact that "a very large proportion of the delegates" were "men accustomed to represent their government in various League activities and in some cases in the Assembly itself."[28]

With each successive aggression, the pro-League sentiment in many countries waned, and in the Secretary General's Report for April 1, 1935 to March 31, 1936 we find:

It cannot be denied however that a number of Societies seem paralysed. The reports of some are extremely meagre and others, far too many, conspicuous by their absence. This seems to be due less to an oversight on the part of overworked secretaries than to a hesitation on the part of those who, having done very little, have little to say. In general, it cannot be pretended that the enthusiasm which buoyed the League of Nations movement in the ten years following the framing of the Covenant has not slackened, if not, indeed, in certain countries quite subsided.[29]

International Consultative Group (For Peace and Disarmament)

The establishment of the International Consultative Group in 1932 represents the widespread pooling of efforts on the part of many *INGO's* which were supporting the Geneva Disarmament Conference of that year. The steps which led to its founding are worth noting. Before an Extraordinary Session of the Conference, on February 6, 1932, there occurred probably the most striking demonstration of international public opinion that had ever taken place. At this session the representatives of four special Disarmament Committees (set up by the International Federation of League of Nations Societies, the women's international organizations,[30] the Christian international organizations,[31] and the students international organizations)[32] and of the International League for the Rights of Man and Citizenship, the International Federation of Trade Unions, and other bodies, both national and international, all voiced their desire for disarmament and presented numerous petitions and resolutions. It was said that over two hundred million people were represented.[33] The petition presented by the women's international organizations alone bore more than nine million signatures.[34]

At the end of the first phase of the Disarmament Conference in July, 1932, the representatives in Geneva of various international organizations and national bodies (including many of the *INGO's* just previously mentioned) issued a joint statement dealing with some of the chief issues then undecided. This statement attracted widespread attention and comment. It was written not in vague or general terms but with "technical and political precision." The representatives were able to be concrete, "because most of the organizations in question had themselves adopted policies on disarmament as the result of careful preparation, study and consultation, which were precise and far from vague."[35]

On July 23, 1932 the International Consultative Group (For Peace and Disarmament) was established, its membership consisting of the Peace and Disarmament Committee of the Women's International Organizations, the Joint Disarmament Committee of the Christian International Organizations, the student international organizations, the International Federation of League of Nations Societies, the International Conference of Associations of Disabled Soldiers and ex-Service Men, the Inter-Parliamentary Union, the International Student Service, and three national organizations.[36]

On October 15, 1933, another great demonstration was organized by this Group. Eminent speakers appeared, messages were received from the Prime Ministers of Great Britain and France, the President of the Council of the People's Commissars of the U.S.S.R., and the Secretary of State of the United States. Five thousand messages from organizations all over the world were received and presented to Arthur Henderson, the President of the Disarmament Conference. Germany had just withdrawn. It was thought that, "but for the wide public demand for disarmament revealed by the Demonstration and the campaign preceding it, the Conference might have there and then collapsed in consequence of Germany's withdrawal."[37]

In addition to the organization of public demonstrations, the Group performed a useful service in supplying its constituents with information and suggestions for political action and propaganda.

From 1935 on, after the failure of the Disarmament Conference, the Group turned its attention to other problems of international affairs, making public statements and issuing surveys and reports.

International Peace Campaign

The International Peace Campaign was organized in 1936 at Geneva, with the following objects:

> To coordinate the activities of international organisations directly or indirectly interested in the question of peace and international understanding. To establish National Committees in every country to carry on concrete action for the defense of peace on the basis of the following Four Points:
> 1. Recognition of the sanctity of Treaty obligations.
> 2. Reduction and limitation of armaments by international agreement and the suppression of profit from the manufacture of arms.
> 3. Strengthening of the League of Nations for the prevention and stopping of war by the more effective organisation of Collective Security and Mutual Assistance.
> 4. Establishing within the framework of the League of Nations of effective machinery for the remedying by peaceful means of international conditions that might lead to war.[38]

In 1938, its membership included twenty-four international organizations and National Committees (which in turn were composed of various organizations) in forty-two countries.

The *IPC* was an attempt to halt the growing disintegration in international relations. Its first Peace Congress (Brussels, September, 1936) was attended by four thousand delegates representing 750 organizations. The

17th Assembly of the League of Nations received its Delegation. It constructed the Peace Pavilion at the Paris Exhibition in 1937. It secured the support of many prominent men and women and its work received a great deal of publicity. Efforts to stimulate the organization of national committees and to increase their efficiency and basis of membership were important in the work of the *IPC*.[39]

The *IPC* was convinced that through unified efforts on the part of organizations, both nationally and internationally, the drift toward war could be stopped, and as Philip Noel-Baker pointed out, the Brussels Congress proved that the various organizations could work together and that if they continued, "their power to inspire the peace movement throughout the world would be far greater than the influence of each of those organizations acting individually and by itself."[40]

Pan-European Union

On October 1, 1923, the Pan-European Union was organized, with headquarters at Hofburg, Vienna. Its first Congress was held three years later, followed by Pan-European Congresses in Berlin, 1930, Basle, 1932, Vienna, 1935. Several economic conferences were organized, in December 1933 and May and November 1934, at Vienna, and a Pan-European Agricultural Congress was convened in September 1936, also at Vienna. Its periodical, *Paneurope*, issued in French and German, appeared ten times a year. It carried on a propaganda campaign—through lectures, publications and congresses—for a United States of Europe, but in 1938 it consisted only of small groups of enthusiasts in fifteen European countries and some supporters in the United States. Before the outbreak of war no major progress had been achieved to advance its program. But, in view of the postwar developments, the Union as a pioneer movement working for European unity assumes a certain significance—another example of how an idea which appears to have little influence within a few years becomes widely accepted.

STUDY AND RESEARCH

Before 1914, with the exception of the international law societies and to some degree the Inter-Parliamentary Union, no *INGO* can be said to have been concerned with scientific study and research on international affairs. But since the twenties, there has been a growing understanding of the need for such investigation to serve as the foundation for action, whether by governments acting independently or through official international organizations. *INGO's* of many kinds have, in this respect, performed most useful and necessary work. They have brought together experts on particular subjects from many different countries to discuss international questions from the point of view both of their own nationality and their own particular school of thought. Also, there has developed on the part of foundations the practice of utilizing the experience of *INGO's* in furthering research on particular problems. One such endeavor was the Joint Committee for the study of international economic relations set up by the International Chamber of Commerce and the Carnegie Endowment for International Peace, which held its first meeting in 1935 and began work upon the problem of the removal of trade barriers and monetary stabilization; it brought together men of great prominence and competence in business and economics.

S. H. Bailey in his *International Studies in Modern Education* points out that one of the "isolated instances" of research which had begun "to break down the rigid frontiers between law and politics by embarking upon studies of international organization and of the practice of the machinery of diplomacy" was the Union of International Associations whose publications "contained an impressive body of work of this kind."[41] Although research in international affairs was neither its exclusive nor primary aim, we will start this discussion with the Union of International Associations.

Union of International Associations

Established in 1910 at Brussels, the Union, representing the most ambitious effort to group international organizations, had an impressive early history. Its purpose was to establish permanent relations between international organizations and thus to assist their activities; to study all questions relative to the organizations—coordination, unification of methods which they had in common—and to promote cooperation between them in research, documentation, and extension of influence. Its membership prior to World War I grouped over two hundred *INGO's*. The principal tasks of the Union were:

> 1. Representation of the international organizations in a world Congress.
> 2. The determination of the legal, economic, and social status of international organizations and the status of the relationships between public and private international organizations.
> 3. The establishment of an International Center: a center of meetings, services, collections, offices; a scientific, educative, and documentary center constituted by a Foundation common to both the public and private international organizations and accessible to the public.
> 4. A systematic and permanent survey of international organizations, activities, and facts.
> 5. The coordination of the resolutions of International Organizations, the codification of these resolutions, their confirmation with or without amendments by the Congress of International Organizations; the passing

of general resolutions tending to summarize various resolutions on particular subjects, the passing of resolutions on neglected subjects, the formation of a general plan and common methods.

6. The formulation of scientific and encyclopedic conclusions, composed in a spirit of synthesis, on the most important questions of the different branches of knowledge, these conclusions to be subject to constant revision, codification, and coordination, in order to furnish, in all matters, recent, the best, and most authoritative conclusions.

7. The presentation of annual reports on the progress realized in all the fields of its activity.

8. An annual general debate at the Congress of International Organizations on the great present-day questions concerning the future of humanity and on which important recommendations might be made.[42]

However much one may sympathize with the purpose of the Union, its major aim of coordinating the activities of so many organizations with such diverse interests seemed to lack practicality. What can be useful is the grouping of *INGO's* which have specific common interests, combined with a close and cooperative relationship with the intergovernmental organizations working in the same fields. Such cooperation already has been well established, is constantly being developed, and will no doubt continue to become more and more important.

Among the Union's publications were two books, *Annuaire de la vie Internationale* (for 1908–09 and 1910–11) containing descriptions of numerous international organizations, followed by a periodical, *La Vie Internationale*, which appeared from January 1912 until the outbreak of the war in 1914.[43] This material still remains the best source for the structure and activities of the *INGO's* functioning at that time. The early significance and influence of the Union were described by H. R. G. Greaves as follows:

> If the League [of Nations] was born in the storm and havoc of war, it was conceived in peace during the early years of this century. Many movements went before it to prepare the way. Perhaps the most important of these was that which led from the establishment of the International Office of Bibliography at Brussels in 1895 to the Union of International Associations, which held its first World Congress in 1910. This was essentially an attempt to promote literary and scientific cooperation between peoples. Its pioneers were M. La Fontaine and M. Otlet. They organized the International Library and the International Museum at Brussels. The Union of International Associations was restricted to noncommercial bodies; it aimed at "a world organization founded on law, on scientific and technical progress, and on free representation of all the interests which are common to the human race." By 1914, 230 international societies belonged to it. Its interest in questions of education and intellectual cooperation is shown, to give but one example, by the resolutions passed by the Congrès Universel

de la Paix urging an "internationalization of education."* These looked toward a common plan of study, a much more frequent and easy interchange of students and professors, and an International University.

These currents of opinion have developed since the War in two directions —in the establishment of an International Summer University at Brussels and an Institute of Higher International Study both at Geneva and at Paris, and, secondly, in the creation—largely under the inspiration of M. La Fontaine—of the Committee for Intellectual Co-operation, which has also developed an Institute of Intellectual Co-operation at Paris and a Cinematographic Institute at Rome.

But in general it may be said that the Union of International Associations was one of the chief pioneers of the idea of a League of Nations. Its Congress proclaimed before the War that "a League of Nations was the ultimate end of all international movements." And in this sense the Brussels activities were not merely the precursors of the Committee on Intellectual Co-operation, they were responsible to a not inconsiderable degree for the materializing of the League itself. Their welcome of the League when it came into existence, and their readiness to subordinate their work to it, is additional evidence of their sincere support. "During the War the leaders of the Union drew up drafts of a Covenant and of the international constitution."†

The origins of the Intellectual Co-operation section, therefore, are intimately bound up with those of the League itself. The movements for bringing both into existence were intermingling and contemporaneous. To some extent the educational element was older. "If an intellectual life had not long been in existence," as M. Bourgeois said, "our League would never have been formed."‡ In consequence, the Intellectual Committee can claim over the League a certain degree of priority in conception, and even of parentage or responsibility in its immediate originators.[44]

Its work after World War I was not significant, and by 1938 the Union had few, if any, members. In spite of the claims of its officers, it had practically ceased to exist.

Institute of Pacific Relations

One of the most interesting associations, whose contribution to scientific investigation has been outstanding, is the Institute of Pacific Relations, founded in 1925, as a result of the initiative of the *YMCA*, with the object, "To study the conditions of life of the Pacific peoples with a view to the

---

* See Union des Associations Internationales, *Code des Voeux Internationaux,* i. 172, 4, p. 96.

† 14 c. 51 (Memorandum of the Secretary-General on Educational Activities). And see *Les Problemes Internationaux et la Guerre,* written by M. Paul Otlet in 1916, also his charter for a League, written in October 1914.

‡ 14 c. 48.

improvement of their mutual relations."[45] A more complete description of its purposes follows:

> Being an unofficial body it can have no part, nor does it seek a part, as mediator between governments. It passes no resolutions, makes no pronouncements. It does, however, aspire to serve the peoples of the Pacific countries and indirectly their governments by undertaking studies of economic, social and political problems, particularly those which seem chiefly to endanger the friendly relations of governments and peoples. As a means to this end, the Institute holds biennial conferences, promotes and coordinates research by other agencies, conducts research through its own Secretariat and endeavours to stimulate the mood of inquiry regarding Pacific problems on the part of the public generally.[46]

In 1938 the Institute, with headquarters in New York City, was composed of National Councils in twelve countries bordering on or having territory in the Pacific area. Its Conferences every two or three years brought together eminent economists, scientists, labor leaders, bankers, publicists, manufacturers, religious and social workers, journalists, and men who have held the highest governmental posts, (but government officials are excluded).[47] They have dealt with "the international bearings of such problems as the pressure of population upon food resources, differing standards of living as a cause of economic and political difficulty, foreign investments, tariffs, the problems of government of the dependent Pacific peoples, the machinery of international diplomacy, and the causes and consequences of . . . economic depression."[48] Prof. Quincy Wright has commented on the value of the Conferences in the following terms:

> However, the value of conferences of this type does not lie in the opinions which emerge but in the processes by which they are formed. This process involves, in the case of the Institute of Pacific Relations, long-time researches which assemble and publish new data and new points of view; preparation, distribution and reading of data papers focussing the results of research and experience upon concrete contemporary problems; discussion and comparison of attitudes at the round tables. To an increasing extent, since its first conference in 1925, the Institute of Pacific Relations has succeeded in integrating these processes. The participants understand the bases of opinions, although they may not agree, and they hope that this understanding may spread to a wider public and provide the necessary foundation for eventual agreement both of governments and peoples.[49]

Although not planned for action, the conferences have resulted in practical achievements. For example, the discussion on the Japanese exclusion law at the first meeting in 1925 had an important influence; an "experienced observer" is quoted in a publication of the Institute as stating, "It is not too much to say that the more patient attitude in Japan and the more generous attitude in America, ever since, can be attributed in large part to the discussions at this conference and their repercussions in the two countries." Also, it was said that discussions at the Honolulu Conference of the Institute in 1927, "opened up avenues which individual British and Chinese members were able to explore and which had undoubtedly resulted in a considerable improvement in the relations between Britain and China."[50]

The conferences of the Institute and its publications are based on research undertaken in part by the International Secretariat. However, "most of the work of the Secretariat is to act as the agent of the International Research Committee in determining which researches are most urgent and which national councils or universities should be asked to undertake them, under the general supervision of the International Research Secretary. Thus [by 1937], most of the thirty major projects . . . sponsored by the International Research Committee have been assigned to scholars in the countries most closely concerned."[51] The National Councils have often been granted financial help for research projects beyond their own resources. Such help is granted by the Pacific Council, the governing body of the Institute, upon the recommendation of the International Research Committee of the Institute.

The Institute has greatly stimulated research on Pacific problems in the member countries by financial grants, generally conditional upon local contributions of equal amounts, which often have made it possible to direct to Pacific studies funds available for research in these countries or to capitalize on a great volume of already well advanced research work, by encouraging individuals or institutions to publish the results of their studies, by liaison work leading to collaboration with other organizations, and at times by turning over projects initiated by the Institute to other bodies. During its first ten years (1926 to 1935) the International Research Fund of the Institute (contributed by the Rockefeller Foundation) expended about $340,000. The National Councils, affiliated groups, and the Pacific Council spent on research approximately $560,000 making a total of almost $900,000 on research alone.[52]

The Secretary of the American Council has stated that its membership in the Institute "greatly increases its opportunity to secure and distribute authoritative information, furnish Far Eastern contacts for Americans, or keep abreast of significant cultural and economic changes abroad which must modify the nature of its work at home."[53]

The Institute has published a magazine, *Pacific Affairs, I.P.R. Notes,* and numerous books (the 1936 catalogue and supplement of the publications of the Institute and the national Councils takes up forty-two pages). The published *Proceedings* of its Conferences have been highly praised. The first, which appeared in 1927, was declared by the *Manchester Guardian* to be "the most valuable contribution to Pacific literature in recent years"; later (1933), the *New York Evening Post* said, "For a summary of relationships among Pacific peoples, we can recommend nothing more highly than these biennial reports."[54]

Henry F. Angus in his *The Problem of Peaceful Change in the Pacific Area,* which is a study of the work of the Institute, states strongly the position that research, though essential, by itself can accomplish very little; that the findings of research on international issues must be made popular knowledge, for if national policies are based upon full knowledge, including consultation with other peoples, they are less likely to lead to conflict. For example, he points out that the prewar Japanese demand for opportunities of emigration were based on ideas easy to assume but difficult to prove, such beliefs as that emigration would be of economic benefit to Japan, that there was no preferable alternative, etc. A correct judgment, however, would have depended upon knowledge of the possibilities of land utilization, trends of population, possibilities of industrialization, effects of migration in the past, etc.[55]

He stated that the Institute within its own circle often had brought "international controversy into the atmosphere of scientific research," but, he added, "the Institute has, as yet, made no very determined effort to diffuse this atmosphere among the general public and to do well what the Press is often charged with doing badly, by making accurate information and its thoughtful interpretation widely available." He concludes his book with the statement:

> This, then, is the limit of the research work of the Institute of Pacific Relations. It has increased human knowledge of economic and social conditions. It has made it clear that human welfare demands international planning and that this planning would carry peaceful change with it. It has not established that there is likely to be any readiness on the part of existing political entities to commit themselves to a policy of planning, still less that the mass of popular opinion is likely to demand, encourage, or even tolerate such participation.[56]

However, it must be pointed out that the Institute has been eminently successful in its chosen field, which is to stimulate research on Pacific problems and to make the results of that research available. That in itself is a great achievement. But, the problem presented by Mr. Angus is, of course, one of the great problems of our time—how to get the knowledge of experts into general operation more quickly. The process is fairly rapid in such fields as chemistry, but exasperatingly slow in the social, political and international fields. The failure is not that of the Institute or any other *INGO,* but that of society as a whole.

International Studies Conference

The International Studies Conference has been operating in Europe as "a permanent organ of cooperation, liaison and coordination for national institutions engaged in the scientific study of international affairs." It endeavored "to develop a system of technical collaboration among its affiliated institutions and to organise collective research on specific problems in international relations." It was established in March 1928 on the initiative of and under the control of the League of Nations' International Committee on Intellectual Cooperation. However, in March 1934 the Committee declared the Conference to be autonomous and independent, and since then it has been responsible solely to its constituent members. The Institute of Intellectual Co-operation, however, continued to furnish its administrative services and bore the cost of the Conference's work. Before the war, the Conference met annually and dealt with such subjects as "The State and Economic Life," "Collective Security," "Peaceful Change," and "Economic Policies in Relation to World Peace." Much of the material presented to its conferences was published by the Institute of Intellectual Co-operation.[57]

S. H. Bailey in his *International Studies in Modern Education* evaluates the work of the Conference as follows:

> The International Studies Conference . . . has proved of peculiar value so far in two directions; first, in making scholars working in the same field known to one another, and, secondly, in helping to encourage the formation of institutions for the study of international relations in countries where none previously existed.
>
> The experiment with collective study, which may be defined as the preliminary study of a given problem simultaneously by groups of scholars in different countries leading up to a common discussion of its different aspects at the meetings of the Conference itself, has thrown into relief some of the formidable obstacles barring the way to successful intellectual co-operation. Some of these difficulties are technical and may be removed without great difficulty. More serious, however, are the divergence of intellectual method in different countries and the consequent difficulty of conducting a discussion in which progress is made towards both a clearer understanding of the problem in its different aspects and the establishment of agreement upon any general principles of conduct which the study of the subject may have suggested.
>
> It is possible that the regular association of scholars in biennial meetings may, little by little, smooth away the rougher edges of these differences, and the spread of familiarity in intellectual commerce forge a useful instru-

ment for international discussion. But the continuity of composition which would be required for this purpose would almost certainly prejudice the authoritative character of a conference discussing subjects demanding different competences or "expertises."[58]

The Conference was chiefly responsible for the creation of the *Centre d'Etudes de Politiques Étrangère,* the first and only prewar institution in France devoted entirely to research in international affairs; this is but one example of the influence of the Conference in the creation of such Centers. It also influenced already existing institutions to extend their studies beyond what they had originally planned.[59] Before the war, the Conference had been rapidly increasing both its membership and its influence, and had become perhaps the leading institution in Europe for the organization on an international scale of international studies.

Geneva Research Centre

The Geneva Research Centre, founded in 1920 by an American Committee, did not become international until 1936, when it expanded its activities considerably. In 1938 its membership consisted of fourteen individuals all of whom were holding high positions as professors, directors of institutes of international relations, members of the Secretariat of the League of Nations, Institute of Intellectual Co-operation, *ILO,* etc. Before the war, it was well known among students of international affairs for its highly competent studies, of which it had published a considerable number dealing with many aspects of international relations; it had awarded a number of scholarships, had held several conferences of experts, and had acted as a center of information and liaison with other research organizations.[60]

WOMEN'S ORGANIZATIONS

Many of the women's *INGO's* have devoted a large share of their program to the advancement of peace. We have seen evidence of this for such groups as the World's *YWCA,* the International Federation of University Women, the Associated Country Women of the World, the International Council of Women,[61] the International Alliance of Women For Suffrage and Equal Citizenship, and the Women's International League for Peace and Freedom. Such *INGO's* have helped to propagandize for peace, have helped in the training of women as workers for peace, and have provided strength in fighting for the adoption of pertinent measures both by intergovernmental agencies and by national legislatures. They strongly supported the League of Nations. The International Co-operative Women's Guild closely associated with, but not part of, the International Co-operative Alliance, was founded in 1921 at London. It had national organizations in twelve countries (1938). It arranged exchanges of visits and correspondence and campaigns for peace education and disarmament. On the other hand, the International Federation of Business and Professional Women, like the European Federation of Soroptomist Clubs, has promoted peace interests among professionally trained women. By 1938, after eight years of existence, this International Federation, with headquarters in New York City, had as members national organizations in twenty-four countries. It has helped in the dissemination of information and in the formulation and expression of policy to governments. Others which may be mentioned to illustrate still further bases of membership are the League of Mothers and Educators of Peace, the League of Jewish Women, and the Association of Slavic Women, all of which participated in disarmament campaigns. Since 1925 there has been in existence, at London, the Liaison Committee of Women's International Organizations which has served as a channel for discussion of common problems.

MEN'S SERVICE ASSOCIATIONS

Little can be said about the peace efforts of the men's service associations before World War II. Kiwanis International, founded in 1915, has been limited to the United States and Canada. The International Association of Lions Clubs, 1917, did not set up an International Relations Committee until 1937. The prewar policy of Rotary International, Chicago, founded in 1912, was to encourage its clubs (4,200 in eighty countries in 1938) to discuss international affairs, but it itself did not advocate any particular policy. The international secretariat provided material for these "international service programs." Although not concentrating its efforts on a study of world affairs, Rotary has contributed something to international good will. It enabled men of different nations to meet in an atmosphere conducive to the development of understanding and friendship and has taught that "Leagues of nations can only function when they have the sanction and support of leagues of men living in various lands, animated by similar purposes, and drawn into mutual confidence by a common understanding, fellowship and good will."[62] Also, through its "Intercountry Committees" of Rotarians from clubs in two or more neighboring countries, quietly and without publicity, efforts were made to solve problems which were disturbing relations.

One organization whose efforts deserve special attention is the Inter-Allied Federation of Ex-Service Men, *FIDAC*, from its French title.

Inter-Allied Federation of Ex-Service Men

FIDAC came into being in 1920, with headquarters at Paris. Composed in 1938 of sixty-five veterans' associations of eleven countries with a total of eight million members, *FIDAC* was described in 1937 by Bernhard Ragner, Chairman of its Propaganda Committee, as "a volunteer fire department for Europe." He stated that *FIDAC* had brought to a peaceful conclusion some twenty difficulties, which if left alone might have imperiled the peace of Europe. He quotes Edward Benes, then President of Czechoslovakia, as saying of *FIDAC,* "Your peace work is incomparably more effective than that of the diplomats." One instance of *FIDAC's* peace work, described by Ragner, was the creation of better relations between Italy and Jugoslavia, where in 1928 frontier incidents had inflamed passions and created a dangerous situation. *FIDAC* summoned the leaders of the Jugoslav and Italian ex-service men to a meeting in Paris, where a plan of action was decided upon. "The Jugoslav delegation, returning home, arranged for a series of informative talks to be delivered throughout the entire nation by the Jugoslav Associations of Reserve Officers and World War Volunteers. In Italy, the Italian Section of *FIDAC,* by means of calm, factual, conciliatory articles in the press, was able to effect a gradual change in public opinion." This effort was continued in both countries for over a year and when the *FIDAC* congress assembled in Belgrade in September 1929, the Italians and Jugoslavs were able to congratulate each other on their mutual success.

The Italo-Jugoslav trouble, however, broke forth afresh in 1934 and feelings were so bitter that the Italian delegation refused to attend the *FIDAC* congress in London. Nevertheless, Jean Desbons, the newly elected President of *FIDAC,* "visited Italy and Jugoslavia; he had long heart-to-heart talks with their ex-service leaders; he contrived practical ways for getting them together . . . it took time, tact, patience and faith, but in the end Desbons succeeded. Slowly but perceptibly, the newspapers of each country ceased their recriminations; one wise, pleasant, friendly phrase provoked another on the other side, and by degrees the atmosphere of hostility disappeared." Finally, a meeting of Italian and Jugoslav war veterans was held in Belgrade where an agreement was signed embodying means for putting into effect "the policy of the good neighbor." Ragner, writing in 1937, states that this document "marks the official beginning of the present Italo-Jugoslav friendship. Never have Jugoslavia and Italy been on such amicable terms as today."[63]

Ragner states that Franco-Polish relations (upset by trouble over Polish workers in France and French capitalists in Poland) were improved by similar action and that, "Franco-Polish statesmen were able to bring to a successful termination the work started by members of *FIDAC.*" General Edward Smigly-Rydz, head of the Polish state, praised *FIDAC* for the "essential role" it had played in making possible an accord between the two countries.

When, in January 1935, "a Franco-Italian treaty of friendship was signed in Rome, both Benito Mussolini and Pierre Laval publicly acknowledged that this accord was 'the work of the ex-service men of the two countries who have never ceased to prepare public opinion for its acceptance.' Unfortunately the Ethiopian war . . . again cooled Franco-Italian friendship."[64]

FIDAC acted too in bringing about the Italo-British agreement signed in Rome on April 16, 1938, which was said to have removed "a constant danger to world peace." (In it Britain agreed to recognize Italian sovereignty over Abyssinia and the Italians made certain concessions regarding their action in the Spanish Civil War and the reduction of their forces in Libya.) In accordance with a resolution of *FIDAC's* Peace and Foreign Relations Committee, the President of this Committee, beginning when League of Nations sanctions against Italy went into effect, made various representations to governments urging a peaceful solution. He later requested representatives of the British, Italian and French National Sections to meet; they urged "an honourable solution of the Italo-Ethiopian conflict." A delegation called on Prime Minister Laval, who promised that if Mussolini would agree to withdraw some of the troops from Libya, he would use his influence to get the British to withdraw some of their ships from the Mediterranean. This was accomplished within a week.[65] In retrospect this achievement does not appear to have contributed to peace; it was, however, a sincere effort and in line with the thought of the time.

Ragner states:

> In this and other ways less dramatic but equally useful, *FIDAC* has carried the message of peace across international boundaries. In addition, it has organized let's-get-acquainted visits to eleven countries for 250,000 Allied veterans, "escorting" Poles to France, Czecho-Slovakians to Rumania, Canadians to Belgium, and so forth. It has also originated and managed 227 reunions between allied ex-service men, of the face-the-facts variety; the dominant aims were to keep reverently the memory of the comrade dead, and to review with impartiality current problems. Finally, perhaps its most far-reaching achievement, it has carried its peace-is-possible gospel to youth, to its sons and daughters, by means of special courses, destined to promote good will between nations, given in some 250 educational institutions scattered about Europe (and America).[66]

Beginning in 1925, it endeavored to establish friendly relations with the ex-service men of the Central Powers, and in this cooperated first with the left groups of German ex-soldiers and later, when the left groups were abolished, with the Nazi organization. In 1935 *FIDAC* decided that an international association to include ex-service men of all the belligerent

(World War I) countries should be organized not only to promote peace between former enemies but also generally to defend peace. The new organization, the International Committee of Ex-Service Men, came into being in 1937, with the President of *FIDAC* as its first head. *FIDAC*, of course, continued as a separate organization.[67]

In 1938 Henri Pichot, President of the French veterans' organization, criticized severely the peace education work of *FIDAC* which was inclined, he says, to prefer social functions rather than "dry discussions and the necessary confrontations." Its peace efforts, he acknowledged, "permitted and favoured . . . happy conjunctions tending to calm public opinion, and this is not without merit," but, he adds, "to tell the truth the doctrine of peace of the *FIDAC* has gradually thinned down with years. The desire of peace remains, and nothing else. And indeed, how is it possible to preconise means for peace, to censure, even respectfully, the ruptures of pacts and aggressions by word of mouth or not, without provoking collisions, dangerous to the very life of the Federation?" He charged that the desire for unanimity and the fear of losing members resulted in weak resolutions.[68] *FIDAC* did not survive World War II.

INGO'S OF AND FOR YOUNG PEOPLE

Much has been done by *INGO's*, between both wars, to promote international friendship and understanding among young people and, particularly, to train them as workers for peace—with the view in mind that such work would exert a potent influence on the "international relations of the future." Two approaches were widely utilized, the international exchange of correspondence and the establishment of international camps. S. H. Bailey in his study gives credit to the International Junior Red Cross Society for initiating "collective or group correspondence between schools in different countries"; (in 1936, 7,472 such exchanges took place under Junior Red Cross auspices).[69] The World's Alliance of *YMCA's* receives credit for having organized, in 1925, the first postwar international camp for older boys from the nations which had been at war with each other (twenty such camps were held in Europe up to 1936). The Alliance also organized the first Pacific Area Older Boys' Camp-Conference in 1929, which met in Japan.[70] Other groups which organized camps were the International Student Service, the International Boy Scouts and Girl Guides Bureaux, the International Confederation of Students, and the International Federation of Camping Clubs.

An interesting example of the influence of such international camps follows: In 1913 José Maza, a law student from Chile, attended the International Student Camp of *YMCA's* of South America at Piriápolis, Uruguay. The last evening in the farewell talk for his delegation he stated that the ties of friendship made at the camp should not be broken, and he gave his word of honor that if he gained influence he would use it to bring about a peaceful settlement between his country and Peru, whose relations had been strained for years. It is said that, "About ten years later a protocol was signed in Washington between the two nations, which was the first in a series of steps that finally led to the solution of the 'problem of the Pacific.' It was before the Chilean Parliament for ratification and was on the point of being lost for lack of sufficient majority—not on its merits but for the internal political party situation. But Dr. José Maza was now a powerful figure in the House of Deputies, and he threw all the weight of his personal prestige and influence into the struggle and succeeded in rallying a sufficient number of votes regardless of party lines to pass the measure. . . . So he redeemed his pledge to his friends of the Piriápolis *YMCA* Camp." (Letter from secretariat, April 21, 1938, enclosing copy of letter from P. A. Conrad, Federacion Sudamericana de Asociaciones Cristianas de Jovenes, March 25, 1938.) The letter continues, "Dr. Maza is a national Senator, has been a Minister on the Cabinet at various times, is author of the present Constitution of Chile. The above story has been told in a public meeting with Dr. Maza present, and he has accepted it as true to the facts."

The international organization of the Boy Scouts, founded in 1920, and of the Girl Scouts, 1928, represents another approach. Located at London, the Boy Scouts International Bureau representing, in 1938, Scout Associations in forty-five countries, with a membership of more than two million Scouts, has done much to promote international friendship through its World Jamborees and through cruises and visits of Scout troops from one country to another. The Jamborees have brought together as many as fifty thousand Scouts from forty-two nations (1929); twenty-eight thousand Scouts from thirty countries attended the 1937 Jamboree.[71] Throughout all these activities the idea of international friendship, regardless of race, creed or class, has been emphasized. Also located at London, the World Association of Girl Guides and Girl Scouts, which in 1938 had full member organizations in twenty-seven countries and "Tenderfoot members" in six countries, has acted in a similar way. Neither organization, however, promotes particular international policies, nor do they engage in the study of international problems.[72]

Still other approaches were the promotion of "Goodwill Day" by the Junior Red Cross, "Children's Peace Sunday" by the World's Sunday School Association, "Youth Sings Over the Frontiers" by the International Broadcasting Union.[73]

Concerning the training of youth as peace workers, we need to recall the work of a number of the religious organizations, that of several of the women's organizations, and the youth activities of the International Federation of League of Nations Societies. However, the World Youth Congress which this group brought into being in 1936 was indeed short-lived. To this should be added the peace activities of the Joint Committee of the Major International Associations and those of the International Student Service, an outgrowth of the European Student Relief of the World's Student Christian Federation.

Joint Committee of the Major International Associations

This Joint Committee was created in 1925, with headquarters at Paris, by action of the International Institute of Intellectual Co-operation, at the request of a number of international associations, especially the International Council of Women.[74] In 1938 it grouped about thirty *INGO's*, including some of the most influential, and among them *INGO's* in the fields of international relations, education, social service, and religion. It was devoted to promoting the idea of better international collaboration, especially among young people. Although closely associated with the official International Institute of Intellectual Co-operation, it was "exclusively responsible to the Major International Associations which it serves as a common organ." Its primary function was "to ensure a certain coordination of thought and efforts between these associations of such varied tendencies."[75] Its 1936 Report states, "In a word, both by their large membership in every country and by the diversity of their respective aims, the Major Associations grouped together in the Joint Committee can rightly be regarded as one of the most authoritative expressions of world opinion."[76] In the field of peace education, this report describes the work of the Joint Committee as follows:

> From time to time . . . the Joint Committee formed sub-committees and specialized study groups composed of representatives of the associations more particularly interested in the visits of young persons to foreign countries, in school textbooks, films, broadcasting, literature for juvenile readers, unemployment among young people, etc. For each of the problems which they investigate, these groups draw up a statement setting forth, firstly, the general principles that seem to meet with the approval of the majority (in most cases they are unanimously endorsed), and, secondly, the chief results already obtained, followed by an indication of those which it would seem possible to obtain in the near future. These statements are communicated to the associations and their principal international congresses for approval and then brought to the notice of the League of Nations and Intellectual Co-operation Organisation in the annual report of the Joint Committee
>
> Since 1932, the February plenary session has been held in close contact with the International Institute of Intellectual Co-operation, that is to say

the Director of the Institute and some of its principal officers explain to the Joint Committee the essential items of the educational programme adopted for the current year by the International Committee on Intellectual Cooperation, and indicate the points for which that Committee hopes to secure the moral support and effective collaboration of the associations. The associations, for their part, freely state their views and wishes.

This procedure has proved to be useful and creative, but owing to the fact that on the one hand, the Joint Committee is engaged in a collective effort made conjointly by the different organs of the League of Nations and by various private organisations, and, on the other, that it possesses no executive organ—for it can only submit suggestions to its member associations and possibly to other unofficial organisations—it is not always easy to determine exactly what results can be attributed directly to is own efforts.[77]

Of the various problems tackled, the Joint Committee possibly achieved its best results in effecting more widespread distribution of literature about the League of Nations and a greater use of educational films, in securing a wider appreciation of the seriousness of the problem of unemployment among young people, and in promoting travel for young people. [78] Concerning its study on films, the Report states:

Its influence on public opinion undoubtedly contributed to the drawing up of the Convention on the international circulation of educational films, adopted by the Diplomatic Conference in the autumn of 1933 and already signed by a large number of States.[79]

Concerning the promotion of travel for young people, the Report indicates that the Committee's program achieved a considerable coordination of the activities of the affiliated associations, and states:

. . . most of the Joint Committee's recommendations have been accepted. The railway and shipping companies have granted considerable reductions. Tourists associations and firms, as well as official and private international organisations, do all they can to promote tours for young people.[80]

International Student Service[81]

The *ISS* held quite a number of study conferences between university people of different countries to discuss general international problems. For example, a series of international conferences was organized in 1936–37 on "The Breakdown of the 1919 Peace Settlement and the Rebuilding of Peace in Europe." Also, an annual course for students of journalism was held in Geneva to acquaint student journalists from various countries with the information and press services of the League of Nations and the *ILO*, and to discuss the responsibilities of journalists in relation to international affairs. The Service was able to secure eminently qualified people to speak before these conferences, and it was generally recognized that the conferences of *ISS* were extremely well run. *ISS* also contributed to international understanding and education through study-tours, work-camp exchanges, and lecture tours of its international secretaries.[82]

ISS also organized relief work for students whenever such aid became necessary.[83] In 1934, following the socialist uprising in Austria, it aided some two hundred working class students who "had been in receipt of scholarships from organizations which were, for political reasons, dissolved."[84] It raised $112,000 in the years 1933–1936 to help German refugee students, and up to 1937 about 2,500 students applied for assistance other than financial aid and for information on recognition of completed courses, professional openings, possibilities of residence and naturalization. Financial help to continue academic studies was given only to the most brilliant; others were assisted in getting started in professions or manual work. Other kinds of aid were given—securing free hospitality, supplying introductions, negotiating with authorities for residence permits, securing reduction of university fees, etc.[85] Its student relief work helped to promote international understanding.

PART III

RELATIONSHIP OF *INGO'S* WITH INTERGOVERNMENTAL ORGANIZATIONS

RELATIONSHIP OF INGO'S WITH INTERGOVERNMENTAL ORGANIZATIONS

SUFFICIENT EVIDENCE has been presented in Part II to prove that private international organizations exert an extensive and significant influence on both national governments[1] and intergovernmental organizations. We have seen this influence at various stages, (1) in relation to diplomatic conferences—in the decision to convene such a conference, in the preparatory and research work essential for its success, in the actual proceedings, and in the results achieved by the conference; (2) in the founding of intergovernmental organizations (in this part we shall examine still more cases of this influence); and, (3) in affecting the activities and policies of such organizations. We have seen this influence in connection with various administrative bodies and in relation to the work of the League of Nations and its allied organs. This relationship has ranged from the agreement between the International Red Cross and the official International Relief Union, under which the international non-governmental organization (*INGO*) provided the "permanent and central services" for the official body,[2] to the action of the League of Nations Institute of Intellectual Co-operation which furnished the "permanent and central services" for two *INGO's*, the Joint Committee of the Major International Associations and the Committee of International Students' Organizations. Since in this study of the prewar influence of *INGO's* their relationship with the League of Nations system is of special import, we will examine it still further, and then look also to see what the future role of *INGO's* can be vis à vis the United Nations.

In the establishment of intergovernmental organizations, the *INGO's* at times have performed the function of precursor while at other times it has been their initiative that has spurred on official action to create an intergovernmental body. For example, the International Bureau of Education, the Institute of Refrigeration, the International Sugar Office, the International Tin Committee, all evolved from non-governmental organizations, while the International Union for the Protection of Literary and Artistic Works, the International Union for the Protection of Industrial Property, the International Relief Union, the International Institute of Agriculture are all examples of intergovernmental bodies whose establishment was due to the demand of private groups.

The International Institute of Refrigeration was converted to an intergovernmental body by a convention in 1920.[3] The International Sugar Office would not have come into being if it had not been for the work of the International Sugar Committee, which, besides promoting the general idea of the international regulation of sugar, prepared much of the material for the diplomatic conference which established the Office. As we have already seen in our discussion of cartels, the Tin Committee came into being when the private Tin Producers Association was unable to enforce the restriction of production, and as a result of its appeal to governments the official agency was established.[4] On the other hand, the International Bureau of Education came into being because of the success of its private forerunner. In 1925 the Rousseau Institute of Geneva founded the private Institute of Educational Sciences, which in 1929 was composed of about four hundred dues-paying members and about seventy odd national and international organizations. According to the 1936 Annual Report of the Rockefeller Foundation it had had "remarkable success." On July 25, 1929, it became the intergovernmental Bureau of Education. Some of its leaders, particularly M. Pedro Rosselló, who later became assistant director of the Bureau, felt that it would be desirable to transform the *INGO* into a governmental organ for several reasons: (1) It was felt that as a private organization the Institute was duplicating the work of the World Federation of Education Associations; (2) there was no intergovernmental organization concerned with education; (3) after becoming governmental, it could concentrate on the educational authorities, leaving the teachers for other organizations to deal with; (4) a governmental organization would be able to secure a more adequate financial support. The success of the private organization, in spite of limited funds, in showing what could be done and the need for such an organization certainly were important factors, however, in its transformation into a governmental organization. In passing, it is interesting to note that at the time of the author's visit to its headquarters, the officials expressed the opinion that the Bureau was as free under governmental direction as it was when private. The reason advanced was that the Bureau was dealing with education objectively, that is, concerned with the collection and publication of information and not with political matters. If it had been acting otherwise, it would have found itself very much hampered by governmental control. If, for example, it had attempted to promote certain particular educational ideas, it could have operated successfully only as an *INGO*.[5]

Concerning the intergovernmental bodies mentioned above which owe their existence to the demand and initiative of *INGO's:* The first draft convention for the establishment of the International Relief Union was prepared by the legal adviser of the League of Red Cross Societies, which played an important part also in getting the matter presented to the governments through its national societies.

William Kaufmann in his lectures before the Academy of International Law at The Hague in 1924 summarized how private international action led to the establishment of the Unions for the Protection of Industrial Property and for the Protection of Literary and Artistic Works. He stated that among the items on the agenda of a private international congress held at Paris in 1878 was the "question of creating an International Union of States for the protection of industrial property." This congress "established a permanent commission and an executive committee which took up the matter with the French government and drew up, at the latter's request, a proposed convention for such an international Union." The French Government in 1880 convoked an official conference at Paris which "prepared on this basis another proposed convention, the Convention setting up the Union for the protection of Industrial Property." This Convention was finally "signed at the second official Conference, at Paris on March 20th, 1883, by eleven States."[6]

Kaufmann adds that, "Following the example of what had been done in regard to industrial property," in 1878 the Association Littéraire et Artistique Internationale (founded in Paris in 1878 under the auspices of Victor Hugo for authors of all nationalities) "for the purpose of ameliorating the protection of literary and artistic property . . . elaborated in 1883, during a conference held at Berne, a proposed convention for an International Union of Literary and Artistic Property. The Swiss government to which this project had been transmitted, convoked the first diplomatic Conference at Berne in 1884, then two others followed in 1885 and 1886. The result was the Convention creating the International Union for the Protection of Literary and Artistic Works . . . signed at Berne, September 9th, 1886 by ten States."[7]

M. Mintz points out that the Association "has throughout done valuable propaganda work for the protection of author's rights at thirty-seven congresses in different countries and, in cooperation with the interested groups, has taken an active part in the extension of legislation on such matters. The further development of the Berne Convention is also largely due to its efforts and the voice of the Association has always carried decisive weight in the legislation adopted in various countries."[8]

We have seen in Part II how much *INGO's* contributed in paving the way for the League of Nations and its related organs: for example, the contribution of the international law societies and the Inter-Parliamentary Union in laying the foundation for the World Court; the important role played by labor in the creation of the *ILO;* the influence of the International Federation of Trade Unions in the founding of the Nansen International

Office for Refugees which, of course, also had the backing of other international associations in the religious and social welfare fields; the influence of the international peace organizations in the creation of the Institute of Intellectual Co-operation and the League of Nations itself. In fact, the efforts of all *INGO's* for the establishment of techniques and procedures for international collaboration deserve mention.

It should be noted that we have described a number of *INGO's* which owe their establishment to the influence of intergovernmental bodies: the International Institute of Statistics, which succeeded the International Congress of Statistics, the International Agricultural Co-ordination Commission, which was created by the International Institute of Agriculture, and the International Studies Conference, the Joint Committee of the Major International Associations and the Committee of International Students' Organizations, which all came into being as the result of the work of the Institute of Intellectual Co-operation. It might be possible to discover other cases in which intergovernmental organizations have taken an important part in the establishment of *INGO's*. However, on the basis of the evidence available to the writer, it appears that official action in establishing *INGO's* has not been very important, while *INGO's* have been decidedly influential in the establishment of intergovernmental bodies. A careful study of each of the hundred or so intergovernmental bodies now in existence would probably bring to light other cases, in addition to those mentioned above.

RELATIONSHIP OF *INGO'S* TO THE LEAGUE OF NATIONS SYSTEM

Personal connections between the League of Nations and the *INGO's* were numerous. The League invited *INGO's* to send representatives to League committees, conferences, etc., and the League itself was often officially represented at the international conferences of the private organizations. In addition to this type of formal relationship, there were many indirect connections. Official delegates to the League's Assembly were often prominent in the activities of *INGO's*[9] and in many cases members of the League Secretariat were closely associated with *INGO's* as were many experts appointed to serve on special League Committees. Here are a few examples of the relationship which existed, by no means complete nor the most significant, for throughout Part II of this book many detailed cases of *INGO* participation in League activities are to be found.

The Communications and Transit Committee of the League of Nations was in constant collaboration with other international organizations. Eight *INGO's* were invited to send representatives to the nineteenth session of the Consultative and Technical Commission on Communications and Transit. From February 1936 to June 1937 the Communications and Transit Section of the Secretariat was represented at twenty-two meetings sponsored by twelve *INGO's*.[10] The Committee on Social Questions of the League had nearly twenty international associations as "corresponding members." The International Federation of League of Nations Societies was represented on the League's Advisory Committee on League of Nations Teaching.

As a result of the joint effort of the women's international organizations to secure positions for women on League committees, they obtained a representative on the League's Commission on Traffic in Women, on the committee for child welfare, on the commission of inquiry into the position of women in the Orient, on the commission dealing with slavery, and on the Saar plebiscite commission.[11]

The League of Nations Committee on Statistical Methodology was nominated jointly by the League and the International Institute of Statistics and "the recommendations put forward by the Committee were submitted to the general conferences of the Institute before circulation to the Member States for their consideration."[12] In 1924 the Council of the League of Nations appointed Professor Pittard, on the nomination of the International Red Cross Committee and the League of Red Cross Societies, as administrator of the relief funds granted to Albania by the League.[13] When, in 1933, the High Commission for Refugees coming from Germany was set up by the League, the International Student Service was made "officially responsible for the student section of the work, and Dr. Walter Kotchnig, the former General Secretary of *ISS,* was made a Director of the Commission." *ISS* relations with the High Commission were thus "particularly close" and *ISS* was "represented on its advisory Council, and on the special committee set up in 1934 to deal with Academic Refugees."[14]

About eight *INGO's* were invited to the League conference held in Java (1936) to consider the problem of the traffic in women and children in the Far East. The international transport workers organizations were regularly invited to designate representatives to take part in the general Conferences of the League's Communications and Transit Organization. Berenstein mentions a number of other organizations which also were represented in these Conferences and states they enjoyed extensive rights, "not only the right of speaking, but also of presenting, in the same manner as other participants in the Conference, propositions to be voted upon."[15] Although these organizations could not vote, we have come across a number of cases (see particularly the International Chamber of Commerce) where *INGO's* were given voting rights equal to those of governments.

The Assembly and Council of the League "never officially heard the representatives of private organizations, but the presidents of each body . . . on a number of occasions invited the representatives of [*INGO's*] to present their point of view. On these occasions other members of the Assembly or Council [were] often present."[16] For example, it was an annual event for the International Federation of League of Nations Societies to present to the President of the Assembly of the League of Nations the resolutions it had adopted at its annual conference.[17]

The writer was unable to secure any complete information on the number of private conferences at which the League officially was represented, but the following statement from a League publication will illustrate how widespread this participation was and the attitude which governed this relationship:

> A wide field of liaison is maintained with unofficial organisations dealing with some aspect or other of League problems. International and national societies—political, commercial, economic, medical, social—are kept informed of League developments of interest to them, and there is a well-developed system of exchanges. Members of the Secretariat attend conferences in all parts of the world for the purpose of giving and gaining information. They are not able to express opinions or to take part in decisions, but they can often usefully draw attention to facts bearing on the subjects of discussion and can acquaint themselves with facts and trends of opinion of which the League should be aware. Secretariat officials have attended meetings of the International Chamber of Commerce, the Inter-Parliamentary Union, international women's organisations, the Institute of Pacific Relations, the Institute of International Relations, international education conferences, international law meetings, international students' organisations, the Imperial Press Conference, the International Federation of Journalists, the international organisations of ex-soldiers, the Federation of League of Nations Societies, etc.[18]

There were still other types of connection between the League and *INGO's*. On various occasions the League requested an *INGO* to secure needed information. In addition to the illustrations given elsewhere, the League asked the World's Alliance of *YMCA's* to prepare a report on the work of the Associations of certain countries in the campaign against narcotic drugs.[19] The League Assembly of 1935 requested eight international women's organizations to prepare reports on the status of women throughout the world. These reports were published by the League.[20] Also, *INGO's* were known to present information (for example, on child welfare) which was not available to the League (because the governments concerned would not forward it) and of a nature which the League would have preferred not to receive. And, there are cases also where officials in the League approached an *INGO* with the suggestion that it start a public campaign for a particular proposal. For example, the writer was told that the European Central Bureau for Inter-Church Aid was approached with a request that it launch a campaign for an Assyrian national home. Such a campaign would have given the League officials a pretext for taking up the problem. One relationship which was most important concerned the activities of *INGO's* regarding ratification of League conventions. For example, the League's Convention of 1931 for limiting the manufacture and regulating the distribution of narcotic drugs needed twenty-five ratifications by April 13, 1933 in order to go into force. The League Assembly of 1932 was about to cancel the appropriation necessary for the carrying out of the Treaty, apparently on the assumption that it would never go into effect, when an appeal to retain the appropriation was made by a number of international Christian organizations in Geneva. As a result, the appropriation was retained.[21] Also, the author is convinced that without the energetic action taken by *INGO's* the Convention would never have gone into effect. The work of the Inter-Parliamentary Union was particularly effective in this respect, and the writer has seen convincing evidence from official sources (which he is not at liberty to name) that the Universal Christian Council for Life and Work influenced several governments to ratify the Convention.[22]

The League, on the other hand, helped private international organizations and made concessions to them on various occasions. For example, it granted certain privileges concerning the use of the League Library and provided "special facilities at League of Nations meetings for duly accredited representatives of unofficial organizations" at the request of the Federation of Private and Semi-Official International Organizations Established at Geneva.[23] In the early days the League subsidized the publication of the "Code des Voeux et Resolutions des Congrès internationaux" by a grant of £1,500 to the Union of International Associations.[24] The resolutions of *INGO's* were often printed in official publications of the League of Nations. For example, the resolutions of the International Federation of League of Nations Societies were printed in the Official Journal or the Journal of the Assembly year after year.[25] In its documents, the League published yearly summaries of the activities of some seven organizations concerned with penal and penitentiary problems, with which the League, by decision of the Assembly in 1931, maintained close contact. Among these were the International Law Association and the International Association of Penal Law.[26] Most important, however, was the fact that association with the League helped and influenced many a private international organization. For example, the connection of International Federation for Aid to Young Women with the social work of the League, particularly representation on the Committee on the Protection and Welfare of Children and Young People, led to the following significant statement:

> [Our Federation] has not ceased . . . to be represented each year at the session of this Committee, where it has had the opportunity of making known to the government representatives all the services which a preventive work like ours can render against the white slave trade. It is also a means of affirming ourselves and of making contacts with other associations to secure greater coordination of work. We do not hesitate to say that our participation in the work of the League of Nations has opened a new era for us. We have had to enlarge our scope of activity and to occupy ourselves more or less closely with many questions new to us. Furthermore, our official collaboration with governments in the Committee has given us a certain prestige in relation to the public.[27]

Generally speaking it can be said that the early League attitude toward the private organizations was one of wholehearted cooperation. For example, in 1921 the Secretary-General of the League of Nations actually wrote a *Memoire* entitled, "The League of Nations and the Union of International Associations" in which he praises the Union and its founders.[28] This was soon followed by a more reserved attitude under which there was nevertheless a considerable amount of cooperation and liaison. However, in the last few years before the outbreak of war there appeared a growing tendency on the part of the League to withdraw from collaboration with private organizations.

Bertram Pickard, who spent many years in Geneva in close touch with both official and nonofficial international organizations, commented on the first stage of this development as follows:

> In an interesting publication of the Geneva Research Centre entitled *The League of Nations and other International Organisations* (Geneva Special Studies, Vol. V, No. 6, 1934) Prof. Pitman B. Potter writes as follows on unofficial organisations:
>
> "In one sense it is here that private initiative and variation can and should be given full rein. On the other hand, the extravagant amount of duplication, subdivision and recombination, multiplication and disappearance, of organisations, often without good cause, which goes on in this field, seems to cry aloud for regulation."
>
> At one time it seemed as though the League of Nations itself might become the chief regulating influence. Under Article 24 of the Covenant it is provided: (1) that all existing international bureaux "established by general treaties" (*i.e.* official bodies) shall be placed, if the parties desire, under the League's direction; and (2) that all new bureaux of this kind shall in any case be placed under League auspices of one kind or another. It will

be seen that no specific reference is made to *unofficial* international organisations. Nevertheless, in the early optimistic days of the League, an extensive interpretation was given to Article 24, witness the fact that on June 27th, 1921, the "Council decided . . . to make it possible for the patronage of the League to be given to all international bureaux," under certain conditions. Two years later, however (July 1923), the Council, at its twenty-fifth Session, reversed this decision, decided that Article 24 could only apply to official (*i.e.* intergovernmental) bodies, and gave as reason that "it is not desirable to risk diminishing the activity of these voluntary organisations, the number of which is fortunately increasing, by even the appearance of an official supervision."

It may be doubted whether the pleasure of Council members or of the higher Secretariat officials, at the increasing number and activity of the private organisations was in fact as unqualified as appears.[29]

No lengthy discussion of the relations between the League and *INGO's* during the second stage is needed here, for that has been amply covered already. However, two points may be made which have not yet been noted. First, the point that Bertram Pickard makes that "helpful cooperation" was given by "some Secretariat Services—notably the International Bureaux Section," but the most helpful was the "generous cooperation given by many individual members of the Secretariat who [were] alive to the advantages of an offensive-defensive alliance between the International Civil Service, debarred from open advocacy of policy, and the unofficial organisations, often insufficiently informed of facts without which policy cannot be accurately devised and pursued."[30] Secondly, it should be noted that the success or failure of particular *INGO's* in developing their relations with the League in the final analysis depended upon their power and influence as well as upon the aims which they were pursuing. A good illustration of this was the strong influence of the International Chamber of Commerce on the League as compared with the lack of influence of the International Co-operative Alliance. (See p. 31.)

An official of wide experience, in discussing with the writer in 1937 the relations of *INGO's* with official international organizations, made some very interesting comments, the significance of many of which is to be clearly seen in the discussion of individual *INGO's* in Part II. He stated at the time that: (1) Private organizations do not specialize enough. (2) Those that are specialized should undertake research not done officially and send the results to the official organization concerned. This, he said, was rarely being done at the time. (3) The unspecialized organizations, which often have greater influence and a wider constituency, should work with the specialized ones, giving them every possible support. (4) Private organizations rely too much on resolutions. The resolutions by themselves are not sufficient. Concrete proposals should be made. (5) The private organizations should keep the official agencies regularly informed by bulletins and by personal contacts. They should not be satisfied by merely asking for information and inquiring how they can help. They should express their own desires and know what they want. (6) They should be more active in informing the public in general and their own constituency in particular regarding international problems and their desires concerning them. (7) They should take every means to increase their prestige; they should protest when neglected and not show themselves too easily pleased by a little attention. They should not so readily accept the position of inferiors. They should be more conscious of their own power.

In the latter years of the League's existence, we find considerable dissatisfaction among the *INGO's* regarding what they considered to have been a growing tendency of the League to withdraw from collaboration and cooperation. This tendency may have been due to the fact that as certain ways of doing things became firmly established, officials became more and more reluctant to accept proposals which would upset the established routine or which would mean additional work. Furthermore the League was avoiding action with regard to political problems; therefore, the insistence of *INGO's* that action be taken was very irritating. Events had gone so far as to lead some officials of *INGO's* to state that they felt that the League wished to have as little as possible to do with private organizations. Even the International Chamber of Commerce felt that the League was less interested in having its cooperation than had previously been the case. The author in his interviews met this attitude over and over again.[31]

One example, in a typewritten statement of the World's *YWCA*, dated December 6, 1937, of this attitude is as follows:

> The League of Nations Committee on Social Questions until last year was composed of Government delegates and also of Assessors who represented certain voluntary organisations. . . . These Assessors were not able to vote but had all the rights and privileges of membership possessed by the Government representatives. . . .
>
> They were able: (1) To bring to the direct notice of the Committee, and there ultimately to the Assembly of the League of Nations, the views of the interested public in the various countries on the questions dealt with on the Agenda. (2) These Assessors were able to initiate discussion upon questions of the utmost importance. . . .
>
> In 1936 this Committee was reorganized because it had become unwieldly and for other reasons. As a result the Committee now consists of *Government representatives* only . . . but when a particular subject is to be studied one or more assessors may be nominated because of his or her special experience and qualification. . . .
>
> Instead the former assessors and some twenty-two international organi-

sations, carrying on social work of an international character, were invited individually to become *Correspondent Members* of the Committee for a period of three years. . . .

Since these developments the feeling has grown on the part of a number of the organisations which formerly were directly or indirectly represented on the Committee that:

1. No longer is public opinion expressed in the Committee by persons who are in *close contact with practical work*. Up to now only a few Governments have sent trained social workers to this Committee, in a number of cases representatives have a very limited knowledge of the questions to be discussed.

2. Nothing more is heard of the Annual Reports—whereas they were formerly discussed in Committee and questions of importance emerged from them. To rely on Governments' reports today is inadequate. They require the effective action of public opinion, so that progress may be made.

3. That it is by no means easy to assist in carrying out the decisions and recommendations of the Social Questions Committee.

It was pointed out that the combined pressure of the voluntary organisations interested in fighting the Traffic in Women and Children had brought about since 1922 a remarkable change in the situation. Hence the question arose as to whether or not it would be wise for the voluntary organisations to initiate some sort of Liaison Committee to strengthen and coordinate their efforts.

The relations of *INGO's* with allied organs of the League should also be noted, the closest and most extensive having been with the *ILO*.

Nansen International Office for Refugees: The International Red Cross, the "Save the Children" International Union, the World's Alliance of *YMCA's,* and to a lesser extent the Alliance of Reformed Churches throughout the World holding the Presbyterian System, and other *INGO's* had important although not continuous contact with the Nansen Office. For example, the International Red Cross Committee was able to obtain for the Nansen Office documents for refugees from Russia which the Office was unable to secure by itself or through its connections with the League of Nations, such documents as birth certificates, diplomas or certificates for doctors and other professional people, without which the refugees would have been unable to obtain work. The Red Cross Committee handled hundreds of such cases for the Office and in the fall of 1937 had fifty cases on hand. The League of Red Cross Societies helped to maintain the health of refugees in transit or in the process of settling, and the other organizations provided funds and other services.[32]

International Institute of Intellectual Co-operation:[33] As we have seen, the International Institute of Intellectual Co-operation maintained close working relations with a number of private organizations. For example, the agreement it established in 1937 with the International Council of Scientific Unions, under which the Council acted as adviser to the Institute and the Institute agreed to consult the Council on all scientific problems submitted to it; the secretariat services it performed for the Joint Committee of the Major International Associations and the Committee of the International Students' Associations; the special activities it undertook at the expressed wishes of private groups—the publication of a list of Vacation Courses for the International Confederation of Students in 1927,[34] its study of the problem of coordinating secondary education, on the request of the Advisory Committee for Intellectual Workers of the International Labor Office and the Committee of International Students' Organizations,[35] its establishment of the International Bureau of University Statistics on the request of the students' and other organizations in order to secure information needed for dealing with the problem of unemployment in the intellectual professions.[36]

Permanent Court of International Justice: Article 66 of the rules of the Court provided "that notice of the requests for consultative opinions shall be given to such international organizations as the Court or the President thereof shall decide"; such organizations could come "before the Court to express their point of view."[37] Private international organizations were not excluded. In the case determining the competence of the *ILO* "to propose legislation which, in order to protect workers, incidentally regulated the same work when done personally by the employer," the World Court sent a notice of the case to the International Federation of Industrial Employers, the International Federation of Trade Unions, and the International Federation of Christian Trade Unions. These private associations, except the last, sent memoranda to the Court and all three sent representatives to furnish information.[38] According to Berenstein in his labor study, in at least four cases labor organizations were asked to give their opinion: "The *IFTU* was represented for the Consultative Opinions, Nos. 1, 2, 13, and 50; the International Federation of Christian Trade Unions in Nos. 1, 13, and 50; the International Federation of Christian Landworkers in No. 2; and the International Landworkers' Federation in No. 2."[39]

International Labour Organization: The *ILO* in the prewar years served as a center of the great network of both governmental and non-governmental international organizations concerned with labor, social and humanitarian matters. In contrast to the League of Nations it would seem that the *ILO* constantly maintained a friendly, one might say "democratic," attitude toward the private organizations. It sought their collaboration and valued their support. It encouraged its Secretariat officials to join and take an active part in their work. This policy evidently created a very sympathetic and often enthusiastic attitude toward the *ILO*, for, in talking to officials of *INGO's* about the *ILO*, the writer came across none of that resentment so often evident when they spoke of their relations with the League of Nations. Also, this policy resulted in widespread support from these private groups which proved to be the most important element supporting the *ILO* in the prewar years and contributed to its lasting vitality in contrast with the moribund state of the League in the later nineteen thirties.

The very Constitution of the *ILO* pulled *INGO's* into its work. It was the provisions for workers and employers representatives on both its Governing Body and at its Conferences which made it possible for the International Federation of Trade Unions to play such a prominent part in the *ILO*,[40] enabled the International Federation of Industrial Employers to take a similar, although not so influential part,[41] and permitted the International Shipping Federation to play its limited role.[42]

It should be emphasized that within the *ILO* the labor and employer representatives have complete equality of status with representatives of governments. This direct and "official" representation made it easy for the labor organizations to influence the trend of *ILO* policy. On the whole, it can be said that it has been the workers' representatives who have always pushed for change, that the employers' representatives, while not always obstructive, usually preferred the status quo[43] and that the government representatives have held the balance of power. These, in voting, have usually sided with the workers. From various interviews, the author has gathered the impression that the employers, not being able to secure as much cooperation among themselves, envy the discipline of the workers' group in presenting a united policy on *ILO* questions. However, as we have seen in detail, the employers do make preparation for "a common attitude," and as Francis Graham Wilson has stated, "The solidarity of the workers is reflected in the solidarity of the employers, though it must not be forgotten that both groups perceive that compromise is necessary for common action."[44]

Another channel through which the *ILO* maintained close working relations with *INGO's* in the prewar period was its Intelligence and Liaison Division, which Howard Ellis in his League study described as follows:

> The Intelligence and Liaison Division includes the Library of the Office, but exists for keeping in touch with national or international organizations of employers, workers, cooperative societies, League of Nations unions, etc., that are interested in the International Labour Organization. This division, with the Press service, fulfills approximately the functions of the Information Section in the League Secretariat, but differs from the

latter in that it exists as much to receive information from these bodies of interest to the Office as to impart knowledge to them.[45]

The *ILO* owes much to *INGO's* for ratification of its Conventions, and furthermore, as we have seen, the labor organizations particularly accepted the responsibility of gathering information on infringements within the countries, and the labor delegates at the Conferences "furnished with a more or less abundant documentation," have been able "to place the representatives of a defaulting country in a difficult position."[46]

We may conclude that the *ILO* before the war was an example of an intergovernmental organization largely dependent for its existence on the continued support of one private organization, for it is no exaggeration to state that if the International Federation of Trade Unions had decided to cease cooperation with the *ILO,* that Organization would have become a lifeless shell, if indeed it had been able to exist at all. The *ILO* has been conscious of what it owes to *INGO's* and they, particularly the labor and social groups, on the other hand fully realize the great importance to themselves that the *ILO* continue as a vital, active organization for it embodies their very aspirations.

INGO'S AND THE UNITED NATIONS

The most significant official recognition of the importance of *INGO's* is to be found in Article 71 of the Charter of the United Nations. This Article reads as follows:

> The Economic and Social Council may make suitable arrangements for consultation with non-governmental organizations which are concerned with matters within its competence. Such arrangements may be made with international organizations and, where appropriate, with national organizations after consultation with the Member of the United Nations concerned.

It was on the 21st of June 1946 that the Economic and Social Council, in accordance with Article 71, put into effect arrangements for consultation with non-governmental organizations. These arrangements, as since modified, went further in extending to non-governmental organizations opportunities for the presentation of their views than have ever been granted to such groups by any national government. The United Nations thus began a great experiment in relations between the governmental and the non-governmental aspects of society—an experiment which was intended to bring to the United Nations public opinion as expressed by the organizations set up by the people themselves according to their different professions, vocations and interests, and which was also intended to make available to the Council the expert technical advice and information which many of these organizations had acquired through long years of work on particular economic or social problems. The United Nations thus took a great step forward toward the establishment of a true and full democracy on the international level.

Among the principles guiding the determination of eligibility for "consultative status" are: "The organization shall be concerned with matters falling within the competence of the . . . Council with respect to international economic, social, cultural, educational, health and related matters and to questions of human rights," its aims and purposes "shall be in conformity with the spirit, purposes and principles of the Charter," it "shall be of recognized standing and shall represent a substantial proportion of the organized persons within the particular interest field in which it operates," it "shall have authority to speak for its members through its authorized representatives" and "shall be international in structure with members who exercise voting rights" (national organizations may be admitted in exceptional cases).

There are three categories of organizations in consultative relationship:

(a) Organizations which have a basic interest in most of the activities of the Council, and are closely linked with the economic or social life of the areas which they represent (to be known as organizations in category A);
(b) Organizations which have a special competence in and are concerned specifically with only a few of the fields of activity covered by the Council (to be known as organizations in category B).
(c) Other organizations, not in continuous consultative relationship, but entered on the "register" of the Secretary-General for the purpose of *ad hoc* consultations.

An up-to-date listing of the organizations in category A or B status is to be found in the appendix.

The *INGO's* in categories A and B and on the register have the right to send their authorized representatives to attend the meetings of the Council and its Commissions. These representatives have ample opportunity to engage in private discussions with government representatives. The organizations in categories A and B may submit written statements which are distributed as official documents to all Members of the United Nations and to the specialized agencies. The representatives of these organizations have on many occasions made oral statements to the Commissions. They also have the privilege of expressing their views to the Council on the report of a Commission, or on other matters, through the Council Committee on Non-Governmental Organizations, which is composed of the President of the Council and seven members of the Council. This type of consultation is arranged if the Council or the Committee or the organization so requests. The Committee may recommend that the Council or a committee of the Council receive the representatives of organizations in category A for the purpose of hearing their views.[47]

An *INGO* in category A has additional privileges. It may ask the Committee to request the Secretary-General to place an item on the provisional agenda of the Council. The Committee then takes into account the adequacy of the documentation, whether or not the item "lends itself to early and constructive action" and the "possibility that the item might be more appropriately dealt with elsewhere than in the Council." A decision of the Committee not to grant the request is final. If the request is granted the organization concerned may present its views through its representative at any meeting of the Agenda Committee at which the question of the inclusion of the item is discussed. (The Agenda Committee recommends to the Council what its definitive agenda should be.) Category A organizations may also propose items for the provisional agenda of the Functional Commissions of the Council; these items are included if accepted by a two-thirds majority. The Economic Commission for Latin America and the Economic Commission for Asia and the Far East (but not the Economic Commission for Europe) may also accept items proposed by category A organizations. When the Council or a committee of the Council discusses an item which was originally proposed by a category A organization its representative is entitled to make "an introductory statement of an expository nature" in support of the proposal. If it is so decided, the representative may make in the course of the debate "an additional statement for the purpose of clarification."[48]

In addition to the consultative arrangements with the Economic and Social Council, *INGO's* may send written statements on matters before the General Assembly, the Security Council, and the Trusteeship Council. Lists of non-official communications are prepared and circulated and the communications themselves may be seen by any interested member of these organs of the United Nations. The Trusteeship Council may and does, in fact, often examine petitions from non-governmental organizations in trusteeship territories which allege that the government of the territory in question is not fulfilling its obligations toward the peoples concerned.

For *INGO's* without consultative status, there are special facilities, which may also be utilized by the consultative organizations. A special Section for Non-Governmental Organizations has been set up in the Department of Public Information, which accredits "observers" of non-governmental organizations which are "able to act as a clearing-house for information, or undertaking information programs through lectures, publications, or other means calculated to develop public understanding of the United Nations." The "observers" are granted special facilities for attending meetings, securing documents, and using the Library of the United Nations and are invited to special "background conferences on the activities of the United Nations and the specialized agencies."[49]

Some of the specialized agencies of the United Nations, such as *UNESCO,* the *ILO,* the World Health Organization, also have procedures for consultation with *INGO's.* A list of the *INGO's* recognized by the specialized agencies is to be found in the appendix.

Thus, the facilities for *INGO's* to function in relation to the United Nations have been greatly advanced over those provided by the League of Nations, and a stronger link exists between official effort and organized public opinion in the establishment of international cooperation. The detailed role of the *INGO's* under the United Nations must be left for later consideration; here we can give only a short general survey of what these organizations have done and can do to assist the United Nations in the economic and social fields.[50] One great field is the promotion of respect for, and universal observance of, human rights and fundamental freedoms for all. This is considered first because the concept of human rights is at the very basis of the United Nations, which exists to serve the peoples of the world, and because human rights are related to and deeply affect all aspects of life.

The Universal Declaration of Human Rights was proclaimed by the General Assembly of the United Nations on December 10, 1948, without a single dissenting vote. The preamble states that "recognition of the inherent dignity and of the equal and inalienable rights of all members of the human family is the foundation of freedom, justice and peace in the world," that "the peoples of the United Nations have in the Charter reaffirmed their faith in fundamental human rights, in the dignity and worth of the human person and in the equal rights of men and women and have determined to promote social progress and better standards of life in larger freedom," and that the "Member States have pledged themselves to achieve, in cooperation with the United Nations, the promotion of universal respect for and observance of human rights and fundamental freedoms." The Declaration is proclaimed "as a common standard of achievement for all peoples and all nations, to the end that every individual and every organ of society, keeping this Declaration constantly in mind, shall strive by teaching and education to promote respect for these rights and freedoms and by progressive measures, national and international, to secure their universal and effective recognition and observance." This noble document is now being translated into all languages and distributed throughout the world. A high standard has been set and everywhere the poor and downtrodden will lift up their heads and demand that their rights, as proclaimed by the highest international authority in the world, be respected. By this act alone the United Nations has justified its existence and repaid to the peoples of the world their investment in it. The role played by the non-governmental organizations in the endeavor to achieve human rights has been and will continue to be of immense importance: without their support the Declaration could hardly have come into being; without their continued efforts the rights proclaimed therein will never be respected.

The broad field of human rights on which the United Nations is working includes, however, not only the Universal Declaration of Human Rights but also the Covenant, now being prepared, which, when ready and ratified by governments, will be legally binding. There is also the Genocide Convention, unanimously adopted by the General Assembly in December 1948, providing that individuals, even the rulers of States, must be tried and, if guilty, punished for this crime. Work is also going on for the prevention of discrimination and the protection of minorities, for the upholding of trade union rights, for the abolition of forced labor, for freedom of information, and for equal rights for women.

In all these matters the non-governmental organizations have played a great role. It was largely through the influence of American organizations at the San Francisco Conference on International Organization that the promotion of universal respect for and observance of human rights was given a foremost place among the aims or purposes of the United Nations. The Charter furthermore specifically provided that a Commission on Human Rights should be established by the Economic and Social Council. This is particularly significant since the Charter, with this one exception, leaves the question of establishing commissions entirely in the hands of the Council. Dr. Charles Malik, former President of the Council and a member of its Human Rights Commission, has stated that the tendencies at San Francisco leading to these results were "greatly aided by reasoned pressure from certain powerful non-governmental organizations."

It will now be explained, with particular reference to the Declaration on Human Rights, what the organizations with consultative status have done.

In the first place, they have worked out and presented ideas in advance of official action. The first international bill or charter of human rights was drawn up in 1929 by an *INGO*. This organization, however, has never applied for and, therefore, does not have consultative status. Two of the consultative organizations have also drawn up international bills of human rights, one of which appeared in 1939 and the other in 1947; these documents, although they were but a few among many sources of ideas, had an important influence.

Early in 1946, another organization, even before it acquired consultative status, distributed a suggested program of action for the Commission on Human Rights. An interesting comparison may be drawn between these suggestions and the actual duties of the Commission as later determined by the Economic and Social Council.

In the second place, a number of these organizations have sent their representatives day after day to attend the meetings of the Human Rights Commission. There they have, in numerous oral statements, presented to the assembled representatives of governments the views of their organizations. Let us take the fifth session of the Commission as an example. At that session, which lasted from May 9 to June 20, 1949, eleven different organizations spoke a total of twenty times. In addition to these formal statements, the representatives of these organizations engaged in hundreds of conversations with government representatives and with officials of the United Nations Secretariat for the purpose of presenting their views, both giving and receiving information.

One organization even released its "international law advisor" to enable the United Nations Secretariat to employ him in preparatory work for the Human Rights Commission.

In the third place, twenty-eight consultative organizations have presented nearly a hundred written communications on human rights which have been issued as official documents of the United Nations. In addition, many letters in reference to human rights have been sent.

One of the organizations set up a special panel of distinguished authorities to assist it in the preparation of studies on human rights, which when ready were communicated to the Economic and Social Council.

Another organization presented both a preliminary and a final report of many pages prepared by one of the leading international lawyers of the world.

As Dr. Malik said, "many non-governmental bodies, especially church groups (Roman Catholic, Protestant, and Jewish)—showed the keenest interest [in the work of the Human Rights Commission] and, in many instances, contributed actual texts." Some of these communications have been recognized by the Human Rights Division of the UN Secretariat as representing great technical competence.

Fourthly, the organizations through their national branches have expressed their views directly to the member governments, requesting their support.

Fifthly, the consultative organizations have carried on an educational campaign among their own members and the general public. This has effectively stimulated widespread interest in and support of the human rights program of the United Nations. When the Declaration was adopted the General Assembly invited the "non-governmental organizations of the world to do their utmost to bring this Declaration to the attention of their members." The organizations, not content with simply informing their members, will undoubtedly do more than this. They have already made great efforts to educate people everywhere in the world to respect the high principles which have been proclaimed.

One organization, for example, has distributed over twenty-seven thousand copies of the Declaration. Two organizations working together have prepared a study guide designed to stimulate discussion, which contains many suggestions on how respect for human rights may be promoted.

Another has kept 175 church leaders in fifty-five countries fully informed of all matters relating to human rights by sending them many carefully prepared memoranda.

Yet another took the lead in forming a group of non-governmental organizations which considers cases of the violation of human rights and decides what action may be taken. In a number of cases the international officials of these organizations have traveled extensively calling attention to the problem and urging effective action.

Many organizations have adopted resolutions in their international conferences in support of the Declaration, and in their publications have urged that it be studied and respected.

By these and other efforts the non-governmental organizations having consultative status have truly earned the high praise of the Human Rights Division of the United Nations Secretariat, which has stated in regard to certain organizations, which cannot be named, that they have "contributed a great deal to the work on the Universal Declaration of Human Rights," that they have sent memoranda and letters "which are stimulating and helpful," that the Division is "grateful" for the publicity work they have done, and that their continued collaboration "is highly desirable."

This brief discussion has been primarily related to the Universal Declaration. The field of Human Rights is, however, a broad and vital one and other points need to be mentioned.

A considerable number of women's organizations have been concerned, among other matters, with the work of the Commission on the Status of Women. They have, in fact, watched with the closest attention all activities of the United Nations which might affect the status of women and have been quick to express their views. These efforts have not been fruitless—the working of the Universal Declaration on Human Rights, for example, always uses such expressions as "all human beings," "everyone," or "no one," making it unmistakably clear that women as well as men are covered by its provisions.

They have also, among other things, supplied suggestions and information in relation to the questionnaire on the status of women which was sent by the United Nations Secretariat to the member governments.

A Jewish organization submitted a number of communications on the situation of the Jewish people in the Arab countries. Hearings on this question were held by the Economic and Social Council's Committee on Non-Governmental Organizations. The representatives of various Arab countries as well as the representative of the organization spoke at these hearings. A resolution on the matter was passed by the Economic and Social Council. The organization to which reference is made is convinced that this action exercised an important influence in improving the situation of minorities in the Middle East.

Organizations have been particularly concerned that the right of individuals and organizations as well as of governments to petition the United Nations in regard to alleged violations of human rights should be recognized. Until recent years it has always been maintained that violations of human rights were a matter of purely domestic concern, that is to say, not within the jurisdiction of international law nor of intergovernmental bodies. This old theory has been broken down as far as governments are concerned, as is shown, for example, by the action of the General Assembly of the United Nations, which has discussed alleged violations of human rights by several of the member countries. The proposal to grant the right of petition to individuals and organizations goes even further. This matter is still under consideration.

Finally, it should be mentioned that certain non-governmental organizations have submitted items relating to human rights which the Economic and Social Council has placed upon its agenda: items on the protection of migrant and immigrant labor, on forced labor and measures for its abolition, on trade union rights, and on equal pay for equal work for men and women workers. Thus attention has been drawn to matters of vital concern to millions of human beings, long discussions have taken place, and conventions open to ratification by governments have been prepared or are in the course of preparation. An example is the Convention on Freedom of Association, protecting the right of workers to organize, which was prepared by the International Labour Organization at the request of the Economic and Social Council in 1948. It will take time, but these initiatives of the non-governmental organizations with consultative status may in the end lead to very important results.

Leaving the subject of human rights, we now turn to the social welfare program of the United Nations which is developed by the Social Commission, a subsidiary body of the Economic and Social Council. This Commission is working out concrete measures to deal with such matters as child and family welfare, prevention of the white-slave traffic, penal reform, housing and standards of living. These are the matters which, next to human rights, have attracted the greatest attention from the *INGO's* having consultative status with the Economic and Social Council. The work of these organizations in relation to this social welfare program may be placed under the same five headings which were used above in speaking of their work in relation to the human rights program. Let us take up each of these five points, giving a few concrete examples of what the consultative organizations have done.

The first point is that they have worked out and presented ideas in advance of official action. Only one of many instances will be mentioned. The Social Commission is now working on a proposed Charter of the Rights of the Child. One of the basic documents used in this study is the famous Declaration of Geneva on the rights of the child, formulated in 1923 by an organization which now has consultative status.

The second point is that the consultative organizations have sent their representatives to the meetings of the Social Commission. These representatives have made during the last three sessions of the Commission a total of thirty-five formal statements before the Commission itself. They have also engaged in many private conversations with representatives of governments and with United Nations Secretariat officials. As an example of personal assistance, let us mention the Secretary-General of one of the consultative organizations, who helped in the preparation of a proposed convention for the suppression of the traffic in women, and who received from the Secretariat a strong letter of appreciation.

The third point is the presentation of ideas and suggestions in writing. Almost forty such communications in this field have been issued as official documents. This number does not of course include the far more numerous letters and memoranda addressed to the Secretariat. These have included such important matters as studies on the impact of war on juvenile delinquency, one on practical measures to stimulate, educate and guide public opinion in order to promote modern methods in the prevention of juvenile delinquency and in the treatment of offenders; a proposed program of action for the United Nations in regard to prevention of crime and the treatment of offenders, a study on short-term imprisonment, and one on probation. In addition, information on social service schools, on methods of training social workers and on family aid measures has been supplied, as well as a synoptic table indicating for various countries, colonies, territories, etc., the present situation regarding the regulation of prostitution. It is interesting to note that an investigation into the effects of modern contacts on African family life and marriage customs is now being made by another of the consultative organizations. A number of these studies have been especially prepared at the request of the United Nations.

The fourth point is that the national branches of these organizations have often influenced the attitudes of their governments toward questions dealt with by the Economic and Social Council.

The fifth point is that these organizations have carried on an educational program among their own members and for the general public, including publications, the adoption of resolutions by international conferences, talks given by the members of these organizations, and so forth.

In addition to these and many other important actions of a similar character, certain other matters relating to the social welfare field should be mentioned. One of the organizations, for example, has offered to take the lead in coordinating the activities of *INGO's* interested in the field of protection for migrants. This organization, with some technical help from the United Nations, did the preparatory work for a conference which met in Geneva. Another organization proposed that a conference of *INGO's* interested in the prevention of crime and the treatment of offenders should be called. The United Nations took up this suggestion and as a result a conference attended by five *INGO's* with consultative status and one intergovernmental organization met in Paris under United Nations auspices on October 15 and 16, 1948. This conference led to an agreement among the organizations represented, including the United Nations, for collaboration and coordination of their activities in this important field.

At least two of the organizations having consultative status have acted for the United Nations in the actual distribution of foodstuffs and in giving other relief to Palestine refugees.

We should not forget to call to mind the great contributions made by national organizations in forty-six countries and thirty territories in support of campaigns in aid of the United Nations Appeal for Children. During 1948 over thirty-five million dollars was raised, a substantial part of which went to the United Nations International Children's Emergency Fund. Many of the national organizations which took part in the campaign are affiliated with the *INGO's* having consultative status, which did a great deal to stimulate their national branches to support this campaign.

We now pass on to what consultative organizations have done to assist the United Nations in its work for the improvement of international transport and communications. Here again we find that the same five points might be mentioned. Instead, however, of repeating them we will mention only a few specific instances in which the organizations have been helpful. In April 1947 the United Nations held a meeting of experts to prepare for a World Conference on Passport and Frontier Formalities. The non-governmental organizations submitted much preparatory material and contributed to the discussion at the meeting. Another example of helpful action was the submission of an item for the agenda of the Transport and Communications Commission. This item on "Barriers to International

Transport of Goods" was accompanied by a report on these barriers which was transmitted by the Commission to the Members of the United Nations. Another organization sent data on transport visas and frontier formalities. This information was considered so useful that the Transport and Communications Commission gave a vote of thanks to the organization and requested that it should submit a similar report to the next session. During August and September of 1949, the United Nations held an important conference in Geneva for the purpose of drawing up new conventions on road traffic. This conference had become necessary because the regulations contained in the prewar conventions relating to international road traffic had become largely obsolete. A number of organizations with consultative status, some of which had been working for many years, already had to their credit significant achievements in lowering barriers to international road transport. These organizations, familiar with all the problems involved because they represented the automobile associations and organizations of road transport users, were able to furnish much technical information and advice regarding such matters as frontier formalities, drivers' licenses, safety rules and regulations such as those relating to brakes, lights, and road signs. For these reasons, the United Nations Secretariat has expressed its appreciation of their cooperation and has emphasized the importance of close liaison between their officials and those of the United Nations who are engaged in the preparation of studies in the same or related fields.

The next field in which the organizations have been helpful is the economic one. Here also the organizations have carried on all the types of activities which have been previously mentioned. Among the particular items which might be mentioned is the special study being made by one of the organizations on the coordination of the work of the many offices, agencies and organizations presently active in the sphere of standardization.

The non-governmental organizations have contributed to the fiscal work of the United Nations in several ways. Their national branches have, for example, in certain cases, prepared comprehensive statements on the tax treatment of foreign enterprises, information which the governments needed for the work of the Fiscal Commission. The organizations have also sponsored research on subjects under study by the Fiscal Commission, such as reciprocal administrative assistance among tax administrations in the assessment and collection of taxes and international double taxation of estates. Finally, these organizations have put before the Fiscal Commission, either orally or in writing, their views, ideas and suggestions on various fiscal matters. Regarding the assistance given by the non-governmental organizations in relation to the statistical work of the United

Nations, it may be mentioned that one of the organizations has undertaken a program of education and training in statistics in collaboration with the United Nations and the United Nations Educational, Scientific and Cultural Organization. As part of this program the organization is sponsoring a permanent educational institute in Calcutta. Other non-governmental organizations have shown a spirit of cooperation by contributing statistical data to the United Nations.

Among the economic matters dealt with by the United Nations there is one in particular which we will be hearing about for many years to come. This question, which has suddenly risen to great prominence, is President Truman's Point 4, otherwise known as technical assistance for the underdeveloped areas. It has become clear that with a small amount of help the economically underdeveloped areas of the world can greatly increase their production and raise the standard of living of their peoples. It has also become clear that a low standard of living, wherever it may exist, holds back the progress of even the most advanced areas and leads to social unrest.

The United Nations, which at the General Assembly held in Paris during the fall of 1948 had already initiated this work, has recently decided to take it up on a greatly increased scale. The role of the United Nations will be largely to plan, to advise, and to coordinate, that is, to make the arrangements through which this technical assistance can best be provided. The United Nations will draw to a large extent on private industry and non-governmental organizations having expert knowledge in one field or another for help in this program.

Non-governmental organizations of both a profit and a nonprofit-making character have, of course, for many years been active in spreading throughout the world knowledge of a most varied nature essential to economic development. This knowledge has related to everything from standardization of mechanical equipment to methods of preparing governmental budgets and from the management of specific industrial enterprises to the collection of statistics.

There will be occasions when the United Nations will gladly turn to these organizations to draw upon their long experience for ideas and information which can greatly assist the planning officials of the United Nations. These organizations may also help by informing their members of the needs of the underdeveloped countries in order to create a favorable climate for the reception of proposals designed to promote economic development so that those types of technical assistance most likely to be fruitful may be offered. They could, for example, study the report of the United Nations Mission to Haiti in order to understand the types of continuing technical aid which may be needed. The organizations may also promote and assist in the setting-up of actual operating establishments. These might take the form of factories, agricultural enterprises, cooperative societies, health work or any other kind of practical demonstration of modern methods on the spot. Many such efforts might arise out of a study of the technical assistance program. These demonstrations would not only be beneficial in themselves, but if properly managed, would have an immense value in showing the people concerned how the adoption of new methods would improve their living standards. Of course, many such practical demonstrations are already in operation. What is needed is more of them and a greater effort to spread throughout the underdeveloped areas knowledge of the advanced methods they use.

At the present time the General Assembly of the United Nations has before it not only the technical assistance program but also the question of action to achieve or maintain full employment and economic stability. This last question arose from the initiative of a non-governmental organization which proposed it as an item for the agenda of the Economic and Social Council. The consultative organizations have presented various reports bearing on both these matters and have thus contributed to an understanding of the problems involved.

A few general remarks which do not relate specifically to human rights, social welfare nor any of the other subjects discussed above may be added.

A well-rounded presentation requires mention of the fact that too high a proportion of the organizations granted consultative status by the Economic and Social Council have made little or no use of the opportunities which have been theirs. In some cases they have been financially unable to do so; this is unfortunate. In other cases they have failed to realize the importance of the opportunity which has been open to them; this is deplorable. In still other cases they apparently were interested only in the prestige which attaches to the grant of consultative status.

Then there are organizations which appear to be promoting the special interests of the groups they represent. This is not unuseful, as the Council should have before it the views of all important elements of public opinion. Nevertheless, every organization should consider whether the promotion of the general interest would not, in the long run, be a greater service to their members, who are all members of the world community. Surely we all should understand by now that the state of the world is of primary importance, since it determines the very course of all our lives.

But, these criticisms in no way detract from the great contributions made to the United Nations by the consultative organizations. The faith of those who believed in the consultative process has been fully vindicated.

To give an idea of how important consultative work is considered by some of the organizations, it may be pointed out that one of them was represented at more than eight hundred days of United Nations meetings in one year. From October 1946 to June 1, 1949, this organization was represented at ninety-five sessions of United Nations bodies, not counting seventeen sessions of specialized agencies bodies. Just to list the attendance of this organization, that is to say, the names of the bodies attended and the names and positions of the persons representing the organization at these sessions, takes thirteen typewritten pages. This organization also submitted thirty communications to the Economic and Social Council, some of which were of considerable length. Finally it established special offices, both in New York and Geneva, for the purpose of carrying on its consultative work. Another organization employed an expert to make a special study which was published under the title "Coordination of Economic and Social Activities." This study was considered to be of great value by many representatives of the Member Governments. Another organization set up what it called an "Observer-Consultant Team" composed of six members. The members of this team were asked to keep in mind the following objectives:

(a) To understand the scope and *modus operandi* of the Economic and Social Council, the various organs and agencies related thereto.

(b) To identify the subjects and issues of the greatest relevance to the organization they represented.

(c) To locate materials, ideas and emphases that should be channeled to the national organizations belonging to the international non-governmental organization.

(d) To evaluate the United Nations efforts and advise how they could be strengthened through the cooperation of the organization or as to how attempts could be made to modify and improve them.

(e) To counsel with the governing body of the organization as to the contribution it might make to the United Nations through studies and research, indicating attitudes, or any other ways.

We should also mention the activity in which many of the organizations engage which is directed toward stimulating thinking and action at the national or even local level on the issues before the Economic and Social Council. One organization, for example, has held for a number of years a summer school with lectures on these activities. It has also held seminars for teachers. Another organization prepared a 152-page booklet entitled "The World at Work" which describes in detail the economic and social activities of the United Nations. This booklet has gone out in tens of thousands of copies and it is expected that it will be used in many schools as well as by the local clubs affiliated with the organization.

So far we have cited many ways in which the organizations have been helpful to the United Nations. However, probably the most important way in which they have been helpful has not yet been mentioned. The United Nations is working for the economic and social welfare of humanity. The international non-governmental organizations are also doing this and their activities along these lines, even when they are not related directly to the work of the United Nations, nevertheless constitute a contribution to the success of the United Nations which cannot be overestimated. It should also be pointed out that we have omitted any discussion of the work done by these organizations in relation to the specialized agencies of the United Nations such as the United Nations Educational, Scientific and Cultural Organization, the World Health Organization, and the United Nations Food and Agricultural Organization. In addition to all this we have no more than mentioned the work done by the consultative organizations, and many others without consultative status, in encouraging schools to teach about the United Nations and in assisting the Department of Public Information to inform the public on all matters concerning the United Nations.

It is clear that the non-governmental organizations and the United Nations have the same general interests. If they work together in the closest possible cooperation there can be no doubt, to paraphrase the United Nations Charter, that succeeding generations will be saved from the scourge of war which twice in our lifetime has brought untold sorrow to mankind, that fundamental human rights will be respected, and that social progress and better standards of life for all will be achieved.

As has been indicated, we have already progressed far along the road toward this complete cooperation. If it is asked what the organizations should do to help the United Nations the answer would be that they should do what they have done—that they should keep it up. It might be added that all men of goodwill should support these organizations in order that they may be strengthened and thus be better able to contribute to the great task of creating a truly peaceful world which is common to the United Nations, the governments and the peoples of the world.

CONCLUSIONS:
PARTNERS FOR PEACE

WE HAVE tried in this volume to present an over-all picture of the influence of international non-governmental organizations (*INGO's*) on world affairs. From this survey some important conclusions may be drawn.

Teaching of International Relations. Students of international affairs traditionally have been "officially" minded, that is, largely concerned with the relations between states or governments, their struggle for power and their conflicts. The expression "the international mind" has, in fact, meant the "official international mind." The development of the kind of mind which leads one to think of the relations among groups of people of different nationalities and how they may promote their common interests has been neglected. In this connection an interesting parallel can be drawn between the study of government and the study of international affairs. Some decades ago, political science was largely confined to the study of the structure, powers and duties of the legislative, executive and judicial branches of the government. However, as time went on it became evident that careful consideration of political parties is necessary for the understanding of government. Later still, political science was expanded further to include the study of what the political scientists call "pressure groups," *i.e.,* the chambers of commerce, trade unions, churches, farmers' organizations and other like bodies which exercise a tremendous influence on the course of legislation. It is now generally recognized that no government, no political party, nor indeed the life of any country where such groups operate, can be understood without careful study of their activities and influence.

The writer believes that this book shows the need for a similar expansion of the study of international relations to include the international non-governmental organizations. These *INGO's*, taken as a whole, constitute a great unexplored continent in the world of international affairs.

The following concrete suggestions may be offered:

(1) Teachers can help their students to become conscious of the fact that when they join any organization not of a strictly local character, either as students or in later life, they probably belong to a world organization which groups together peoples of many countries; and that they can, by working through these organizations, contribute greatly to better inter-

national relations and the progress of humanity. In almost every community such organizations as the Red Cross, the Boy and Girl Scouts, the *YMCA,* the *YWCA,* the Chamber of Commerce, trade unions, the local cooperative society, and churches may be found. These organizations are the channels through which every citizen can enter and affect the main stream of international life.

(2) Students should be informed that, no matter what lifework they may choose, there is an international non-governmental organization already working in that field which they can help and from which they can gain a great deal.

(3) Young people who are interested in a career within the field of international relations should be aware that the non-governmental organizations as well as the intergovernmental organizations offer great opportunities for the highly qualified.

(4) A great deal of effort is being given to the promotion of the teaching of the principles and activities of the United Nations in our schools. This teaching usually fails to inform the students of the relations between the United Nations and non-governmental organizations and how through these organizations the individual can contribute to the success of the United Nations.

(5) International relations clubs, study conferences, and model General Assemblies, or better yet, model Economic and Social Councils should not neglect the role of the non-governmental organizations.

(6) Many students visit Europe during the summer months. They could be put in touch with the international organizations dealing with subjects of interest to them, either to attend their conferences or to visit their headquarters.

(7) Graduate students writing theses on any subject in the field of international relations should be expected to take into consideration the influence of international non-governmental organizations whenever that is appropriate. Graduate students should also become aware of the fact that there are many suitable subjects for theses within the field of international non-governmental organization.

(8) The writers of textbooks on international relations should endeavor to cover adequately the activities and achievements of the international non-governmental organizations.

(9) Some consideration is already being given to international non-governmental organizations in some courses for graduate students. These examples should be more widely followed and increasing attention should be given this subject. Perhaps some of the leading universities might pioneer by offering special courses in this field.

If these things were done appreciation of, and greater support for, the international non-governmental organizations might be gradually built up which would contribute significantly to their efforts for human progress and the achievement of peace.

Suggestions for Peace Workers. The writer believes that the peace movement needs a new and more constructive approach. Up to the present time, it has dissipated its energies to a large extent in unrealistic, sentimental and negative proposals for preventing war. Much attention has been given to: (1) pointing out the evils of war, (2) promoting conscientious objection to participation in it, (3) the movement for disarmament and against the munitions manufacturers, (4) outlawry of war or the securing of promises not to fight, (5) collective security, (6) alliances and other threats of superior force, (7) appeasement, and (8) propaganda for a world government. The attention given to these matters has far outweighed their real importance. Workers for peace are, in fact, too preoccupied by war—their fear and their hatred of it keep them from realizing the true nature of peace and the means they must use to build it. Both their conscious and their unconscious attitudes are too often based on the fallacious idea that peace is the absence of war, and that what is needed is to abolish or control the causes of war. This idea does not contain the dynamic power necessary for success. It places the peace workers in a psychologically weak position—the position of those who are "against" rather than "for," who appeal to fear rather than to courage, and who exhort us to hate evil rather than to do good.

Since men are brave and will fight even under the most terrible circumstances, if they think it necessary, appeal should not be made to the vision of the horrors of war. It is futile to attempt to frighten men into peace! Attention should be concentrated on the "causes of peace" rather than on the "causes of war." Above all, people who wish to contribute to peace must realize that the bricks and the mortar with which peace will eventually be built are the non-governmental and intergovernmental organizations which exist to promote the common interests of mankind. Each international organization works toward unity in one or more fields of human activity. Alongside hundreds of other international associations, they can create world unity on every subject of international concern. This process is analogous to what happens within nations by the creation and development of national organizations of every kind, each drawing its strength from individuals or organizations scattered throughout the country. By this process the interests of the individuals or groups in any particular political or geographical subdivision become so subordinated to interests of a national character that any strife between one geographic section and another becomes "unthinkable." Thus the basis of any conflict is transferred to national bodies representing all sorts of functional interests. In view of the national point of view thus created it becomes exceedingly difficult for any sectional group to organize a shooting war. Any conflict between national bodies tends to be resolved on the national political level. Until this process is well developed war is possible, even within territories under one government. There would not have been a civil war in the United States if the railroads had run north and south as well as east and west, if trade between the North and South had been more developed, and the process of the organization of interests on a national basis rather than a sectional basis had been more fully developed. It is on this process that we must rely to unify the world. In the words of David Mitrany in his "A Working Peace System," we need to "overlay political divisions with a spreading web of international activities and agencies in which and through which the interests and life of all the nations would be gradually integrated." Mitrany's principles are, in fact, being carried out through such functional services as those of the World Health Organization, the International Civil Aviation Organization and other specialized agencies of the United Nations. Mitrany, however, confines his proposals to intergovernmental action. The need to "overlay political divisions with a spreading web of international activities and agencies" is perhaps just as important on the non-governmental level and, indeed, is a necessary foundation for the type of intergovernmental action for which Mitrany argues, as it also is for world government.

Each individual can contribute his share to this world unity, for no matter what his particular interest may be, it is almost certain that one or more international organizations are already at work advancing it. Today we have the machinery for dealing with almost every conceivable international common need, on both the governmental and non-governmental level. Neither can function successfully without the other. There are mutual benefits in a close working relationship between the two. To obtain these benefits people everywhere must make sure that their governments wholeheartedly support the intergovernmental organizations, and as active members of national associations, induce these groups to join and support the *INGO's* working in their particular field. By developing common aims, by creating habits of cooperation, and by establishing international attitudes, these *INGO's* have been influential and will be a still greater force in creating the conditions which eventually will bring about peace. If supported, their strength can create unity, among peoples, across frontiers, in all areas of endeavor, which will diminish the importance of any national aspiration organized on a purely geographical basis. It is upon this organized public opinion and action that the success of intergovernmental organizations depends. Under the United Nations system, as under the League of Nations, there seems to be one relatively unexploited and effective method open to the individual who wants to contribute his share to peace, and that is to identify his efforts with those of an organization whose structure is international and whose purpose is consistent with the Charter.

In the history of the *INGO's* there is a special message for those who are basically concerned with the organization of peace. We must cease to look for the keys to peace solely in the action of governments. The factors toward internationalism inherent in the work of *INGO's* must be fully analyzed and exploited. The peace worker must realize that his success is dependent upon utilizing the favorable forces in the society in which he lives. Today our world is bound together by material unity, through invention, science, transportation, etc. It has not yet been brought together morally and intellectually. In order to bring about these new bonds, the peace worker, the student of international affairs, the statesman must take advantage of the possibilities latent in the *INGO's*.

At a hasty glance conflicting interests seem to be far more important than common interests. People everywhere, whipped up by sensational treatment of news, tend to concentrate in an almost pathological manner on the things which divide rather than unite them. Still, as we have shown, there is also inherent drama in cooperation. Moreover, the life of men everywhere in the world is becoming more and more interdependent. Only by cooperation can man hope to meet even his basic needs. It is, therefore, evident that the common interests of man are actually far more important than his conflicting interests. The United Nations and the *INGO's* provide the machinery for promoting these common interests. Both deserve the fullest attention and support from all men of good will. The *INGO's* in particular, should be given far more consideration than they have so far received, for it is they who lead the way on the road to world unity.

The Future Influence of INGO's. It is evident that for the past hundred years there has been a strong tendency for *INGO's* to increase in number, to take up new activities, and to expand in membership and influence. This movement has gained in intensity as the existence of common interests and of the practical advantages to be obtained from private cooperation has been more and more clearly recognized. In this process there has been a steady integration of hopes, of aims and of efforts on the part of groups of individuals of different races, nationalities and religions scattered throughout the world. Within specific fields we have seen that integration take place, and a world attitude in relation to particular problems come to the fore. No new factor able to halt this process is likely to appear. It has been suggested to the author that as intergovernmental organizations expand their activities, *INGO's* will come to occupy a less important position in world affairs. Only if democracy is destroyed will this happen, for the function of *INGO's*, particularly their role as pressure groups, will be still more essential as official bodies widen their scope. We have seen this happen on the national level. For example, in the United States the influence of trade unions, farmers' associations, churches and other non-governmental bodies has at least kept pace with the expansion of the activities of the Federal Government during and since the 1930's.

Conclusion. Man in the last hundred years has developed through science and invention the basic tools for building the good life for all. He can eliminate poverty and want. He can protect himself from disease. He has developed a whole series of social sciences which he can use to promote human welfare. He has devised and put into operation machinery by which a true and lasting peace can be achieved.

In this book we have proved that the international non-governmental organizations are an essential and tremendously important part of this machinery. We have demonstrated that they contribute to almost every aspect of human progress. We have pointed out that their international efforts in whatever field, directly or indirectly, promote peace, which is not merely the absence of war but a cooperative way of life. We have shown that it is through these organizations that the individual can most effectively contribute to the building of a better world.

This book is an appeal to the men and women of all lands to work more and more closely together for human welfare. It is a demonstration of the primacy of the common interests of mankind. It has been written with the belief that once this great truth is fully recognized, our hopes for the future will become realities as the peoples of the world join together as partners for peace.

NOTES AND REFERENCES

PART I. THE ROLE OF INTERNATIONAL NON-GOVERNMENTAL ORGANIZATIONS IN WORLD AFFAIRS

1. For Article 71 see p. 258.
2. United Nations document E/INF/23, 30 April 1948, "Arrangements of the Economic and Social Council of the United Nations for Consultation with Non-Governmental Organizations, Guide for Consultants," p. 16.
3. Even disregarding the large sums spent by the Roman Catholic Church in the international administration of its activities, *INGO's* had considerable annual incomes, sometimes ranging into millions. However, after 1939, IGO budgets reached fantastic proportions, the budget of *UNRRA* alone exceeding two billion dollars.
4. In the League of Nations *Handbook of International Organizations* (Geneva, 1938) the World's Evangelical Alliance, founded in London in 1846, and the International Order of Good Templars, founded in 1851 in the United States, are credited as being the oldest. The writer has determined from a visit to the headquarters of the Alliance in London that it is not an international organization; its so-called members in other countries are mere subscribers to its publications, without any voting rights. The Good Templars spread into Canada in September 1853 when two Lodges were instituted in Greenville County, Canada (I. Newton Pierce, *The History of the Independent Order of Good Templars*, Philadelphia 1869, p. 85), but was not established in other countries until 1868 when it was introduced into Great Britain. (*Encyclopaedia Britannica*, 1948 edition, Vol. 21, p. 919.)
5. Of the 546 organizations considered, 9 were founded in the twenty year period from 1846 (see footnote 4 above) to 1865; 29 from 1866 to 1885; 96 from 1886 to 1905; 289 from 1906 to 1925; and 123 in only six years from 1926 to 1931. Of the total, 84 per cent had been founded since 1899; 59 per cent after World War I. The League of Nations *Handbook* shows that 163 *INGO's* were established in the seven years 1932–1938, but this was not a complete list.
6. Lyman C. White, *The Structure of Private International Organizations*, Philadelphia, 1933, p. 90.
7. Otto D. Tolischus, in the *New York Times* (August 25, 1937), stated, "This was taken to mean the end not only of the Rotary Clubs in Germany . . . but also German participation in all international organizations of which the German sections are not directly under National Socialist control or management."
8. W. A. Visser 't Hooft, *Students Find the Truth to Serve: The Story of the World's Student Christian Federation, 1931–1935*, pp. 64–65.
9. Cesar Saerchinger, "Radio as a Political Instrument," *Foreign Affairs*, January 1938, p. 247.
10. See *Règlement pour la Commission Permanente des Associations Agricoles*, Institut International d'Agriculture, 1928 (annual report).
11. International Relief Union, *Official Texts*, Second Edition, Geneva, December 1935, pp. 37–39.
12. See Article 11, *Convention Européenne de Radiodiffusion*, Lucerne, 1933.
13. Simeon E. Baldwin, "The International Congresses and Conferences of the Last Century as Forces Working Toward the Solidarity of the World," *American Journal of International Law*, Vol. 1, 1907, p. 576.

PART II. THE CONTRIBUTION OF *INGO's* IN SPECIFIC FIELDS

BUSINESS AND FINANCE

1. *Annuaire de la Vie Internationale, 1908–1909*, Brussels, pp. 941–43; *ibid.*,

1910–1911, pp. 1727–1730; and *La Vie Internationale,* Vol. 5, 1914.06—No. 6, Brussels, pp. 562–63.

2. John F. Fahey, *The International Chamber of Commerce, An Explanation of Its Purposes, Plan, and Scope, Two Speeches by Étienne Clementel, President of the International Chamber of Commerce and John H. Fahey, Chairman of the Organization Committee,* July 5, 1920, Paris, pp. 14–15.

3. International Chamber of Commerce, information pamphlet, 1938, p. 3.

4. To indicate the scope of this work, in addition to the publications which are discussed in the text, among the titles appearing in 1938 were: Passport Regime, showing up-to-date regulations concerning passports and visas for all the countries of the world; International Code of Standards of Advertising Practice; Commercial Aviation, existing barriers to commercial air traffic and proposals for abolishing them; Function of Foreign Lending, reviewing future prospects of investment abroad; International Ententes; Practical Use of "Distribution Figures"; Bankruptcy and Rights of Creditors. *Ibid.,* p. 13.

5. Pierre Vasseur, "Economic Information, Essential Factor in Modern Business Organization," *World Trade,* June 1937, p. 68.

6. *ICC Brochure No. 77,* p. 6; *World Trade,* August 1931, p. 312.

7. The *ICC's* attitude against trade barriers is categorically expressed in the resolutions adopted at its 1937 Berlin Congress.

8. Édouard Dolléans, *La Chambre de Commerce Internationale et les Conférences Internationales, Annexe à la note personnelle d'Édouard Dolléans sur l'activité de la Chambre de Commerce Internationale,* typewritten, October 18, 1932.

9. Sir Arthur Salter, in League of Nations, *International Economic Conference, Geneva, Guide to the Documents of the Conference,* C.E.I. 40 (1), 1927.

10. Dolléans, *op. cit.*

11. "General Survey and Summary," by M. Theunis, President of the Conference (speech made at the closing meeting on May 23, 1927), quoted in League of Nations Information Section pamphlet *Economic and Financial Organization,* p. 55.

12. Nicholas Murray Butler in the preface to *International Conciliation,* No. 338, March 1938.

13. "International Economic Reconstruction, Text of Report by Paul van Zeeland," *International Conciliation, op. cit.,* pp. 86, 90, 107.

14. *Plenary Sessions, Third Congress, International Chamber of Commerce,* Brussels (June 21–27, 1925), Brochure No. 42, p. 5.

15. "Incoterms 1936, Simplifying International Business Contracts . . . extracts from an introduction by Messrs. C. B. Ingwersen . . . Thor Caslander . . . and James Mordan . . .," *World Trade,* October, 1936, p. 5.

16. F.O.B., F.A.S., F.O.R., Free Delivered, C.I.F., and C. & F.

17. Information pamphlet, *op. cit.,* p. 12.

18. See p. 207.

19. See p. 206.

20. *World Trade,* July–August, 1927, p. 50; and information pamphlet, *op. cit.,* p. 11.

21. Charles S. Haight, "The Hague Rules, A Big Step to Facilitate International Trade, Advantages of Uniform Law Now Virtually Assured for 70 per cent of World's Tonnage," *World Trade,* July–August, 1936, p. 5.

22. For a fuller account see "Reciprocal Tax Exemption for Ocean Carriers" by Charles S. Haight, *Brochure No. 43, International Chamber of Commerce, Third Congress (Brussels, June 21–27, 1925, Group Sessions),* pp. 17–21.

23. Kenneth W. Colegrove, *International Control of Aviation,* World Peace Foundation, Boston, 1930, p. 118. Membership was automatic with ratification of the Convention.

24. K. M. Beaumont, "Air Transport Documents," *World Trade,* February 1937, p. 29. Major Beaumont was then legal adviser to the International Air Traffic Association and at the same time *Rapporteur* of the Air Transport Committee of the ICC.

25. See p. 64.

26. Laurence C. Tombs, *International*

Organization in European Air Transport, New York, Columbia University Press, 1936, p. 198.

27. *Ibid.,* p. 162.

28. Dolléans, *op. cit.*

29. Brig. Gen. Sir Osborne-Mance, *International Road Transport, Postal, Electricity and Miscellaneous Questions,* Oxford University Press, 1947, p. 119.

30. Letter from secretariat of the International Air Traffic Association, October 25, 1937.

31. Hermann Schaub, *The New International Convention for the Carriage of Goods by Rail,* Standing Committee on Rail Transport (meeting of February 3, 1936), Document No. 5760 tr. 23, I. 1936 hkm Transport Department, International Chamber of Commerce.

32. Information pamphlet, *op. cit.,* p. 11.

33. Lord Riverdale, "Great Britain and International Trade, The Place of the International Chamber of Commerce in the World," *World Trade,* January, 1936, p. 8.

34. International Chamber of Commerce, *International Telegraph Regulations and Rates,* Document No. 9, Berlin Congress, 1937, p. 1.

35. *Methods of Allocating Taxable Income,* League of Nations Document No. C. 399 M. 204. 1933. II. A., Geneva, June 26th, 1933, F. Fiscal. 76.

36. *Journal of the International Chamber of Commerce,* February, 1926, p. 16.

37. *International Chamber of Commerce, Brochure No. 42, Third Congress (Brussels), 1925, Plenary Session,* p. 24.

38. "Public Opinion and Business Leadership," *World Trade,* August, 1931, pp. 227–229.

39. *Quelques Résultats Pratiques des Travaux de la Chambre en ce qui Concerne la Section Financière.* Note par M. Thor Caslander, Commissaire Administratif Suédois en vue de son voyage de propagande en Suéde, typewritten, International Chamber of Commerce 7.2.1938.

40. Arthur K. Kuhn, "The International Conferences for Unification of Laws on Bills of Exchange, Promissory Notes and Cheques," *American Journal of International Law,* April, 1931, p. 318.

41. See "Arbitration" in index for specific instances.

42. Nicolas Politis, "The Court of Arbitration of the International Chamber of Commerce," International Chamber of Commerce, *Exceptional Group Meeting, June 25, 1935, Paris Congress, J. A. 4,* mimeographed, p. 1.

43. Information pamphlet, *op. cit.,* p. 15.

44. Where the importance of the dispute warrants it, or if the parties so request, the dispute may go before a board of three arbitrators. In such cases, each party nominates one arbitrator and the Court the third, or the Court selects the three. Information pamphlet, *op. cit.,* p. 14.

45. Politis, *op. cit.,* pp. 3–5.

46. Information pamphlet, *op. cit.,* p. 14.

47. *Ibid.*

48. *Ibid.*

49. *International Chamber of Commerce,* information pamphlet, 1935, p. 8.

50. Manley O. Hudson, "The Friendly Settlement of Economic Disputes Between States," *American Journal of International Law,* April, 1932, pp. 353–57. Paul van Zeeland in his report on *International Economic Reconstruction* recommended that where conciliation failed, the States agree "to accept the award of an appropriate arbitral body," and suggested that the good offices of the arbitral bodies then in existence, such as the ICC Court, be utilized. *International Conciliation, op. cit.,* pp. 90–91.

51. Dolléans, *op. cit.*

52. Wallace McClure, *World Prosperity Through the Economic Work of the League of Nations,* New York, The Macmillan Company, 1933, pp. 128–29.

53. *Review of International Co-operation,* May, 1930, pp. 166–68.

54. The definitions of the terms "exhibition," "general and special fairs," found in the Convention are mainly *ICC* proposals. Chapter IV of the Convention, dealing with the obligations of the host countries as well as the obligations of the countries participating in the exhibitions, contains, in substance, under articles 15 to 26, all *ICC* proposals, par-

ticularly those dealing with customs regulations and the operations of monopolized services. International Chamber of Commerce, Paper No. 3708, *Committee on International Fairs and Exhibitions. Work of the Committee on International Fairs and Exhibitions of the International Chamber of Commerce.* (Draft) Mimeographed, p. 1.

55. International Chamber of Commerce, Paper No. 3590, *Committee on International Fairs and Exhibitions, Report on the Diplomatic Conference on International Exhibitions*, VDR 1 MM, April 22, 1929, mimeographed, p. 1.

56. *Conférence Diplomatique relative aux Expositions Internationales, Paris, 12–22 November 1928, République Francaise*, Paris, 1930, pp. 240–241, 533.

57. Dolléans, *op. cit.*

58. J. H. May, *International Cooperation*, leaflet, London, 1930, p. 5; and *Handbook, op. cit.*, p. 340.

59. James P. Warbasse, *Cooperation as a Way of Peace*, New York, London, 1939, p. 62.

60. Letter from Secretariat, April 29, 1938.

61. *Agenda and Reports, Fifteenth Congress of the International Co-operative Alliance, Paris, 6th to 9th September 1937*, p. 176.

62. *Ibid.*, pp. 181–82.

63. *Ibid.*, p. 175.

64. *Ibid.*, p. 51.

65. "Report of the Central Committee on the Work of the International Cooperative Alliance 1934–1936," in *Agenda and Reports*, 1937, *op. cit.*, p. 71.

66. *Agenda and Reports*, 1937, *op. cit.*, p. 54; and "Report of the Central Committee, 1934–1936," *op. cit.*, p. 27.

67. Interview, William Chalmers, U.S. Vice-Commissioner of Labor, Geneva.

68. Mary L. Fleddérus, Director, *Ten Years I.R.I., Report of the Industrial Relations Institute since its inception in 1925*, 1935, inside back cover.

69. *Handbook, op. cit.*, pp. 354–55. Among its other prewar studies were *Essential Relations between all Categories of Industrial Collectivity*, Vol. I, 1928, Vol. II, 1929; *Rational Organisation and Industrial Relations*, 1930; *International Unemployment*, 1932; *World Social Economic Planning*, 1932.

70. Fleddérus, *op. cit.*, p. 9 and passim.

71. The International Federation of National Standardizing Associations was succeeded by the International Organization for Standardization, which was founded in 1946 as the successor to the United Nations Standards Co-ordinating Committee (unofficial), created in 1944.

72. Maurice Berger, "Principes Généraux de Normalisation, Normes Fondamentales d'Application Courante," in *SIA, Journal de la Société des Ingénieurs de l'Automobile, Paris*, février, 1938, pp. 31–49.

73. *Ibid.*

74. *International Electrotechnical Commission, Its Aims, Objects, and Procedure*, October, 1937, p. 1.

75. *Ibid.*

76. *Ibid.*

77. *Handbook, op. cit.*, p. 380.

78. *Ibid.*, pp. 18–19.

79. Berger, *op. cit.*

80. Frederick Haussmann and David Ahearn, "International Cartels and World Trade, an Explanatory Estimate," *Thought*, Fordham University Quarterly, September, 1944, p. 429, cited in United Nations, Department of Economic Affairs, *International Cartels, a League of Nations Memorandum*, Lake Success, New York, 1947, p. 2. Laurence Ballande, *Les Ententes Économiques Internationales, Étude Monographique et Statistique*, Paris, 1937, gives general information on 178 cartels.

81. Haussmann and Ahearn, *op. cit.*

82. See Karl Pribram, *Cartel Problems, An Analysis of Collective Monopolies in Europe with American Application*, the Brookings Institution, Washington, D.C., 1935; and Clemens Lammers, *International Ententes*, Berlin Congress Document No. 4, Paris, 1937.

83. Pribram, *op. cit.*, footnote p. 142.

84. Lammers, *op. cit.*, p. 33.

85. *Ibid.*, pp. 44–45.

86. This agreement was reported in *Time* magazine for February 28, 1938, which quoted the New York *Journal of*

Commerce: "The International Steel Cartel and the Steel Export Association of America have decided on common export levels for the ensuing fiscal, or cartel, year at lower levels than previously in effect. . . . Moreover, export quotas on some dozen steel commodities have been assigned to various member countries. Thus the U.S. has been assigned definite tonnages which it can sell monthly to Brazil, Argentina, Japan, China and other important steel-consuming countries. . . ." No denial was made of this report. *Time,* p. 58.

87. Björn Prytz, Introduction, Clemens Lammers' Report, *op. cit.,* p. 7.
88. Ballande, *op. cit.,* pp. 320–22.
89. Lammers, *op. cit.,* pp. 33–35. Despite the decline in the price of aluminum, Donald H. Wallace of Harvard University stated in the comprehensive study on *International Control in the Non-Ferrous Metals:* "The Alliance cartel has contributed to the maintenance during depression of relatively high published quotations accompanied by price discrimination. This price policy must be regarded as operating on the side of those factors which tend to prolong the depression. Lower prices might have stimulated greater consumption directly or indirectly by lessening the deflationary pressure on immediate consumers which must have tended to diminish their efficiency in production and marketing." (W. Y. Elliott, *International Control in the Non-Ferrous Metals,* New York, 1937, p. 274. Quotations from this book by permission of The Macmillan Company, publishers, and the Bureau of International Research, Harvard University.) On the other hand, Lammers reported that "leading manufacturers' associations confirm that the Alliance has not taken advantage of its monopoly to impose unreasonable prices." (Lammers, *op. cit.,* p. 35.)
90. Lammers, *op. cit.,* p. 40.
91. *Ibid.,* p. 44.
92. *Ibid.*
93. *Ibid.,* p. 43.
94. The Continental Tube Cartel, founded in 1926, included the tube plants of Germany, Czechoslovakia, France, Poland and Hungary. In 1929 a series of agreements were concluded with the British, American, and Canadian producers "to which was given the name of International Tube Cartel." Later, both the Swedish and Japanese producers joined. The Cartel was dissolved in 1935, for due to the trade policy of several governments, "it became impossible to allocate orders to members in accordance with the Cartel Agreement, neither could the fixed export prices be any longer enforced." More particularly, it proved impossible to reach agreement with the German plants on their export quota. However, the former members remained in contact with each other and concluded an agreement for the protection of their domestic markets, which was in force from 1935 on, based on the former Cartel provisions, and in 1937 negotiations were under way for a new over-all agreement. *Ibid.,* pp. 54–55.
95. *Ibid.,* pp. 53–55.
96. Elliott, *op. cit.,* p. 103.
97. Lammers, *op. cit.,* pp. 20–21.
98. See Alex Skelton, "The Mechanics of International Cartels," in Elliott, *op. cit.,* p. 182.
99. Lammers, *op. cit.,* p. 34.
100. *Ibid.,* pp. 34, 46.
101. Elliott, *op. cit.,* pp. 13–14, 17–18.
102. Sir Arthur Salter, *Recovery, the Second Effort,* London, 1932, p. 207.
103. Werner Kaufmann, *L'Organization Scientifique dans les Grands Magasins,* Comité National de l'Organization Francaise, Paris, 1934, pp. 20–22; see also H. Pasdermadjian, *The International Association of Department Stores, Management Research in Retailing,* Newman Books, London, 1950.
104. *Minutes of the Third General Meeting of the International Credit Insurance Association,* p. 5.
105. *Fédération Internationale du Bâtiment et des Travaux Publics (Confédération Patronale),* mimeographed, no date.
106. Federation publication, *Aims and Objects of the International Cotton Federation,* no date.
107. *International Hotelmen's Association,* leaflet, 1937.
108. *Collaboration des Hôtels avec les Agences de Voyages,* mimeographed;

and *Accord stipulé entre l'Alliance Internationale de l'Hôtellerie (AIH) et l'Association entre les Grandes Organisations Nationales de Voyages et Tourisme (AGOT)*, mimeographed.

109. *Bulletin de l'Alliance Internationale de l'Hôtellerie*, March, 1938, pp. 21–27.

110. *Handbook, op. cit.*, p. 336.

111. *Compte Rendu Officiel, Congrès Internationale des Fabricants de Chocolat et de Cocoa, Anvers, 1930 (du 8 au 11 septembre)*, p. 191; and, *Bulletin Officiel de l'Office Internationale du Cocoa et du Chocolat*, September 1935, pp. 347–51, 369–77, 412.

112. *Ministère des Affaires Etrangères*, Royaume de Belgique, Compte Rendu Officiel, *Conférence Internationale du Cocoa, Bruxelles, 12, 13, et 14 septembre 1932*.

113. Letter from secretariat, October 15, 1937.

114. *Compte Rendu et Documents Officiels, IX Conférence Lainière Internationale, Budapest, 4 et 5 octobre 1933*, pp. 11–12.

115. *Statutes of the International Wool Textile Organisation*, Articles 6, 1, 3.

116. *Compte Rendu et Documents Officiels, IX Conférence Lainière Internationale, Budapest, 4 et 5 octobre 1933*, p. 66.

117. Bureau Permanent International des Constructeurs d'Automobiles, *Autorizations des Expositions et Compétitions (courses et concours), Procès-Verbaux des Séances des 11 novembre 1920, 31 mars 1924, 30 novembre 1928, 21 octobre 1931 et 21 mars 1936*.

COMMUNICATIONS, TRANSPORT, AND TRAVEL

1. In June 1946 a new body called the International Broadcasting Organization was set up with headquarters at Brussels for the purpose of replacing the Union. Its membership included radio broadcasting organizations of twenty-eight European countries. The new organization operated the Brussels Checking Centre. In 1949 many member organizations resigned and the headquarters were moved to Prague. A European Broadcasting Association was then established, with members in the Western European countries. The International Broadcasting Union was terminated.

2. *Radiodiffusion*, No. 1, October 1935, Union Internationale de Radiodiffusion, Geneva, p. 84.

3. Introduction, *Broadcasting: An Instrument for the Creation of a Better Understanding Between the Peoples*, Being the English version of a Document presented to the International Organisation of Intellectual Co-operation (June 1937) by the International Broadcasting Union. Hereafter cited as *Broadcasting*.

4. Vice-Admiral Sir Charles Carpendale, "Dix Années de Collaboration Internationale dans le Domaine de la Radiodiffusion," *Radiodiffusion, op. cit.*, pp. 18–19.

5. Raymond Braillard, "Le Controle Technique à Distance des Stations de Radiodiffusion," *Radiodiffusion, op. cit.*, pp. 73–74.

6. *Convention Européenne de Radiodiffusion*, Lucerne, 1933 Article 11.

7. International Institute of Intellectual Co-operation, *The Educational Role of Broadcasting*, Paris, 1935, p. 280.

8. International Institute of Intellectual Co-operation, *School Broadcasting*, Paris, 1933, Introduction, p. 6.

9. *Broadcasting, op. cit.*, pp. 88–92.

10. League of Nations, International Committee on Intellectual Co-operation, *Report of the Committee on the Work of its Nineteenth Plenary Session* (C. 327 M. 220. 1937. XII August 9th, 1937), p. 61.

11. *Ibid.*, Appendix, pp. 97–98. For additional information on the efforts of the IBU to further international good will, see Institute of Intellectual Co-operation, *Broadcasting and Peace, Studies and Projects in the Matter of International Agreements*, Paris, no date, pp. 31–33, 49–50, 77–78, 94–95, 100–102, 118–19, 123–36, 213–14; and A. R. Burrows, "Broadcasting and International Rapprochement," International Institute of Intellectual Co-operation, *The Educational Role of Broadcasting*, Paris, 1935, pp. 280–89.

12. *Handbook, op. cit.*, p. 384.

13. Keith Clark, *International Com-*

munications, New York, Columbia University Press, 1931, pp. 187–89.
14. Letter from secretariat, April 8, 1938.
15. *Handbook, op. cit.,* p. 386.
16. Sir Ralph L. Wedgwood, *International Rail Transport,* Oxford, 1946, p. 13.
17. *Ibid.,* pp. 126–27.
18. *Handbook, op. cit.,* p. 396; *1885–1930, Union Internationale de Tramways, de Chemins de Fer d'intérêt local et de Transports Publics Automobiles,* Brussels, March 1930, p. 25; *Publications de L'Union.*
19. Sir Osborne Mance, *International Sea Transport,* Oxford, 1945, p. 6.
20. *The Baltic and International Maritime Conference, 1905–1930,* p. 5 and Mance, *op. cit.,* p. 5.
21. *Conference, 1905–1930, op. cit.,* p. 6.
22. *Ibid.,* and Mance, *op. cit.,* p. 6.
23. The Conference recently changed its name to International Chamber of Shipping to avoid confusion with the international shipping conferences, shortly to be discussed, which regulate passenger and trade traffic on all leading routes.
24. *Handbook, op. cit.,* p. 391.
25. Mance, *op. cit.,* pp. 4–5.
26. Charles Hodges, *The Background of International Relations,* New York, John Wiley and Sons, 1931, pp. 368–69.
27. Mance, *op. cit.,* pp. 96, 99–100.
28. *Ibid.,* p. 96.
29. Kenneth W. Colegrove, *International Control of Aviation,* Boston, 1930, p. 123.
30. Lawrence C. Tombs, *International Organization in European Air Transport,* New York, 1936, Columbia University Press, pp. 148 and 202. Tombs in this study centered his attention on those organizations established or supported by governments, because of the fact that European air transport "depends on the direct and indirect subsidies granted by governments." Nevertheless, of the twenty-eight organizations mentioned in the book, ten are private, and it is quite evident from the reading of the volume that *INGO's* have greatly influenced the work of governmental organizations and have achieved important results in those phases which they directly control.
31. *Handbook, op. cit.,* p. 369.
32. Tombs, *op. cit.,* pp. 148–49.
33. Letter from secretariat, October 25, 1937.
Here we should be reminded of the technical contributions in this field made by the International Federation of National Standardising Associations, whose activities we have reviewed, and mention the work of the International Commission on Illumination which is concerned with all photometric problems. Tombs reports that both these *INGO's* have influenced the official International Commission for Air Navigation (*op. cit.,* p. 99). (In 1913, the Illumination Commission became the successor to the Commission Internationale de Photométrie, founded in 1900.)
34. For role of International Chamber of Commerce in this, see pp. 24–25.
35. Tombs, *op. cit.,* p. 129.
36. Letter, *op. cit.*
37. Tombs, *op. cit.,* p. 131.
38. Letter, *op. cit.* Herman Doring, "Les Tâches Juridiques de l'IATA," *Revue aéronautique internationale,* March 1935, contains a great deal of information on the work of the IATA and how it has influenced the international law of the air.
39. Letter, *op. cit.*
40. In 1934, air insurance companies in Britain, Denmark, Finland, France, Germany, Italy, Norway, Sweden and Switzerland founded the International Union of Aviation Insurers to serve as their clearing house.
41. Tombs, *op. cit.,* pp. 157–58.
42. Sir Osborne Mance, *International Air Transport,* Oxford University Press, 1943, p. 28.
43. *10 Years of Travel,* Commission for International Relations and Travel, London, 1934.
44. Letter, October 20, 1937, from International Association of Recognized Automobile Clubs, and Alliance Internationale de Tourisme, *Annuaire,* 1937, pp. 15–21.
45. *Annuaire, op. cit.,* pp. 15–21, and L'Association Internationale des Automobile-Clubs Reconnus, *Recueil de*

Renseignments de Tourisme, 11e Édition, April 1937, Index and pp. 6–7.

46. In 1926, by intergovernmental conference action, the old 1909 *Certificate International de Route* "which inconveniently linked together on the same document the vehicle and its driver," serving as a joint international driving permit and automobile license, was replaced by the present documents, the International Certificate for automobiles, "which is a sort of automobile license good in all countries," and the International Driving Permit. The Automobile Federation in 1936 expressed its intention to achieve one further step, the standardization of national driving permits and automobile licenses, so that even the present international documents will no longer be necessary. "L'Association Internationale des Automobiles-Clubs Reconnus *(AIACR),*" *Revue Internationale de l'Automobile,* August, 1936, pp. 5-6.

47. *Ibid.*
Claiming full credit for the triptyque, the Touring Alliance terms the *Carnet* "but a booklet of which each page is a triptyque." *Verbatim Report of the General Assembly of the Alliance Internationale de Tourisme, Budapest, 16–19 September 1935,* pp. 17–18. On the Agenda of its 1936 Assembly, at Monaco, there was a proposal that the Alliance support jointly with the Automobile Federation the adoption of the *Carnet* in countries which had not yet done so. This question was removed from the Agenda, for: "When the Automobile Association placed this question on the Agenda, it was under the impression that the relations between the *AIT* and the *AIACR* were based upon a policy of mutual support. The mistake was ours, and only recently in the 'Auto' there appeared an article which was certainly due to the influence of the *AIACR* in which very little cordiality was displayed towards the *AIT* [*Revue, op. cit.*]. Among other things, it was stated that everything done for motor tourist was due to the AIACR: it was the Automobile Clubs that have created the carnet de passages en douanes, the international road certificate, the use of the triptyque, etc. This article is an almost textual rendering of an article in the AIACR's Official Bulletin. Faced with a policy of this kind, imbued with such bad faith, we refuse to discuss the possibility of mutual support, and as we meet with so little cordiality on the part of this Association we withdraw question No. 23 from the Agenda." *Verbatim Report of the General Assembly of the Alliance Internationale de Tourisme, Monaco, September 16–19, 1936,* p. 87.

48. *Revue, op. cit.,* p. 6. This claim is supported by the League of Nations official report of the Conference. At an earlier conference, in 1926, the nations had agreed that the triangle would be reserved exclusively for danger signs, a decision which the Federation had been pressing in order to avoid confusion between danger signs and advertisements.

49. International Touring Alliance, *Note sur la Route Londres-Istanbul,* July 1935, pp. 24–27, and *Verbatim Reports, op. cit.,* 1935, pp. 36–40.

50. The nine international organizations were: International Touring Alliance (Private); International Association of Recognized Automobile Clubs (Private, now the International Automobile Federation); International Railway Union; International Federation of Travel Agencies (P); International Union for the Issue of Combined Coupon Tickets; Association of the Major Tourist Organisations; International Hotel Alliance (P); International Union of Official Organs of Tourist Propaganda; International Aeronautic Federation (P). *Handbook, op cit.,* pp. 417–18.

51. *Ibid.*
52. *Ibid.*

LABOR

1. There are a number of international organizations, other than those discussed in this chapter, whose work should be mentioned. The functions and contributions of the International Organization of Industrial Employers, the International Shipping Federation and the International Industrial Relations Institute, have already been discussed. Then, there are such groups as the International Federation of Business and Professional Women, the Y's, the Inter-

NOTES AND REFERENCES

national Federation of Intellectual Workers, as well as the many *INGO's* devoted to social and humanitarian interests (see the chapter on Social Welfare) whose work is related to labor.

2. According to Alexandre Berenstein (*Les Organisations Ouvrières, Leurs Compétences et Leur Rôle dans la Société des Nations*, Brussels and Paris, 1936, p. 17), "Probably the earliest expression of desire for the creation of an international institution for labor legislation, by an international organization, was that of the First International in 1866."

3. Carol Reigelman, "War-Time Trade-Union and Socialist Proposals" in *The Origins of the International Labor Organization*, James T. Shotwell, Ed., New York, 1934, pp. 55–56; and Francis Graham Wilson, *Labor in the League System, A Study of the International Labor Organization in Relation to International Administration*, Stanford University Press, 1934, p. 31.

4. Shotwell, *op. cit.*, pp. 55–56.

5. C. Howard-Ellis, *The Origin, Structure and Working of the League of Nations*, London, 1928, p. 220.

6. Paul S. Reinsch, *Public International Unions*, Boston, 1911, p. 43; and Sir Malcolm Delevingne, "The Pre-War History of International Legislation," in Shotwell, *op. cit.*, p. 33.

7. Reinsch, *op. cit.*, p. 43.

8. Delevingne, *op. cit.*, p. 33.

9. Reinsch, *op. cit.*, pp. 43–45; and Delevingne, *op. cit.*, pp. 29–30, 49.

10. *Ibid.*, p. 30.

11. C. Howard-Ellis, *op. cit.*, p. 212; and Ernest Mahaim, "The Historical and Social Importance of International Labor Legislation," in Shotwell, *op. cit.*, p. 9.

12. Reinsch, *op. cit.*; and Delevingne, *op. cit.*, pp. 50–51.

13. C. Howard-Ellis, *op. cit.*, p. 220.

14. The *IFTU* was formally dissolved in 1946 after the establishment of the World Federation of Trade Unions in October, 1945.

15. Berenstein, *op. cit.*, p. 16.

16. Lewis L. Lorwin, *Labor and Internationalism*, New York, 1929, pp. 398–400.

17. Lorwin, *op. cit.*, pp. 622–23. Its fund for relief work in Spain was administered jointly with the Labor and Socialist International. *The International Trade Union Movement*, January–July 1937, pp. 5–6.

18. Lorwin, *op. cit.*, p. 399.

19. Edo Fimmen, *The International Federation of Trade Unions, Development and Aims*, Amsterdam, 1922, pp. 15–16; and Lorwin, *op. cit.*, pp. 206–207.

20. Lorwin, *op. cit.*, p. 400.

21. Edo Fimmen, *op. cit.*, p. 16.

22. International Federation of Trade Unions, *Report on Activities During the Years 1924, 1925, and 1926, Submitted to the Fourth Ordinary Congress, Paris, August, 1927*, pp. 81–82. See also the statement concerning the part played by the International Chamber of Commerce in regard to the Dawes Plan in the chapter on Business and Finance.

23. Léon Jouthaux, in International Federation of Trade Unions, *Report Fourth Congress*, 1927, p. 111.

24. International Federation of Trade Unions, *Triennial Report, 1933–1935, Congress London 1936*, Paris, 1937, p. 126.

25. Berenstein, *op. cit.*, pp. 30–31.

26. *Ibid.*, p. 139.

27. Wilson, *op. cit.*, pp. 15–18.

28. *Ibid.*, p. 19.

29. *Ibid.*, p. 20.

30. *Ibid.*

31. *Ibid.*, pp. 317–18.

32. Jean Zarras, *Le Contrôle de l'Application des Conventions Internationales du Travail*, Institut de Droit Comparé, Paris, 1937, pp. 202–03.

33. *Handbook, op. cit.*, p. 304.

34. *Ibid.*, p. 289.

35. *Reports and Proceedings, Fourth Congress of the Labour and Socialist International, Vienna, 25th July to 1st August 1931*, pp. 6–7.

36. C. Howard-Ellis, *op. cit.*, p. 467.

37. *Reports and Proceedings, 1931, op. cit.*, p. 144.

38. *The Activities of the International Federation of Trade Unions, 1933–35*, London, 1936.

39. Translation, Alexandre Berenstein, *op. cit.*, p. 7.

40. Carlton J. H. Hayes, *A Political and Cultural History of Modern Europe*, New York, 1936, Vol. 2, p. 378. By

permission of the Macmillan Company, publishers.

41. V. I. Lenin, *State and Revolution,* International Publishers, New York, 1932, pp. 5, 99.

42. A. Losovsky, *The World's Trade Union Movement,* 1925, quoted in *Encyclopaedia Britannica,* 1948, Vol. 22, p. 388.

43. *Encyclopaedia Britannica, op. cit.,* p. 389.

44. *The Activities of the International Federation of Trade Unions, 1930–1932,* Brussels, 1933, p. 13.

AGRICULTURE

1. Translation, F. Houillier, *L'Organisation Internationale de l'Agriculture, Les Institutions Agricoles internationales et l'action internationale en agriculture,* Paris, 1935, pp. 2–3.

2. *Handbook, op. cit.,* p. 313; and Marcel Rieul Paisant, *La Commission Internationale d'Agriculture et son rôle dans l'Économie Européenne* (Extrait des Annales de la Commission Internationale d'Agriculture—No. XV, Paris, 1936), pp. 103, 110–11.

3. Houillier, *op. cit.,* pp. 4, 17–18; and International Institute of Administrative Sciences, Brussels, *A Directory of International Organizations in the Field of Public Administration,* 1936, p. 36.

4. Paisant, *op. cit.,* pp. 47–49.

5. The United Nations Food and Agricultural Organization (*FAO*) in 1945 voted to propose the termination of the Convention of 1905 which had established this Institute. At a meeting of the members of the Institute in July 1946 arrangements were made to dissolve the convention. The work of the Institute ended July 31, 1946.

6. Paisant, *op. cit.,* p. 115.

7. This Commission, although composed of private agricultural associations, was completely under the dominance of the Institute. See p. 9.

8. Composed of both *INGO's* and intergovernmental organizations, such as: the *ILO,* the Secretariat of the League of Nations, and among the *INGO's,* the International Chamber of Commerce, and the International Statistical Institute.

9. Houillier, *op. cit.,* pp. 15, 30.

10. Paisant, *op. cit.,* pp. 116–17.

THE ARTS AND SCIENCES

1. J. B. Condliffe, *Possibilities of Cooperation Among Research Institutions, Address Given on the Dedication of the Brookings Institution Building,* Washington, D.C., May 1931, Geneva Research Centre, Doc. 1938. I. 4, mimeographed, pp. 2–4.

2. L. L. Bernard and Jessie Bernard, *Sociology and the Study of International Relations,* Washington University Studies, No. 4, February, 1934, pp. 96–97.

3. One hundred and three *INGO's* dealing with "Arts and Sciences" are listed in the League of Nations *Handbook of International Organizations,* 1938; only under "Religion, Humanitarianism and Morals" are there a larger number.

4. In this field, there are many *INGO's* not treated below which have made valuable contributions; to name some: International Association for Bridge and Structural Engineering, International Entomological Association, International Geological Congress, Hoerbiger Institute, International Commission on Illumination, International Ornithological Congress, International Photogrammetric Society, Permanent Commission of International Congresses of Scientific and Applied Photography, Foundation "Pour La Science"—International Centre for Synthesis, International Association on Quaternary Research, International Society of Radiobiology, International Commission on Radium Standards.

5. *Message from the President of the United States transmitting A Report from the Secretary of State to the end that legislation may be enacted requesting the President to invite the World Power Conference to hold the Third Power Conference in the United States in 1936 and 1937, and providing an appropriation of the sum of $75,000 for the necessary expenses of organizing and holding such a meeting.* Document No. 240, House of Representatives, 74th Congress, 1st Session.

6. *The Transactions of the Second World Power Conference, 1930,* are twenty large volumes totaling 8,200 pages; the printed proceedings of its Third Congress, published by the U. S. Printing Office, number more than 7,000 pages in addition to 2,500 pages devoted to the transactions of the Second Congress on Large Dams which was held in conjunction with the Washington meeting. Carl Kottgen, "The Second World Power Conference, Berlin, 1930," *Engineering Progress,* March 1930, pp. 60–64; and Prospectus, *Transactions of the Third World Power Conference, 1937.*

7. *Program, World Power Conference, Washington, D.C., September 7–12, 1936,* pp. 13–14, 15, and 34–35.

8. Letter from secretariat, World Power Conference, November 3, 1937, with extracts from meetings of the International Executive Council of the World Power Conference for 1930–1934 and 1936–1937, and extract from League of Nations Advisory and Technical Committee for Communications and Transit, Records of the Work of the Twentieth Session, Geneva, August 31st to September 4th, 1937.

9. *L'Union Internationale des Producteurs et Distributeurs d'Énergie Électrique,* MP.—Juin 1937, typewritten, *passim.*

10. *Handbook, op. cit.,* p. 380. Individual membership comprised "about 1,100 manufacturers of electrical materials, power companies, professors, consulting engineers, government engineers, etc., in 46 countries," while group affiliation included "government departments, technical and scientific societies, [commercial] companies, and public electrical undertakings." *Directory, 1936, op. cit.,* p. 49.

11. Conférence Internationale des Grands Réseaux Électriques, *Compte Rendu Sommaire dex la Neuvième Session, 24 juin—2 juillet, 1937,* p. 3.

12. *International Association for Testing Materials, London Congress, April 19–24, 1937,* London, 1937, Preface and "Statement by the President, Sir William Bragg," pp. xiii–xix, and xxvi.

13. Since World War II, four new Unions have been added: the International Unions of Crystallography, of Theoretical and Applied Mechanics, of the History of Sciences, and the International Mathematical Union.

14. *Handbook, op. cit.,* p. 164.

15. George Hale (President of the Council) quoted in, Sir Henry Lyons, Editor, *Reports of Proceedings, The Second General Assembly of the International Council of Scientific Unions held at Brussels, July 9th to 13th, 1934,* London, 1935, p. 6.

16. *Ibid.,* p. 5.

17. International Institute of Intellectual Co-operation, *Plan of Work 1938,* Report No. 10, November 1937, C.A. 60. 1937, p. 17.

18. League of Nations, International Committee on Intellectual Co-operation, *Report of the Committee on the Work of its Nineteenth Plenary Session, August 9th, 1937,* C. 327 M. 220. 1937 XII, p. 63.

19. International Institute of Intellectual Co-operation, *Document, D. 41.* 1937.

20. The task, since the date of this report, has been multiplied a hundredfold, with the completion of the 200-inch Mount Palomar telescope.

21. Letter from secretariat, April 27, 1938; and report, "Co-operation in astronomy and the recent activities of the International Astronomical Union."

22. International Council of Scientific Unions, *Proceedings, 1934, op. cit.,* pp. 24–35.

23. *Ibid.,* pp 36–51.

24. The International Meteorological Organization, founded in 1878, has had a worldwide membership consisting of the Directors of the official meteorological services of all countries. (*Handbook, op. cit.,* p. 141.) In 1938, although technically an *INGO,* its membership was completely official. It has been reorganized lately so as to transform it into an intergovernmental organization, and has become a specialized agency of the United Nations (World Meteorological Organization). Before the war, it had eighteen Commissions and thirty-five sub-commissions, and one of its major concerns was that of weather forecasting. (*Liste des Membres du Comité Météorologique International et*

des Commissions de l'Organisation Météorologique Internationale, Édition 1938, pp. 85–86.)
25. International Council of Scientific Unions, *Proceedings, 1934, op. cit.,* pp. 52–53.
26. *Ibid.,* pp. 58–63.
27. *Ibid.,* pp. 68–79.
28. *Handbook, op. cit.,* p. 115.
29. *Proceedings, 1934, op. cit.,* p. 83; *Handbook, op. cit.,* pp. 118–19, 150–51; and M. J. Timmermans, *Rapport sur les Exercises 1930, 1931, 1932, 1933; Bureau International des Étalons Physico-Chimiques,* p. 3.
30. Union International de Chimie, *Comptes Rendus de la Douzième Conférence, Lucerne et Zurich, 16–22 Août, 1936,* pp. 20–21.
31. Dr. D. la Cour, "L'Année Polaire Internationale 1932–1933, Les Buts, Les Méthodes et Quelques Résultats Préliminaires," *Proceedings, 1934, op. cit.,* pp. 192, 196.
32. Translation, *ibid.,* pp. 193–94.
33. *Ibid.,* pp. 195, 201–03.
34. See Friedrich Zahn, *50 Années de l'Institut International de Statistique,* 1934, pp. 4–5.
35. Translation, *ibid.,* pp. 3–4.
36. *Ibid.,* pp. 8–10.
37. *Ibid.,* p. 12.
38. *Ibid.,* pp. 29 and 79.
39. *Ibid.,* p. 145.
40. *Ibid.,* pp. 26, 43, 62, 126, 154, 171–73.
41. *Ibid.,* pp. 44–45.
42. *Ibid., pp.* 46–49.
43. *Ibid.,* pp. 88–89.
44. *Ibid.,* pp. 116–17.
45. *Ibid.,* pp. 97, 149, 155.
46. *Ibid.,* p. 173.
47. A few other organizations especially concerned with the social sciences but not discussed here are: International Institute of Constitutional History, International Committee on Historical Sciences, International Institute of History of the French Revolution, International Institute of Sociology, the Islamic Research Association, International Psychological Congress.
48. *Handbook, op. cit.,* p. 105.
49. American Council of Learned Societies, *Bulletin,* May, 1932, pp. 19–21; letter from secretariat, January 5, 1933; and Union Académique Internationale, *Liste des Publications,* June 15, 1937.
50. Other *INGO's* concerned to a greater or lesser extent with the field of public administration are the World Power Conference—especially at its Washington Conference—the International Academy of Comparative Law, the American Institute of Comparative Law and Legislation, the International Association of Penal Law, the International Bureau for the Unification of Penal Law, the International for Criminal Law (Droit Pénal), the General Association of Municipal Health and Technical Officers, the International Police Conference, and the International Institute of Public Law.
51. Rowland Egger, "The Brussels Public Administration Center," *Public Management,* September, 1937, p. 268.
52. *Handbook, op. cit.,* p. 229.
53. Institut International des Sciences Administratives, *Compte Rendu du Vléme Congrès International des Sciences Administratives,* Warsaw, July, 1936, pp. 19, 57, 241, 647.
Present at this Conference were such well known Americans as Leonard D. White of the Civil Service Commission, Louis Brownlow, Director of the Public Administration Clearing House of Chicago, and Charles E. Merriam, Chairman of the Political Science Department of the University of Chicago.
54. Institut International des Sciences Administratives, *Objet, Membres, Activités, Publications,* 1937.
55. *Local Government Administration,* The Organ of the International Union of Local Authorities, September, 1937, p. 156.
56. *Ibid.,* p. 155.
57. International Housing Association, Permanent International Association of Road Congresses, International Federation for Housing and Town Planning (which later merged with the International Housing Association and entered into close cooperation with the Union and Institute), International Federation of Employees in Public and Civil Services, International Institute of Public Law, International Institute of Statistics.

58. Organ of Union, *op. cit.*, pp. 125–27, 155f. See also *Compte Rendu des Délibérations de la Réunion de Paris—Juillet 1937, consacrée à la Recherche d'une Coopération Rationnelle entre les Grandes Associations Internationales,* Institut International des Sciences Administratives, Union Internationale des Villes et Pouvoirs Locaux, Brussels; and "Coopération entre les Grandes Associations Internationales," Extrait de la *Revue Internationale des Sciences Administratives,* année 1937, No. 4.

59. Directory, 1936, *op. cit.,* p. 68; and *International Federation for Housing and Town Planning,* leaflet.

60. Leaflet, *op. cit.*

61. *Handbook, op. cit.,* p. 106.

In the field of linguistics and anthropology we may also mention the following associations: International Congress of Anthropological and Ethnological Sciences, International Anthropological Institute, International Committee for the Unification of Anthropological Methods, Anthropos Institute, Permanent International Committee of Linguists, International Society for Logopedy and Phoniatry, International Phonetic Association, Universal Esperanto Association.

62. *Handbook, op. cit.,* p. 106; and Edwin W. Smith, *The Story of the Institute, A Survey of Seven Years,* International Institute of African Languages and Cultures, 1934, p. 9.

63. *Ibid.,* pp. 12–13.

64. Diedrich Westermann, "The Work of the International Institute of African Languages and Cultures," *The International Review of Missions,* October, 1937, p. 494.

65. "Documentation—Congrès mondial de la Documentation universelle (Paris 16–21 aout 1937)," *La Co-operation Intellectuelle,* January–February, 1937, pp. 73–74; *Sommaire, Congrès Mondial de la Documentation Universelle, Paris, 16–21 août 1937,* Exposition International des Arts et Techniques, Paris 1937, 12 août 1937; Pierre Vasseur, "Economic Information, Essential Factor in Modern Business Organization," *World Trade,* June 1937, pp. 68–69.

66. *Handbook, op. cit.,* p. 120.

67. *Ibid.,* p. 113.

68. *Inter-Auteurs, Bulletin Officiel de la Confédération Internationale des Sociétés d'Auteurs et Compositeurs,* June–July 1937, pp. 483ff.

69. *Compte Rendu du Onzième Congrès de la Confédération Internationale des Sociétés d'Auteurs et Compositeurs—Tenu à Berlin du 28 septembre au 30 octobre 1936,* pp. 36–37.

70. Confédération Internationale des Sociétés d'Auteurs et Compositeurs, *Statuts, Réglements des Fédérations, des Commissions et des Congrès, Annexe III, Réglement d'Arbitrage Confédéral;* Rene Jeanne, "Rapport annuel de Secrétaire Général," *Douzième Congrès, Paris 1937, Confédération Internationale des Sociétés d'Auteurs et Compositeurs,* pp. 45–46.

71. *Rapports, Congrès International des Editeurs, Onzième session (Londres, 7–12 Juin 1936)*, London, pp. 18–20; "Texte définitif des Voeux adoptés à la XIe Session du Congrès International des Éditeurs (Londres 1936)," *Bulletin du Bureau Permanent,* No. 5 (du 15 mars 1937); and Congrès International des Éditeurs, *Bulletin* No. 2 (January 30, 1936), pp. 15–16 and No. 3 (May 25, 1936), p. 12.

72. Congrès International des Éditeurs, *Réglement d'arbitrage international,* Berne, 1914.

PRESS

1. Robert W. Desmond, *The Press and World Affairs,* New York, London, D. Appleton-Century Co., 1937, p. 50.

2. *Ibid.,* p. 219.

3. *Ibid.,* pp. 65–66.

4. The members of the League are listed here according to countries. The status of the organization is indicated as follows: * private or "independent," † "semi-official," ‡ official, § unknown:

‡ Austria	† France
† Belgium	‡ Germany
‡ Bulgaria	* Great Britain
* Canada	† Greece
* China	† Hungary
§ Czechoslovakia	‡ Italy
* Denmark	† **Japan**
§ Estonia	§ Latvia
§ Finland	§ Lithuania

‡ Netherlands
* Norway
‡ Poland
† Portugal
‡ Rumania
‡ Russia
‡ Spain
† Sweden
§ Switzerland
† Turkey
* United States
† Yugoslavia

Ibid., pp. 66–67.
5. *Ibid.,* p. 68.
6. *Ibid.*

EDUCATION

1. World Association for Adult Education, *Eighteenth Annual Report and Statement of Accounts, 1936–37,* pp. 12–13.
2. *New Education Fellowship,* pamphlet, London, 1937 (?), pp. 3–4; and letter from secretariat, October 19, 1937.
3. Pamphlet, *op. cit.,* p. 3.
4. *Handbook, op cit.,* pp. 187–88.
5. *Ibid.*
6. *Ibid.,* p. 195.
7. *Ibid.*
8. *Annuaire de la Confédération Internationale des Étudiants, 1935–1936–1937,* pp. 30–36.
9. Michael Poberezky, "La Crise de la Confédération Internationale des Étudiants," *Vox Studentium,* October-December, 1931, *passim,* and *Annuaire, op. cit.,* pp. 25–26.
10. *Dix Ans de Cooperation entre les Organisations Internationales d'Étudiants,* Rapport présenté par l'Institut international de coopération intellectuelle, Onzième Session du Comité des Organisations internationales d'étudiants, Genève, 27–28 avril 1936, pp. 7–8, 13, 18; and International Institute of Intellectual Co-operation, *Les Associations Internationales d'Étudiants,* Paris, 1931, pp. 6–7.
11. *Ibid.,* p. 17.
12. *Ibid.,* p. 24.
13. *Handbook, op. cit.,* p. 197.
14. The *ISS* has no members; prior to the last war it had offices or "collaborators" in a number of countries. Its governing body, "The Assembly," was composed of twenty persons from various countries.
15. International Student Service, *The Universities and the Future, A Report and a Forecast,* 1935, pp. 3–4.

16. Foreword by John R. Mott in Ruth Rouse, *Rebuilding Europe, The Student Chapter in Post-War Reconstruction,* London, 1925.
17. *Handbook, op. cit.,* p. 194.
18. *Ibid.*
19. *International Student Service, Annual Report, 1936–1937,* pp. 5–6; ISS, *The Universities and the Future,* 1936, p. 12; and Walter Kotschnig, *Unemployment in the Learned Professions,* London, Oxford University Press, 1937, p. 1.
20. *Ibid.,* p. 310.
21. *Handbook, op. cit.,* pp. 176–77.

RELIGION

1. These three have been the most important œcumenical bodies; as Henry Smith Leiper (*World Chaos or World Christianity, A Popular Interpretation of Oxford and Edinburgh, 1937,* Chicago, New York, 1937, p. 8) has pointed out, they are "all partly ecumenical (none can be fully ecumenical which does not actually include the *whole* of the church throughout the world)."
2. This Alliance was dissolved on June 30, 1948, and was reorganized to include other than Christians under the title, World Alliance for International Friendship through Religion.
3. Eric Fenn, *That They Go Forward, An Impression of the Oxford Conference on Church, Community and State,* London, 1938, p. 16.
4. John R. Mott, *Cooperation and the World Mission,* New York, 1935, pp. 7–10.
5. W. W. Gethman, "Days of Transition and Re-orientation," *Youth in the New World,* Report of the World's Committee of Young Men's Christian Associations to the Twenty-first World's Conference at Mysore, India, January 2–10, 1937, p. 151.
6. Leiper, *op. cit.,* p. 179.
7. Charles S. Macfarland, *International Christian Movements,* New York, 1924, pp. 94–95.
8. William Paton, *Jerusalem 1928,* International Missionary Council, p. 39.
9. John R. Mott quoted in Leiper, *op. cit.,* p. 167.
10. "Facing a World Crisis," *Report*

NOTES AND REFERENCES

of the World's Committee of Young Men's Christian Associations to the XXth World's Conference at Cleveland, August 4th–9th, 1931, p. 65.

11. John R. Mott, *op. cit.*, pp. 10–11.

12. Paton, *op. cit.*, p. 39.

13. "Appendix E., Report of the Department of Social and Industrial Research and Counsel," *Minutes of the Committee of the International Missionary Council, Northfield, Massachusetts, September 27–October 7, 1935,* p. 49.

14. *Ibid.*, p. 50.

15. Leiper, *op. cit.*, p. 7. The League of Nations *Handbook* states that the delegates at this conference came from thirty-seven countries.

16. J. H. Oldham, "Introduction," *The Churches Survey Their Task, The Report of the Conference at Oxford, July, 1937, on Church, Community, and State,* London, 1937, p. 11.

17. *Ibid.*, p. 17.

18. *Handbook, op. cit.*, p. 60.

19. Leiper, *op. cit.*, p. 8.

20. "Foreword," *Programme for the second World Conference on Faith and Order to be held at Edinburgh, Scotland, August 3–18, 1938,* published by Continuation Committee, Winchester, England, New York, 1935, pp. 3–5.

21. Leiper, *op. cit.*, p. 9.

22. William Adams Brown, *Next Steps on the Road to a United Church,* prepared for the Commission on the Church's Unity in Life and Worship in preparation for the World Conference on Faith and Order, Edinburgh, 1937, pp. 2–5.

23. See footnote 2 above.

24. Lord Dickinson of Painswick, "Foreword," *Handbook,* World Alliance for International Friendship through the Churches, 1935, pp. 3–5.

25. *Ibid.*, pp. 10–15.

26. *Ibid.*, pp. 10–11, 60.

27. Charles S. Macfarland, *op. cit.*, pp. 188–89.

28. World Alliance for International Friendship through the Churches, *Annual Report, 1936–1937,* pp. 14–15.

29. *Bulgarian–Yugoslav Relations,* Report presented by Professor Stefan Zankow, to the General Secretary of the World Alliance for International Friendship through the Churches, May 11, 1937.

30. Interview, H. L. Henriod.

31. *Facing a World Crisis, Report of the World's Committee of Young Men's Christian Associations to the XXth World's Conference at Cleveland, August 4th–9th, 1931,* p. 38.

32. *Handbook, op. cit.*, p. 102.

33. *Minutes of the Plenary Meeting of the World's Committee of the Young Men's Christian Association,* 1927, p. 44.

34. The International Committee of Young Men's Christian Associations of the United States and Canada, *YMCA International, 1935–1936,* New York, 1936, p. 27; and International Committee of YMCA's of the U. S. and Canada, *The Story of the YMCA International, 1844–1934,* New York, pp. 1, 2, 13.

35. *Ibid.*, p. 10; and *YMCA International, 1935–36, op. cit.*, p. 25.

36. *Ibid.*, pp. 5, 10, 16.

37. *International Survey of the Young Men's and Women's Christian Associations, An Independent Study of the Foreign Work of the Christian Associations of the United States and Canada,* The International Survey Committee, 419 Fourth Avenue, New York, 1932, p. 403.

38. Clarence P. Shedd, *Two Centuries of Student Christian Movements, Their Origin and Intercollegiate Life,* New York, 1934, p. 362.

39. *Ibid.*, p. 372.

40. John R. Mott, *The World's Student Christian Federation, Origin, Achievement, Forecast,* 1920, p. 15.

41. Tissington Tatlow, *The Story of the Student Christian Movement in Great Britain and Ireland,* London, 1933, pp. 882–87.

42. W. A. Visser 't Hooft, *Students Find the Truth to Serve (1930–1935),* World's Student Christian Federation, 1935, pp. 20–21 and 24–25.

43. For discussion of the significance of the 1911 Conference of the Federation at Constantinople, see W. A. Visser 't Hooft, Editorial, "The Federation and the Eastern-Orthodox Nations," *The Student World,* Second Quarter, 1935, pp. 94–95; and Tatlow, *op. cit.*, p. 418.

44. *The World's Student Christian Federation, What It Is, What It Does, How Students Can Participate,* Third Revised Edition, Geneva, 1934, pp. 11–12.

45. Brown, *op. cit.,* pp. 43ff.

46. Leiper, *op. cit.,* p. 161.

47. The Council was finally established at the Amsterdam conference (August 22–September 4, 1948) with headquarters at Geneva. Ninety-one churches of thirty-three countries affiliated, representing a membership of about three hundred and fifty million.

48. "The Churches and the International Crisis, 1939," *Bulletin,* Commission to Study the Organization of Peace, January–February, 1942, pp. 4–5.

49. *Handbook, op. cit.,* p. 61.

50. Francis Younghusband, "Preface," *The World's Need of Religion, Being the Proceedings of the World Congress of Faiths, Oxford, July 23–27th, 1937,* London, 1937, pp. vxi–xvii, xix.

51. *Handbook, op. cit.,* p. 66.

52. *Report of the Meeting of the Executive Committee of the European Central Office for Inter-Church Aid at Ridley Hall, Cambridge, August 19th–23rd, 1937,* mimeographed.

53. *The World's Sunday School Association, What It Is and What It Does,* leaflet.

54. *The Unique Service of the World's Sunday School Association,* leaflet; and Handbook, *op. cit.,* p. 95.

55. *Handbook, op. cit.,* p. 87; corrected from *Salvation Army Year Book,* 1938, p. 41.

56. See *Acts of Parliament and Schedules attached hereto cited as 21 and 22 Geo. 5, Salvation Army Act 1931, Ch. XCIV.*

57. *Year Book, op. cit.,* pp. 1, 41, 47.

58. *Ibid.,* pp. 14–16.

59. *Ibid.,* p. 30.

60. Macfarland, *op. cit.,* pp. 94–95.

61. J. H. Rushbrooke, *The Baptist World Alliance, Origin, Constitution, Achievements, Objects,* typewritten, p. 6.

62. J. H. Rushbrooke in *Official Report, Fifth Baptist World Congress, Berlin, August 4–10, 1934,* London, 1934, p. 23.

63. *Ibid.,* pp. 7–8.

64. Rushbrooke, *op. cit.,* pp. 9–10.

65. *Handbook, op. cit.,* p. 58.

66. *Ibid.*

67. *Time,* June 6, 1938, p. 54; and *New York Times,* May 26 and 29, 1938.

68. *The Christian Young Workers,* no date, leaflet.

69. *Ibid.*

70. Union Internationale des Ligues Féminines Catholiques, *Apercu Historique,* leaflet, 1936; Union Internationale des Ligues Féminines Catholiques, *Ce que pensent et réalisent dans le monde 30 millions de femmes catholiques,* 1937, p. 5; Union Internationale des Ligues Féminines Catholiques, leaflet, no title; and *Handbook, op. cit.,* p. 49.

71. *Aperçu Historique, op. cit.*

72. Translation, *Ibid.*

73. *Ibid.*

74. Leaflet, no title, *op. cit.*

75. Translation, *Aperçu Historique, op. cit.*

76. *Apostleship of the Sea,* leaflet.

77. Letter from Cardinal Pizzardo, the Vatican, to the AMIC, February 12, 1938.

78. Leaflet, *op. cit.*

79. The following letter from Cardinal Pizzardo of the Vatican gives an indication of the position of *AMIC* in the Catholic world: "It gave me great pleasure to learn of the laudable work which the Apostolatus Maris International Council is achieving, and since this enterprise is such an important part of Catholic action, it has my hearty approval. It is, indeed, very gratifying to hear that so many 'Service Centers' have been established in the various ports, and I hope that this good work will continue until each and every port will have its own centre, Hostel and Club. The Holy Father has insisted that Catholic sailors should be trained to be apostles to their fellow seamen. . . . The Holy Father takes a deep personal interest in the world of the Apostolatus. . . ." Signed, G. Card. Pizzardo; dated, February 12th, 1938.

80. *Apostleship of the Sea Quarterly,* March, 1938, p. 2.

81. *Handbook, op. cit.,* p. 44.

82. *Ibid.,* p. 53.

83. *Ibid.,* p. 62.

Social Welfare

1. Elsie M. Zimmern, *Facts Concerning the A.C.W.W. as given at The International Speakers' School, January, 1938*, mimeographed, p. 3.
2. "Midwifery Services in Rural Areas, Report prepared by the Associated Country Women of the World," Special Supplement to *The Countrywomen*, August, 1937, p. 2 and *passim;* and, letter from secretariat, May 2, 1938.
3. David Horowitz, *Jewish Colonization in Palestine*, Institute of Economic Research, Jewish Agency for Palestine, Jerusalem, 1937, pp. 45–47.
4. A number of *INGO's* in the field of "Medicine and Hygiene," in addition to those mentioned in this section, may be found in the League of Nations *Handbook of International Organisations*, 1938.
5. *The Florence Nightingale International Foundation*, 1935, pp. 6–7, 9.
6. *Handbook, op. cit.*, p. 215.
7. Isabel M. Stewart and committee members, *The Educational Programme of the School of Nursing*, The International Council of Nurses, Geneva, 1934, pp. 9–12.
8. Translation, Association Professionnelle Internationale des Médecins, *Statuts*, Article 2.
9. Translation, Association Professionnelle Internationale des Médecins, *Règlement intérieur*, Article 1.
10. Association Professionnelle Internationale des Médecins, *Ce qu'est l'A.P.I.M., Sa constitution, ses buts, ses moyens et ses travaux*, 1937, pp. 3–4.
11. *Bulletin de la Fondation Documentaire Dentaire*, No. 3, 1933.
12. Foundation Bulletin, *op. cit.*, No. 2, 1935; and letter from secretariat, November 16, 1937.
13. Federation Dentaire Internationale, *Bulletin Annuel*, 1937, pp. vi, 6–11; and *Handbook, op. cit.*, p. 204.
14. See, for example, "Report on the Activities of the International Association for the Prevention of Blindness, since its foundation, 1929–1936," *The Number of the Blind and the Protection of the Eyes in Different Countries, International Association for Prevention of Blindness, XV Concilium Ophthalmologicum*, Paris, 1937.
15. *Ibid.*, p. 13.
16. Association Internationale de Pédiatrie Préventive, *Quatrième Conférence, Lyon 27–28 Septembre 1934;* and *Compte Rendu de la Cinquième Conférence, Bâle, 20–21 Septembre 1935, passim.*
17. Following the War, the Committee held such Congresses in 1929, 1930, and 1935. In 1938 its membership consisted of some fifty experts on industrial medicine from nineteen countries. *Handbook, op. cit.*, p. 208.
18. *Activities of the Health Service, International Labour Office, 1919–1937*, typewritten (furnished by Prof. L. Carozzi), no author given.
19. Report of the International Secretariat of Stone Workers in International Federation of Trade Unions, *Triennial Report, 1933–1935*, Paris, 1937, p. 343; and Activities of the *ILO* Health Service, *op. cit.*
20. *Third Conference on the Health and Welfare of Seamen convened by the League of Red Cross Societies* [etc.], October 5, 1936, Preface, pp. 1–11, 63–78.
21. *Handbook, op. cit.*, p. 222; and interview, Secretariat, League of Red Cross Societies.
22. *Les Informations de L'OCIC*, No. 10, January 15, 1938, *passim;* and *L'Office Catholique International du Cinématographie, Son Histoire, Sa Mission, Ses Premières Réalisations, Son Avenir, passim.*
23. *Revue Internationale de Legislation pour la Protection de la Nature, Congo Belge 1930–1934*, 1936, inside cover; *Handbook, op. cit.*, p. 432; *Deuxième Congrès International pour la Protection de la Nature, Paris, 30 juin–4 juillet 1931, Procès-Verbaux, Rapports et Voeux*, Paris, 1932, p. 537.
24. *Conference Report, Third International Conference on Social Work, London, 12–18 July, 1936*, London, 1938, Preface.
25. *Ibid.*, pp. 175–77.
26. *A Study of the World's Y.W.C.A.*, Geneva, 1932, pp. 21–22.
27. "Qu'est-ce l'International Migration Service?" *Extrait de la Revue Inter-*

nationale de la Croix-Rouge, seizième année, no. 189, septembre, 1934, pp. 721–31, pp. 5–6.

28. *Handbook, op. cit.,* pp. 71–72.

29. Extract, Red Cross Review, 1934, *op. cit.,* p. 7.

30. Porter Lee, "Beyond Our Own Shores," *Migrants 1930, New Standards of International Practice,* International Migration Service, Geneva, 1930, pp. 42–43.

31. *Catholic International Union for Social Service,* leaflet, June, 1935.

32. *Note sur les resultats de l'activité de l'Union Catholique Internationale de Service Social,* typewritten, 1938 (?).

33. The Editor, *Bulletin d'Information,* Union Catholic Internationale de Service Social, October 1936, p. 3.

34. League of Nations, *Statut de la Femme,* document A. 54. 1937, V. p. 1.

35. International Alliance of Women for Suffrage and Equal Citizenship, *Congress Report,* 1929, p. 179.

36. *Report of the Joint Demonstration on Nationality of Married Women held 14th March, 1930, at The Hague,* International Council of Women, International Alliance of Women for Suffrage and Equal Citizenship, passim.

37. *The Associated Country Women of the World,* leaflet.

38. *Ibid.*

39. Elsie M. Zimmern, *op. cit.,* p. 1.

40. *Minutes of the Triennial Conference of the Associated Countrywomen of the World, June 1st to 8th, 1936, Washington, D. C., U.S.A,* p. 8.

41. Paul S. Reinsch, *Public International Unions,* Boston, 1911, p. 65.

42. In 1938, the International Abolitionist Federation had national sections in thirteen countries, all European except Syria and Uruguay, and individual members in five countries. Its last Congress before 1938 was in 1931. *Handbook, op. cit.,* p. 38.

43. Reinsch, *op. cit.,* p. 65.

44. Translation, *Cinquante ans d'activité de la Fédération internationale des Amies de la Jeune Fille, 1877–1927,* pp. 10–11.

45. In child welfare, as in other phases of activity, for an over-all view of what *INGO's* have accomplished, the work of organizations in other fields should be noted. For example, to make the sum total of their efforts more effective, the Joint Committee of the Major International Associations endeavoured to coordinate the work of its member associations in dealing with the effect of the depression on young people (*Joint Committee of the Major International Associations, Ten Years' Activity,* Paris, 1936, p. 38); the *ILO* considered the World's *YWCA* to be the best source of information on child labor in China. Much of the industrial work of the Chinese National *YWCA,* and the inquiry undertaken by the Shanghai Municipal Council on child labor, was influenced by a representative of the World's *YWCA* (Interview, World's *YWCA*).

46. *Save the Children International Union, 1934,* leaflet.

47. *Ibid.*

48. *Ibid.* Above quotations from leaflet.

49. *Sommaire, XIIe Session de l'Association Internationale pour la Protection de l'Enfance, Paris, 19–22 juillet 1937;* "Liste des publications," *Bulletin International de La Protection de l'Enfance,* No. 148, Brussels, 1937; and *Mission et activité de l'A.I.P.E., Association Internationale de la Protection de l'Enfance,* typewritten.

50. *Constitution* and *Deuxième Assemblée Générale de l'Association Internationale des Juges des Enfants, Journées des 15, 16 et 17 Juillet 1935,* pp. 52–55, *passim.*

51. The organizational features of the International Red Cross are explained fully in Laszlo Lederman, "The International Organization of the Red Cross and the League of Red Cross Societies," *The American Journal of International Law,* July, 1948, pp. 635–44.

52. John Barton Payne quoted in B. de Rougé, "Thirteen Years, What the League Owes to Judge Payne," *Monthly Bulletin,* League of Red Cross Societies, May, 1935, p. 87.

53. *The International Red Cross,* 1937, and *Facts and Figures about the Junior Red Cross,* mimeographed, June 1937. It should be noted that a high

proportion of these eighteen million members merely contributed small amounts of money and did not actively participate in any Red Cross activities.

54. This statement is made without minimizing the tremendous work of the League of Nations and the *ILO* in checking certain epidemics, in the collection of information on epidemic diseases, the interchange of health specialists, the standardization of sera, assistance to governments in improving their public health services, etc.

55. T. B. Kittredge, Secretary General, League of Red Cross Societies, "1919–1929: A Survey," *The World's Health*, April–June, 1929, p. 152.

56. See p. 167.

57. League of Red Cross Societies, *Proceedings, XVIth Meeting of the Board of Governors, Paris, November 25th to 27th, 1936*, p. 72.

58. *League of Red Cross Societies*, Paris, 1937, p. 10; and Dr. René Sand, in 1936 Proceedings, *op. cit.*, p. 42.

59. *Facts and Figures, op. cit.*

60. International Red Cross Committee, *Rapport-Général, 1912–1920*, p. 14.

61. International Red Cross Committee, *343me Circulaire, Action de la Croix-Rouge en Espagne*, p. 7.

62. League of Red Cross Societies, "Relief Operations in Spain," *Monthly Bulletin*, January, 1938, p. 3.

63. *Ibid.;* and *The International Red Cross, 1937*, p. 18.

64. *The International Red Cross Committee and Its Missions Abroad (1918–1923)*, pp. 15–16.

65. *Rapport Général du Comité International du Croix Rouge, 1912–1920*, pp. 111ff.

66. *General Report of the International Red Cross Committee on Its Activities from 1921 to 1923*, Document 40a., pp. 60–61. The League of Nations, in *Ten Years of World Co-operation* (pp. 265–67) places more emphasis on its own contributions than on that of the Red Cross.

67. *The International Red Cross*, 1937, p. 18.

68. "Relief Operations in Spain," *op. cit.*, p. 3.

69. Rougé, *op. cit.*, p. 87.

70. *Handbook, op. cit.*, p. 77.

71. *Service Civil International*, International Service for Peace, 1934.

72. We need to recall the work already discussed of the International Migration Service, the Jewish Association for the Protection of Girls, Women and Children, the International Federation for Aid to Young Women; also note, student aid to refugees, religious aid, Red Cross aid, etc.

73. *Handbook, op. cit.*, p. 64.

74. *Bulletin d'Information de la HIAS-JCA Emigration Association (HICEM)*, December 1936, p. 3.

75. Translation, quoted in John L. Bernstein, *The Migration of Jews in Recent Years*, New York, The American Jewish Committee, 1936, reviewed in *Bulletin, op. cit.*, p. 10.

76. *Handbook, op. cit.*, p. 71.

77. V. de Tworkowski, "Bienfaisance Internationale," *Dictionnaire de Sociologie*, Paris, 1934 (?), p. 899.

78. "Organized groups of the Bulgarians of Roumania and Yugoslavia; the Catalans of Spain; the Basques and Galicians of Spain; the Germans of Czechoslovakia, Denmark, Estonia, Hungary, Italy, Latvia, Poland and Romania (Bessarabia); the Slovenes and Croats of Austria and Italy; the Slovaks of Hungary; the Czechoslovaks of Austria, the Hungarians of Czechoslovakia, Roumania and Yugoslavia; the Lithuanians of Germany and Poland; the Ukrainians of Poland and Roumania; the White Russians of Poland," *Handbook, op. cit.*, p. 59.

79. See White, *op. cit.*, pp. 139–43.

80. See Nathan Feinberg, *La Question des Minorités à la Conférence de la Paix de 1919–1920 et l'Action Juive en Faveur de la Protection Internationale des Minorités*, Conseil pour les Droits des Minorités Juives, Paris, 1929, and *Le Comité des Délégations Juives, Dix-Sept ans d'Activité*, 1936, p. 9. The influence of the "Union des Nationalitiés" and the "Organization centrale pour la Paix durable" is also discussed.

81. Antiprohibitionist *INGO's* include the following: the International League of Anti-Prohibitionists, the Permanent International Committee on Wine-Growing, the International Union of the Development of Grape-Cure Re-

sorts and the Consumption of Grapes, the International Committee on the Trade in Wines, Ale, Ciders, Spirituous Liquors, and Kindred Industries.

82. The International Federation for the Protection of Native Races Against Alcoholism (see *Handbook, op. cit.,* p. 39), dissolved before the war.

83. *Unification du droit pénal et codification progressive du droit pénal international, Memorandum adressé aux Nations Unies par le Bureau International pour l'Unification du Droit Pénal,* Edité par La Revue de Droit International de Sciences Diplomatiques et Politiques (A. Sottile), Genève, 1947, *passim.*

SPORTS

1. *New York Times,* July 29, 1932, p. 19.

2. Translation, "L'Association Internationale des Automobile-Clubs Reconnus," *Revue Internationale de l'Automobile,* August, 1936, p. 5.

3. Translation, letter from secretariat, January 10, 1933.

4. Baillet-Latour, President of the *IOC*, "The Rights and duties of the International Olympic Committee, the National Olympic Committees and the International Federations," *Bulletin Official du Comité International Olympique,* January 1927, English section, p. 15.

5. *Statutes of the International Olympic Committee,* Article 2.

6. *Ibid.,* Article 17.

7. *Bulletin Officiel de Comité International Olympique,* June, 1932, pp. 3–5. Before the war, there were fifty-four national Olympic Committees, and twenty-two international sporting federations.

8. *Regulations for the Olympic Congresses,* Article 2.

9. Baillet-Latour, *op. cit.,* p. 5.

10. *By-Laws of the International Amateur Athletic Federation.*

INTERNATIONAL LAW AND THE LEGAL SETTLEMENT OF DISPUTES

1. In this connection, we need to note the contribution of those *INGO's* whose work is discussed under the section, *Pursuit of Peace,* and those in the religious field, like the World Alliance for International Friendship Through the Churches, which have helped to erase bitter antagonisms at the official level.

2. William Martin, "Le Role de la Croix-Rouge dans le développement du droit international," *Revue Internationale de la Croix-Rouge,* March, 1927, pp. 161–73.

3. Translation, *Statuts de l'Institut de Droit International,* Article 1.

4. Codification of the international law of peace; Admission and expulsion of foreigners; Nationality of married women; Reprisals in time of peace; Creation of an international organization to deal with questions regarding the high seas; International rivers and waterways of international interest; The legal nature of consultative opinions of the Permanent Court of International Justice: their value and their positive effect in international law; Recognition, determination and significance, in international law, of the domain left by international law to the exclusive jurisdiction of the state; The problem of the access of individuals to international courts; Competence of international courts; Recognition of new states and governments; Consular immunities and immunities of persons invested with functions of international interest; Revision of the rules concerning bills of exchange and promissory notes; Conclusion of international treaties: signature, ratification, adhesion; The effects of the most favored nation clause: The extraterritorial effect of foreign repressive decisions; Conflicts of law over the condition and the capacity of individuals; The legal effects of changes in territorial sovereignty; Diplomatic protection of nationals abroad; Conflict of laws over aerial navigation; sources of international law; protection of minorities; The legal foundation for the conservation of the riches of the sea. *Annuaire de l'Institut de Droit International,* 1931, pp. 233ff.

5. James Brown Scott, Editor, *Resolutions of the Institute of International Law,* New York, 1916, pp. V–VI.

6. Quoted from American Society of

International Law, *Proceedings*, 1915, pp. 164–65, in letter from George A. Finch, August 23, 1937.

7. *Ibid.*

8. James Brown Scott, Editor, *The Reports to the Hague Conferences of 1899 and 1907, being the official explanatory and interpretative commentary accompanying the draft conventions and declarations submitted to the conferences by the several commissions charged with preparing them, together with the texts of the final acts, conventions and declarations as signed, and of the principal proposals offered by the delegations of the various powers as well as of other documents laid before the commission,* Oxford, 1917, pp. 75, 144.

9. *Ibid.*, pp. 503, 504, 604, 656, 659, 662, 673, 679, 697, 732, 761, 762, 847.

10. Translation, Discours de M. James Brown Scott, *Annuaire de l'Institut de Droit International, Session de New York, Octobre 1929,* pp. 58–59.

11. James P. Hendrick, "An International Bill of Human Rights," in *The Department of State Bulletin,* February 15, 1948, p. 195.

12. Stevan Tchirkovitch, *L'Institut Américain de Droit International,* Paris, 1926, p. 95.

13. George A. Finch, *The Sources of Modern International Law,* Washington, 1937, p. 72.

14. J. S. Reeves, "The Montevideo Resolution on Codification," *American Journal of International Law,* 1934, p. 319.

15. Translation, Tchirkovitch, *op. cit.,* p. 124.

16. *Ibid.*, pp. 126–27. Following mention of the League of Nations action, Tchirkovitch states, "Let us note following this repercussion the project for the International Institute for the Unification of Private Law which the Italian Government offered to establish at Rome." Some connection seems to be implied.

17. Translation, *ibid.,* p. 116.

18. Manley O. Hudson, "The Development of International Law Since the War," *American Journal of International Law,* Vol. 22, 1928, p. 346.

19. *Handbook, op. cit.,* p. 247.

20. Colegrove, *op. cit.,* pp. 116–17.

21. The Association was one of the seven international organizations with which the League of Nations, by Assembly action, kept in close contact concerning penal and penitentiary problems.

22. International Law Association, *Report of the Thirty-Ninth Conference held at Paris . . . September 10th to 15th, 1936,* 1937, pp. XI–XII.

23. George Rupert Rudolf, *The York-Antwerp Rules, Their History and Development, with Comments on the Rules of 1924,* London, 1926, pp. 1, 2, 4, 17, 18, 20, 23, 25, 26, 28, 29, 31.

24. *Handbook, op. cit.,* pp. 241–42.

25. V. V. Pella, *L'Association International de Droit Penal et la Protection de la Paix,* Paris, 1947, pp. 1–10.

PURSUIT OF PEACE

1. Herbert H. Shenton, *Cosmopolitan Conversation, The Language Problems of International Conferences,* 1933, pp. 23, 32.

2. A. C. F. Beales, *The History of Peace,* London, 1931, pp. 259–62.

3. In its early years the Inter-Parliamentary Union "had no permanent organisation, the Conferences merely inviting members to form 'Inter-Parliamentary Committees' in their Parliaments; out of these the present National Groups have grown." *The Inter-Parliamentary Union,* 1929 (?), p. 5.

4. *Statutes of the Inter-Parliamentary Union,* Article 1.

5. *The Inter-Parliamentary Union, Its Work and Organization,* Third Edition, 1930, p. 5.

6. Chr. L. Lange, "The Interparliamentary Union," reprinted from *Advocate of Peace,* March, 1932, pp. 3–4.

7. John Hay, quoted in James Brown Scott, *The Hague Peace Conferences of 1899 and 1907, A series of lectures delivered before the John Hopkins University in the year 1908,* Baltimore, 1909, pp. 168–69.

8. James L. Tryon, *The Interparliamentary Union and its Work,* American Peace Society, March, 1910, p. 4.

9. Translation, Christian L. Lange, "Histoire de la Doctrine Pacifique et de son influence sur le développement du

droit international," Académie de Droit International, *Recueil des Cours, 1926,* Vol. III, Paris, 1927, pp. 403–04. See also Michael Priklonsky, "Die Vorgesschichte der ersten Haager Friedenskonferenz," in Alfred H. Fried, Editor, *Die Friedens-Warte,* May, 1929, pp. 129ff.

10. Lange, *op. cit.,* pp. 5–6; and James Brown Scott, *op. cit.,* pp. 90–91.

11. Lange, *op. cit.,* p. 6.

12. *Ibid.,* pp. 7–8.

13. Chr. L. Lange, "Introduction, Part I," *Resolutions adopted by Inter-Parliamentary Conferences and Principal Decisions of the Council, 1911–1936,* Geneva, 1937, p. 13.

14. *Ibid.,* p. 18.

15. Lange, "The Interparliamentary Union," *op. cit.,* p. 9.

16. William Martin, *Disarmament and the Inter-Parliamentary Union, 1931, passim.*

17. *Ibid.,* p. 13.

18. Beales, *op. cit.,* p. 299; and John H. Latané, Ed., *Development of the League of Nations Idea, Documents and Correspondence of Theodore Marburg,* New York, 1932, Vol. II, pp. 821–22.

19. *Ibid.,* pp. 281–82.

20. This has been acknowledged in U. S. peace literature, public magazines and newspapers.

21. Letter to writer, November 22, 1937; and Dorothy Detzer, *Memorandum on the History of the Munitions Campaign of the Women's International League for Peace and Freedom,* mimeographed, June, 1934.

22. This Federation was liquidated after the war, and in 1946 the World Federation of United Nations Associations was founded.

23. *Bulletin of the International Federation of League of Nations Societies,* April–July, 1930, No. III, *passim;* and *Handbook, op. cit.,* p. 20. In 1930, the Federation had national societies in thirty-eight countries (Bulletin, *op. cit.*); likewise in 1938, with societies in the Union of South Africa, Argentina, Canada, China, Haiti, Iran, Japan, Palestine, Tangier, United States, and twenty-eight European countries. (*Handbook, op. cit.*)

24. Federation *Bulletin,* Nos. I and II, January–March, 1930, pp. 6–7, Nos. III–IV, April–August, 1936, pp. 122–23; and *Handbook, op. cit.*

25. Federation *Bulletin,* Nos. I and II, January–March, 1930, pp. 8–9.

26. Federation *Bulletin,* No. 2, April–May, 1926, p. 10.

27. Federation *Bulletin,* Nos. I and II, January–March, 1930, pp. 11–12.

28. Felix Morley, "The Federation's Fourteenth Congress," *League of Nations News,* July–August, 1930, p. 5.

29. Federation *Bulletin,* Nos. III–IV, April–August, 1936, pp. 65–66.

30. The Peace and Disarmament Committee of the Women's International Organizations was composed of representatives of thirteen INGO's and five national organizations: International Council of Women; World's *YWCA;* International Alliance of Women for Suffrage and Equal Citizenship; Women's International League for Peace and Freedom; World Union of Women for International Concord; League of Mothers and Educators for Peace; International Federation of Business and Professional Women; League of Jewish Women; European Federation of Soroptimist Clubs; World's Women's Christian Temperance Union; International Co-operative Women's Guild (observer); International Federation of University Women (ob.); National Committee on Cause and Cure of War; Women's Polish Organizations; Association of Slavic Women; Women's Peace Committee (G.B.); Federation of American Women's Clubs Overseas. *Handbook, op. cit.,* p. 26.

31. Joint Disarmament Committee of the Christian International Organizations represented the World's Committee of the YMCA's; World's Committee of *YWCA's,* World's Student Christian Federation, World Alliance for International Friendship through the Churches, Universal Christian Council on Life and Work, Friends International Service. *Ibid.,* p. 25.

32. The student organizations were: Pax Romana—National Federations of Catholic Students; International Federation of University Women; International Confederation of Students; World's Student Christian Federation; Interna-

NOTES AND REFERENCES

tional University Federation for League of Nations; World Union of Jewish Students. *Ibid.*, p. 25.

33. *Vox Populi,* Vox Populi Committee, Geneva, 1933, pp. 9–10; and the *International Consultative Group (For Peace and Disarmament), Its Origin, Aims and Development,* Geneva, 1937, pp. 4–5.

34. Peace and Disarmament Committee of the Women's International Organisations, *Documents Illustrative of the Activities of the Committee,* 1931–1937, p. 44.

35. *International Consultative Group, op. cit.,* pp. 6–7.

36. *Ibid.,* pp. 2, 3, 7.

37. *Ibid.,* p. 9; League of Nations, *Conference for the Reduction and Limitation of Armaments, Journal,* Special Supplement, No. 5, October 26, 1933; and *International Consultative Group, op. cit.,* p. 10.

38. *Handbook, op. cit.,* pp. 28–29.

39. *Ibid.,* pp. 28–30; and International Peace Campaign, *Report of the International Secretariat, VIth General Council,* Geneva, September 13th–14th, 1937, pp. 4–11.

40. "Eighteen Months' Work for Peace, Mr. Noel-Baker's Report on I.P.C.'s International Development," *Monthly Bulletin of the International Peace Campaign,* November–December, 1937, p. 34.

41. S. H. Bailey, *International Studies in Modern Education,* London, Oxford University Press, 1938, pp. 1–2.

42. "Les Tâches principales de l'Union des Associations Internationales," *Compte-Rendu sommaire, Conférence des Associations Internationales,* Geneva, September, 1924, Publication No. 115, pp 10–11.

43. One number appeared after the war.

44. H. R. G. Greaves, *The League Committees and World Order,* Oxford, 1931, pp. 111–12.

45. *Constitution of the Institute of Pacific Relations,* Article II.

46. *The Origin and Present Activity of the Institute of Pacific Relations,* (undated, but about October, 1931), pp. 3–4.

47. Galen M. Fisher, *A Bird's-Eye View of the Institute of Pacific Relations,* Institute of Pacific Relations, New York, 1937, p. 7.

48. Condliffe, *op. cit.,* p. 2. For a discussion which throws much light on the procedure, subject matter and the general results of one of these conferences, see Chester H. Rowell's "The Kyoto Conference of the Institute of Pacific Relations," in *International Conciliation,* No. 260, May, 1930.

49. Quincy Wright, "Yosemite Conference of the Institute of Pacific Relations," *American Journal of International Law,* 1936, p. 712.

50. Rowell, "The Kyoto Conference," *op. cit.,* pp. 11–12, 54.

51. Fisher, *op. cit.,* p. 8.

52. *Ibid.,* p. 16.

53. American Council, Institute of Pacific Relations, *Annual Report of the Secretary,* 1936, p. 6.

54. *Publications on the Pacific, 1936, Catalogue of the Institute of Pacific Relations and its National Councils,* New York, 1936, pp. 31–33.

55. Henry F. Angus, *The Problem of Peaceful Change in the Pacific Area, A Study of the Work of the Institute of Pacific Relations and its Bearing on the Problem of Peaceful Change,* London, and New York, 1937, pp. 67–68.

56. *Ibid.,* pp. 10–11, 193.

57. International Institute of Intellectual Co-operation, *The International Studies Conference, Origins, Functions, Organisation,* Paris, 1937, pp. 11, 15, 29, 37–50, 76ff., 123.

58. Bailey, *op. cit.,* pp. 22–23.

59. Interview, Mr. Leo Gross, Institute of Intellectual Co-operation.

60. *Handbook, op. cit.,* pp. 14–16; and John B. Whitton, "The Re-organization of the Geneva Research Centre," *Geneva Special Studies,* Vol. VIII, No. 10, 1936–37, *passim.*

61. Established in 1888, with headquarters at Brussels; in 1938 its membership consisted of National Women's Councils in thirty-five countries with a total membership of forty million.

62. Rotary International, *International Service,* September, 1938, p. 4.

63. Bernhard Ragner, "One Up on

the Diplomats," *The American Legion Monthly*, March, 1937, pp. 24–25.
64. *Ibid.*, pp. 48–49.
65. H. W. Dunning, "The Italo-British Agreement," *FIDAC*, June, 1938, pp. 4, 29.
66. Ragner, *op. cit.*, p. 50.
67. *Ibid.*, pp. 50–51.
68. Henri Pichot quoted in "International Ex-servicemen," *FIDAC*, April 1938, p. 18.
69. Bailey, *op. cit.*, pp. 251–52; and *Facts and Figures About the Junior Red Cross*, mimeographed, June 1937, *passim*.
70. World's Alliance of the Y.M.C.A., Announcement, *Fifth Pacific Area YMCA Older Boys' Camp-Conference*.
71. Boy Scouts International Bureau, *Jamboree*, October 1929, p. 1020; and The Boy Scouts Association, *The History and Organisation of World Scouting*.
72. *Ibid., passim*.
73. *Facts and Figures About the Junior Red Cross, op. cit., Educational Service Bulletin of the World's Sunday School Association*, July 1937; and International Broadcasting Union, *Broadcasting, op. cit.*
74. *Règlement Interieur et Directives du Comité D'Entente des Grandes Associations Internationales.*
75. *Handbook, op. cit.*, pp. 428–29; and Joint Committee of the Major International Associations, *Ten Years' Activity*, Paris, 1936, p. 30.
76. *Ibid.*, p. 31.
77. *Ibid.*, pp. 32–33.
78. *Ibid.*, pp. 32–46.
79. *Ibid.*, p. 35.
80. *Ibid.*, p. 36.
81. For its work in the field of education, see pp. 131–132.
82. International Student Service, *A Three Years Plan, 1937–1938–1939*, pp. 6, 10–11; and *Annual Report, 1936–1937*, pp. 9–11.
83. For relief work under title, European Student Relief, see p. 130.
84. *The Universities and the Future, op. cit.*, p. 7.
85. *Annual Report, op. cit.*, pp. 5–7; and *Three Years Plan, op. cit.*, statement inside back cover.

PART III

RELATIONSHIP OF *INGO'S* WITH INTER-GOVERNMENTAL ORGANIZATIONS

1. An especially interesting case of the relationship of *INGO's* to national governments is the Jewish Agency for Palestine (the World Zionist Organization). There were "regular relations between the Government [of Palestine] and the Executive of the Jewish Agency, which, according to the terms of the Mandate, [had] the right of 'advising and cooperating with the Administration of Palestine in such economic, social and other matters as may affect the interests of the Jewish national home and the interests of the Jewish population in Palestine.' " Israel Cohen, *The Progress of Zionism*, Zionist Organisation, London, 1935, p. 22.
2. International Relief Union, *Official Texts*, Second Edition, Geneva, December, 1935, pp. 18, 23, 37–39.
3. Clyde Eagleton, *International Government*, New York, 1932, p. 256.
4. Clemens Lammers, *op. cit.*, p. 20.
5. Pierre Bovet, *Vingt Ans de Vie, L'Institut J. J. Rousseau de 1921 á 1932*, Neuchatel, Switzerland, 1932, pp. 117, 171; *Rockefeller Foundation Annual Report for 1936*, New York, p. 142; P. Rossello, *Le Bureau International d'Éducation*, brochure, Geneva, no date, p. 6.
6. Translation, Wilhelm Kaufmann, "Les Unions Internationales de Nature Économique," *Recueil des Cours*, Academie de Droit International, 1924, Vol. II, Paris, 1925, p. 199.
7. *Ibid.*, p. 205.
8. M. Mintz, "World Problems of Copyright," *World Trade*, August 1931, pp. 283–84.
9. C. Howard-Ellis, *op. cit.*, p. 467.
10. Information from Secretariat, League of Nations.
11. Charlotte T. Niven, "The Y.W.C.A. in the World," *The Women's Press*, December, 1926, p. 531; and International Alliance of Women for Suffrage and Equal Citizenship, *Report of the Twelfth Congress, Istanbul, April 18th to 24th, 1935*, p. 72.
12. *Economic and Financial Organi-*

NOTES AND REFERENCES

zation of the League of Nations, Information Section pamphlet, Revised Edition, about 1930, pp. 107–108.

13. League of Nations, Secretariat, *Ten Years of World Cooperation,* Geneva, 1930, pp. 264–65.

14. International Student Service, *The Universities and the Future,* 1935, p. 5.

15. Berenstein, *op. cit.,* p. 237.

16. *Ibid.,* p. 245.

17. *Bulletins* of the Federation.

18. *Ten Years of World Cooperation, op. cit.,* p. 412.

19. *Youth in the New World, Report of the World's Committee of Y.M.C.A.s to the Twenty-first World's Conference at Mysore, India, January 2–10, 1937,* p. 69.

20. League of Nations, *Statut de la Femme, Rapport présenté par la première Commission à l'Assemblée,* A. 54. 1937. V., Geneva, September 25, 1937.

21. *News Letter of the Universal Christian Council for Life and Work,* No. 8, October 15, 1932, p. 5.

22. *Inter-Parliamentary Bulletin,* June, 1933, pp. 105–106; see also "Annexe II, Résponses des organizations internationales á M.L. 5. 1935. XI," in C.C. 1622, Genève, le 3 mars 1936, Commission Consultative du Trafic de l'Opium et autres Drogues Nuisibles, *Enquete sur les mesures prises par les gouvernments et par les associations nationales et internationales en vue d'organiser la lutte contre la toxicomanie et contre le trafic illicite des stupefiants.* Résponses à C.L. 199. 1934. XI et à M.L. 5. 1935. XI. League of Nations, *passim.*

23. *The Federation of Private and Semi-Official Organizations Established at Geneva, Its Aims and Activities,* Geneva, 1937, pp. 5 and 9. This Federation in 1938 grouped forty-two INGO's and devoted its efforts to promoting the interests of its members regarding such matters as taxes, use of the former League of Nations Secretariat building (Palais Wilson) and the Disarmament Buildings, and with securing special facilities at League meetings for the accredited representatives of unofficial organizations.

24. Union of International Associations, *La Société des Nations et l'Union des Associations Internationales,* Publication No. 118, 1926, p. 14.

25. International Federation of League of Nation Societies, *Bulletin,* January–March, 1930, p. 17; and subsequent *Bulletins.*

26. League of Nations document A. 62. 1937. IV., *Penal and Penitentiary Questions, Report submitted by the Fifth Committee of the Assembly, September 30th, 1937;* and document A. 23. 1937. IV., *Penal and Penitentiary Questions, Report by the Secretary-General to the Assembly,* September 1st, 1937.

27. Translation, *Cinquante ans d'activité de la Fédération internationale des Amies de la Jeune fille, 1877–1927,* Bureau Central International, Neuchâtel, pp. 11–12.

28. See also *La Société des Nations et l'Union des Associations Internationales,* published by the Union (Publication No. 118) in 1926.

29. Bertram Pickard, "The Greater League of Nations. A Brief Survey of the Nature and Development of Unofficial International Organisations," reprinted from *The Contemporary Review,* October, 1936, pp. 6–7.

30. *Ibid.,* p. 8.

31. The International Migration Service, however, felt that its relations with the League were very good, better than they had been in the beginning.

32. G. Zwerner, Nansen International Office for Refugees; and Mlle. Posnansky, International Red Cross Committee.

33. This Institute was directly attached to the League of Nations.

34. International Confederation of Students, *Yearbook 1930,* p. 13.

35. Prospectus, International Institute of Intellectual Cooperation, *La Coordination des Enseignements du Second Degré,* 1938.

36. League of Nations Committee on Intellectual Co-operation, *Nineteenth Session, op. cit.,* pp. 51–53.

37. Berenstein, *op. cit.,* p. 230.

38. The American Foundation, *The World Court,* Ninth Edition, New York, February, 1931, pp. 50–51.

39. Berenstein, *op. cit.*, pp. 230–34.
40. See pp. 81–84.
41. See pp. 35–38.
42. See p. 64.
43. Some observers of the employers' group in Geneva expressed the opinion that this attitude of the employers has been very much influenced by the fact that they have been in almost all cases paid *employees* and not really *employers* in the true sense.
44. Wilson, *op. cit.*, p. 135.
45. C. Howard-Ellis, *op. cit.*, p. 264. Quoted by permission of George Allen and Unwin Ltd., Publishers. For further information on how collaboration between governmental and private groups is not only mutually useful but even necessary, see Henri Fuss, "Collaboration of Private Societies with Official Institutions," *Migrants, 1930,* International Migration Service, Geneva; and A. Arnou, *L'Organisation Internationale du Travail et les Catholics,* Paris, 1933, pp. 95–110.
46. Jean Zarras, *op. cit.*, p. 202.
47. United Nations, Economic and Social Council, Resolution 288 (X), 27 Feburary 1950, document E/1646, 2 March 1950. This resolution revised the arrangements for consultation which had been adopted by the Council on June 21, 1946 and subsequently modified from time to time. See also "Non-Governmental Organization Consultative Methods Revised," *United Nations Bulletin,* April 15, 1950, pp. 370–72.
48. *Ibid.*
49. United Nations, Economic and Social Council, *Arrangements for Consultation with Non-Governmental Organizations, Guide for Consultants,* document E/INF/23, April 30, 1948, pp. 10–12.
50. The following material is adapted from Lyman C. White, "The Emerging Age of World Cooperation," address before the Commission on World Peace of the Methodist Church, Chicago, November 8, 1949, UN Press Release PM/1520, 7 November 1949. In view of the author's connection with the United Nations, as a member of the Secretariat, names of the organizations are omitted. Full details may, however, be found in "Activities Undertaken by Non-Governmental Organizations up to 1 June 1949 in Connexion with their Consultative Status, Report of the Secretary-General," UN document E/C.2/231 (and Add. 1–4). 25 November 1949.

APPENDIX

INGO'S OFFICIALLY RECOGNIZED BY THE UNITED NATIONS AND ITS SPECIALIZED AGENCIES[1]

GRANTED CONSULTATIVE OR SIMILAR STATUS (JANUARY 1951)

KEY

\# Established during or after World War II
1 Economic and Social Council of the United Nations[2]
2 Food and Agricultural Organization
3 International Civil Aviation Organization[3]
4 International Labour Organization
5 International Refugee Organization[4]
6 International Telecommunications Union[5]
7 United Nations Educational, Scientific and Cultural Organization
8 Members of the Temporary International Council for Educational Reconstruction (an advisory committee of *UNESCO*)
9 World Health Organization

1. Concerning specialized agencies not included above: The conventions establishing the International Trade Organization, the International Maritime Consultative Organization and the World Meteorological Organization have not yet gone into effect. The International Monetary Fund, the International Bank for Reconstruction and Development, and the Universal Postal Union do not maintain official relationships with *INGO's;* the *UPU,* however, cooperates closely with the International Air Transport Association in regard to air mail postal rates.

2. A number of national organizations have been brought into consultative relationship with *ECOSOC:* All-India Women's Conference, Anti-Slavery Society (United Kingdom), Carnegie Endowment for International Peace (United States), Howard League for Penal Reform (United Kingdom), Indian Council of World Affairs, National Association of Manufacturers (United States), Society of Comparative Legislation (France).

3. *ICAO* invites organizations to attend particular meetings. Organizations which have been so invited are included in this list, since they are considered to be in "consultative or similar status."

4. Many private national organizations are participating on a widespread scale in the field operations of *IRO.* They are, of course, omitted from this listing of *INGO's.*

5. The convention establishing the *ITU* provides for cooperation with international organizations having allied interests, and although *INGO's* are not brought into direct relationship with the governing body (the Plenipotentiary Conference) of the *ITU,* they are invited to participate in the Administrative Conferences of the Union and in the meetings of its International Consultative committees. Several *INGO's* were invited to participate in the 1947 Conference, which drew up the Convention and General Regulations governing the *ITU*—among them, the International Broadcasting Union, the International Chamber of Commerce, the International Air Transport Association, the International Shipping Federation.

10 Organizations not listed in connection with one of the above bodies, but placed on the register of the Secretary-General of the United Nations for *ad hoc* consultations by request of *ECOSOC*. (Note: The register also includes the organizations in "consultative or similar status" with any of the specialized agencies, provided that they are not already in category A or B status with *ECOSOC* and that they conform to *ECOSOC* resolution 214 C (VIII) on *INGO's* having members in Spain)

3	Aero Medical Association
1, 7	Agudas Israel World Organization
#, 7	Asian Relations Organization
2, 7	Associated Country Women of the World
#, 6	Association Internationale der interets radio-maritimes (A.I.I.R.M.)
#, 9	Biometric Society
7, 8	Boy Scouts International Bureau
1, 7, 8	Catholic International Union for Social Service
#, 1, 2, 7, 8	Commission of the Churches on International Affairs (representing the World Council of Churches and the International Missionary Council to *ECOSOC* and *UNESCO*)
#, 1	Consultative Council of Jewish Organizations (representing the Alliance Israelite Universelle, the American Jewish Committee and the Anglo-Jewish Association)
#, 1	Co-ordinating Board of Jewish Organizations for Consultation with the Economic and Social Council of the United Nations (representing the British Board of Jewish Deputies, the South African Board of Jewish Deputies and B'nai B'rith)
#, 7, 9	Council for the Co-ordination of International Congresses of Medical Sciences
10	Econometric Society
#, 10	Engineers Joint Council
6	European Broadcasting Union
#, 1, 7, 8	Friends' World Committee for Consultation
#, 9	Inter-American Association of Sanitary Engineering
#, 4	Inter-American Confederation of Workers
#, 1	Inter-American Council of Commerce and Production
1	International Abolitionist Federation
9	International Academy of Forensic and Social Medicine
3	International Aeronautical Federation
1	International African Institute
#, 3, 6	International Air Transport Association
1, 7, 8	International Alliance of Women—Equal Rights, Equal Responsibilities
6	International Amateur Radio Union
7	International Association for Bridge and Structural Engineering
#, 7	International Association for the Exchange of Students for Technical Experience
#, 1	International Association of Independent Enterprises, Trades and Crafts
3	International Association of Oceanography

APPENDIX 307

1	International Association of Penal Law (jointly represented with the International Bureau for the Unification of Penal Law)
9	International Association for the Prevention of Blindness
#, 7	International Association on Soil Mechanics and Foundation Engineering
#, 7	International Association of University Professors and Lecturers
6	International Astronomical Union
1, 3	International Automobile Federation (jointly represented with the International Touring Alliance)
#, 6	International Broadcasting Organization
1	International Bureau for the Suppression of Traffic in Women and Children
1	International Bureau for the Unification of Penal Law (jointly represented with the International Association of Penal Law)
1	International Carriage and Van Union (jointly represented with the International Wagon Union)
1, 2, 3, 6	International Chamber of Commerce
6	International Chamber of Shipping (formerly: International Shipping Conference)
3	International Commission on Illumination
7	International Committee on Modern Literary History
6	International Committee on Radio-Electricity
1, 9	International Committee of the Red Cross
1, 7, 8	International Committee of Schools of Social Work
1, 7	International Committee of Scientific Management
#, 1, 4, 7	International Confederation of Free Trade Unions
7	International Confederation of Societies of Authors and Composers
6, 7	International Conference of Large Electric Systems
1, 7, 8, 9	International Conference of Social Work
#, 7	International Congress for Modern Architecture
1, 2, 4	International Co-operative Alliance
1	International Co-operative Women's Guild
10	International Council of Commerce Employers
#, 7	International Council of Museums
9	International Council of Nurses
#, 7	International Council for Philosophy and Humanistic Studies (composed of: International Academic Union, International Commission on Folk Arts and Folklore, International Committee on Historical Sciences, International Committee on History of Art, International African Institute, International Federation of Philosophic Societies, International Federation of the Societies of Classical Studies, International Institute of Philosophy, Permanent International Committee of Linguists)
7	International Council of Scientific Unions (composed of: International Astronomical Union, International Geographical Union, International Scientific Radio Union, International Union of Biological Sciences, International Union of Chemistry, International Union of Crystallography, International

	Union of Geodesy and Geophysics, International Union of History of Science, International Union of Pure and Applied Physics, International Union of Theoretical and Applied Mechanics)
1, 2, 7, 8	International Council of Women
1	International Criminal Police Commission
9	International Dental Federation
#, 7	International Economic Association
#, 1, 2, 4	International Federation of Agricultural Producers
#, 3	International Federation of Air Lines Pilots Associations
10	International Federation of Building Employers and Public Works (Confederation)
1	International Federation of Business and Professional Women
1, 4	International Federation of Christian Trade Unions
7	International Federation for Documentation
1	International Federation of Friends of Young Women
1	International Federation for Housing and Town Planning
#, 3	International Federation of Independent Air Transport
7, 8	International Federation of Library Associations
#, 7	International Federation of Musical Youth
1, 7	International Federation of Newspaper Publishers (Proprietors) and Editors
#, 7, 8	International Federation of Organizations for School Correspondence and Exchanges
7	International Federation of the Phonographic Industry
6	International Federation of Radiotelegraphists
8, 10	International Federation of Secondary School Teachers
7	International Federation of Surveyors
8	International Federation of Teachers Associations
1	International Federation of Unions of Employees in Public and Civil Services
1, 7, 8	International Federation of University Women
#, 7	International Federation of Workers' Educational Associations
1	International Fiscal Association
#, 7	International Folk Music Council
3	International Geographical Union
9	International Hospital Federation
1, 7	International Institute of Administrative Sciences
7	International Institute of Political and Social Sciences concerning countries of differing civilizations
1, 7	International Institute of Public Finance
1	International Institute of Public Law
2	International Landworkers Federation
1, 3, 7	International Law Association
9	International League Against Rheumatism
#, 1	International League for the Rights of Man
9	International Leprosy Association
7	International Literary and Artistic Association
6	International Maritime Radio Committee
	International Missionary Council (see Commission of the

APPENDIX

	Churches on International Affairs)
10	International Music Council
1	International Organization of Employers
#, 7	International Organization of Journalists
#, 1, 3, 6, 7	International Organization for Standardization
7	Internation P.E.N. Club
9	International Pharmaceutical Federation
#, 7	International Political Science Association
#, 7, 8	International Relief Committee for Intellectual Workers
#, 1	International Road Transport Union
6	International Scientific Radio Union
	International Shipping Conference (see International Chamber of Shipping)
6	International Shipping Federation
1, 5, 7	International Social Service
7	International Society for Contemporary Music
1, 7	International Society of Criminology
7	International Society for Musical Research
1	International Society for the Welfare of Cripples
#, 7	International Sociological Association
1, 7	International Statistical Institute
	International Student Service (see World University Service)
7	International Studies Conference
1	International Temperance Union
#, 7	International Theatre Institute
1, 3	International Touring Alliance (jointly represented with the International Automobile Federation)
1	International Transport Workers' Federation
9	International Union Against Cancer
9	International Union Against Tuberculosis
9	International Union Against Venereal Diseases
3	International Union of Aviation Insurers
#, 1, 7	International Union of Architects
1, 7, 8	International Union of Catholic Women's Leagues
#, 1, 2, 7, 8, 9	International Union for Child Welfare
#, 1, 7, 8	International Union of Family Organizations
3	International Union of Geodesy and Geophysics
#, 7	International Union of Institutes of Archaeology, History, and the History of Art
1	International Union of Local Authorities
#, 1, 3	International Union of Official Travel Organizations
6	International Union of Producers and Distributors of Electric Power
1, 3	International Union of Railways
7	International Union for the Protection of Nature
1, 7	International Union for the Scientific Study of Population
#, 7	International Union of Students
7, 8	International Voluntary Service for Peace (the organization prefers to use its French title only *Service Civil International*)
1	International Wagon Union (jointly represented with the International Carriage and Van Union)

7, 8	International Youth Hostel Federation
1, 7	Inter-Parliamentary Union
#, 7	Joint Committee of International Teachers' Federations
6	Joint International Committee for tests relating to the protection of telecommunication lines and underground ducts (C.M.I.)
7, 8, 9	League of Red Cross Societies
1	Liaison Committee of Women's International Organizations (composed of: Associated Country Women of the World, International Alliance of Women—Equal Rights, Equal Responsibilities, International Co-operative Women's Guild, International Council of Women, International Federation of Business and Professional Women, International Federation of Friends of Young Women, International Federation of University Women, International Federation of Women Magistrates and Members of the Legal Profession, Open-Door International for the Economic Emancipation of the Women Workers, Pan-Pacific Women's Association, St. Joan's International Social and Political Alliance, World's Woman's Christian Temperance Union, World Union of Women for International Concord)
1	Lions International—International Association of Lions Clubs
#, 5	Lutheran World Federation
5	Mennonite Central Committee (United States and Canada only)
7	New Education Fellowship
#, 1	Nouvelles Équipes Internationales (no English title)
5, 7, 8	O.R.T. World Union
8	O.S.E. Union
#, 1, 7	Pax Romana—International Catholic Movement for Intellectual and Cultural Affairs (in relation to ECOSOC and UNESCO, jointly represented with Pax Romana—International Movement of Catholic Students)
1, 7	Pax Romana—International Movement of Catholic Students
1, 7	Rotary International
1	Salvation Army
	Service Civil International (see International Voluntary Service for Peace)
7, 8	Soroptimist International
#, 10	South American Petroleum Institute
#, 5	Standing Conference of Voluntary Agencies
#, 6	Union sudanéricaine de Radiodiffusion (*USARD*)
#, 1, 7	Women's International Democratic Federation
1, 7	Women's International League for Peace and Freedom
#, 1, 7	World Assembly of Youth
7	World Association of Girl Guides and Girl Scouts
#, 5	World Council of Churches (represented to *ECOSOC* and *UNESCO* through the Commission of the Churches on International Affairs)
#, 1, 7	World Engineering Conference
#, 7, 8	World Federation of Democratic Youth

APPENDIX

#, 7, 9	World Federation for Mental Health
#, 1, 2, 4, 7	World Federation of Trade Unions
#, 1, 2, 7, 8, 9	World Federation of United Nations Associations
1, 7, 8	World Jewish Congress
#, 9	World Medical Association
#, 1	World Movement of Mothers
#, 7, 8	World Organization for Early Childhood Education
#, 1, 7, 8	World Organization of the Teaching Profession
6, 7	World Power Conference
7	World Student Christian Federation
#, 5, 7, 8	World Student Relief
7	World Union of Jewish Students
1	World Union for Progressive Judaism
7	World University Service (formerly: International Student Service)
1, 5, 7, 8	World's Alliance of Young Men's Christian Associations
1	World's Woman's Christian Temperance Union
1, 5, 7, 8	World's Young Women's Christian Association
7	Young Christian Workers

BIBLIOGRAPHY

This bibliography is intended to cover only the more important general material. References to sources on particular international organizations will be found in the appropriate places throughout the book.

GENERAL SOURCES

Office Central des Associations Internationales, Brussels, *Annuaire de la Vie Internationale,* 1908–09 and 1910–11.

———, *La Vie Internationale,* a monthly periodical appearing from January 1912 to the outbreak of World War I. One number appeared after the war.

League of Nations, *Handbook of International Organizations (Associations, Bureaux, Committees, etc.),* Geneva, 1938 (XII. B.) International Bureaux, 1937. XII. B. 4.

———, *The Quarterly Bulletin of Information on the Work of International Organizations,* compiled by the Section of International Bureaux of the League of Nations Secretariat, published from 1922 to 1938.

International Institute of Intellectual Co-operation, Paris, *La Co-operation intellectuelle.*

International Institute of Administrative Sciences, Brussels, *A Directory of International Organizations in the Field of Public Administration,* 1936.

Masters, Ruth D., and others, *Handbook of International Organizations in the Americas,* Carnegie Endowment for International Peace, Washington, 1945.

Union of International Associations, *Annuaire des Organisations Internationales [Yearbook of International Organizations],* Geneva, 1950 edition.

Bulletin Mensuel [Monthly Review], Union des Associations Internationales [Union of International Associations], Palais d'Egmont, Brussels, Belgium (published since January 1949).

United Nations Bulletin, published twice a month by the United Nations, contains occasional articles on non-governmental organizations. See the Index, issued every six months.

United Nations document E/INF/23, 30 April 1948, "Arrangements of the Economic and Social Council of the United Nations for consultation with Non-Governmental Organizations, Guide for Consultants." (A revised edition is to be issued as E/C, 2/INF/2, February[?] 1951.)

United Nations, Department of Public Information, "Non-Governmental Organizations" Background Paper No. 61, ST/DPF/SER.A/61, May 20, 1950.

United Nations document E/INF/224, 31 August 1949, "Non-Governmental Organizations in Consultative Status, Information regarding the ninety non-governmental organizations in consultative status, compiled by the Secretariat."

Gregory, Winifred, ed., *International Congresses and Conferences, 1840–1937, A Union List of their Publications available in Libraries of the United States and Canada,* under Auspices of the Bibliographical Society of America, New York, 1938, 229 pp.

Congresses, Tentative Chronological and Bibliographical Reference List of National and International meetings of Physicians, Scientists, and Experts, Second Supplement, Fourth Series, Index-Catalogue, United States Army (Army Medical Library), Government Printing Office, Washington, 1938. See also *First Addition to the Reference List of Congresses,* Published in the Third Volume, Fourth Series, of the Index-Catalogue.

White, Lyman Cromwell, *The Structure of Private International Organizations,* Philadelphia 1933.

———, "Peace by Pieces—The Role of Non-Governmental Organizations," *The Annals of the American Academy of Political and Social Science,* July 1949, pp. 87–97.

———, "Nouvelles méthodes pour l'organisation de la Pax internationale," *La Revue de Droit International de Sciences Diplomatiques et Politiques (Sottile),* No. 3/1949, pp. 1–10.

———, "Preventing War versus Peace Making," *The Bulletin of the World Federation for Mental Health,* Vol. 1, No. 6, December, 1949, pp. 16–21.

———, "The Conference of International Non-Governmental Organizations, Palais des Nations, Geneva, Switzerland, May 15th to 21st 1948," in *World Affairs,* Fall, 1948, pp. 160–66.

Graven, Jean et Bouzat, Pierre, "La Conference des Organisations Consultatives Non Gouvernementales des Nations Unies," *Revue Internationale de Droit Pénal,* No. 3–4, 1948, pp. 311–357.

Mander, Linden A., *Foundations of Modern World Society,* 2nd Edition, New York, 1947.

Potter, Pitman B., *An Introduction to the Study of International Organization,* 5th Edition, New York and London, 1948. See Chapter III.

Schrag, Paul, *Internationale Idealvereine,* Bern-Leipzig, 1936.

Woolf, L. S., *International Government,* 2nd Edition, New York, 1916.

Hodges, Charles, *The Background of International Relations,* New York, 1931.

Otlet, Paul, "L'Organisation Internationale et les Associations Internationales," in *Annuaire de la vie Internationale, 1908–09,* Brussels, pp. 31–166.

Baldwin, Simeon E., "The International Congresses and Conferences of the Last Century as Forces Working Toward the Solidarity of the World," *American Journal of International Law,* Vol. I, 1907, pp. 565–78, 808–29.

Parkes, J. W., International Conferences, *A Handbook for Conference Organizers and Discussion Leaders,* Published in collaboration with The Inquiry, New York City, by International Student Service, Geneva, 1933.

MATERIAL ON PARTICULAR ORGANIZATIONS OR GROUPS THEREOF

Lorwin, Lewis L., *Labor and Internationalism,* New York, 1929.

Scheler, Michael S., "The World's Trade Unions Today," *Current History,* December 1931.

International Labor Office, Geneva, *International Labor Review* and *Industrial and Labor Information*.

Ridgeway, George L., *Merchants of Peace, Twenty Years of Business Diplomacy Through the International Chamber of Commerce*, New York, 1938.

Noailly Frédérique, *La Croix-Rouge au point de vue National et International, son histoire, son organisation*, Paris, 1935.

The following excellent series on "International Transport and Communications," issued under the auspices of the Royal Institute of International Affairs and published by the Oxford University Press, contains a wealth of information on both inter-governmental and non-governmental organizations working in this field:

Mance, Brig.-Gen. Sir Osborne, *International Telecommunications*, 1943.

———, *International Air Transport*, 1943.

———, *International River and Canal Transport*, 1944.

———, *International Sea Transport*, 1945.

———, *Frontiers, Peace Treaties, and International Organization*, 1946.

———, *International Road Transport, Postal, Electricity and Miscellaneous Questions*, 1947.

Wedgwood, Sir Ralph, *International Rail Transport*, 1946.

Spahr, Walter E., and Swenson, Rinehart J., *Methods and Status of Scientific Research*, New York, 1930.

"Les organisations internationales d'étudiants," *La Co-operation intellectuelle*, Revue de l'Institut International de Co-operation Intellectuelle, 15 Juillet, 1929, pp. 409–42.

Pochon, Roger, *Les Associations Internationale d'Étudiants*, Fribourg, Suisse, 1928.

Harley, John Eugene, *International Understanding, Agencies Educating for a New World*, Stanford University Press, 1931, pp. 291–342.

Bureau International Permanent de la Paix, Genève, *Annuaire des Associations Internationales à Tendances Pacifistes*, Dole, Suisse, 1929.

Ware, Edith E., *The Study of International Relations in the United States, Survey for 1937*, Published for the American National Committee on International Intellectual Co-operation, New York, 1938.

INDEX

Academy of International Law, 211, 247.
Advisory Committee for Intellectual Workers (of the ILO), 256.
Air transport, 24–26, 64–69, 99.
All-Asian Conference of Women, 180.
Alliance Aluminum Cie., 42, 43, 46, 283 (n. 89).
Alliance of Reformed Churches Throughout the World Holding the Presbyterian System, 136, 159, 255.
Allied Supreme Council, 81.
American Federation of Labor, 7, 78.
American Friends Service (Philadelphia), 165.
American Institute of Comparative Law and Legislation, 290 (n. 50).
American Institute of International Law, 13, 204–205.
American Political Science Association, 14.
American Society of International Law, 13, 203.
Amsterdam International, 78.
Anglo-American Press Association in Paris, 121.
Anthropos Institute, 291 (n. 61).
Anti-Alcohol movement, 196.
Apostolatus Maris Internationale Concilium, 69, 163–164, 173, 294 (n. 79).
Arbitration, private, 29–31, 49, 52–53, 63–64, 119, 120, 198–200, 201 (*see also* Cartels).
Arts, 118–120.
Associated Country Women of the World, 166, 180, 181, 233.
Association of Foreign Correspondents in the United States, 121.
Association entre les Grandes Organisations Nationales de Voyages et Tourisme, 51, 286 (n. 50).
Association Littéraire et Artistique Internationale, 247.
Association of Slavic Women, 234, 300 (n. 30).
Astronomy, 102–104.
Atlantic Conference (shipping), 63.
Aviation (*see* Air Transport).

Bahai Cause, 165.
Baltic and International Maritime Conference, 61–62.
Bank for International Settlements, 6, 22.
Baptist World Alliance, 159–161.
Bills of exchange, 29, 207.
Boy Scouts International Bureau, 11, 237, 238.
Broadcasting (*see* International Broadcasting Union, International Broadcasting Organization, European Broadcasting Organization).
Burschenschaft, 14.

Calcutta Conference (shipping), 62.
Camps, international, 237–238.
Carnegie Endowment for International Peace, 28, 174, 203, 226.
Cartels, 41–47.
Catholic International Union for Social Service, 179.
Central Commission on the Navigation of the Rhine, 4.
Central Council of International Touring, 51, 73–74.
Central Organization for a Durable Peace, 218, 219.
Chemistry, 105–106.
Child welfare, 184–187.
Christian Working Youth (*see* Christian Young Workers).
Christian Young Workers, 161–163.
Comité Consultatif International Télégraphique, 56.
Commission for International Relations and Travel (of the International Confederation of Students), 69–71.
Commission Internationale de Photométrie, 285 (n. 33.)
Committee of International Students' Associations, 128–129, 131, 245, 248, 256.
Committee of Jewish Delegations, 195.
Communism, 84, 85, 134 (*see also* Communist International, Red International of Labor Unions, Communist Manifesto).

315

INDEX

Communist International, 75, 85, 86–88.
Communist Manifesto of 1848, 86–87.
Comptoirs, 44.
Congress of European Nationalities, 195, 297 (n. 78).
Consultative Committee of Women on Nationality, 180.
Continental Tube Cartel, 45, 283 (n. 94).
Correspondence, international exchange of, 237.
Council of the Friends' Service (London), 165.
Court of Arbitration of the International Chamber of Commerce, 29–31, 201.

Dawes Plan (*see* Reparations and war debts).
Disarmament, 81, 217, 218, 220, 223–224.

Emigrants (*see* Migrants).
Engineering, 96–100.
Equal Rights International, 180.
Eucharistic Congress (*see* International Eucharistic Congress Movement).
European Broadcasting Association, 284 (n. 1).
European Central Office [or Bureau] for Inter-Church Aid, 155, 251.
European Christian Endeavour Union, 165.
European Federation of Soroptimist Clubs, 234, 300 (n. 30).
European Student Relief, 130, 239.

Fascism, 6–7, 82–83, 84, 85, 86, 134, 213.
Federation of Private and Semi-Official Organizations Established at Geneva, 251, 303 (n. 23).
FIDAC (*see* Inter-Allied Federation of Ex-Service Men).
First International, 87, 287 (n. 2).
Florence Nightingale International Foundation, 167, 188, 189.
Foreign Press Association in London, 121.
Foundation "Pour La Science"—International Centre for Synthesis, 288 (n. 4).
Friends International Service, 300 (n. 3).
Friends, Society of, 165.
Friends World Committee for Consultation, 165.

General Association of Municipal Health and Technical Officers, 290 (n. 50).
Geneva Research Centre, 233, 252.
Geodesy and Geophysics, 104–105.

Hague Court (*see* Permanent Court of International Justice).
Hague Peace Conferences of 1899 and 1907, 13, 201, 203–204, 213, 216–217.
Hague rules for uniform bills of lading, 23–24, 208.
Health, 166–173, 188–190, 297 (n. 54).
HIAS–JCA Emigration Association (*"HICEM"*), 193–194.
High Commission for Refugees (of the League of Nations), 81, 247, 249, 255.
Highway transport, 26, 268.
Hoerbiger Institute, 288 (n. 4).
Hoover moratorium (*see* Reparations and war debts).
Howard League for Penal Reform, 196.
Human rights, 204, 261–265.

IGO, 3–4
ILO (*see* International Labour Organization).
INGO (*see* International non-governmental organization).
Institut de Droit International, 13, 202–204, 225, 298 (n. 4).
Institute of Educational Sciences, 246.
Institute of Intellectual Co-operation (of the League of Nations), 57, 70, 101–102, 112, 117, 119, 128–129, 131, 228, 232, 233, 239, 245, 248, 255–256.
Institute of International Law (*see Institut de Droit International*).
Institute of Pacific Relations, 94, 146, 228–232, 250.
Inter-Allied Federation of Ex-Service Men, 11, 69, 234–237.
Inter-Allied Trade Union Congress, 75.
Inter-American Commission of Women, 180.
Intergovernmental organizations (*IGO's*), defined, 3–4.
International Abolitionist Federation, 182, 296 (n. 42).
International Academic Union, 112–113.
International Academy of Comparative Law, 290 (n. 50).

INDEX

International Advisory Committee on Wireless Communications, 56.
International Aeronautic Federation, 286 (n.50).
International African Institute (*see* International Institute of African Languages and Cultures).
International Agrarian Bureau, 90.
International Agricultural Co-ordination Commission, 92, 248.
International Air Traffic Association, 14, 25, 64–68.
International Air Transport Association, 64.
International Alliance of Socialist Lawyers, 85.
International Alliance of Women for Suffrage and Equal Citizenship, 179, 180–181, 182, 233, 300 (n. 30).
International Amateur Athletic Federation, 198, 200.
International Amateur Radio Union, 58–59.
International Anthropological Institute, 291 (n. 61).
International Association of Automobile Manufacturers, 199.
International Association for Bridge and Structural Engineering, 288 (n. 4).
International Association for Business Education, 124.
International Association of Children's Court Judges, 187.
International Association of Department Stores, 47–48.
International Association for the Fight against Unemployment, 110.
International Association of Industrial Accident Boards and Commissions, 173.
International Association of Journalists Accredited to the League of Nations, 121, 250.
International Association for Labor Legislation, 75–76, 171, 172.
International Association of Libraries (*see* International Library Association).
International Association for Life-Saving and First Aid to the Injured, 173.
International Association of Lions Clubs, 234.
International Association of Mercantile Marine Officers, 173.
International Association of Penal Law, 196, 211–212, 251, 290 (n. 50).
International Association for Prevention of Blindness, 171, 189.
International Association for Preventive Pediatrics, 171, 186.
International Association for the Promotion of Child Welfare, 184, 186–187.
International Association on Quaternary Research, 288 (n. 4).
International Association of Recognized Automobile Clubs, 53, 71–73, 198–199, 286 (n. 46, 47, 50).
International Association of Registers, 68–69.
International Astronomical Union, 101, 102–104.
International Automobile Federation (*see* International Association of Recognized Automobile Clubs).
International Bank for Reconstruction and Development, 28.
International Broadcasting Organization, 284 (n. 1).
International Broadcasting Union, 9, 10, 54–58, 214, 238, 284 (n. 1).
International Bureau Against Alcoholism, 196.
International Bureau of Automobile Standardization, 39–40, 53.
International Bureau of Education, 14, 245, 246.
International Bureau of Musicians, 118.
International Bureau for Physico-Chemical Standards, 101.
International Bureau for the Suppression of Traffic in Women and Children, 182.
International Bureau for Technical Training, 124.
International Bureau for the Unification of Penal Law, 196–197, 290 (n. 50).
International Catholic Association of Girls Friendly Societies, 182.
International Catholic Film Bureau, 174.
International Catholic League Against Alcoholism, 196.
International Centre for Workers' Education, 124.
International Chamber of Commerce, 6, 19–32, 33, 54, 62, 64, 66, 110, 111, 112, 117, 211, 226, 249, 250, 253, 254, 288 (n. 8).
International Chamber of Shipping (*see* International Shipping Conference).
International Chemistry Office (*see* International Office of Chemistry).

INDEX

International Civil Aviation Organization, 64, 276.
International Commission of Agriculture, 34–35, 89, 90–93.
International Commission for Air Navigation, 24–25, 65–66, 285 (n. 33).
International Commission of Congresses for Family Education, 124.
International Commission on the Educational Use of Films and Broadcasting, 125.
International Commission on Illumination, 285 (n. 33), 288 (n. 4).
International Commission on Radium Standards, 288 (n. 4).
International Commission for Resistance to Fascism, 85.
International Commission for Testing Electrical Installation and Wiring Equipment, 98.
International Commission for Testing Materials, 98, 100.
International Committee of Ex-Service Men, 237.
International Committee on Historical Sciences, 290 (n. 47).
International Committee on the History of Art, 118.
International Committee on Industrial Medicine, 171, 295 (n. 17).
International Committee of Inter-Cooperative Relations, 35, 93.
International Committee of Legal Experts on Technical Air Matters (*see* International Technical Committee of Legal Experts on Air Matters).
International Committee for the Polar Year, 1932–33, 106–107.
International Committee for the Publication of Annual Tables of Chemical, Physical, Biological and Technological Constants, 106.
International Committee of the Red Cross, 10, 173, 187–188, 190–192, 249, 255 (*see also* International Red
International Committee of Schools for Social Work, 126, 127.
International Committee on the Trade in Wines, Ale, Ciders, Spirituous Liquors, and Kindred Industries, 297 (n. 81).
International Committee for the Unification of Anthropological Methods, 291 (n. 61).

International Committee of *YMCA's* of the United States and Canada, 148–149.
International Concert Federation, 118.
International Confederation of Agriculture (*see* International Commission of Agriculture).
International Confederation of Authors' and Composers' Societies, 118–119.
International Confederation of Free Trade Unions, viii.
International Confederation of Intellectual Workers, 131.
International Confederation of Students, 69–71, 127–128, 237, 256, 300 (n. 32).
International Conference of Associations of Disabled Soldiers and Ex-Service Men, 223.
International Conference of Large Electric Systems (*see* International Conference of the Principal High-Tension Electrical Systems).
International Conference of National Unions of Mutual Benefit Societies, 170.
International Conference for the Prevention of Accidents, 173.
International Conference of the Principal High-Tension Electrical Systems, 99–100.
International Congress of Anthropological and Ethnological Sciences, 291 (n. 61).
International Congress on Modern Architecture, 118.
International Congress of Public Health Work, 189.
International Congress of Statistics, 107–108, 248.
International Consultative Committee on Long-Distance Telephonic Communications, 56.
International Consultative Group (For Peace and Disarmament), 223–224.
International Consultative Telephone Committee (of the International Union of Telecommunications), 26.
International Cooperative Alliance, 6, 30, 32–35, 112, 233, 253.
International Cooperative Banking Committee, 34.
International Cooperative School, 34.
International Cooperative Trading Agency, 34.

INDEX

International Co-operative Wholesale Society, 34.
International Co-operative Women's Guild, 34, 233, 300 (n. 30).
International Cotton Federation (*see* International Federation of Master Cotton Spinners and Manufacturers' Associations).
International Council of Nurses, 167–168.
International Council of Scientific Unions, 101–106, 256.
International Council of Women, 173, 180, 233, 239, 300 (n. 30), 301 (n. 61).
International Credit Insurance Association, 48.
International for Criminal Law (*Droit Pénal*), 290 (n. 50).
International Criminal Police Commission, 8, 196.
International Dental Federation, 11, 170.
International Economic Conference of 1927, 21–22, 43, 80, 92.
International Educational Cinematograph Institute of Rome, 139, 228.
International Electrotechnical Commission, 40–41, 56, 98, 99, 173.
International Entomological Association, 288 (n. 4).
International Eucharistic Congress Movement, 11, 161.
International Exhibition Bureau, 32.
International Federation of Agricultural Producers, 89.
International Federation for Aid to Young Women, 182–184, 251, 297 (n. 72).
International Federation of Arts, Letters and Sciences, 118.
International Federation of the Blue Cross Temperance Societies, 196.
International Federation of the Building Trades, 49.
International Federation of Business and Professional Women, 180, 234, 286 (n. 1), 300 (n. 30).
International Federation of Calvinists, 165.
International Federation of Camping Clubs, 237.
International Federation of Christian Factory and Transport Workers' Syndicates, 84.
International Federation of Christian Landworkers, 256.
International Federation of Christian Trade Unions, 82, 84, 256.
International Federation of Christian Trade Unions of Railway and Tramway Men, 84.
International Federation of Christian Workers in the Building Trades and of Wood-workers, 84.
International Federation of Dramatic and Musical Criticism, 118.
International Federation of Employees in Public and Civil Services, 290 (n. 57).
International Federation of European Beet Growers, 89.
International Federation of Friends of Young Women (*see* International Federation for Aid to Young Women).
International Federation for Housing and Town Planning, 9, 113–115, 290 (n. 57).
International Federation of Intellectual Workers, 286 (n. 1).
International Federation of League of Nations Societies, 15, 196, 220–223, 239, 249, 250, 251, 300 (n. 22).
International Federation of Master Cotton Spinners and Manufacturers' Associations, 49–50.
International Federation of National Standardizing Associations, 39–40, 98, 173, 285 (n. 33).
International Federation of Olive Growers, 89.
International Federation of the Phonographic Industry, 119.
International Federation of Professional Societies of Men of Letters, 118.
International Federation for the Protection of Native Races Against Alcoholism, 298 (n. 82).
International Federation of Secondary School Teachers, 126–127.
International Federation of Teachers' Associations, 126.
International Federation of Technical Agriculturalists, 90.
International Federation of Textile Workers Associations, 15, 78.
International Federation of Trade Unions, 6, 7, 15–16, 75, 77–84, 85, 88, 112, 172, 223, 247, 256, 257, 258, 287 (n. 14).

International Federation of Travel Agencies, 50–51, 286 (n. 50).
International Federation of University Women, 127, 128, 129–130, 233, 300 (n. 30, 32).
International Game-Shooting Council, 174.
International Geographical Union, 101.
International Geological Congress, 288 (n. 4).
International Goat Breeding Federation, 89.
International Guild of Hospital Librarians, 189.
International Health Bureau, 173.
International Hospital Association, 167, 189.
International Hotel Alliance, 50–51, 286 (n. 50).
International Hotelmen's Association, 50–51.
International Housing Association, 290 (n. 57).
International Industrial Relations Institute, 38–39, 286 (n. 1).
International Institute of Administrative Sciences, 113–115.
International Institute of African Languages and Cultures, 115–117, 139.
International Institute of Agriculture, 9, 22, 31, 91, 92, 110, 245, 248, 288 (n. 5).
International Institute of Constitutional History, 290 (n. 47).
International Institute of Documentation, 117–118.
International Institute of History of the French Revolution, 290 (n. 47).
International Institute of Public Law, 290 (n. 50, 57).
International Institute of Refrigeration, 245, 246.
International Institute at Rome for the Unification of Private Law, 119, 205, 299 (n. 16).
International Institute of Sociology, 290 (n. 47).
International Institute of Statistics, 107–112, 248, 249, 288 (n. 8), 290 (n. 57).
International Labour Organization, 5, 6, 22, 25, 35, 36, 37, 49, 64, 75, 76, 77, 79, 81, 82, 83, 93, 110, 111, 117, 127, 131, 132, 157, 171, 172, 173, 178, 233, 247, 256–258, 261, 297 (n. 54).

International Landworkers' Federation, 256.
International Law Association, 23, 197, 207–211, 212, 225, 251.
International League Against Alcoholism, 196.
International League Against Epilepsy, 171.
International League Against Rheumatism, 171.
International League of Anti-Prohibitionists, 297 (n. 81).
International League for the Campaign Against Trachoma, 171.
International League for the Rights of Man and Citizenship, 223.
International Legal Committee on Aviation, 206–207.
International Leprosy Association, 171.
International Library Association, 117.
International Maritime Committee, 23, 206.
International Maritime Radio Committee, 59–60.
International Mathematical Union, 289 (n. 13).
International Metal Workers' Federation, 78.
International Meteorological Organization, 104–105, 106, 289 (n. 24).
International Migration Service, 69, 177–179, 297 (n. 72), 303 (n. 31).
International Miners' Federation, 78.
International Missionary Council, 112, 134, 136–139, 152, 159.
International Monetary Fund, 28.
International Montessori Association, 125.
International non-governmental organizations (*INGO's*): definition, ix, 3; membership, 7–10; functions, 10–14; historical development, viii, 4–7, 75, 133ff., 213, 225, 279 (n. 4, 5); importance, vii–viii, 94–96, 124, 166–167, 245, 273–278; and conventions, treaties, intergovernmental agreements, 23–25, 29, 49, 55, 59, 66, 67, 68, 76, 83, 89, 90, 91, 110, 111, 119, 136, 172, 173, 180, 181, 182, 183, 184, 185, 186, 187, 190, 197, 201, 203, 204, 205, 206, 216, 217, 222, 235, 236, 240, 246, 247, 251, 258, 262, 265, 266; and creation of intergovernmental organizations, 14, 75–77, 81, 154, 172, 192, 201, 205, 213, 216, 217, 218, 219, 220, 227, 228, 245–248;

INDEX

International non-governmental organizations (*INGO's*): (*cont.*)
and intergovernmental conferences, 21–22, 25–28, 31–32, 52, 62, 72, 73, 76, 80–81, 91, 111, 172, 173, 180, 183, 206, 223, 224, 267 (*see also* Hague Conferences, International Economic Conference of 1927); and national governments and national legislation, 9–10, 14, 24, 67, 68, 79, 83, 84, 87, 104, 111, 116, 119, 120, 122, 138, 139, 145–146, 161, 186, 187, 191, 194, 197, 202–203, 205, 207, 208, 229, 234, 235, 247; relations with each other, 14–16, 189 (*see also* Committee of International Students' Organizations, Federation of Private and Semi-Official Organizations Established at Geneva, International Consultative Group [For Peace and Disarmament], International Peace Campaign, International Trade Secretariats, Joint Committee of the Major International Associations, Liaison Committee of Women's International Organizations, Union of International Associations); relations to the League of Nations, 248–258; relations to the United Nations, vii–viii, 258–272.

International Office for the Application of Aluminum, 46.

International Office of Chemistry, 105, 117.

International Office for Cocoa and Chocolate, 51–52.

International Olympic Committee, 199–200.

International Order of Good Templars, 196, 279 (n. 4).

International Organization of Industrial Employers, 16, 35–38, 64, 256, 257, 286 (n. 1), 303 (n. 43).

International Organization for Standardization, 40.

International Ornithological Congress, 288 (n. 4).

International Peace Bureau, 4, 213, 214–215.

International Peace Campaign, 224–225.

International Penal and Penitentiary Commission, 110, 196.

International Phonetic Association, 291 (n. 61).

International Photogrammetic Society, 288 (n. 4).

International Police Conference, 290 (n. 50).

International Professional Association of Medical Practitioners, 168–170.

International Protestant Loan Association, 155.

International Psychological Congress, 290 (n. 47).

International Public Transport Union (*see* International Union of Tramways, Light Railways and Motor Omnibuses).

International Publishers' Congress, 119–120.

International Railway Congress Association, 54, 60, 173.

International Railway Union, (*see* International Union of Railways).

International Red Cross, 4, 146, 166, 174, 187–193, 202, 237, 238, 245, 255, 296 (n. 51). (*See also* International Committee of the Red Cross, League of Red Cross Societies).

International Relief Union, 10, 192, 245, 246.

International Scientific Agricultural Council, 92.

International Secretariat of Stone Workers, 172.

International Secretariat of Women's Rural Associations, 90.

International Service of the Society of Friends (Quakers), 165.

International Shipping Conference, 62, 285 (n. 23).

International Shipping Conferences, 62–64.

International Shipping Federation, 64, 257, 286 (n. 1).

International Social Service (*see* International Migration Service).

International Society for Contemporary Music, 118.

International Society for Logopedy and Phoniatry, 291 (n. 61).

International Society of Musicology, 118.

International Society of Radiobiology, 288 (n. 4).

International Special Commission of Radio Interference, 41.

International Student Service, 127, 128, 130–132, 194, 224, 237, 239, 240–241, 249.

International Studies Conference, 232–233, 248.
International Sugar Committee, 246.
International Sugar Office, 245, 246.
International Technical Committee of Legal Experts on Air Matters, 25, 66, 206.
International Technical Fire Committee, 173.
International Telephone and Telegraph Company, ix.
International Tin Committee, 14, 46, 245, 246.
International Touring Alliance, 51, 71–73, 286 (n. 47, 50).
International Trade Secretariats, 15, 78, 84, 172.
International Transport Workers Federation, 15, 69, 78, 173.
Internatonal Tube Cartel, 283 (n. 94).
International Union Against Cancer, 171.
International Union Against Tuberculosis, 171, 189.
International Union Against the Venereal Diseases, 171, 173.
International Union of Aviation Insurers, 285.
International Union for Biological Sciences, 101.
International Union of Building Workers, 78.
International Union of Catholic Women's Leagues, 163, 180.
International Union for Child Welfare, 184–187.
International Union for Combatting Venereal Diseases, 171, 189.
International Union of Crystallography, 289 (n. 13).
International Union of the Development of Grape-Cure Resorts and the Consumption of Grapes, 297 (n. 81).
International Union of Forest Research Organizations, 8.
International Union of Geodesy and Geophysics, 101, 104–105, 106.
International Union of the History of Sciences, 289 (n. 13).
International Union for the Issue of Combined Coupon Tickets, 286 (n. 50).
International Union of Local Authorities, 8, 110, 113–115.
International Union of Official Organizations for the Promotion of Tourist Traffic [or Propaganda], 51, 286 (n. 50).
International Union of Penal Law, 197.
International Union of Producers and Distributors of Electric Power, 98, 99–100.
International Union for the Protection of Industrial Property, 245, 247.
International Union for the Protection of Literary and Artistic Works, 245, 247.
International Union of Pure and Applied Chemistry, 101, 105–106.
International Union of Pure and Applied Physics, 101.
International Union of Railways, 23, 54, 60, 68, 173, 286 (n. 50).
International Union of Scientific Radio-Telegraphy, 101, 106.
International Union of Telecommunications, 26, 54.
International Union of Theoretical and Applied Mechanics, 289 (n. 13).
International Union of Tramways, Light Railways and Motor Omnibuses, 60–61.
International Union of Wood Workers, 78.
International University Federation for the League of Nations, 128, 300 (n. 32).
International Voluntary Service for Peace, 193.
International Wool Textile Organization, 52–53.
International Workingmen's Association (see First International).
International Youth Hostel Association, 71.
Inter-Parliamentary Union, 4, 8, 13, 212, 213, 214, 215–218, 224, 225, 247, 250, 251, 299 (n. 3).
Islamic Research Association, 290 (n. 47).

Jeunesse Ouvrière Chrétienne (see Christian Young Workers).
Jewish Agency for Palestine, 6, 166, 302 (n. 1).
Jewish Association for the Protection of Girls, Women and Children, 182, 297 (n. 72).
Joint Committee of the Major International Associations, 132, 239–240, 245, 248, 256, 296 (n. 45).

INDEX

Joint Disarmament Committee of the Christian International Organizations, 223, 300 (n. 31).
Journalism (*see* Press).

Kiwanis International, 234.

Labor and Socialist International, 75, 78, 80, 84–86, 87, 287 (n. 17).
League to Enforce Peace, 215.
League of Jewish Women, 234, 300 (n. 30).
League of Mothers and Educators of Peace, 234, 300 (n. 30).
League of Nations, 5, 6, 21–22, 25, 27, 29, 31, 35, 56, 58, 62, 72, 75, 80, 85, 92, 98, 110, 111, 119, 131, 136, 139, 145, 157, 166, 173, 178, 180, 182, 183–184, 185, 186, 187, 189, 191, 192, 195, 196, 197, 205, 212, 213, 217, 218, 225, 227, 228, 232, 233, 236, 239, 240, 245, 247, 248–258, 261, 277, 297 (n. 54). (*See also* International Federation of League of Nations Societies.)
League of Red Cross Societies, 15, 167, 168, 173, 174, 188–190, 192–193, 246, 249, 255, 296 (n. 51). (*See also* International Red Cross.)
Liaison Committee of Women's International Organizations, 234.
Ligue Internationale Aéronautique, 174.
Lions International (*see* International Association of Lions Clubs).

Migrants, 177–179, 182, 193–194, 267. (*See also* Refugees.)
Minorities, 144, 195–196, 221–222, 262.
Mixed organizations: definition, 8–10; examples, 39, 40, 55, 60, 73, 92, 99–100, 101, 113, 115, 121–122, 171, 173, 196.
Monetary stabilization, 226.

Nansen International Office for Refugees (*see* High Commission for Refugees).
National non-governmental organizations (*NNGO's*), ix, 3.
Near East Association, 194.
New Education Fellowship, 125–126.
NNGO, (*see* National non-governmental organizations).
North Atlantic Passenger Conference, 62–63.

Oecumenical movement, 134–154 *passim*, 159.

Office Central des Institutions Internationales, 214.
Office International d'Hygiène Publique, 173.
Olympic Games, 199–200.

Pan-American Union, 5.
Pan-European Union, 225.
Pax Romana—International Secretariat of National Federations of Catholic Students, 127, 128, 300 (n. 32).
Peace and Disarmament Committee of the Women's International Organizations, 223, 300 (n. 30).
PEN—a World Association of Writers, 118.
Penal law, 196–197.
Permanent Bureau of Analytical Chemistry, 105.
Permanent Commission of the International Congresses of Scientific and Applied Photography, 288 (n. 4).
Permanent (or Standing) Committee of the International Conferences on Social Work, 174–177, 189.
Permanent Committee of the International Congresses of Open-Air Schools, 189.
Permanent Council for the Exploration of the Sea, 106.
Permanent Council for International Co-operation between Composers, 118.
Permanent Court of Arbitration, 31, 216.
Permanent Court of International Justice, 6, 31, 38, 82, 212, 218, 247, 256.
Permanent International Association of Road Congresses, 290 (n. 57).
Permanent International Bureau of Motor Manufacturers, 53.
Permanent International Commission on Acetylene and Autogenous Welding, 172.
Permanent International Commission of Agricultural Associations, 9, 92.
Permanent International Committee of Architects, 118.
Permanent International Committee of Linguists, 291 (n. 61).
Permanent International Committee for the Study of Industrial Accidents, 172.
Permanent International Committee on Wine Growing, 16, 297 (n. 81).

INDEX

Permanent International Conference of Private Organizations for the Protection of Migrants, 194.
Point 4 (*see* Technical assistance).
Press, the, 121–123, 240.
Press Congress of the World, 122–123.
Prisoners of war, 190–192.

Railway transport, 23, 26.
Red Cross (*see* International Red Cross).
Red International of Trade Unions, 88.
Refugees, 184–185, 193–194, 241, 267. (*See also* High Commission for Refugees, Relief, Migrants.)
Relief, 130, 155, 160, 184–185, 187–194, 241, 267.
Reparations and war debts, 27–28, 80.
Rockefeller Foundation, 106, 168, 230, 246.
Roman Catholic Church, 4, 7, 11, 133–134, 142, 157, 163, 165.
Rotary International, 6, 234, 279 (n. 7).
Ruhr, 80.

St. Joan's Social and Political Alliance, 179.
Salvation Army, 7, 156–159.
"Save the Children" International Union, 171, 184–186, 255.
Scandinavian Co-operative Wholesale Society, 34.
Sciences, natural and exact, 96–100.
Sciences, pure, 101–112.
Sciences, social, 112–118.
Second International (*see* Labor and Socialist International).
Service Civil International (*see* International Voluntary Service for Peace).
Shipping (ocean), 23–24, 29, 59–60, 61–64, 206. (*See also* Hague Rules, York-Antwerp Rules.)
Social and humanitarian activity, 174–197, 265–267.
Socialism, 78. (*See also* Labor and Socialist International, Socialist . . .)
Socialist Workers' Sport International, 85.
Socialist Youth International, 85.
Social service, 174–179.
Standardization, 38–41, 53, 97–98, 109, 268.
Standing Committee on the Health and Welfare of Seamen, 189.
Steel Cartel, 42–43, 44, 47, 282 (n. 86).

Stock Exchange Bureau, 29.
Students, 127–132, 223.
Surface Transport, 60–61.

Taxation, 27.
Technical assistance for underdeveloped areas, 269–270.
Telegraph and cable, 26.
Telephone, 26.
Third International (*see* Communist International).
Tin Producers' Association, 14, 46, 246.
Trade barriers, 21–23, 226, 267–268.
Trade terms, 22–23.
Transport, 23, 26, 60–69, 249, 267–268. (*See also* Shipping).
Travel, 69–74, 236, 240, 241.

Union of International Associations, 226–228, 251, 252. (See also *Office Central des Institutions Internationales.*)
United Nations, vii, ix, 3, 121, 154, 204, 258–272, 276, 277; Article 71 of the Charter of, vii, 3, 258; Economic and Social Council of, vii, ix, 3, 258–272 *passim;* General Assembly of, 260; Security Council of, 260; Trusteeship Council of, 260.
United Nations Educational, Scientific and Cultural Organization, 261, 272.
United Nations Food and Agricultural Organization, 272, 288 (n. 5).
Universal Christian Council on Life and Work, 134, 139–141, 152, 251, 300 (n. 31).
Universal Esperanto Association, 213, 291 (n. 61).
Universal Postal Union, 54.
Universal Theatre Society, 118.

Van Zeeland Report of 1938, 22, 28.

War crimes, 211–212.
White slave traffic (*see* Women, traffic in).
Women, status of, 179–184, 249, 250, 262, 264; traffic in, 181–182, 197, 249, 252.
Women's International League for Peace and Freedom, 5, 180, 219–220, 233, 300 (n. 30).
World Alliance for International Friendship Through the Churches, 11, 134, 144–146, 195, 292 (n. 2), 298 (n. 1.), 300 (n. 31).

INDEX

World Alliance for International Friendship Through Religion, 292 (n. 2).
World Association for Adult Education, 124–125.
World Association of Girl Guides and Girl Scouts, 237, 238.
World Conference on Faith and Order, 134, 141–144, 152.
World Congress of Documentation, 15.
World Congress of Faiths, 154–155.
World Council for Christian Education (*see* World's Sunday School Association).
World Council of Churches, 134, 136, 144, 153–154, 294 (n. 47).
World Court (*see* Permanent Court of International Justice).
World Economic Conference of 1927 (*see* International Economic Conference of 1927).
World Federation of Education Associations, 132, 246.
World Federation of Trade Unions, viii, 287 (n. 14).
World Federation of United Nations Associations, 300 (n. 22).
World Health Organization, 261, 272, 276.
World Jewish Congress, 195.
World League of Press Associations, 121–122, 291 (n. 4).
World Meteorological Organization, 289 (n. 24).
World Organization of the Teaching Profession, 132.
World Power Conference, 11, 96–98, 99, 290 (n. 50).
World Prohibition Federation, 196.
World's Alliance of Young Men's Christian Associations, 4, 15, 134, 146–148, 228, 237, 238, 250, 255, 286 (n. 1), 300 (n. 31).
World's Christian Endeavor Union, 165.
World's Evangelical Alliance, 147, 165, 279 (n. 4).
World's Poultry Science Association, 89.
World's Student Christian Federation, 7, 127, 128, 130, 134, 146, 149–152, 239, 300 (n. 31, 32).
World Student Federation Against Alcoholism, 196.
World's Sunday School Association, 154–156, 238.
World's Woman Christian Temperance Union, 16, 196, 300 (n. 30).
World's Young Women's Christian Association, 134, 146–147, 177, 179, 182, 233, 254, 286 (n. 1), 296 (n. 45), 300 (n. 30, 31).
World Touring and Automobile Association, 73.
World Union of Freethinkers, 165.
World Union of Jewish Students, 128, 300 (n. 32).
World Union of Women for International Concord, 300 (n. 30).
World Youth Congress, 239.

York-Antwerp Rules of General Average, 207, 208–211.
Young Italy, 14.